Rethinking the Social in Innovation and
Entrepreneurship

Rethinking the Social in Innovation and Entrepreneurship

Edited by

Beniamino Callegari

Oslo New University College and Kristiania University College, Norway

Bisrat A. Misganaw

NEOMA Business School, France

Stefania Sardo

Technical University of Munich, Germany

Cheltenham, UK • Northampton, MA, USA

© Beniamino Callegari, Bisrat A. Misganaw and Stefania Sardo 2022

All rights reserved. No part of this publication may be reproduced, stored in a retrieval system or transmitted in any form or by any means, electronic, mechanical or photocopying, recording, or otherwise without the prior permission of the publisher.

Published by
Edward Elgar Publishing Limited
The Lypiatts
15 Lansdown Road
Cheltenham
Glos GL50 2JA
UK

Edward Elgar Publishing, Inc.
William Pratt House
9 Dewey Court
Northampton
Massachusetts 01060
USA

A catalogue record for this book
is available from the British Library

Library of Congress Control Number: 2022931264

This book is available electronically in the **Elgar**online
Law subject collection
http://dx.doi.org/10.4337/9781839108174

Printed on elemental chlorine free (ECF)
recycled paper containing 30% Post-Consumer Waste

ISBN 978 1 83910 816 7 (cased)
ISBN 978 1 83910 817 4 (eBook)

Printed and bound in the USA

Contents

List of figures	vii
List of tables	viii
List of contributors	ix
Preface	x

1   Introduction to *Rethinking the Social in Innovation and Entrepreneurship Studies*   1
Beniamino Callegari, Bisrat A. Misganaw and Stefania Sardo

PART I   THE CONTEXTUAL APPROACH

2   Entrepreneurial team formation, task allocation in new ventures and the theory of imprinting   26
Bisrat A. Misganaw

3   Exploring the social dimension of regional industrial restructuring   43
Jan Ole Rypestøl

4   Collective resources in entrepreneurship: a reconceptualisation of resource mobilisation   67
Karin Wigger and Thomas Lauvås

5   Innovation and adaptation strategies during the front-end phase of an industry downturn   89
Jakoba Sraml Gonzalez

6   "Is that my problem?" A study of motivation for knowledge sharing   113
Stian Bragtvedt

PART II   THE IDENTIFICATION APPROACH

7   Playing around with the 'rules of the game': social entrepreneurs navigating the public sector terrain in pursuit of collaboration   133
Mikhail Kosmynin

8	Integrating responsible research and innovation into smart specialization: a question-machine approach *Nhien Nguyen, Jens Ørding Hansen, Are Jensen and Carlos Álvarez Pereira*	152
9	Making a thousand diverse flowers bloom: driving innovation through inclusion of diversity in organisations *Marte C.W. Solheim*	174

PART III   THE ESSENTIALIST APPROACH

10	Schumpeter's social ontology: before and beyond pure economics *Beniamino Callegari*	191
11	The naturalized disharmony of a socio-technical system: understanding safety in the oil and gas drilling industry *Stefania Sardo*	210
12	Interactions in innovation processes of medical devices: systemic and network perspectives *Olga Mikhailova*	234
Index		257

Figures

1.1	Classification of the integration of the social dimension in Innovation and Entrepreneurship studies	6
2.1	Entrepreneurial team formation process as an imprinter	37
3.1	Analytical framework of the role of social relations in regional industrial restructuring	52
8.1	The RIS3 process in action	156
12.1	Illustration of the TAVI networks in Denmark	246

Tables

3.1	Asset types and scales	48
4.1	Theoretical insights on resource mobilisation	75
4.2	Arrangements for the mobilisation of collective resources	79
5.1	Overview of the case companies characteristics and data	97
5.2	Overview of the codes and thematic categories	98
5.3	Five adaptation strategies and the specific sets of actions	100
7.1	Data collection methods	140
8.1	Summary of assumptions underlying the approach	160
8.2	Smart specialization stages: Analysis	163
8.3	Smart specialization stages: Vision and Prioritization	164
8.4	Smart specialization stages: Policy Mix and Monitoring	165
12.1	Comparison of system and network perspectives	241
12.2	Interviews overview	243

Contributors

Carlos Álvarez Pereira, Innaxis Foundation & Research Institute, Madrid, Spain

Stian Bragtvedt, Nordland Research Institute, sbr@nforsk.no

Beniamino Callegari, Oslo New University College and Kristiania University College, callegari.ben@gmail.com

Jakoba Sraml Gonzalez, University of Oslo, j.s.gonzalez@tik.uio.no

Jens Ørding Hansen, Nordland Research Institute, joh@nforsk.no

Are Jensen, Nordland Research Institute, aje@nforsk.no

Mikhail Kosmynin, Nord University, mikhail.kosmynin@nord.no

Thomas Lauvås, Nord University Business School, thomas.a.lauvas@nord.no

Olga Mikhailova, Norwegian University of Life Sciences, olga.mikhailova@nmbu.no

Bisrat A. Misganaw, NEOMA Business School, bisrat.misganaw@neoma-bs.fr

Nhien Nguyen, Nordland Research Institute, Bodø and Norwegian University of Science and Technology, Trondheim, Norway, nhien.nguyen@ntnu.no

Jan Ole Rypestøl, University of Agder, jan.o.rypestol@uia.no

Stefania Sardo, Technical University of Munich, stefania.sardo@tum.de

Marte C.W. Solheim, University of Stavanger, marte.solheim@uis.no

Karin Wigger, Nord University Business School, karin.a.wigger@nord.no

Preface

The idea for this anthology originated from debates among alumni and current students of the Nordic Research School in Innovation and Entrepreneurship (NORSI) – a research school in the Nordic countries that embraces the fields of Innovation and Entrepreneurship (I&E). Given that the NORSI school gives students the opportunity to explore and specialize in different subfields within these two disciplines, we realized how different our conceptualizations and research practices were with regard to something as simple and basic as "the social". *Are entrepreneurship and innovation processes inherently social? Should one explain innovation and entrepreneurship processes by including selected social elements external to them? Is the social element adding further complexities, producing spurious studies and threatening generalizations?* Indeed, when not openly discussed, these differences inevitably produce misunderstandings, unnecessary theoretical departures, or overlapping concepts multiplications. The spectre of a devolution into highly specialized yet contentious niches and schools, unable to constructively interact with each other, pushed us to confront one of the "elephants in the room" and open up a space of dialogue focused on variegated understandings of *the social* in our research activities.

The chapters comprising this anthology emerged from a face-to-face discussion organized in 2019 around the theme of *the social* within Innovation and Entrepreneurship Studies. Even though the unexpected Covid-19 pandemic has meanwhile challenged all of us in unpredictable ways and has inevitably delayed the publication of this book, we stuck to our promises and brought it to a conclusion. Managing this project has been an important experience for the three of us, as it requires not only an intellectual effort, but also a managerial one. Of course, not less important, it was quite a lot of fun; certainly a way to meet again since our departure towards different institutes from that of our academic beginnings.

As will be clear from the introductory chapter of this book, finding a common way to relate *the social* to all the I&E research subfields was a somewhat impossible task. Indeed, our attempt was not one of reducing divergences, but to openly acknowledge them. To solve this conundrum, we have proposed a non-exhaustive spectrum of how *the social* is analytically understood in Innovation and Entrepreneurship Studies, ranging from it being not considered at all to defining it as foundational. We hope that our reflections

Preface xi

will stimulate a discussion in the I&E fields concerning the importance of dialogue between disciplines and a self-reflection on the way we do research. The attempt at categorization is extensively explained in the Introduction and is reflected in the book structure, which is divided into three main parts. Not only do the chapters comprising this anthology belong to different sub-disciplines within I&E studies, but they are aimed at different audiences. Therefore, we hope this book will be interesting to academics at all career stages, as well as to practitioners.

We are indeed grateful to the NORSI Board and Scientific Committee for trusting us as editors and encouraging NORSI students and alumni in taking part in this first (and hopefully not last) common endeavour. In particular, we want to thank Professor Bjørn Asheim for his experienced guidance, and Birte Horn-Hanssen for her invaluable emotional and organizational support. Moreover, we want to thank the Research Council of Norway for its generous support of NORSI activities, including this one.

We certainly acknowledge the reviewers for their comments on the chapter drafts: Bjørn Asheim (University of Stavanger, NO); Stian Bragtvedt (Nordland Research Institute, NO); Beniamino Callegari (Kristiania University College, NO); Rune Dahl Fitjar (University of Stavanger, NO); Petter Gullmark (Nord University, NO); Jens Ørding Hansen (Nordland Research Institute, NO); Debbie Harrison (BI Norwegian Business School, NO); Mikhail Kosmynin (Nord University, NO); Arne Isaksen (University of Agder, NO); Hans Landström (Lund University, SE); Olga Mikhailova (Norwegian University of Life Sciences, NO); Bisrat Agegnehu Misganaw (Neoma Business School, FR), Somendra Narayan (NEOMA Business School, FR); Einar Rasmussen (Nord University, NO); Jan Ole Rypestøl (University of Agder, NO); Stefania Sardo (Technical University of Munich, DE); Jonas Söderlund (BI Norwegian Business School, NO); Marte C.W. Solheim (University of Stavanger, NO); Taran Thune (University of Oslo, NO); and Sudip Tiwari (Nord University, NO).

For assistance in the preparation of the manuscript we thank the Edward Elgar team: Matthew Pittman, Elizabeth Ruck, Karen Jones and Kate Norman; and freelance copy editor Brian North. We also extend our thanks to NORSI at large and in particular to Birte Marie Horn-Hanssen, Bjørn Asheim and Roger Sørheim for their continued support.

Beniamino Callegari, Bisrat A. Misganaw, Stefania Sardo
July 2021

1. Introduction to *Rethinking the Social in Innovation and Entrepreneurship Studies*

Beniamino Callegari, Bisrat A. Misganaw and Stefania Sardo

Since the turn of the twenty-first century, we have witnessed an increasing academic interest in phenomena such as social innovation and social entrepreneurships, which have led to a plethora of definitions. For example, Mulgan et al. (2007, p. 2) define social innovation as "new ideas that address unmet social needs – and that work". This definition points at innovation processes targeted for a "social goal". Similar interpretations abound within the entrepreneurship field as well, where it is, for example, understood as "the innovative use and combination of resources to pursue opportunities to catalyse social change and/or address social needs" (Mair & Marti, 2006, p. 37). Within this field, scholars focus on the conditions for social entrepreneurship to happen, on the opportunity recognition skills, on specific obstacles such as financing and networking, by referring back to, for example, the institutional perspective as a theoretical lens (Kimmitt & Muñoz, 2018). This overall tendency has been echoed by public institutions, which have designed research and development (R&D) funding programmes to gather solutions for social goals – more recently placed under the banner of Grand Challenges (Kuhlmann & Rip, 2018; Mazzucato, 2018). Examples can be found as early as 2010, when a European Union coming out of a financial crisis was remarking once again on the necessity of putting innovation "at the heart of the Europe 2020 strategy". Here, the "social" element was highlighted as a new (or rediscovered) category for innovation and entrepreneurship. In the Innovation Union initiative document, "social innovation" is described as being about "tapping into the ingenuity of charities, associations and social entrepreneurs to find new ways of meeting social needs which are not adequately met by the market or the public sector (…) to tackle the major societal challenges" (European Commission, 2010, p. 21).

To us, the theoretical and policy trend endorsing the social aspects of the entrepreneurship and innovation processes has enforced a separation between innovation and entrepreneurship processes with social aims, and those guided by economic profit, either entirely lacking a social goal, or where the social goal is not the primary driving motive. Adding the "social" label seems to specify a normative predisposition towards some types of activities, an attempt to elevate existing processes by indicating what "an acceptable good" should be. This trend might have stemmed from the recognition of the widespread negative consequences germinated by former innovations (see e.g. Mulgan et al., 2007; Murray et al., 2010), a veiled condemnation of our – more or less collectively participated – past decisions (e.g. disasters caused by power plants, asbestos, Bhopal, Deepwater Horizon, plastics). And, connected to this, from an attempt to "correct" the longstanding predominant attention for the technical and economic aspects of these processes.[1]

In this introductory chapter, we dig more into how selected subfields within Innovation and Entrepreneurship (I&E) studies have been dealing with the social in recent years, and we put forward a spectrum of four categories of approaches based on a non-systematic literature review of the I&E fields in the next section. This review was conducted by selecting leading academic journals in these fields (e.g. *Research Policy*; *Technological Forecasting and Social Change*; *Journal of Evolutionary Economics*; *Industrial and Corporate Change*; *Science, Technology & Human Values*; *Technology Analysis & Strategic Management*; *Technovation*; *Entrepreneurship Theory and Practice*; *Strategic Entrepreneurship Journal*; *Entrepreneurship and Regional Development*), and keywords such as social value, social theory, social dimension, social context, and social ontology. Our aim was not to cover all the subfields within the I&E disciplines, but to give a glimpse on how the social is approached analytically. As a result of this review, we have developed a preliminary classification of the approaches to the social dimension dominant in I&E studies, which also provides the main structure of the book.

Scholars within the disciplinary approach conceptualize the primary causal mechanisms of their object of study while intentionally ignoring the residual social dimension. This category will not be represented in our anthology, as we specifically collected contributions that explicitly integrate the social within their analytical framework. Within the contextual approach one can find contributions introducing selected social aspects as factors to explain innovation and entrepreneurship mechanisms and outcomes (Chapters 2, 3, 4, 5 and 6). Scholars employing the identification approach, identify a specifically social subset of the main phenomena under study (e.g. social entrepreneurship) and develop their analysis around the specific mechanisms influencing these phenomena (Chapters 7, 8 and 9). Finally, some scholars adopt an essentialist approach (Chapters 10, 11 and 12), focusing on the essentially social nature of innovation and/or entrepreneurship, bringing to the fore marginal and poten-

Introduction 3

tially controversial social mechanisms and characterizing them, such as power and conflict.

THE SOCIAL DIMENSION IN INNOVATION AND ENTREPRENEURSHIP STUDIES

Although there is a consensus that entrepreneurship and innovation are disciplines in social sciences, studies in the fields are predominantly characterized by an individualistic orientation, largely inherited from economics (Goss, 2005; Lundvall, 2013). In the last couple of decades, however, research acknowledging the importance of the social dimension has been growing in influence over the field (e.g. Anderson, 2015; Shepherd et al., 2020; van der Have & Rubalcaba, 2016). These studies have, for example, contrasted a humanistic conceptualization of entrepreneurship (Kupferberg, 1998) supported by a logic of social processes, relations and changes, as opposed to entrepreneurs "investigated as undersocialized economic animals or robots" (Zafirovski, 1999, p. 354). Yet, there is a tremendous variation in the analytical use of the social, ranging from implicit assumption to explicit conceptualization to defining methodological foundations. This variety is a potential source of critical tensions within disciplines and fields composing Social Science, as social assumptions are commonly associated with contentious implicit or explicit epistemological, methodological and normative assumptions. This is a consequence of the holistic nature of the social sphere. Human life is, by and large, a social affair. From a fleeting tryst to a global war, most human phenomena are performed in interaction, and are, therefore, social. Thus, little escapes the potential grasp of Social Science, leading to a complexity unsuitable to the precision requirements of analysis.

A common analytical response has been to restrict the object of study to a more manageable size, to operate a distinction between what comprises the theoretical core and what belongs to the contextual phenomenological sphere. This distinction provides a first explanation for the common understanding of the social as a residual component, identifying the phenomena lying outside the theoretical core of the analysis. The cut can be operated across two different lines. The first option is to identify a specific frame of social life, a dimension present in the entirety of the social, although with varying intensity, and develop a pure analysis of that frame, discarding all other aspects in the pursuit of precise, abstract theorizations. This is the disciplinary solution, characterizing, for example, Economics, which focuses on the analysis of *Homo economicus* and its interactions, discarding, prima facie, every other social aspect. The considerable influence held by economic thought over both Innovation and Entrepreneurship studies is reflected in how common is the analytical approach in which "the social is often treated solely as a background factor, the ceteris paribus of the economists" (Korsgaard & Anderson, 2011, p. 135). The second option is to specify a set of actual phenomena of peculiar interest to be analysed in their actual complexity. From this type of analysis, domain-specific theories can be developed to explain the most relevant causal mechanisms at play. This is the phenomenological solution, applied by I&E studies among others. The complex nature of the phenomena under study gives rise to a multitude of both competing and complementary theorizations, each focusing on a specific set of active mechanisms (e.g. novelty generation, entrepreneurial disposition and innovation diffusion) based on different theoretical cores usually borrowed, although often adapted, from existing social disciplines.

Both options have limits. The holistic nature of social life resists any attempt to cleave it in neat, distinct slices. While a specific, internally consistent dimension can be identified and described, providing a disciplinary core, its actual reach and relevance for the multitude of real-life phenomena can hardly be defined with any certainty. Similarly, any phenomenon, no matter how narrow, influences and is influenced by a potentially unlimited amount of other phenomena, leaving any phenomenological core with unclear borders. In general, the complex nature of the social process implies that, no matter how limited the dimension chosen as object of study, or the original set of phenomena included in the analysis, every social science has a potentially unlimited field of expansion. Successful disciplines can extend their analytical frame to the analysis of more and more phenomena. The obvious example is provided by the apparently unstoppable imperialistic trend of economics, applying economic theory to the analysis of phenomena as diverse as fertility (Becker, 1960), criminal law (Posner, 1985), prostitution (Edlund & Korn, 2002) and torture (Yakovlev, 2011). Similarly, successful phenomenological fields are bound to gradually discover that more and more phenomena are intimately connected to their original set, and their inclusion within the analysis is a necessity to achieve superior theoretical validity. The success of the Triple Helix perspective (Etzkowitz & Leydesdorff, 1995) has already spawned a potential expansion to the Quadruple, the Quintuple Helix and beyond (Carayannis & Campbell, 2009; Carayannis et al., 2012; Leydesdorff, 2012). Similarly, the National Innovation System perspective (Freeman, 1987; Lundvall, 1988) has spawned a Regional (Cooke & Morgan, 1994), Technical (Nelson & Rosenberg, 1993), and now even Global variant (Lee et al., 2020).

These expansions can be understood as a gradual colonization of the phenomenological residual by the successful theoretical core. This process, however, is a primary driver for contention and academic division within social science. In a disciplinary context, phenomena outside the theoretical core can be used as alternative empirical settings on which to apply existing theoretical constructs, thus extending the validity of the disciplinary core by demonstrating its ability to be gainfully applied to phenomena once thought far removed from the disciplinary reach, a sign of disciplinary vigour. Critical perspectives inside the discipline, however, may point to the phenomenological residual to argue that social aspects currently excluded from the theoretical core mediate key disciplinary mechanisms and therefore should be included (Dequech, 2012). Within a discipline, then, the social dimension can be a frontier, appearing simultaneously as a target for ambitious researchers looking for new grounds to settle, and a refuge for outsiders wanting to challenge the status quo.

The phenomenological approach taken by I&E studies implies both theoretical and methodological pluralism. Consequently, the distinction between theoretical core and phenomenological residual depends on the epistemological assumptions, methodological choices and theoretical frame adopted by each researcher. Indeed, the line between theoretical core and social residual is contentious, giving rise to several alternative conceptualizations of what the social means and which role it plays in regard to the main object of study. The generally acknowledged pluralist approach inherent to phenomenological fields facilitates the acceptance of differences even within the definition of the theoretical core. However, the influential position of the economic approach within I&E studies (Anderson, 2015; Godin, 2012; Minniti & Lévesque, 2008), have motivated some researchers into adopting the social dimension in explicit opposition with the economic framework: another manifestation of the social frontier as a refuge for critical analysis.

Following these considerations, we can identify four main categories with respect to how the social dimension is analytically integrated within the context of I&E studies (Figure 1.1).

The most peripheral approach is the disciplinary approach, focusing on an abstract conceptualization of the main object of study and its primary causal mechanisms, limiting the analysis to a single interpretative frame. This approach is usually associated with economics (Schumpeter, 2010) and consequently with all those approaches to I&E studies which adopt an economic framework of analysis (e.g. Dosi, 1982; Nelson & Winter, 1982; Rosenberg, 1982). While innovation and entrepreneurship are acknowledged as social phenomena, the social dimension is not explicitly conceptualized to reduce complexity and avoid losing the ability to generalize analytical results. While we acknowledge the disciplinary approach as both legitimate and common within I&E studies, in this book we focus our attention on those approaches which explicitly integrate the social dimension in the analysis.

The second is the contextual approach, which introduces specifically social aspects as background factors affecting the primary causal mechanisms, such as team composition characteristics, the consequences of economic crisis to innovation processes, the influences of social relations on processes of regional renewal, and so on. A significant heterogeneity exists in regard to which factors are associated with the social sphere and their relevance for explanatory purposes. This approach is more commonly found in empirical studies, where social aspects can be used to explain some phenomenological variance (Landry et al., 2002), or in systemic theoretical work, aiming to integrate a variety of related phenomena with the main objects of study (Godin, 2009). Yet, it can be found also in analytical efforts aiming to either enlarge the phenomenological areas of interest associated with the field of study, supporting the validity of existing theoretical structures, or integrating new explanatory factors to clarify contentious areas of present debates.

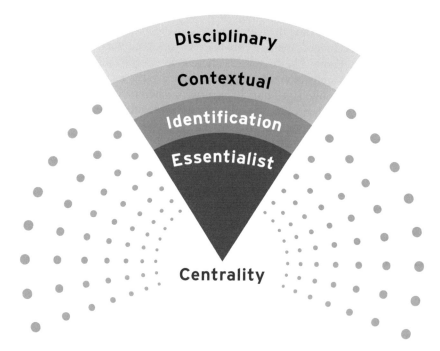

Figure 1.1   *Classification of the integration of the social dimension in Innovation and Entrepreneurship studies*

Examples of these approaches are numerous. Within the entrepreneurship literature, social interaction is widely acknowledged as one of the most important factors affecting entrepreneurs' ability to recognize and pursue entrepreneurial opportunities (Shepherd et al., 2020), as well as to acquire the resources they need (Davidsson & Honig, 2003; Stam & Elfring, 2008). This is why Gedajlovic et al. (2013) suggest that social capital theory should be one of the foundational theories in entrepreneurship. Social capital is the "sum of actual and potential resources embedded within, available through, and derived from the network of relationships possessed by individuals or social units" (Nahapiet and Ghoshal, 1998, p. 243). Studies in entrepreneurship have then utilized social capital theory to examine the role of social capital at the individual (Davidsson & Honig, 2003), regional (Kleinhempel et al., 2020; Rypestøl, Chapter 3 in this book) and national levels (Kwon & Arenius, 2010). Social networks are also found to facilitate the acquisition of resources by entrepreneurs (Lee et al., 2019), and to affect firm performance (Hernández-Carrión, et al., 2017). Combining the two perspectives, Shepherd et al. (2020) suggest that individual characteristics of the entrepreneur mediate the usefulness of social networks for resource acquisition purposes. The social dimension is introduced in the analysis as a specific source of resources for entrepreneurs to tap.

Social capital theory also finds application within innovation studies. Baba and Walsh (2010) argue that embedded social capital is a key resource for overcoming the uncertainty involved in radical innovation, and for securing and maintaining control over the resources required for achieving a breakthrough. At a macro level, social capital has been correlated with innovative performance (Dakhli & De Clercq, 2004), although both the conceptualization and measurement of the construct remain challenging and open to various interpretations (Landry et al., 2002). Scholars within the Innovation System approach (Isaksen, 2015; Martin, 2010) have used social capital theory to understand the extent to which industrial clusters, regions and industries can evolve. Social capital needs to be "activated" by policy interventions when missing (Tödtling & Trippl, 2004). Indeed, authorities at different levels can "shape local learning and innovation processes (…) by providing R&D infrastructure and educational infrastructure, supporting academic spin-offs, enhancing human capital and encouraging the formation of social capital" (Cooke et al., 2007, p. 54). The social dimension, reified in a specific factor (i.e. social capital), supports and extends the previously developed theoretical core, entering the analysis as an explicit and active context.

The third is the identification approach, aiming to define and analyse a specifically social subset of the main phenomena under study, resulting, for example, in the creation of concepts such as social innovation (Avelino et al., 2019; van der Have & Rubalcaba, 2016), social entrepreneurship (Mair & Marti, 2006), and also Responsible Research and Innovation (Owen et al., 2012; von Schomberg, 2013). Here we have an implicit or explicit critique towards the assumption of self-interest, under the guise of either profit- or rent-seeking, underlying most of the literature. At the same time, altruistic, lifestyle, democratic and inclusive practices are identified as either absent or instrumental in the transactional dimension. These concepts are commonly associated with patterns of behaviour oriented towards social and/or communitarian welfare improvement, the realization of altruistic goals and/or the pursuit of non-monetary aims. This approach enlarges the I&E fields by bringing under analysis previously marginalized phenomena.

The concept of social innovation has gradually emerged in recent years (Avelino et al., 2019; Cajaiba-Santana, 2014; Fougère et al., 2017). Although it is still ambiguous (van der Have & Rubalcaba, 2016), scholarly efforts have focused on developing it further towards the state of middle-range theory (Pel et al., 2020), where it is displayed as both a process of changing social relations and a qualitative property of ideas, objects, activities or persons. This definition has the advantage of operating a clear distinction with the more common definitions of innovation originating from an economic background (Schumpeter, 1934), and of identifying a potentially vast area of analytical expansion for both the fields of innovation and entrepreneurship studies. For example, social entrepreneurship has established itself as a subfield since the early 2000s and it has been defined as the "process involving the innovative use and combination of resources to pursue opportunities to catalyse social change and/or address social needs" (Mair & Marti, 2006, p. 37). By addressing social needs and problems, the common mission of social enterprises is the creation of social value (Chell, 2007; Dacin et al., 2011), with a varying degree of ambition towards the creation of economic value (Stevens et al., 2015). Even though there is no consensus in the literature on what social value is (Stevens et al., 2015), the activities of social entrepreneurs and social entrepreneurship are affected by the contextual settings in which they operate (Gupta et al., 2020). The way in which entrepreneurs perceive and interpret what the social challenge is may define their actions and in turn the beneficiaries of their project (Kimmitt & Muñoz, 2018). To mobilize their social capital and gain legitimacy from different stakeholders, these entrepreneurs often use a rhetorical strategy, especially against the antagonists (Ruebottom, 2013), that is, those who do not support the "social change" that the enterprise intends to bring about. All in all, "the social" is conceptualized as a specific type of entrepreneurial opportunity that entrepreneurs identify and pursue, as well as the type of value they seek to create, as part of an entrepreneurial process whose contents remain highly context-dependent.

A recent addition to I&E studies comes from the science, technology and innovation policy and academic discourses in relation to the concept of responsibility (Flink & Kaldewey, 2018; Guston et al., 2014; Owen et al., 2013; Stilgoe et al., 2013). According to Burget et al. (2017, p. 14), Responsibility in Research and Innovation (RRI) promotes "an idea of science governance that is essentially about responsible processes, as opposed to processes that are not supervised responsibly". While this field of study openly recognizes innovation and entrepreneurship as intrinsically social processes – and therefore close to our fourth categorization (see below) – it identifies a specific subcategory of research and innovation activities aligned with societal values and expectations, although both context-based and project-dependent. RRI scholars study cases and refine practices to either "correct" existing innovation and entrepreneurship processes, or design new and better ones according to the principles of inclusivity and sustainability (see Chapter 8 by Nguyen et al. in this book). Von Schomberg (2015, p. 1), for example, maintains that "Responsible innovation will be established when public authorities and private actors work together and create incentives for becoming mutually responsive to each other and anticipate research and innovation outcomes (…) for which they share responsibility."

The fourth categorization, the essentialist approach, argues that the social nature of innovation and entrepreneurship should be explicitly integrated within the main concepts and causal mechanisms of the fields. According to many socially essentialist scholars (e.g. Bijker et al., 1987; Sismondo, 2010; Winner, 1980), mainstream I&E studies have obscured the social nature of the object of study and the relevance of specifically social mechanisms – such as power and identity – for the analysis, resulting in a severely limited and, worse, skewed academic debate, which ignores or outright conceals key real-world dynamics. The recent review of the more influential schools of thought in innovation studies conducted by Geels (2010) brought to light the assumptions, and analytical consequences of essentialism. Constructivists, for example, see innovations as socially constructed processes (Sismondo, 2010): technologies, as well as science, are human products and emerge out of the frames of related circumstances. When innovating, entrepreneurs, designers and engineers combine heterogeneous resources and try to enrol several actors, who might have discordant ideas on what the innovation should be and which problem it should solve (Pinch & Bijker, 1987). This controversial process affects technologies in the making, introducing a specifically social source of uncertainty not only in technological development, but also in adoption. The final result is influenced by the different power wielded by the individuals, organizations and groups involved. Combining this school of thought with evolutionary economics and institutional theory, transition theorists try to understand the dynamics and governance of system transitions (Geels, 2005). Transition processes are intrinsically social and uncertain endeavours, but agents are assumed to be imbued with agency, while constrained by a semi-coherent system of rules. Therefore, instead of proposing causal mechanisms as outcome of their studies, these scholars work with interaction patterns (Geels & Schot, 2007; Markard & Truffer, 2008; Rip & Kemp, 1998). More recently, critical realism has also acquired some influence within the Innovation field (Vega & Chiasson, 2019). Behind purely ontological and epistemological assumptions, however, hides the controversial issue of value judgements, and their key role in affecting scientific endeavours (Schumpeter,

1949). In this regard, the recent contribution from Beal and Cavalieri (2019), criticizing the pecuniary canons of value implicitly assumed by most social science approaches, highlights how deeply our understanding – especially the normative dimension of our understanding of the social – affects the objects of study, the methods applied and, crucially, the results so obtained.

Highlighting the bias in mainstream entrepreneurship research for economic approbation as the main focus (Minniti & Lévesque, 2008) and the individual as the analytical starting point (Goss, 2005), critical research has suggested the need to develop a social ontology of entrepreneurship (Anderson, 2015). Although orthodox economic theory postulates that the main motivation behind entrepreneurs is profit, Zafirovski (1999) suggested that entrepreneurship has an eminent social character and entrepreneurial motives are rather culture-specific and constrained by institutional incentives. A key assumption here is that "entrepreneurship, development and related economic activities are primarily complex social processes, and only secondarily physical, technological or psychological" (p. 354). Ignoring these social conditions and processes can only lead to a partial explanation of the phenomenon, and a lens adjustment is required to bring other mechanisms into focus (Goss, 2005). According to Anderson and Miller (2003), entrepreneurship draws on the social in at least two ways. First, entrepreneurs are conditioned by their social environment; in particular, their perception of opportunities is a function of their social background. Second, businesses conduct their economic activities within a social web of interactions. Korsgaard and Anderson (2011) extend this argument by arguing that the social is not only the context through which the entrepreneurial process occurs or the arena for enabling mechanisms; the outcome of the entrepreneurial process itself is social. Thus, "the examination of entrepreneurial processes should include a focus on the social as an enabler, as context and as outcome" (p. 136). The motives and preferences of entrepreneurs as decision makers should be taken as endogenous to the culture, institutions and the societal context where the phenomenon is taking place rather than an exogenous, homogeneous factor (Zafirovski, 1999).

We believe that the continuum identified by these categories provides a complete description of the role played by the social sphere within innovation and entrepreneurship studies. This taxonomy conceals a significant degree of heterogeneity, with each category containing significantly different conceptualizations and theorizations of the social dimension. However, these categories should not be intended as clear-cut, but as having porous borders: several authors, schools of thought and single contributions straddle them. This diversity cannot be reduced, as it follows from foundational differences within the analytical traditions employed, and it should be understood as an unavoidable consequence of the pluralistic nature of phenomenological approaches to social science.

From the preceding discussion, the following conclusions can be drawn in regard to the role of the social dimension within the context of I&E studies. First, innovation and entrepreneurship are fundamentally social phenomena, independent from the methodological apparatus employed in the process of analysis. Second, I&E studies, as phenomenological fields rather than disciplines, are necessarily characterized by a plurality of analytical interpretations of the social dimension. This diversity should not be considered a sign of immaturity of the field, or a preliminary exploratory phase to be reconciled through further analytical development, but rather a permanent feature. If anything, the success of these fields will only lead to an expansion of the phenomena analysed, both empirically and theoretically, resulting in even more diversity in the near future. Third, understanding the epistemological roots of these varieties of views, found in the conflict between the social sphere's complexity and the requirements of scientific analysis, allows for a reconciliation of these differences, not in a single perspective, but rather within a pluralist field, capable of admitting and fostering constructive interaction between different camps, in contrast with the rigidities and conflicts characterizing disciplinary approaches. Fourth, essentialist conceptualizations of the social play a systemic critical function of checking the growth of transactional and individualist assumptions nested in mainstream approaches to I&E studies, and providing spaces for new and alternative analytical traditions to grow.

While, in this introduction, we have endeavoured to argue that social ontology and epistemology are relevant for all social sciences, they hold a central position in I&E studies particularly. Lacking a clearly defined and generally accepted theoretical core, the demarcation between object of study and social context is bound to remain contentious and, consequently, a potential source of academic division, hindering the main process of scientific development, namely academic debate. Once the issue is framed as a necessary consequence of the phenomenological nature of these fields, the heterogeneity of positions in regard to the analytical role played by social elements can receive a pluralist interpretation as evolving richness, rather than early confusion.

BOOK OVERVIEW

The proposed classification greatly simplifies the complexity of the actual debate and provides a convenient structure for the book. Even though this allows for manageable and, hopefully, meaningful discussion, it is necessary to underline how its categories are not distinct, but rather identify a broad continuum, with individual contributions often straddling the classification borders. While some chapters neatly fit the proposed classification, others find themselves in a potentially contentious position; a useful reminder that analytical convenience should not blind us to the complexity of the real.

The Contextual Approach

In Chapter 2, Misganaw links the literature on entrepreneurial team formation with the literature on organizational imprinting theory, and argues that the type of positions created in new ventures could partially be predicted by looking at the way the entrepreneurial team is formed. In his essay that created the basis for organizational imprinting theory, Stinchcombe (1965) suggested that the present structure of organizations is the reflection of the social conditions and structure at the time of founding. The argument is that the social structure, which includes "groups, institutions, laws, population characteristics, and sets of social relationships that form the environment of the organization" (Stinchcombe, 1965, p. 142), leaves its imprints on organizations, which will be reflected in, among others, the organization's strategies, capabilities and routines (Marquis & Tilcsik, 2013; Simsek et al., 2015). The imprinting process is largely assumed to start at venture founding and venture founders are considered as imprinters in organizational imprinting theory. The imprints of the venture founders are reflected in new organizations, among others, in terms of the positions created and maintained. In this chapter, Misganaw argues that organizational imprinting begins long before the formal founding of the new organization. By linking the literature on entrepreneurial teams and organizational imprinting, he has developed propositions suggesting the positions created in new organizations can be predicted by looking at how the entrepreneurial teams behind the ventures are formed. The chapter contributes to organizational imprinting theory by extending it to the entrepreneurial team (ET) level and suggesting the ET formation, which is a reflection of the social conditions at the time of founding itself, is an antecedent as well as predictor of the organizational imprinting process.

In Chapter 3, Rypestøl focuses on issues of regional development and industrial restructuring provoked by processes such as globalization, sustainability and digitalization. According to the existing literature, strategic change agency is crucial in initiating and moderating the transformation of firm- and system-level assets, thus leading to regional restructuring. Indeed, what is crucial is the close coordination between different types of agency, both at the firm and at the system level (Isaksen et al., 2019). However, while the recent literature has mainly focused on the relation between firm- and system-level assets and successful regional restructurings, Rypestøl invites us to take into consideration the role of social relations. The analytical framework that he presents highlights the role of the structural, relational and cognitive dimensions of relationships on the ability of regions to identify the need for asset modification and to carry on such processes. In short, the structural dimension refers to the position one has in a network and to the value associated with it (Rutten et al., 2010); the relational dimension highlights the nature of social interactions (e.g. questions of trustworthiness, norms, sanctions); the cognitive dimension relates to the resource exchange capability founded on shared codes, values, goals, and so on. Rypestøl's framework is substantiated by a case study on the creation of a system-level material asset (the Mechatronic Innovation Lab) in Norway. Rypestøl finds that this was a complex, expensive and time-consuming social process, involving manifold actors at multiple scales and geographies. Establishing the Lab required a high level of bonding social capital, a network structure of cliques connected by actors holding strategic positions within their cliques, strong and trustful ties, state funding, and a community-based rationality. Therefore, he concludes, one should take care of all these dimensions of social capital when planning a system-level transformation.

In Chapter 4, Wigger and Lauvås challenge the extant views on how entrepreneurial firms mobilize resources by demonstrating how mobilizing collective resources requires a combination of different strategies. They argue that this requires idiosyncratic arrangements, as the ownership of these resources is usually not transferable and firms may not have an exclusive right to use them. Consequently, they identify four types of resource mobilization arrangements used by entrepreneurial firms, where each arrangement has a different design in terms of access, utilization and transferability of the collective resource firms would require. Illuminating their arguments by using cases from the Norwegian salmon industry, the authors argue that in two of the four arrangements, the collaborative and relational arrangements, entrepreneurial firms' ability to mobilize the collective resource(s) rely on social elements, specifically co-dependency and trust, rather than formal contracts. They further argue that these social connections help the involved firms to develop a unique relationship that would be difficult for other firms to imitate, and make the collective resources inaccessible for others who do not have the same social relationships. The chapter draws on a resource-based view, resource dependency theory, and new institutional economics to suggest a reconceptualization of entrepreneurial firms' resource mobilizations by going beyond the widely accepted view that firms create a competitive advantage by owning resources exclusively for themselves and excluding others. Rather, they highlight the importance of social relations to access collective resources and by doing so may increase the barrier for other firms from acquiring the collective resources.

In Chapter 5, Gonzalez studies the relationship between innovation and economic crises. She investigates the adaptation and innovation efforts of companies during the front-end phase of a crisis, and in particular how the constrained resources and learned patterns of work affect innovation processes. Studying crisis has been a flourishing topic of analysis in innovation studies in the past decade, due to the well known 2000s financial crisis and the more recent Covid-19 pandemic (Amore, 2015; Archibugi et al., 2013; Filippetti &

Archibugi, 2011). Gonzalez contributes by exploring the front-end phase of a crisis, where companies try to make sense of what is happening by using and adapting previously learned experiences in the new situation. This is indeed a challenging situation, since the environment they are used to operating in has changed. Her study focuses on a group of suppliers to the oil and gas industry during the industry downturn of 2015–18. Gonzalez finds that companies experienced conflicted situations, for example due to a change in resources and the arising of uncertainty and ambiguity. However, this did not stop their innovation efforts, but it produced a shift in how companies worked and in their position in relation to clients. The type of innovation they introduced was of an incremental type, in line with the pre-crisis learned experiences, and this might be due to the fact that companies first needed to secure their own survival. During the front end of the crisis, they adopted both retrenchment and proactive adaptation strategies for innovation, variously combining them, for example by starting with a retrenchment activity and ending with an innovation effort, or the reverse. Interestingly, retrenchment should not necessarily be perceived as negative for innovation processes, as it can open up space for other forms of innovation.

Chapter 6 tackles the relevance of the social dimension vis-à-vis economic incentives for employees' cooperation with incremental innovation processes on the shopfloor. In this chapter, Bragtvedt confronts the phenomenon of spontaneous and unpaid workers' contribution to incremental process innovation in a Norwegian aluminum smelter, exploring which behavioral mode of operation proposed by existing literature provides the better interpretative fit. The ethnographic fieldwork includes interviews with employees, employers, engineers and trade union representatives taken during a period of direct observation and informal interaction. Bragtvedt finds that employees used to be individually rewarded for offering practical suggestions resulting in incremental operational improvements. However, the incentive scheme was suspended when workers were re-organized as autonomous teams. Despite this, workers continued to contribute their practical knowledge to the management, resulting in an even more rapid pace of operational improvements. Bragtvedt finds several factors contributing to this outcome. First, the desire to do a good job and to be identified by other workers as productive and able (Lindenberg, 2001). Second, the ambition to contribute to the success of the firm, to be seen by managers as benevolent collaborators (Nonaka & Takeuchi, 1995). Third, to reduce waiting times and, more generally, time dedicated to boring tasks, in favour of more productive and personally satisfying activities (Williamson, 1996). These drivers could support each other, leading to a continuous, positive contribution thanks to the key supporting role played by an underlying positive class compromise (Olin Wright, 2015), supported by a clear consensual vision (Lindenberg & Foss, 2011) of the positive social role played by the

Introduction

firm within the region and of the ultimately harmonious relationship between workers, managers and owners.

The Identification Approach

In Chapter 7, Kosmynin investigates how social entrepreneurs enact the context for collaborations. Social enterprises have received growing interest from researchers and policymakers alike, because of the role they play in bringing about social change by combining practices of traditional for-profit and non-profit organizations. Not constrained by established organizational routines and models of thinking, they have capacity to provide innovative solutions to societal challenges. To achieve their objectives, social enterprises need to collaborate with different stakeholders, both in the public and private sector. By using an ethnographic case study approach, Kosmynin studied two social enterprises in Norway operating in sectors traditionally associated with the public sector in the Norwegian welfare system. Given that the context is characterized by a strong welfare structure and societal model with a strong civil society component, social services are typically provided by public bodies. As a result, social entrepreneurs face a challenge in dealing with the conventional wisdom on how welfare services have to be provided and have to find ways to reach their goals. Kosmynin found that although social entrepreneurs are expected to follow certain rules in the context in which they operate, they go beyond that by finding new ways of circumventing existing rules, which leads to the emergence of new practices. He further argues that social entrepreneurs cannot be seen in isolation from their social contexts. This social context not only sets the rules for the entrepreneurs, but the entrepreneurs through their entrepreneurial acts contribute to the emergence of new practices in the context. Building on de Certeau's (1988) practice theory, the chapter extends the notions of "strategy" and "tactics" to the context of social venture–public sector collaboration and provides an enhanced understanding of how social entrepreneurs draw on practices to engage in collaboration and accomplish entrepreneurial doings at the micro level.

In Chapter 8, Nguyen et al. merge the existing approaches of RRI and smart specialization into a framework aimed at guiding policymakers in designing and implementing viable policies to foster and nurture a regional innovation ecosystem, according to locally based specificities. The "smart specialization" approach stems from the attempt to strengthen European economic growth by increasing the regional diversity of R&D investments. According to its proponents, this diversity will mitigate the problem of R&D duplication in the EU, while enabling regions to carve out competitive niches based on inherent strengths. Therefore, smart specialization policies tend to select the regions' unique strengths and advantages and encourage related projects. Instead,

RRI refers to the implementation of governance processes aimed at aligning research and innovation activities with the values and needs of society. This approach stems from a recognition that policymakers cannot exercise complete control over a system; at best, what they can do is to embrace its complexity and seize fleeting opportunities emerging from it. By presenting the case of the formulation of a strategic plan for Nordland in Norway, the authors show how their practice-oriented framework can be practically applied with the aim of bringing stakeholders together and engaging them in a productive dialogue. It is composed of several questions, whose answers should help to define a thematic focus for the region (e.g. a regional challenge), create a common vision and set priorities for smart specialization. The framework included in this chapter should be regarded as an introductory account of how it is possible to promote RRI in the context of smart specialization.

In Chapter 9, Solheim reviews the state of the art of current scholarly research on the relationship between diversity and innovation. Diversity enters the present business landscape both through increased global interactions (Guillaume et al., 2014), and increased workforce diversity in terms of work–life experiences, gender, educational background and skill mix, birthplace diversity and age (Parrotta et al., 2014). Empirical studies have underlined both positive and negative consequences of diversity for the development of innovation capabilities. Diversity contributes to innovation processes by broadening the knowledge base, improving access to network resources and providing new stimuli and creative challenges (Østergaard et al., 2011; Phillips et al., 2009; Van Engen & Van Woerkom, 2010). At the same time, diversity could increase conflicts and miscommunication, but also innovation processes' time and costs (Basset-Jones, 2005; Smith et al., 2017). The main contribution of this chapter, however, lies in pointing out that both analysts and practitioners should not assimilate diversity with the simple presence of people with diverse backgrounds and resources, but rather focus their attention on the actual social practices of integration. Integration is described as the key mediator, determining if the costs or benefits of diversity predominate. In this regard, both the creation of shared identities and common spaces of actions and interactions can play a positive role (Stegmann et al., 2012; Traavik, 2019). However, no "one-size-fits-all" solutions have been identified, leaving significant gaps for future researchers to fill.

The Essentialist Approach

In Chapter 10, Callegari explores the social ontology supporting the defining theoretical and methodological choices of Schumpeter's theory of economic development. The chapter aims to illustrate the relevance of ontological and epistemological assumptions regarding the nature of the social dimension and

Introduction 17

its relationship with the requirements of scientific analysis for the development of Schumpeterian theory. While Schumpeter (2010) initially aimed to develop a purely economic theory of development, the inclusion of monetary transactions within the analysis, necessary to enable individual agency in the context of the economic system, required the introduction of a set of institutional assumptions regarding the nature of the system of social accounting. Consequently, while the Schumpeterian conceptualizations of innovation and entrepreneurship are purely economic, the accompanying theoretical propositions are contextual, depending on the institutional features of the supporting monetary and financial system (Schumpeter, 1942). The resulting theory of economic development was therefore distinct from, and ultimately incompatible with, neoclassical economics (Schumpeter, 1934). Furthermore, the supporting methodology implied a multidisciplinary approach to social sciences, aimed towards understanding and causal explanation rather than prediction and functional modelling (Schumpeter, 1954). In this regard, the current innovation and entrepreneurship studies can be interpreted as a partial realization of the Schumpterian meta-theoretical blueprint (Shionoya, 2007). Indeed, the further development of these fields would benefit from an explicit integration of an ontological and epistemological dimension clarifying the relationship between the social dimension and the conceptualization of the phenomena under study, in particular novelty and agency. The chapter clarifies how Schumpeter tackled the issue, using the results as a basis for the development of an internally consistent and far-reaching theoretical framework; the same results are now offered for fuelling contemporary debates on the role of the social in innovation and entrepreneurship studies.

In Chapter 11, Sardo challenges some of the assumptions of innovation studies describing not-in-transition industries as internally coherent and evolving along shared variables (or socio-technical codes) against which technologies are evaluated and incrementally improved. These studies assume the same moral and societal agendas to be embedded in rules, technological designs, contracts, standards, routines and imaginaries about the future (see e.g. Dosi, 1982; Geels, 2002; Geels and Schot, 2016). Together, these elements form a dynamic socio-technical framework, or regime, which is a constraining and enabling context for action (Geels, 2004). For these reasons, few conflicts or mismatches characterize not-in-transition industries. This chapter challenges these assumptions by resorting to concepts from Science and Technology Studies and focusing on the socio-technical code of safety in the Norwegian offshore oil and gas drilling industry. At first glance, safety appears as a "naturalized" element, a standard criterion routinely applied by everyone. However, a close analysis reveals that it is instead the loose outcome of a distributed – but hierarchical – surveillance system. Tensions and debates on safety constantly tear the industry apart. Rather than being stable, safety is constantly in the making. Sardo shows why industrial and innovation activities cannot be separated from social values, and why it is important to deeply understand which (and whose) criteria are employed in the design of technologies and operations. Indeed, assuming that socio-technical values are shared (and therefore theoretically unimportant) and that decisions on innovations and policies are value- and power-neutral hinders a more democratic construction of safety. This of course raises further questions about whether value homogeneity and coherence are theoretically necessary conditions for explaining the dynamic stability of industries not-in-transition.

Chapter 12, by Mikhailova, compares and contrasts the systemic and network perspectives as applied to the analysis of medical technologies innovation processes. The Health Innovation System (HIS) perspective (Consoli & Mina, 2009) has provided an evolutionary aggregate conceptualization of how the functional interactions between the diverse agents and organizations composing the healthcare ecosystem generate, implement and diffuse new knowledge. On the other hand, network-based approaches (Albert-Cromarias & Dos Santos, 2020; Chiambaretto & Dumez, 2016) offer an empirically focused understanding of the interlocked strategic dynamics of cooperation and competition in which agents engage during actual innovation processes, creating, leveraging and destroying relationships and resources in the process. The complementary nature of these two approaches is illustrated in a case study involving the Transcatheter Aortic Valve Implantation technology innovation process involving producers, hospitals and practitioners active in the Danish context. While the HIS perspective can be gainfully applied to make sense of the complex dynamics between the actors and highlight the emerging functional logic, the network approach reveals the subjective perspective motivating individual agents' behaviour. Used in combination, the two approaches illuminate both the complex, systemic nature of social interactions, and their personal, strategic side, providing a holistic perspective of the role of the social in the process of medical technologies innovation.

NOTE

1. For a critical overview on innovation and its connection to the social dimension, see Godin (2015).

REFERENCES

Albert-Cromarias, A., & Dos Santos, C. (2020). Coopetition in healthcare: Heresy or reality? An exploration of felt outcomes at an intra-organizational level. *Social Science & Medicine*, 252, 112938.

Amore, M. D. (2015). Companies learning to innovate in recessions. *Research Policy*, 44(8), 1574–83.

Anderson, A. R. (2015). The economic reification of entrepreneurship: re-engaging with the social. In A. Fayolle, & P. Riot (Eds.), *Rethinking entrepreneurship: debating research orientations* (pp. 44–56). Abingdon: Routledge.

Anderson, A. R., & Miller, C. J. (2003). 'Class matters': Human and social capital in the entrepreneurial process. *Journal of Socio-Economics*, 32(1), 17–36.

Archibugi, D., Filippetti, A., & Frenz, M. (2013). Economic crisis and innovation: Is destruction prevailing over accumulation? *Research Policy*, 42(2), 303–14.

Avelino, F., Wittmayer, J. M., Pel, B., Weaver, P., Dumitru, A., Haxeltine, A., Kemp, R., Jørgensen, M. S., Bauler, T., Ruijsink, S., & O'Riordan, T. (2019). Transformative social innovation and (dis)empowerment. *Technological Forecasting and Social Change*, 145, 195–206.

Baba, Y., & Walsh, J. P. (2010). Embeddedness, social epistemology and breakthrough innovation: The case of the development of statins. *Research Policy*, 39(4), 511–22.

Basset-Jones, N. (2005). The paradox of diversity management, creativity and innovation. *Creativity and Innovation Management*, 14, 169–75.

Beal, D., & Cavalieri, M. (2019). Connecting institutional economics to communitarian philosophy: Beyond market institutions and pecuniary canons of value. *Journal of Economic Issues*, 53(3), 634–46.

Becker, G. S. (1960). An economic analysis of fertility. In G. S. Becker (Ed.), *Demographic and economic change in developed countries* (pp. 209–40). Princeton, NJ: Princeton University Press.

Bijker, W. E., Hughes, T. S., & Pinch, T. J. (Eds.) (1987). *The social construction of technological systems: new directions in the sociology and history of technology.* Cambridge, MA: MIT Press.

Burget, M., Bardone, E., & Pedaste, M. (2017). Definitions and conceptual dimensions of responsible research and innovation: A literature review. *Science and Engineering Ethics*, 23(1), 1–19.

Cajaiba-Santana, G. (2014). Social innovation: Moving the field forward. A conceptual framework. *Technological Forecasting and Social Change*, 82, 42–51.

Carayannis, E., & Campbell, D. F. J. (2009). "Mode 3" and "Quadruple Helix": Toward a 21st-century fractal innovation ecosystem. *International Journal of Technology Management*, 46(3–4), 201–34.

Carayannis, E., Barth, T., & Campbell, D. F. J. (2012). The Quintuple Helix innovation model: Global warming as a challenge and driver for innovation. *Journal of Innovation and Entrepreneurship*, 1(1), 1–12.

Chell, E. (2007). Social enterprise and entrepreneurship: Towards a convergent theory of the entrepreneurial process. *International Small Business Journal*, 25(1), 5–26.

Chiambaretto, P., & Dumez, H. (2016). Toward a typology of coopetition: A multilevel approach. *International Studies of Management & Organization*, 46(2–3), 110–29.

Consoli, D., & Mina, A. (2009). An evolutionary perspective on health innovation systems. *Journal of Evolutionary Economics*, 19(2), 297–319.

Cooke, P., & Morgan, K. (1994). The regional innovation system in Baden–Wurttemberg. *International Journal of Technology Management*, 9(3–4), 394–429.

Cooke, P., de Laurentis, C., Tödtling, F., & Trippl, M. (Eds.) (2007). *Regional knowledge economies: markets, clusters and innovation.* Cheltenham, UK and Northampton, MA, USA: Edward Elgar Publishing.

Dacin, M. T., Dacin, P. A., & Tracey, P. (2011). Social entrepreneurship: A critique and future directions. *Organization Science*, 22(5), 1203–13.

Dakhli, M., & De Clercq, D. (2004). Human capital, social capital, and innovation: A multi-country study. *Entrepreneurship & Regional Development*, 16(2), 107–28.

Davidsson, P., & Honig, B. (2003). The role of social and human capital among nascent entrepreneurs. *Journal of Business Venturing*, 18(3), 301–31.

de Certeau, M. (1988). *The practice of everyday life*. Berkeley, CA: University of California Press.

Dequech, D. (2012). Post Keynesianism, heterodoxy and mainstream economics. *Review of Political Economy*, 24(2), 353–68.

Dosi, G. (1982). Technological paradigms and technological trajectories: A suggested interpretation of the determinants and directions of technical change. *Research Policy*, 11(3), 147–62.

Edlund, L., & Korn, E. (2002). A theory of prostitution. *Journal of Political Economy*, 110(1), 181–214.

Etzkowitz, H., & Leydesdorff, L. (1995). The Triple Helix: University–industry–government relations: A laboratory for knowledge based economic development. *EASST Review*, 14(1), 14-19.

European Commission (2010). *Europe 2020: flagship initiative innovation union*. Brussels: European Commission.

Filippetti, A., & Archibugi, D. (2011). Innovation in times of crisis: National systems of innovation, structure, and demand. *Research Policy*, 40(2), 179–92.

Flink, T., & Kaldewey, D. (2018). The new production of legitimacy: STI policy discourses beyond the contract metaphor. *Research Policy*, 47(1), 14–22.

Fougère, M., Segercrantz, B., & Seeck, H. (2017). A critical reading of the European Union's social innovation policy discourse: (Re)legitimizing neoliberalism. *Organization*, 24(6), 819–43.

Freeman, C. (1987). *Technology policy and economic performance: lessons from Japan*. London: Pinter.

Gedajlovic, E., Honig, B., Moore, C. B., Payne, G. T., & Wright, M. (2013). Social capital and entrepreneurship: A schema and research agenda. *Entrepreneurship Theory and Practice*, 37(3), 455–78.

Geels, F. W. (2002). Technological transitions as evolutionary reconfiguration processes: A multi-level perspective and a case-study. *Research Policy*, 31(8–9), 1257–74.

Geels, F. W. (2004). Understanding system innovations: A critical literature review and a conceptual synthesis. In B. Elzen, F. Geels, & K. Green (Eds.), *System innovation and the transition to sustainability* (pp. 19–47). Cheltenham, UK and Northampton, MA, USA: Edward Elgar Publishing.

Geels, F. W. (2005). *Technological transitions and system innovations: A co-evolutionary and socio-technical analysis*. Cheltenham, UK and Northampton, MA, USA: Edward Elgar Publishing.

Geels, F. W. (2010). Ontologies, socio-technical transitions (to sustainability), and the multi-level perspective. *Research Policy*, 39(4), 495–510.

Geels, F. W., & Schot, J. (2007). Typology of sociotechnical transition pathways. *Research Policy*, 36(3), 399–417.

Geels F. W., & Schot, J. (2016). Towards a new innovation theory for grand societal challenges. Working Paper for SPRU Anniversary Conference.

Godin, B. (2009). National innovation system: The system approach in historical perspective. *Science, Technology, & Human Values*, 34(4), 476–501.

Godin, B. (2012). "Innovation studies": The invention of a specialty. *Minerva*, 50(4), 397–421.

Godin, B. (2015). Social innovation: From scheme to utopia. In B. Godin (Ed.), *Innovation contested: The idea of innovation over the centuries* (pp. 122–33). London: Routledge.

Goss, D. (2005). Entrepreneurship and "the social": Towards a deference-emotion theory. *Human Relations*, 58(5), 617–36.

Guillaume, Y. R. F., Dawson, J. F., Priola, V., Sacramento, C. A., Woods, S. A., Higson, H. E., Budwar, P.S., & West, M. A. (2014). Managing diversity in organizations: An integrative model and agenda for future research. *European Journal of Work and Organizational Psychology*, 23(5), 783–802.

Gupta, P., Chauhan, S., Paul, J., & Jaiswal, M. P. (2020). Social entrepreneurship research: A review and future research agenda. *Journal of Business Research*, 113, 209–29.

Guston, D. H., Fisher, E., Grunwald, A., Owen, R., Swierstra, T., & Van der Burg, S. (2014). Responsible innovation: Motivations for a new journal. *Journal of Responsible Innovation*, 1, 1–8.

Hernández-Carrión, C., Camarero-Izquierdo, C., & Gutiérrez-Cillán, J. (2017). Entrepreneurs' social capital and the economic performance of small businesses: The moderating role of competitive intensity and entrepreneurs' experience. *Strategic Entrepreneurship Journal*, 11(1), 61–89.

Isaksen, A. (2015). Industrial development in thin regions: trapped in path extension? *Journal of Economic Geography*, 15(3), 585–600.

Isaksen, A., Jakobsen, S.-E., Njøs, R., & Normann, R. (2019). Regional industrial restructuring resulting from individual and system agency. *Innovation: The European Journal of Social Science Research*, 32(1), 48–65.

Kimmitt, J., & Muñoz, P. (2018). Sensemaking the "social" in social entrepreneurship. *International Small Business Journal*, 36(8), 859–86.

Kleinhempel, J., Beugelsdijk, S., & Klasing, M. J. (2020). The changing role of social capital during the venture creation process: A multilevel study. *Entrepreneurship Theory and Practice*, https://doi.org/1042258720913022.

Korsgaard, S., & Anderson, A. R. (2011). Enacting entrepreneurship as social value creation. *International Small Business Journal*, 29(2), 135–51.

Kuhlmann S., & Rip, A. (2018). Next-generation innovation policy and grand challenges. *Science and Public Policy*, 45(4), 448–54.

Kupferberg, F. (1998). Humanistic entrepreneurship and entrepreneurial career commitment. *Entrepreneurship & Regional Development*, 10(3), 171–88.

Kwon, S. W., & Arenius, P. (2010). Nations of entrepreneurs: A social capital perspective. *Journal of Business Venturing*, 25(3), 315–30.

Landry, R., Amara, N., & Lamari, M. (2002). Does social capital determine innovation? To what extent? *Technological Forecasting and Social Change*, 69(7), 681–701.

Lee, S., Lee, H., & Lee, C. (2020). Open innovation at the national level: Towards a global innovation system. *Technological Forecasting and Social Change*, 151, 119842.

Lee, R., Tuselmann, H., Jayawarna, D., & Rouse, J. (2019). Effects of structural, relational and cognitive social capital on resource acquisition: A study of entrepreneurs residing in multiply deprived areas. *Entrepreneurship & Regional Development*, 31(5–6), 534–54.

Leydesdorff, L. (2012). The triple helix, quadruple helix, … , and an N-tuple of helices: Explanatory models for analyzing the knowledge-based economy? *Journal of the Knowledge Economy*, 3(1), 25–35.

Lindenberg, S. (2001). Intrinsic motivation in a new light. *Kyklos*, 54(2–3), 317–42.

Lindenberg, S., & Foss, N. J. (2011). Managing joint production motivation: The role of goal framing and governance mechanisms. *Academy of Management Review*, 36(3), 500–525.

Lundvall, B.-Å. (1988). Innovation as an interactive process: From user–producer interaction to the national innovation systems. In G. Dosi, C. Freeman, R. R. Nelson, G. Silverberg, & L. Soete (Eds.), *Technical change and economic theory* (pp. 349–69). London: Pinter.

Lundvall B.-Å. (2013). Innovation studies: A personal interpretation of "the state of the art". In J. Fagerberg, B. R. Martin, & E. S. Andersen (Eds.), *The future of innovation studies: Evolution and future challenges* (pp. 21–70). Oxford: Oxford University Press.

Mair, J., & Marti, I. (2006). Social entrepreneurship research: A source of explanation, prediction, and delight. *Journal of World Business*, 41(1), 36–44.

Markard J., & B. Truffer (2008). Technological innovation systems and the multi-level perspective: Towards an integrated framework. *Research Policy*, 37(4), 596–615.

Marquis, C., & Tilcsik, A. (2013). Imprinting: Toward a multilevel theory. *Academy of Management Annals*, 7(1), 195–245.

Martin, R. (2010). Roepke lecture in economic geography—rethinking regional path dependence: Beyond lock-in to evolution. *Economic Geography*, 86(1), 1–27.

Mazzucato, M. (2018). Mission-oriented research & innovation in the European Union. https://op.europa.eu/en/publication-detail/-/publication/5b2811d1-16be-11e8-9253 -01aa75ed71a1/language-en.

Minniti, M., & Lévesque, M. (2008). Recent developments in the economics of entrepreneurship. *Journal of Business Venturing*, 23(6), 603–12.

Mulgan, G., Tucker, S., Ali, R., & Sanders, B. (2007). *Social innovation: What it is, why it matters and how it can be accelerated*. Oxford: Skoll Centre for Social Entrepreneurship.

Murray, R., Caulier-Grice, J., & Mulgan, G. (2010). *The open book of social innovation*. London: Nesta.

Nahapiet, J., & Ghoshal, S. (1998). Social capital, intellectual capital, and the organizational advantage. *Academy of Management Review*, 23(2), 242–66.

Nelson, R. R., & Rosenberg, N. (1993). Technical innovation and national systems. In R. R. Nelson (Ed.), *National innovation systems* (pp. 3–21). Oxford: Oxford University Press.

Nelson, R. R., & Winter, S. G. (1982). *An evolutionary theory of economic change*. Cambridge, MA: Harvard University Press.

Nonaka, I., & Takeuchi, H. (1995). *The knowledge-creating company: How Japanese companies create the dynamics of innovation*. Oxford: Oxford University Press.

Olin Wright, E. (2015). *Understanding class*. London: Verso Books.

Østergaard, C. R., Timmermans, B., & Kristinsson, K. (2011). Does a different view create something new? The effect of employee diversity on innovation. *Research Policy*, 40(3), 500–509.

Owen, R., Macnaghten, P., & Stilgoe, J. (2012). Responsible research and innovation: From science in society to science for society, with society. *Science and Public Policy*, 39(6), 751–60.

Owen, R., Stilgoe, J., Macnaghten, P., Gorman, M., Fisher, E., & Guston, D. (2013). A framework of responsible innovation. In R. Owen, J. Bessant, & M. Heintz (Eds.), *Responsible innovation: Managing the responsible emergence of science and innovation in society* (pp. 27–50). Chichester: Wiley.

Parrotta, P., Pozzoli, D., & Pytlikova, M. (2014). Labor diversity and firm productivity. *European Economic Review*, 66, 144–79.

Pel, B., Haxeltine, A., Avelino, F., Dumitru, A., Kemp, R., Bauler, T., … & Jørgensen, M. S. (2020). Towards a theory of transformative social innovation: A relational framework and 12 propositions. *Research Policy*, 49(8), 104080.

Phillips, K. W., Liljenquist, K. A., & Neale, M. A. (2009). Is the pain worth the gain? The advantages and liabilities of agreeing with socially distinct newcomers. *Personality and Social Psychology Bulletin*, 35(3), 336–50.

Pinch, T. J., & Bijker, W. E. (1987). The social construction of facts and artifacts: Or how the sociology of science and technology might benefit each other. In W. E. Bijker, T. P. Hughes, & T. J. Pinch (Eds.), *The social construction of technical systems: New directions in the sociology and history of technology* (pp. 17–50). Cambridge MA: The MIT Press.

Posner, R. A. (1985). An economic theory of the criminal law. *Columbia Law Review*, 85(6), 1193–231.

Rip, A., & Kemp, R. (1998). Technological change. In S. Rayner, & E. L. Malone (Eds.), *Human choice and climate change*, Vol. 2 (pp. 327–99). Columbus, OH: Battelle Press.

Rosenberg, N. (1982). *Inside the black box: Technology and economics*. Cambridge: Cambridge University Press.

Ruebottom, T. (2013). The microstructures of rhetorical strategy in social entrepreneurship: Building legitimacy through heroes and villains. *Journal of Business Venturing*, 28(1), 98–116.

Rutten, R., Westlund, H., & Boekema, F. (2010). The spatial dimension of social capital. *European Planning Studies*, 18(6), 863–71.

Schumpeter, J. A. (1934). *The theory of economic development: An inquiry into profits, capital, credit, interest, and the business cycle*. Cambridge, MA: Harvard University Press.

Schumpeter, J. A. (1942). *Socialism, capitalism and democracy*. New York: Harper and Brothers.

Schumpeter, J. A. (1949). Science and ideology. *American Economic Review*, 39(2), 345–59.

Schumpeter, J. A. (1954). *History of economic analysis*. New York: Oxford University Press.

Schumpeter, J. A. (2010). *The nature and essence of economic theory*. New Brunswick, NJ: Transaction Publishers.

Shepherd, D. A., Sattari, R., & Patzelt, H. (2020). A social model of opportunity development: Building and engaging communities of inquiry. *Journal of Business Venturing*, 106033.

Shionoya, Y. (2007). *Schumpeter and the idea of social science: A metatheoretical study*. Cambridge: Cambridge University Press.

Simsek, Z., Fox, B. C., & Heavey, C. (2015). "What's past is prologue": A framework, review, and future directions for organizational research on imprinting. *Journal of Management*, 41(1), 288–317.

Sismondo, S. (2010). *An introduction to science and technology studies*. Malden, MA: Blackwell Publishing.

Smith, K. W., Erez, M., Jarvenpaa, S., Lewis, M. W., & Tracey, P. (2017). Adding complexity to theories of paradox, tensions, and dualities of innovation and change: Introduction to organization studies [special issue]. *Organization Studies*, 38(3–4), 303–17.

Stam, W., & Elfring, T. (2008). Entrepreneurial orientation and new venture performance: The moderating role of intra- and extra-industry social capital. *Academy of Management Journal*, 51(1), 97–111.

Stegmann, S., Roberge, M.-É., & van Dick, R. (2012). Getting tuned in to those who are different: The role of empathy as mediator between diversity and performance. In B. Beham, C. Straub, & J. Schwalbach (Eds.), *Managing diversity in organizations* (pp. 19–44). Wiesbaden: Gabler Verlag.

Stevens, R., Moray, N., & Bruneel, J. (2015). The social and economic mission of social enterprises: Dimensions, measurement, validation, and relation. *Entrepreneurship Theory and Practice*, 39(5), 1051–82.

Stilgoe, J., Owen, R., & Macnaghten, P. (2013). Developing a framework for responsible innovation. *Research Policy*, 42(9), 1568–80.

Stinchcombe, A. L. (1965). Social structure and organizations. In J. G. March (Ed.), *Handbook of organizations* (pp. 142–93). Chicago, IL: Rand McNally.

Tödtling, F., & M. Trippl (2004). Like a phoenix from the ashes? The renewal of clusters in old industrial areas. *Urban Studies*, 41, 1175–95.

Traavik, L. E. M. (2019). Where differences dwell: Inclusion and the healthy workplace. In R. J. Burke, & A. M. Richardson (Eds.), *Creating psychologically healthy workplaces* (pp. 215–34). Cheltenham, UK, and Northanpton, MA, USA: Edward Elgar Publishing.

van der Have, R. P., & Rubalcaba, L. (2016). Social innovation research: An emerging area of innovation studies? *Research Policy*, 45(9), 1923–35.

Van Engen, M., & Van Woerkom, M. (2010). Learning from differences: The relationships between team expertise diversity, team learning, team performance, and team innovation. In M. Van Woerkom, & R. Poell (Eds.), *Workplace learning: Concepts, measurement and application* (pp. 131–47). London: Routledge.

Vega, A., & Chiasson, M. (2019). A comprehensive framework to research digital innovation: The joint use of the systems of innovation and critical realism. *The Journal of Strategic Information Systems*, 28(3), 242–56.

von Schomberg, R. (2013). A vision of responsible research and innovation. In R. Owen, J. R. Bessant, & M. Heintz (Eds.), *Responsible innovation: Managing the responsible emergence of science and innovation in society* (pp. 51–74). New York: John Wiley & Sons.

von Schomberg, R. (2015). Responsible innovation: The new paradigm for science, technology and innovation policy. In A. Bogner, M. Decker, & M. Sotoudeh (Eds.), *Responsible innovation: Neue impulse fur die technikfolgenabschatzung?* (pp. 47–71). Baden-Baden: Nomos Verlagsgesellschaft.

Williamson, O. E. (1996). Economic organization: The case for candor. *Academy of Management Review*, 21(1), 48–57.

Winner, L. (1980). Do artifacts have politics? *Daedalus*, 109, 121–36.

Yakovlev, P. (2011). The economics of torture. In C. J. Coyne, & R. L. Mathers (Eds.), *The handbook on the political economy of war* (pp. 109–25). Cheltenham, UK and Northampton, MA, USA: Edward Elgar Publishing.

Zafirovski, M. (1999). Probing into the social layers of entrepreneurship: Outlines of the sociology of enterprise. *Entrepreneurship & Regional Development*, 11(4), 351–71.

PART I

The contextual approach

2. Entrepreneurial team formation, task allocation in new ventures and the theory of imprinting

Bisrat A. Misganaw

INTRODUCTION

In his influential essay entitled "Social Structure and Organizations", Stinchcombe (1965, p. 153) suggested that "organizational forms and types have a history, and that this history determines some aspects of the present structure of organizations of that type." This essay laid the foundation of organizational imprinting theory, which predicts that the social structures at the time of venture founding have implications for the future of new firms including their strategies, capabilities and routines (Marquis & Tilcsik, 2013; Simsek et al., 2015). Social structures are defined as "groups, institutions, laws, population characteristics, and sets of social relationships that form the environment of the organization" (Stinchcombe, 1965, p. 142). In order to understand the imprinting process better, Johnson (2007) calls students of organizational imprinting theory to give more attention to the sequence of decisive activities in the venture founding process. In contrast to this, research in the field largely assumes that imprinting begins at venture inception (Mathias et al., 2015) and focuses on what happens after the founding of the venture (Aldrich & Yang, 2012). However, the imprinting process might begin earlier than the day the venture is founded. For instance, Mathias et al. (2015) have shown how individual entrepreneurs themselves are imprinted and how that affects the decision-making process of the entrepreneurs as well as the ventures. Given that a significant proportion of firms are created by teams (Honoré, 2015; Wasserman, 2012), I argue that the genesis of the imprinting process could be understood better by studying how entrepreneurial teams (ETs) themselves are formed. The aim of this chapter is, thus, to link the literature on ET formation with imprinting theory, specifically the position imprinting literature, by discussing how the way teams are formed may affect the composition of founding teams and how that may affect the positions created at the early stages of the venture founding process. Consequently, I suggest that ET formation is an antecedent for ET composition and the position imprinting process, and hence a predictor of the organizational imprinting process.

Why is a discussion about ETs important for the theory of imprinting? According to Stinchcombe (1965, pp. 148–9), the high rate of failure among new organizations is because of the "liability of newness". He further argued that three of the four important factors causing the liability of newness for new ventures are related to the founding team, where new working relationships have to be developed, roles need to be learned, and the financial rewards from the new venture have to be negotiated among the team members. Furthermore, new venture founders are said to have an imprinting effect on organizations in several ways – among others, by influencing the initial strategy of the organization (Boeker, 1989), positions created (Beckman & Burton, 2008; Burton & Beckman, 2007) or exit strategies (Albert & DeTienne, 2016). Indeed, Marquis and Tilcsik (2013) maintain that one of the areas where organizational imprinting research offers convincing evidence is related to the lasting effect of founders in organizations. Similarly, Kriauciunas and Shinkle (2008, p. 7) emphasized that "powerful founders are the sources of imprint and they continue to exert influence on the firm that traditionalizes the imprint." Consequently, imprinting in newly created organizations could be explained as an agent-driven process where the decisions made by nascent entrepreneurs are the mechanisms through which new organizations obtain important features from their contexts (Johnson, 2007; Tornikoski & Renko, 2014). Thus, understanding how the team came into being from the start is crucial as it may have implications for the way the team operates and steers the venture.

This chapter contributes to the literature on imprinting and ETs in several ways. First, it extends the imprinting literature to the team level and suggests that ETs engaged in founding new ventures are not only imprinters but are also imprinted by the social conditions at the time of formation. Existing research on imprinting largely focuses on the organization level (Guenther et al., 2016; Mathias et al., 2015) and considers founders only as imprinters or sources of imprints for new organizations (Beckman, 2006; Boeker, 1989; Simsek et al., 2015). Second, it contributes to the position imprinting literature by suggesting that positions created in new ventures could partly be predicted by looking at how the ETs behind the ventures form. Third, besides predicting positions created in organizations, it suggests that the way ETs form may also have an effect on the future career development and choices of team members. Imprinting research at the individual level suggests "conditions experienced in the early years of organizational tenure or a career exert a lasting influence on subsequent habits, routines, and behaviors" (Tilcsik, 2014, p. 641). I argue that the experiences of individuals during their early years of tenure could differ depending on the way the ETs they are part of are formed.

The rest of the chapter is organized as follows. The next section discusses the main arguments in imprinting theory, specifically on position imprinting. Then perspectives on job position creation are presented followed by perspectives on ET formation. I then discuss how ET formation and position creation as well as position imprinting are linked, followed by concluding remarks.

IMPRINTING THEORY AND POSITION IMPRINTING

The concept of imprinting, originally developed in animal behaviour studies in the late nineteenth century (Marquis & Tilcsik, 2013), has been introduced into organizational studies following Stinchcombe's (1965) seminal essay on social structures and organizations. Although Stinchcombe (1965) did not use the term "imprinting" in his analysis, the concept is attributed to his paper (Marquis & Tilcsik, 2013). The literature on imprinting has been growing since then and the concept has been applied on different levels of analysis such as venture networks (Milanov & Fernhaber, 2009), organizations (Boeker, 1989; Han et al., 2014), entrepreneurial founding teams (Bryant, 2014) and even individuals (Azoulay et al., 2017; Mathias et al., 2015).

In a synthesis of the extant research on imprinting, Marquis and Tilcsik (2013) identified three different but equally important sources of imprints: institutional, economic and technological, and individual. The list of institutional imprinters includes "regulative, normative, and cultural-cognitive factors" (Marquis & Tilcsik, 2013, p. 207), while the economic and technological factors include both macro-level economic conditions or economic conditions within organizations. The imprinting generated from these three sources could be manifested or imprinted on four entities: organizational collectives, single organizations, organizational building blocks and individuals (Marquis & Tilcsik, 2013).

In another review, Simsek et al. (2015, p. 289) suggested that imprinting is not a "once-off episode whereby the environment is merely stamped upon an entity", but it "involves three processes in which an imprint is formed (genesis), evolves and morphs (metamorphosis), and eventually becomes manifest in outcomes (manifestation)". In the genesis phase, they argued, an imprint will be formed because of an interaction between the imprinters (defined as the sources of imprints) and the imprinted (defined as the target entity bearing the imprint). The list of imprinters includes individual founders (e.g. initial position holders), teams (their composition and diversity), and the environment (including regulatory conditions as well as institutional and cultural norms). However, I would argue that founders' composition and diversity of founders may not only be an imprinter but also something that is imprinted during the formation process of ETs. Consequently, I suggest that ET formation is an antecedent for ET composition and diversity. Although some aspects of teams are said to be imprinted in the literature, what is considered to be imprinted is, for example, the team process variables, such as a transactive memory system (Bryant, 2014; Zheng, 2012), not the team composition and diversity itself.

For an imprinting to occur, the entity that receives an imprint should be exposed to the imprinters(s) during a "sensitive period", which is a period of transition for the entity (Marquis & Tilcsik, 2013; Tilcsik, 2014). Although I concur with Marquis and Tilcsik (2013, p. 235) that the extant literature on imprinting demonstrates that imprinting may "exist at multiple levels of analysis and at multiple sensitive periods", the segment that focuses on founders and the founding stage is more relevant for this study. This is because the focus of this chapter is to link the literature on ETs working towards founding a new venture and the positions created in the new ventures.

FIRM FOUNDING AND POSITION IMPRINTING

In the founding process of a new organization, one of the most important activities and decisions that co-founders have to undertake is related to the structure of the organization, which is explained in terms of how roles and positions are assigned, organized, and formalized within the venture (Jung et al., 2017). This is because positions are one of the mechanisms through which firm-level idiosyncrasies prevail over time through the process of position imprinting, which is defined as "legacies left by the first incumbents of particular functional positions" (Burton & Beckman, 2007, p. 239). It is a process through which the bureaucratization and structure of the venture takes shape. Prior research has shown that positions created at venture founding will have a lasting consequence on the venture.

By studying how local firm histories influence individual turnover rates in organizations, Burton and Beckman (2007) argue that positions imprinted at venture founding constrain subsequent position holders. Furthermore, they find that the functional experience of the first occupant of a position in an organization influences the turnover rate of future occupants of the same position. Similarly, Boeker (1989) finds that the founder functional experience is positively related to the importance of that function in the following periods. Beckman and Burton (2008) have demonstrated how initial conditions constrain subsequent outcomes and initial organizational functional structures predict subsequent top manager backgrounds and later functional structures. These findings emphasize the importance of the first positions created in organizations as well as their first occupants. This is because the first occupants should develop the tasks and routines that will be performed within their positions and they will shape the positions to mirror their own experiences and desires (Beckman & Burton, 2008; Burton & Beckman, 2007). Subsequent position holders will then join the organization with a relatively stable and defined position as well as tasks to accomplish, unlike their predecessors. Therefore, entrepreneurial teams influence not only the performance of the ventures they create (Baum & Silverman, 2004; Zhou & Rozini, 2015) but also shape the very nature of the organization (Beckman & Burton, 2008) and constrain later firm action (Beckman, 2006). It is under the positions created in the organization that tasks performed and jobs get done (Cohen, 2013).

Given their consequence on the future of ventures, interesting questions to ask are how and why are initial positions created? Although these are important questions to address, less is known about why and how positions are created from the beginning (Burton & Beckman, 2007; Jung et al., 2017). This is partly because much of what is known about roles and positions is derived from studies of well-established bureaucracies (Burton & Beckman, 2007; Jung et al., 2017). I now briefly discuss what the extant literature says about position creation in organizations.

PERSPECTIVES ON POSITION CREATION

A clear formalization of task positions within entrepreneurial teams is crucial for venture performance (Sine et al., 2006). Yet, there is a relatively little understanding of how founders address one of the critical organizational design questions, which is the creation of a hierarchy of relationships, creation of positions, division of tasks and formalization of roles (Burton et al., 2019). According to Jung et al. (2017), there are two contending perspectives regarding how positions are created in organizations.

In the first view, the internal idiosyncratic jobs view (Barley, 1990; Miner, 1987; Miner & Akinsanmi, 2016) or the constructionist view (Burton & Beckman, 2007), positions are created through negotiation within the organization. The negotiation depends on the local context of the organization as well as the idiosyncratic characteristics of individual incumbents constituting the founding team. Thus, founding team members will have the chance to build distinct (idiosyncratic) positions reflecting their own particular qualities. Idiosyncratic positions and jobs have two traits (Miner, 1987). First, their creation is prompted by the existence of its occupant. Second, the positions and the activities included under the position are designed in accordance with the expertise and desires of the person for whom the position is created, which means that "the bundle of duties in an idiosyncratic job initially matches a specific person" (Miner & Akinsanmi, 2016, p. 69). Therefore, by definition, these kinds of positions and jobs cannot precede their occupants (Miner, 1987). Among other factors, uncertainty in the environment and lack of clarity in mission facilitate the creation of idiosyncratic positions in organizations (Cohen, 2013; Miner, 1987; Miner & Akinsanmi, 2016). These two criteria are among the features that characterize new founding ventures. In fact, one of the sources of the "liability of newness" new ventures suffer from (identified by Stinchcombe, 1965) is the lack of clarity and presence of ambiguity among the founders as they learn their new roles. All in all this view implies that the composition of the founding team – or, in other words, the individuals involved in creating the new venture – is a crucial factor in determining what kinds of position will be created at the beginning.

In the second view, the external institutional view (Edelman, 1990; Tolbert & Zucker, 1983) or the external logic (Burton & Beckman, 2007), positions are created to satisfy some expectations set by the external environment to gain legitimacy (Burton & Beckman, 2007; Jung et al., 2017). This legitimacy is critical because organizations should obtain essential resources for their operation from different stakeholders. The devices for resource acquisition differ across time, and hence organizations need to organize and structure themselves in accordance with the expectations at the time to be able to obtain the resources they require. In the words of Stinchcombe (1965, p. 161), "an organization must have an elite structure of such form and character that those people in the society who control resources essential to the organization's success will be satisfied that their interests are represented in the goal-setting apparatus of the enterprise." Therefore, teams and the new ventures they create will have a limited room to create positions different from the conventional or traditional positions known by the stakeholders and their environment (Jung et al., 2017; Scott, 2001) at a given point in time. In this case, unlike what the idiosyncratic view suggests, positions and jobs could precede their incumbents. Labelling it as the "vacancy assumption", Miner (1987) argued that this is the dominant assumption in organization theory and research on jobs and positions. At the macro level, this view suggests that there is not much variation in positions observed across firms at a given time as positions and roles are historically situated (Burton & Beckman, 2007).

Regardless of how positions are created, initial occupants would still leave their imprint and thereby affect future outcomes (Burton & Beckman, 2007). Yet, as argued by Burton et al. (2019), there is still limited research on the antecedents of the choices made by founding teams in designing, among other things, roles and positions in new ventures. One antecedent that should be considered in analysing the choices made by ETs, I would argue, is the way the teams are formed from the beginning. This is because the formation process and how members came into the team will impact the resources the teams will have at their disposal and the power each of the members will have in negotiating what positions to create and for whom. However, the extant literature assumes that the founding team already exists (Jung et al., 2017) and focuses on addressing what happens after the first incumbent holds the position created in the ventures. Before discussing in detail the implication of the ET formation on positions created in organizations, I now briefly discuss the perspectives on ET formation in the extant literature.

PERSPECTIVES ON ET FORMATION

Prior research has shown that most new ventures are founded by ETs (Klotz et al., 2014; Lazar et al., 2020; Wasserman, 2012). Although it received less attention in the literature as compared to other aspects of ETs (Nikiforou et al., 2018), ET formation, defined as "the process through which founders establish a team to start a new venture" (Lazar et al., 2020, p. 29) is an important dimension that affects team and venture performance. A critical question to address is thus, how do individuals come together to create a venture, that is, how do the teams come into being in the first place?

Generally speaking, there are two dominant and contending models to explain the formation of ETs in the extant literature (Aldrich & Kim, 2007; Forbes et al., 2006; Larson & Starr, 1993; Lazar et al., 2020): the rational model (resource-seeking strategy), and the social-psychological (the interpersonal-attraction strategy). The argument in the first model, the rational model, is that pragmatic instrumental criteria are used in selecting members for a team. This makes the desire to fill a particular resource need the main motive behind adding a new member to an ET (Forbes et al., 2006). This mostly revolves around the functional capabilities of the startup participants, which in turn is echoed in their functional experiences (Ruef, 2010) or their human capital (i.e. knowledge, skills and capabilities) (Lazar et al., 2020). Thus, in order to add a member, the lead entrepreneur will check if there are critical needs that cannot be covered by him/herself by making a resource dependence analysis (Ben-Hafaiedh-Dridi, 2010). Once the need is identified, then a constellation of decisions will follow regarding where to find partners, how to choose them and how to convince them to join the team (Kamm & Nurick, 1993). Nevertheless, these factors, according to Ruef (2010), are found to explain relatively little of the variance in ET formation.

In the second model, the social psychological model, interpersonal relation, rather than an economic consideration, is the key factor in determining who will make up an ET. This approach suggests that individuals from the same demographic group are more likely to form a team (Kim & Aldrich, 2004; Kim et al., 2005; Ruef, 2010; Ruef et al., 2003). It relies on social categorization and social identity theories – two theories that "privilege selection based on the fit of traits, sharing salient identifications, and in-group classifications" (Lazar et al., 2020, p. 41) to explain the formation of ETs. As a result, ETs formed following this strategy tend to be more homogeneous as ET members will be disproportionately from the same friendship network, family relationship, or other actual or perceived similarities (Lazar et al., 2020) and existing team members would desire to duplicate their own qualities while hiring additional team members (Forbes et al., 2006).

Although it is not yet a central part of the ET literature, there is a third perspective on ET formation labelled the institutional view (Forbes et al., 2006). This view suggests that institutional factors such as financers and government regulations are sometimes the main reasons behind who is involved in the team (see e.g. Bruton & Ahlstrom, 2003). Financers could themselves become part of the ET after making an investment at a very early stage of the venture (Lim et al., 2013) or they may require the team to add someone to the team as a requirement to receive finance. Government rules and regulations could also be critical in shaping the formation and composition of a team. For instance, if an ET would like to access some international markets, they could be asked to have someone local in their team. Furthermore, Jevnaker and Misganaw (2017) have also demonstrated that changes in rules and regulations at national level may influence the way ETs form in some settings, such as academic spinoffs.

To summarize, the literature on ET formation largely assumes that ET formation is an endogenous process (Lazar et al., 2020). This, I would argue, is probably why the first two perspectives are the dominant views, as the third view suggests ET formation could also be affected by exogenous factors. Whether the team is formed endogenously following the rational model and the socio-psychological model or exogenously with influence from institutions in place at the time of formation, it is clear that the process followed in ET formation defines the composition of the team. This composition, I argue, in turn defines the positions creation process that the teams follow. In fact, in their recent literature review paper on ET formation, Lazar et al. (2020) suggested that future research should examine how the ET formation process affects different outcomes at the team and venture level. In the following section, I integrate the perspectives on position creation and ET formation, and argue that ET formation is an antecedent for position creation in new ventures.

ET FORMATION AS ANTECEDENT OF POSITION IMPRINTING

As imprinting theory suggests, organizations founded at a particular time build their social system based on the available resources at the time of founding (Stinchombe, 1965). This process involves building the elites who in turn recruit the necessary resources from the external environment and establish the internal structure of the organization. Therefore, founding teams are considered as the source of imprint, and may continue traditionalizing the imprints in the firm (Kriauciunas & Shinkle, 2008) through, among other things, the positions created at founding. However, the literature takes the composition of the entrepreneurial team founding a venture for granted by considering the team only as an imprinter. I argue that ETs themselves are imprinted and a reflection of the formation process they followed. This in turn will have an implication on how the ET will create positions in a venture and what types of position will be created. Hence, the ET formation process is the "window" or "sensitivity period" at which the imprinting would take place as the founders create the team within the social conditions at the time of founding.

When an ET follows the socio-psychological logic, or homophily (Aldrich & Kim, 2007; Ruef et al., 2003) in its formation, interpersonal relationships and the desire of existing members to duplicate their own qualities or preserve the existing ambience in the team determines who will join the team. As a result a team formed following this logic is more likely to be homogeneous in its composition, which makes the position creation and assignment process problematic (Jung et al., 2017). This is because one of the most important factors that determines the position creation and allocation process in new ventures is the preference of the individuals involved (Burton & Beckman, 2007) and matching that with the needs of the organization. The involved individuals will then negotiate and define the boundaries of the initial positions. This implies that in ETs that follow the socio-psychological model it is more likely that individuals will join the team first and positions will be created afterwards.

As it is unlikely that two individuals will hold the same position in a new venture, some of the ET members will then hold a position that may not exactly fit their qualifications and expertise. Therefore, the likelihood that the initial position occupant will have an atypical background will be higher. When the first position holder possesses an atypical background, she or he will define the position to suit her/his own specific background, and hence "he or she is more likely to have created an idiosyncratic job with unusual tasks and responsibilities" (Burton & Beckman, 2007, p. 244). Although this is an advantage for the first occupant, it will have a consequence for future position incumbents to fit in to the position, as the first occupant will leave her or his imprint on the position. Burton and Beckman (2007) found a high turnover rate of subsequent position holders when the first occupant is someone with an atypical background. Since the position creation assignment is through negotiation among the individuals involved in the ET, some of the co-founders may take positions with greater responsibility while others would hold supporting roles (Aldrich & Ruef, 2006). Yet, even the supporting roles could be institutionalized and become formal roles in the venture as time goes by and the venture needs to find future occupants to hold those supporting positions created because of the presence of the first occupants in the ET. Consequently, I propose the following:

Proposition 1. Ventures founded by ETs based on homophily or existing social relations (following the social-psychological models) are more likely to have idiosyncratic positions and jobs at the early stage of their development.

Another model of ET formation is the rational model or the resource-seeking strategy. This model suggests that ETs are formed when the lead entrepreneur(s) identifies a competence or skill that is missing in the team (Aldrich & Kim, 2007; Ben-Hafaiedh-Dridi, 2010; Lazar et al., 2020; Smith, 2007) and decides to recruit additional members to the team to fill the missing qualities and resources. Hence, a team formed following the rational model is more likely to be heterogeneous in its composition, and positions will be created before the holder joins the team. In situations where the positions are not created a priori, position allocation will not be as problematic because of the low degree of overlap in expertise and qualification among ET members.

Those positions could be created for both internal and external reasons. Internally, ETs could create positions when they think that the task at hand is too much to handle for the existing team members or there is a specific skill or expertise required to fill a certain gap. Externally, ETs may need to obtain legitimacy from resource providers essential to their venture creation effort, and hence they may create a position to gain legitimacy from the external environment, although the specific position created might not be as urgent. This is because positions are considered as one of the social signals of the quality of the team. When the required (or perceived) legitimacy is high, positions need to be adjusted based on the expectations. Therefore, an ET formed based on the rational or economic logic would create positions that are common and expected by the external environment. Consequently, I propose:

Proposition 2a. Ventures founded by ETs formed by using instrumental criteria (as the rational or economic model suggests) are more likely to have positions usual or common in the industry or sector in which they operate.

Proposition 2b. ETs formed by using instrumental criteria (as the rational or economic model suggests) are more likely to create positions in their ventures for the purpose of creating external legitimacy as compared to those teams formed following the social-psychological model.

Similar to the two ET formation models that assume the formation process as endogenous, I would argue that ETs formed in line with what the third view of ET formation, the institutional view, suggests would have a different team composition and consequently would follow a different path to position creation. Since the formation process is exogenous, some of the individuals involved in the ET would join the team following a suggestion or at times an instruction from external institutional actors and resource providers. As argued by Stinchcombe (1965), allowing outside organizations to have control over some aspects of the organization with the aim of resource mobilization will also involve infusing a certain structure and institutionalizing it.

If an external resource provider suggests that the ET adds someone (which would mostly be either at a CEO or finance level) into the team as a precondition for resource provision, there are two alternatives to accommodate the newly suggested member: (1) if the position has been assigned to an existing team member already, the team needs to replace him/her. This process will lead to two different possible scenarios for the incumbent: either she or he will leave the position, the team, and the venture, or she or he will take another role in the team and thus a new role will be created to accommodate that change; (2) if the position is not yet occupied, the new member suggested by the external resource provider or institutional actor will be added into the team and assume the new position. In the first alternative, the position will be created first and the occupant will follow, while in the second alternative the occupant will come first. Yet, in both cases, I would argue the position creation will be based on the expectations of the resource providers or the institutional rules and regulations that the ET needs to follow in the venture founding process. Thus, the position creation will be similar to what is expected or common in the industry or market. Consequently, I propose:

Proposition 3. Ventures founded by ETs formed with a strong involvement from external actors (as the institutional view suggests) are less likely to have idiosyncratic positions as the positions would reflect the interest of external actors.

As much as the way ETs form determines the composition of the team and affects the type of positions created in new ventures they create, the position each ET member occupies at venture founding may also have its own imprint on the initial occupants by shaping their future career path and development. Imprinting research at the individual level suggests that "conditions experienced in the early years of organizational tenure or a career exert a lasting influence on subsequent habits, routines, and behaviors" (Tilcsik, 2014, p. 641). For instance, in a study we conducted on ETs in the biotechnology industry in one region in Scandinavia (Misganaw & Jevnaker, 2019), we found that some ET members had no plan to start a company or to work as an executive in a new venture. However, they wanted to continue in that career path after they were convinced to join the ventures they helped to create. Some others, on the other hand, found that their interest lay in creating something new (not being an executive in an established company). Subsequently, they decided to leave the ventures they helped to create after a certain stage and started new ventures from scratch again, thus becoming serial entrepreneurs.

Although we did not investigate why some members wanted to continue in the executive position and others wanted to go back and start new ventures again, the way the teams were formed at the start and their composition seem to play a role in shaping their career choices and by doing so the turnover in the ET. For instance, one of our informants stated that the position she had at the time of venture founding made her a central figure in the venture, which enabled her to learn more about how to run a company, and she eventually decided to continue as an executive. This is in line with Mathias et al. (2015) who found that individual entrepreneurs get their imprints from external conditions. Thus, I propose:

Proposition 4. How an ET forms (whether based on homophily, instrumental criteria, or strong involvement from external actors) and the position created for ET members (whether it is idiosyncratic or a position created to satisfy some expectations set by the external environment) will have imprinting effects on the individual members by shaping their future career choice and development.

To summarize, I contend that ET formation is an antecedent for team composition, position creation and position allocation. This is because how initial positions are created and negotiated could depend on the characteristics and preferences of the initial incumbents in the founding team (Burton & Beckman, 2007), which, in turn, could be a reflection of how the team is formed. The dynamics between ET formation process and position allocation may also affect the structure and turnover in the ETs as positions are negotiated, additional members join, and the venture develops. Figure 2.1 summarizes how the ET formation process is linked with position imprinting and other outcomes at the team and venture levels.

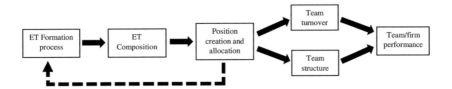

Figure 2.1   Entrepreneurial team formation process as an imprinter

The impact of the ET formation and the initial team configuration could also extend beyond the position and turnover, and affect the performance of the venture (regardless of how it is measured) by affecting the resources that the team and the venture could draw from. For instance, a team composed of members with similar characteristics (when the formation process is based on homophily), may have access to only a redundant network, be it social or economic. A heterogeneous ET, on the other hand, may have the possibility to draw on an extended and diverse network, which in turn could affect the level of resources the team will have at its disposal, and by so doing the eventual performance of the team and the venture. In fact, several studies in the ET literature (Bjørnåli & Aspelund, 2012; Eisenhardt, 2013; Foo, 2011; Kakarika, 2013) show that homogeneity and heterogeneity of ETs has an impact on firm performance and team effectiveness, regardless of how it is measured. Thus, by affecting the team composition, structure and turnover, ET formation process may affect eventual firm and/or team performance.

CONCLUDING REMARKS

This chapter set out to contribute to the imprinting literature by linking the literature on ET formation and position imprinting. The theory of organizational imprinting suggests that the social conditions at time of founding affects the future of new organizations (Marquis & Tilcsik, 2013; Simsek et al., 2015; Stinchcombe, 1965). To understand the organizational imprinting process better, Johnson (2007) suggested that more attention should be given to the sequence of activities in the venture-founding process, and specifically to the intersection between entrepreneurs and their environment in building new organizations. For this, I contend, we need to take the process of ET formation into consideration since ETs are one of the most important agents through which the environment leaves its trace in new ventures and organizations.

I argue that integrating the literature on ET formation may contribute to both the organizational and the position imprinting literatures by moving the point where the imprinting process is assumed to have begun to an earlier period (i.e. before the time of the founding of the venture). I concur with Beckman and Burton (2008, p. 19) that venture founding is not truly the beginning and "future teams may be best understood by a detailed examination of the teams that have come before". Therefore, studying ETs and their formation may help to understand how future teams in an organization might develop as well as how they create and allocate positions among themselves, which will have a lasting consequence on the organization through position imprinting. This is because the first positions in an organization may be created through negotiation among the founding members and the first occupant of the position is the one who will most likely instantiate the newly created position (Burton &

Beckman, 2007). By definition, *ceteris paribus*, the latter occupants of a given position will take over a more established position than their predecessors. Thus, understanding the formation process of ETs may help to answer the question of how positions are started by telling us what the team members bring on board and the power they may have to negotiate their positions in the new venture (Burton & Beckman, 2007). In order to understand this, I argue, we need to know not only what each team member brings to the negotiation table but also how the members themselves are brought on board, which in turn may influence their negotiating power.

To summarize, this chapter contributes to the imprinting literature by suggesting ET formation as an antecedent of the venture-founding process, which the imprinting literature largely assumes as the starting point for organizational imprinting (Mathias et al., 2015). It specifically contributes to the position imprinting literature by discussing how positions created in new ventures could partly be predicted by looking at how the entrepreneurial teams behind the ventures are formed. It extends the imprinting literature to the team level and suggests that ETs engaged in founding new ventures are not only imprinters but are also imprinted by the social conditions at the time of formation. Future research may further develop the propositions posed in this chapter and test them with empirical data.

REFERENCES

Albert, L. S., & DeTienne, D. R. (2016). Founding resources and intentional exit sales strategies: An imprinting perspective. *Group & Organization Management, 41*(6), 823–46.

Aldrich, H., & Kim, P. H. (2007). Small worlds, infinite possibilities? How social networks affect entrepreneurial team formation and search. *Strategic Entrepreneurship Journal, 1*(1–2), 147–65.

Aldrich, H., & Ruef, M. (2006). *Organizations evolving* (2nd edn.). London: Sage Publications.

Aldrich, H., & Yang, T. (2012). What did Stinchcombe really mean? Designing research to test the liability of newness among new ventures. *Entrepreneurship Research Journal, 2*(3), 1–13.

Azoulay, P., Liu, C., & Stuart, T. (2017). Social influence given (partially) deliberate matching: Career imprints in the creation of academic entrepreneurs. *American Journal of Sociology, 122*(4), 1223–71.

Barley, S. P. (1990). The alignment of technology and structure through roles and networks. *Administrative Science Quarterly, 35*, 61–103.

Baum, J. A., & Silverman, B. S. (2004). Picking winners or building them? Alliance, intellectual, and human capital as selection criteria in venture financing and performance of biotechnology startups. *Journal of Business Venturing, 19*(3), 411–36.

Beckman, C. M. (2006). The influence of founding team company affiliations on firm behavior. *Academy of Management Journal, 49*(4), 741–58.

Beckman, C. M., & Burton, M. D. (2008). Founding the future: Path dependence in the evolution of top management teams from founding to IPO. *Organization Science*, *19*(1), 3–24.

Ben-Hafaiedh-Dridi, C. (2010). Entrepreneurial team formation: Any rationality? *Frontiers of Entrepreneurship Research*, *30*(10), 1.

Bjørnåli, E. S., & Aspelund, A. (2012). The role of the entrepreneurial team and the board of directors in the internationalization of academic spin-offs. *Journal of International Entrepreneurship*, *10*(4), 350–77.

Boeker, W. (1989). Strategic change: The effects of founding and history. *Academy of Management Journal*, *32*(3), 489–515.

Bruton, G. D., & Ahlstrom, D. (2003). An institutional view of China's venture capital industry: Explaining the differences between China and the West. *Journal of Business Venturing*, *18*(2), 233–59.

Bryant, P. T. (2014). Imprinting by design: The microfoundations of entrepreneurial adaptation. *Entrepreneurship Theory and Practice*, *38*(5), 1081–102.

Burton, M. D., & Beckman, C. M. (2007). Leaving a legacy: Position imprints and successor turnover in young firms. *American Sociological Review*, *72*(2), 239–66.

Burton, M. D., Colombo, M. G., Rossi-Lamastra, C., & Wasserman, N. (2019). The organizational design of entrepreneurial ventures. *Strategic Entrepreneurship Journal*, *13*(3), 243–55.

Cohen, L. E. (2013). Assembling jobs: A model of how tasks are bundled into and across jobs. *Organization Science*, *24*(2), 432–54.

Edelman, L. (1990). Legal environments and organizational governance: The expansion of due process in the American workplace. *American Journal of Sociology*, *95*, 1401–40.

Eisenhardt, K. M. (2013). Top management teams and the performance of entrepreneurial firms. *Small Business Economics*, *40*(4), 805–16.

Foo, M. D. (2011). Teams developing business ideas: how member characteristics and conflict affect member-rated team effectiveness. *Small Business Economics*, *36*(1), 33–46.

Forbes, D. P., Borchert, P. S., Zellmer-Bruhn, M. E., & Sapienza, H. J. (2006). Entrepreneurial team formation: An exploration of new member addition. *Entrepreneurship Theory and Practice*, *30*(2), 225–48.

Guenther, C., Oertel, S., & Walgenbach, P. (2016). It's all about timing: Age-dependent consequences of founder exits and new member additions. *Entrepreneurship Theory and Practice*, *40*(4), 843–65.

Han, Y., Zheng, E., & Xu, M. (2014). The influence from the past: Organizational imprinting and firms' compliance with social insurance policies in China. *Journal of Business Ethics*, *122*(1), 65–77.

Honoré, F. E. M. (2015). Entrepreneurial teams' human capital: From its formation to its impact on the performance of technological new ventures (doctoral dissertation, University of Minnesota).

Jevnaker, B., & Misganaw, B. A. (2017). Entrepreneurial team formation practices in academic spinoffs: When the rules of the game are changing and players evolve. Paper presented at the 2nd Entrepreneurship as a Practice Workshop, Dublin, Ireland.

Johnson, V. (2007). What is organizational imprinting? Cultural entrepreneurship in the founding of the Paris Opera. *American Journal of Sociology*, *113*(1), 97–127.

Jung, H., Vissa, B., & Pich, M. (2017). How do entrepreneurial founding teams allocate task positions? *Academy of Management Journal*, *60*(1), 264–94.

Kakarika, M. (2013). Staffing an entrepreneurial team: Diversity breeds success. *Journal of Business Strategy, 34*(4), 31–8.

Kamm, J. B., & Nurick, A. J. (1993). The stages of team venture formation: A decision-making model. *Entrepreneurship Theory and Practice, 17*(2), 17–27.

Kim, P., & Aldrich, H. (2004). Teams that work together, stay together: Resiliency of entrepreneurial teams. *Frontiers of Entrepreneurship Research, 24*, 85–95.

Kim, P. H., Aldrich, H., & Ruef, M. (2005). Fruits of co-laboring: Effects of entrepreneurial team stability on the organizational founding process. *Frontiers of Entrepreneurship Research, 25*, 81–92.

Klotz, A. C., Hmieleski, K. M., Bradley, B. H., & Busenitz, L. W. (2014). New venture teams: A review of the literature and roadmap for future research. *Journal of Management, 40*(1), 226–55.

Kriauciunas, A., & Shinkle, G. (2008). Organizational imprinting: Informing firm behavior in domestic and international contexts. Purdue CIBER Working Papers, No. 58.

Larson, A., & Starr, J. A. (1993). A network model of organization formation. *Entrepreneurship Theory and Practice, 17*(2), 5–15.

Lazar, M., Miron-Spektor, E., Agarwal, R., Erez, M., Goldfarb, B., & Chen, G. (2020). Entrepreneurial team formation. *Academy of Management Annals, 14*(1), 29–59.

Lim, J. Y. K., Busenitz, L. W., & Chidambaram, L. (2013). New venture teams and the quality of business opportunities identified: Faultlines between subgroups of founders and investors. *Entrepreneurship Theory and Practice, 37*(1), 47–67.

Marquis, C., & Tilcsik, A. (2013). Imprinting: Toward a multilevel theory. *Academy of Management Annals, 7*(1), 195–245.

Mathias, B. D., Williams, D. W., & Smith, A. R. (2015). Entrepreneurial inception: The role of imprinting in entrepreneurial action. *Journal of Business Venturing, 30*(1), 11–28.

Milanov, H., & Fernhaber, S. A. (2009). The impact of early imprinting on the evolution of new venture networks. *Journal of Business Venturing, 24*(1), 46–61.

Miner, A. (1987). Idiosyncratic jobs in formal organizations. *Administrative Science Quarterly, 32*, 327–51.

Miner, A. S., & Akinsanmi, O. B. (2016). Idiosyncratic jobs, organizational transformation, and career mobility. In L. E. Cohen, M. D. Burton, & M. Lounsbury (Eds.), *Research in the sociology of organizations, Vol. 47, The structuring of work in organizations* (pp. 61–101). Bingley: Emerald Group Publishing.

Misganaw, B. A. & Jevnaker, B. (2019). How do entrepreneurial teams form? On mechanisms leading to entrepreneurial team formation. Paper presented at EURAM conference, Lisbon, Portugal.

Nikiforou, A., Gruber, M., Zabara, T., & Clarysse, B. (2018). The role of teams in academic spin-offs. *The Academy of Management Perspectives, 32*(1), 78–103.

Ruef, M. (2010). *The entrepreneurial group: Social identities, relations, and collective action.* Princeton, NJ: Princeton University Press.

Ruef, M., Aldrich, H. E., & Carter, N. M. (2003). The structure of founding teams: Homophily, strong ties, and isolation among US entrepreneurs. *American Sociological Review, 68*(2), 195–222.

Scott, R. W. (2001). *Institutions and organizations* (2nd edn.). Thousand Oaks, CA: Sage Publications.

Simsek, Z., Fox, B. C., & Heavey, C. (2015). "What's past is prologue": A framework, review, and future directions for organizational research on imprinting. *Journal of Management, 41*(1), 288–317.

Sine, H. M., Mitsuhashi, H., & Kirsch, D. A. (2006). Revisiting burns and stalker: Formal structure and new venture performance in emerging market sectors. *Academy of Management Journal*, *49*, 121–32.

Smith, B. R. (2007). Entrepreneurial team formation: The effects of technological intensity and decision making on organizational emergence (doctoral dissertation, University of Cincinnati).

Stinchcombe, A. L. (1965). Social structure and organizations. In G. J. March (Ed.), *Handbook of organizations* (pp. 142–93). Chicago, IL: Rand McNally.

Tilcsik, A. (2014). Imprint–environment fit and performance: How organizational munificence at the time of hire affects subsequent job performance. *Administrative Science Quarterly*, *59*(4), 639–68.

Tolbert, P. S., & Zucker, L. G. (1983). Institutional sources of change in the formal structure of organizations: The diffusion of civil service reform, 1880–1935. *Administrative Science Quarterly*, *28*, 22–39.

Tornikoski, E., & Renko, M. (2014). Timely creation of new organizations: The imprinting effects of entrepreneurs' initial founding decisions. *M@n@gement*, *17*(3), 193–213.

Wasserman, N. (2012). *The founder's dilemmas: Anticipating and avoiding the pitfalls that can sink a startup*. Princeton, NJ: Princeton University Press.

Zheng, Y. (2012). Unlocking founding team prior shared experience: A transactive memory system perspective. *Journal of Business Venturing*, *27*(5), 577–91.

Zhou, W., & Rosini, E. (2015). Entrepreneurial team diversity and performance: Toward an integrated model. *Entrepreneurship Research Journal*, *5*(1), 31–60.

3. Exploring the social dimension of regional industrial restructuring

Jan Ole Rypestøl

1. INTRODUCTION

Globalisation, digitalisation and the increasing demand for more sustainable production have created unprecedented challenges among regional economies. These mounting challenges affect regional development because regional industries need to restructure to maintain their competitiveness (Grillitsch & Trippl, 2016). This need for regional restructuring has recently become even more pressing as the economic lockdown to combat the spread of Covid-19 has disrupted existing value chains and markets.

A recent topic within the regional industrial restructuring literature has focused on the fundamental role of strategic change agency in industrial restructuring. In this stream of the literature, agency is understood as the actions or interventions introduced to produce a particular effect (Sotarauta & Suvinen, 2018). Grillitsch and Sotarauta (2019) proposed a trinity of change agency that is essential to facilitating regional industrial change. This trinity consists of Schumpeterian entrepreneurship, institutional entrepreneurship and place-based leadership. Isaksen et al. (2019) suggested an alternative framing of change agency, arguing for a distinction between firm-level agency and system-level agency. Here, firm-level agency refers to the agency performed by firm-level actors to benefit their own firm's success, while system-level agency refers to the agency performed by actors to promote collective value. The literature maintains that regional restructuring will benefit from the close coordination between firm- and system-level change agency so that firms can exploit new possibilities facilitated by system-level agency (Kyllingstad & Rypestøl, 2018).

This literature on change agency has been supplemented by research on the importance of assets and their modification to regional industrial restructuring (Isaksen et al., 2020; Rypestøl, 2020; Trippl et al., 2020). In this literature, a firm-level asset is understood as an asset restricted by private ownership, while a system-level asset is defined as an asset freely available to several actors. A fundamental tenet in the regional restructuring literature is that the assets accumulated in firms and regions are primarily tailored to support existing solutions (Asheim et al., 2019). Thus, change agency must involve the modification of existing firm- and system-level assets to support regional restructuring. Trippl et al. (2020) suggest that assets can be modified through three alternative processes: asset reuse, asset creation and asset destruction. Rypestøl (2020) furthers this line of thinking while suggesting that various modification modes support various outcomes. Rypestøl (2020) argues that the emergence of new industries requires new asset creation, while the upgrading of existing industries primarily relies on asset reuse.

Because asset modification for regional industrial restructuring is an emergent field of research, the literature contains several underexplored topics. One such question is how the social dimension influences asset modification processes. Even if the actor's perspective has gained more focus in economic geography and related fields (e.g. Isaksen et al., 2019; Jolly et al., 2020; Njøs & Fosse, 2019; Sotarauta & Suvinen, 2018), most of this research tends to view agency as primarily resulting from internal affairs rather than social interactions, including bargaining, expectations and obligations between multiple actors.

This chapter aims to bridge this gap by shedding light on how the social dimension can influence the processes of asset modification in regional industrial restructuring. Relying on social capital theory and the studies discussing actors and agency in processes of regional industrial restructuring, the chapter suggests an analytical framework that can be useful for increasing our understanding of the role of social relations in the processes of asset modification in regional industrial restructuring. The framework postulates three dimensions of relationships that influence the ability of regions to identify the need for asset modification and to initiate and complete such processes: structural, relational and cognitive.

Empirically, the chapter investigates how the need for a new system-level asset in the Agder region of Southern Norway emerged and how the structural, relational and cognitive social elements have influenced the creation of the new asset. The process of system-level asset creation that is investigated is the establishment of the Mechatronic Innovation Lab (MIL), and the research question explored is to what extent and in what ways structural, relational and cognitive social elements have influenced the process of establishing the MIL in Agder.

The rest of the chapter is organised as follows. In Section 2, we provide a short literature review that includes discussions of change actors and agency (2.1), assets and asset modification (2.2) and social capital theory (2.3). Section 3 introduces the case study and discusses the methods for data collection (3.1).

Section 4 presents the findings and analysis, and Section 5 summarises the study and suggests topics relevant to further research.

2. THEORETICAL UNDERPINNINGS

In this chapter, regional industrial restructuring is understood as a path-dependent process (Martin, 2010; Martin & Sunley, 2006). Anchored in the pioneering work of Paul David (e.g. 1985) and Bryan Arthur (e.g. 1989), path dependence theory conceptualises economic development as an accumulative process in which economic actors are significantly influenced by the decisions made in the past (Martin & Sunley, 2006). Although the canonical version of the theory postulates that new pathways are created mainly from uncontrollable incidents and that their future development will progress in a locked-in manner by increasing return effects (Arthur, 1988, 1989, 1994), contemporary research argues that industrial development can also follow a dynamic evolutionary progression (Martin, 2010); that is, new industries can be intentionally created (Boschma et al., 2017; Grillitsch & Trippl, 2016; Rypestøl, 2017), and existing industries can be unlocked through various planned modification processes (Isaksen et al., 2018; Kyllingstad & Rypestøl, 2018).

In this chapter, we do not focus on the outcomes of regional industrial restructuring. Instead, we seek a deeper understanding of how these dynamic processes of industrial restructuring are initiated and what influences their progression. We begin by investigating the role of actors and agency in the processes of regional industrial restructuring.

2.1 Change Agents and Change Agency in Regional Industrial Restructuring

Grillitsch and Sotarauta (2019) conceptualise a trinity of change agency relevant to regional industrial restructuring. This trinity consists of Schumpeterian entrepreneurship, institutional entrepreneurship and place-based leadership. In this typology, Schumpeterian entrepreneurship represents the introduction of path-breaking innovations, while institutional entrepreneurship involves activities that challenge existing institutions or introduce new ones. Finally, place-based leadership is a type of collective leadership that aims to coordinate and pool 'efforts and resources for the stimulation of new regional development opportunities' (Jolly et al., 2020, p. 3). Thus, in this literature, change agency is performed by Schumpeterian and institutional entrepreneurs as well as by formal and informal leaders that aim to coordinate local initiatives to create increasing momentum for change.

An alternative categorisation of change actors and agency in regional industrial restructuring is presented by Kyllingstad and Rypestøl (2018) and Asheim et al. (2019), who distinguish between two main categories of entrepreneurial change agents. One is the firm-level entrepreneur, a profit-seeking actor who exploits business opportunities. This type of change agent has been thoroughly described by Schumpeter (1934) and other scholars (e.g. Gartner, 1988; Kirzner, 1973), and the potential consequences of their actions have been considered by authors such as Norman Smith (1967), Bruce Kirchhoff (1994) and Erik Stam (Stam et al., 2007; 2012). The main argument in this stream of literature is that entrepreneurs and firms can alter existing pathways by introducing new products, services or processes that radically challenge existing solutions. More recently, Rypestøl (2017) distinguished between four types of firm-level entrepreneurs that influence regional industrial restructuring in different ways. Rypestøl (2017) identified entrepreneurial growth intentions and innovativeness as critical indicators, arguing that the least radical consequences to regional industrial development result from the agency of entrepreneurs who are not innovative or concerned with growth. The most drastic consequences of regional industrial restructuring, conversely, result from the agency of highly ambitious and radically innovative entrepreneurs.

Even if firm-level entrepreneurs are essential players in the processes that generate regional industrial growth, existing research highlights that they are not the only type of entrepreneurial change agent involved in the processes of regional industrial development. An alternative type is the system-level entrepreneur (Asheim et al., 2019; Isaksen et al., 2018; Kyllingstad & Rypestøl, 2018) who, unlike its counterpart, is motivated by alleged system failure and aims to improve collective value through the restoration and creation of systemic assets (Asheim et al., 2019). The literature identifies several types of actors that fall into the category of system-level entrepreneurs. Examples include individuals and cluster administrations (Isaksen et al., 2018) and politicians and regional leaders (Asheim et al., 2019). Thus, what separates firm-level entrepreneurs from system-level entrepreneurs is not the type of actor but rather the kind of motivation that informs the agency employed. Although successful firm-level agency implies an improved strategic firm position or increased firm growth (Kirzner, 1973; Penrose, 1959; Schumpeter, 1939), successful system-level agency is defined as the actions or interventions that transform the regional innovation system (RIS) (Isaksen et al., 2019).

In this chapter, we will use the concepts of firm- and system-level entrepreneurs and firm- and system-level agency in further exploring regional industrial restructuring.

2.2   Regional Restructuring as a Process of Asset Modification

From a strategy perspective, the resource-based view of the firm (e.g. Barney, 2002; Foss, 1996; Prahalad & Hamel, 1990) argues that competitive advantage drives organisational diversity. Maskell and Malmberg (1999) define a competitive advantage as a firm's heterogeneous tangible resources and intangible competencies, arguing that diversity results from the processes in which firms seek to cultivate unique resources and competence. According to Maskell and Malmberg (1999, p. 10), unique resources form when an entity gains access to and control over something desired by others, while unique competence is established when firms can 'do something which its competitors cannot do as well, as rapidly or as cheaply'. An essential notion of the resource-based view is that firm competitiveness is not just the result of summing up a firm's internal resources and competencies. Rather, firms can also benefit from localised capabilities, which are understood as a unique set of region-specific resources.

More recently, from an evolutionary economic geography (EEG) approach, the concepts of resources, capabilities and competencies have been researched under the umbrella of assets. Based on the work of Maskell and Malmberg (1999), MacKinnon et al. (2019) introduced five groups of assets: (i) natural assets, (ii) infrastructural and material assets, (iii) industrial assets, (iv) human assets and (v) institutional assets. Table 3.1 presents examples of these various types of assets at the firm and system levels.

Even if assets accumulate over time – thus forming a central element in the preformation phase of path restructuring – assets can be altered to support the development of industries in new directions. Maskell and Malmberg (1999, p. 10) found that assets are in fact constantly 'modified or reconstructed by the deliberate and purposeful action of individuals and groups within or outside the area'. Following this line of thinking, Trippl et al. (2020) have suggested that assets can be modified via three alternative processes: asset reuse, asset creation and asset destruction. Asset reuse is understood as the redeployment and recombination of assets, while asset creation encompasses various strategies to generate assets that were not previously available. Finally, asset destruction describes the processes in which the assets that hamper productivity are demolished or unlearned. Most recently, Kyllingstad et al. (2021) suggested a fourth mode of modification, asset upgrade, which is defined as a process in which existing assets are renewed and advanced to support changing conditions.

Bathelt and Glückler (2005) suggested a relational conception of resources in economic geography. A fundamental tenet of this relational view is that economic decisions and their consequences are always shaped by the structure of social relationships and dominating institutional arrangements. Taking inspiration from this relational view, we examine more closely how social relationships and dominating institutional endowments can influence the processes of asset modification in firms and systems.

Table 3.1   *Asset types and scales*

Type of asset	Examples of firm-level assets	Examples of system-level assets
Natural assets	Land, water reservoirs, mineral mines, oil wells owned by a firm or an organisation	Climate, waterfalls, coastlines, unrestricted commodity sources
Infrastructural and material assets	Buildings, machines, and vehicles owned by a firm, firm-specific logistics and networks	Physical buildings, machines and equipment not privately owned, knowledge infrastructure and physical infrastructure
Industrial assets	Firm-specific technology, financial leverage, and management	Generic technology, organisational methods, and available risk capital
Human assets	In-house knowledge and skills	Knowledge and skills available in the workforce, access to R&D knowledge
Institutional assets	In-house formal and informal rules and regulations, organisational culture	Institutional settings, laws, and regulations

Source: Modified from Rypestøl (2020).

2.3   The Social Dimension of Regional Industrial Restructuring

The RIS literature maintains that economic actors are social entities embedded in specific institutional environments (Asheim & Gertler, 2005; Asheim et al., 2019; Cooke, 1992). In this context, actors are understood as encompassing all types of private and public sector organisations, including entrepreneurs, incumbent firms, universities, governments, educational organisations, research and development (R&D) organisations and financial representatives. A central understanding here is that a system comprises more than the sum of its components. Thus, we cannot fully understand systemic changes by analysing various parts in isolation. Consequently, we argue here that we also need to examine the social dimension of a system if we want to understand how the processes of asset modification contribute to forming regional industrial restructuring. The importance of social relationships to purposeful change agency is also highlighted by Granovetter (1992), who states, 'Actors do not behave or decide as atoms outside a social context, nor do they adhere slavishly to a script written for them by the particular intersection of the socio-cultural categories they happen to occupy. Their attempts at purposeful action are instead embedded in a concrete, ongoing system of social relations' (p. 32). In the following, we examine the value of these systems of social relationships for understanding the processes of asset modification for regional industrial restructuring from the perspective of social capital theory.

The social dimension of regional industrial restructuring 49

Embracing the early literature on the concept of social capital (e.g. Bourdieu, 1986; Burt, 1992; Coleman, 1988, 1990; Putnam, 2000), Nahapiet and Goshal (1998) define social capital as 'the sum of the actual and potential resources embedded within, available through, and derived from the network of relationships possessed by an individual or social unit' (p. 243). This definition understands social capital as both a multifaceted and multilevel phenomenon. By arguing that social capital is a multilevel phenomenon, the authors agree with the earlier work of Bourdieu (1986) and Coleman (1988), who define social capital as a value that can be capitalised on by individuals, as well as with Burt (1992), Putnam (2000) and Malecki (2012), who argue that social capital is also a macro-level phenomenon that can be capitalised on at the regional and national levels. However, when addressing the multifaceted nature of social capital, Nahapiet and Ghoshal (1998) also expand existing understandings by suggesting a cognitive dimension to predominating structural and relational views.

Rooted in the work of Bourdieu (1986), the structural dimension of social capital refers to the value of who is in one's network, which is understood as who one reaches and how one reaches them. Thus, to a structuralist, networks that include many connections (nodes) will represent more value than networks with fewer connections (Rutten et al., 2010). This structuralist perspective on social capital has inspired a wide range of research using social network analysis to investigate how network structures influence the performance of individual participants, clusters within the network and the network as a whole (e.g. Martin & Rypestøl, 2018). In particular, two concepts have gained attention in this field: the twin concept of bonding and bridging social capital (Putnam, 2000). While bridging social capital refers to the value of a network position that bridges otherwise unrelated actors in a network, bonding social capital is defined as a resource that 'develops among participants who interact over time, build trust, and have common sense of belonging' (Jakobsen & Lorentzen, 2015). Even though a critical level of bonding social capital is important to support collective action, the literature also emphasises that too much bonding capital can hamper asset modification for regional restructuring because tight network structures can exclude the initiatives of outsiders, create conformity and restrict entrepreneurial initiatives (Malecki, 2012). On the other hand, too much bridging social capital can hamper asset modification because the modification of assets relies on the ability to utilise and process new knowledge for innovation, which can be challenging in structures with too many external linkages.

From a relational perspective of social capital, network actors and connections are, in and of themselves, not valuable for analysis. Instead, according to Coleman (1988), the relational dimension of social capital underscores the importance of the nature of the social interactions that unfold between actors.

Hall and Soskice (2001) highlighted that the nature and results of relationships are influenced by variables such as trust, dominating norms and obligations and expectations; they also postulate that the relational dimension of networks can act as a barrier to a well-structured network. Two concepts that have gained particular interest in the relational social capital domain are strong and weak ties (Granovetter, 1973). Strong ties refer to robust connections developed over time in trustworthy relationships, while weak ties refer to connections with more peripheral actors who can be a source of new knowledge and opportunities. In networks, strong ties facilitate bonding social capital, while weak ties facilitate bridging social capital.

Nahapiet and Ghoshal (1998) suggested considering a third dimension to supplement the structural and relational perspective to social capital. This third component is the cognitive dimension, which refers to the value of resources that provide a shared system of meaning and worldviews among network participants. Thus, a high degree of cognitive social capital is seen in networks where actors share the same culture as represented by narratives, language and codes. Therefore, the cognitive dimension is closely linked to the concept of institutions, which includes factors such as formal laws and regulations, as well as informal norms and values (North, 1990). In regional industrial restructuring, cognitively consistent networks facilitate change with less friction than less conventional systems. However, too much cognitive consistency can be harmful because potentially fruitful alternatives can be overlooked (Nooteboom et al., 2007). Thus, cognitive resonance can produce a form of collective blindness that foresees alternative development as less favourable among key regional actors (Martin, 2010), blurring the ability to discover potentially disastrous consequences (Isaksen, 2015).

In conclusion, it is important to emphasise that the three dimensions of social capital influence both the need for asset modification and the ability to perform such modifications. The concepts of bonding and bridging are illustrative in this respect. A high amount of bonding social capital includes a high level of trust, thus reducing the cognitive distance among regional actors. Trust and a common worldview are helpful in creating effective communication and favour the ability of multiple actors to perform collective action, if needed. However, too much social capital might also produce a form of lock-in, which is recognised as a state of development in which agency to modify assets becomes difficult. In such situations, regional industries can suffer from collective blindness, which hampers their ability to recognise and utilise ideas and opportunities. This danger of developing an introvert culture if a region holds too much bonding social capital, illustrates the importance of bridging linkages for modifying assets. However, too many external links might also be harmful because firms and industries need time and capacity to build absorptive capac-

The social dimension of regional industrial restructuring 51

ity (Cohen & Levinthal, 1990) so that imported new assets and the inflow of related knowledge and technology can contribute to upgrading existing assets.

Finally, the literature suggests that the need for firms and regional industries to build structural, relational and cognitive social capital to facilitate asset modification for regional restructuring can vary over time. An example here is presented by Kyllingstad and Rypestøl (2018). When analysing the greening process of the Eyde cluster firms, the authors found that the moderators of change needed to prioritise actions aiming to strengthen cognitive and relational elements in an early phase, while the structural dimension gained increasing attention in later phases.

2.4   Analytical Framework

This chapter aims to shed additional light on regional industrial restructuring processes by exploring the role of social relations in such processes. The literature has highlighted that regional industries restructure through asset modification processes that are initiated and moderated by change agency. The literature also emphasises that this agency is employed by firm- and system-level entrepreneurs. Finally, social capital theory highlights that change agency at the firm and system levels is influenced by a social dimension that can be analysed and understood from its structural, relational and cognitive dimensions. According to a structuralist perspective, the number, nature and diversity of the existing assets in firms and systems will affect the need for asset modification. However, from a relational perspective, the climate for creating and modifying assets depends on the trust, expectations and obligations between relevant actors. As such, the ability to modify assets in firms and regions is heavily influenced by the quality of existing relations. Third, from a cognitive perspective, the ability of firms and systems to form new assets relies significantly on the institutional endowments embedded in the firm's internal culture and regional industrial culture. Such endowments include formal rules and regulations, as well as the informal norms and values that have been gradually shaped throughout history to support existing trajectories (Asheim et al., 2019). The RIS literature argues that the regional institutional framework is formed over time to support existing solutions and that it is less supportive of the processes that include the modification of assets favouring new solutions. Thus, the processes of asset modification will meet less friction if the modification supports strong existing industries than if the modification challenges existing solutions.

Finally, the literature has emphasised the need for firm–system alignment. If the assets at the firm and system levels are not aligned, firms will not be able to utilise system-level assets and system-level assets will not be able to draw from firm-level assets and competencies.

Figure 3.1 presents an analytical framework to increase our understanding of the role of social relations in regional industrial restructuring. This framework suggests that asset modification in firms and systems are social processes that derive from firm- and system-level agency. The model further suggests that this agency is influenced by the structural, relational and cognitive elements that shape the nature of the activity conducted by firm- and system-level entrepreneurs.

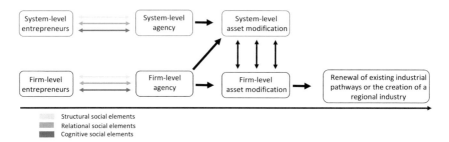

Figure 3.1   Analytical framework of the role of social relations in regional industrial restructuring

In the remainder of this chapter, we investigate how the various elements of social capital spill out in praxis and how they influence the processes of asset modification for regional industrial restructuring. However, in this chapter, it is, of course, not possible to research in depth how social capital influences all forms of asset modifications or to compare how social capital influences the processes of asset modification in various regional settings. Instead, we limited the range of cases to gain deeper knowledge. In the following sections, we present a case study design of how the various dimensions of social capital have influenced one particular process of system-level material asset creation in the Agder region of southern Norway.

3.   PRESENTATION OF THE CASE, RESEARCH QUESTIONS AND METHODS

In this section, we research how the structural, relational and cognitive dimensions of social capital influence asset modification by examining the process of establishing the Mechatronic Innovation Lab in the Agder region of southern Norway. This process lasted nearly ten years, and today, the MIL is a prominent national centre for innovation, piloting and technology qualification in mechatronics and related areas. The MIL has a total of 55 cutting-edge technologies within the fields of robotics, simulation, electrical power, instrumentation, artificial learning and deep learning, mixed reality and more. By offering this variety of state-of-the-art technologies and test services, the MIL aims to strengthen firms' ability to innovate (Mechatronics Innovation Lab, 2020). The lab finances its day-to-day operations by selling various services, such as access to technologies, courses, project leading and research assignments. The MIL is owned by the University of Agder and NORCE Norwegian Research Centre and constitutes a part of the national R&D infrastructure. Thus, in this chapter, the MIL is considered a system-level material asset with particular relevance to the mechatronic industry in the Agder region and beyond.

The Agder region is characterised by being an RIS that is organisationally thick in oil-related firms and infrastructure (Normann et al., 2020; Rypestøl, 2018). The oil and gas industry in Agder has a 50-year history, and today, oil and gas firms in Agder are world-leading producers of drilling equipment and lifting and handling equipment. The RIS in Agder is well developed in oil- and gas-related infrastructure and hosts the NODE cluster, which has been awarded as a Global Centre of Expertise (GCE) by the Norwegian Innovation Cluster program, a Centre for Research-based Innovation (SFI) in mechatronics, the MIL[1] and a university that has developed a master's and a doctoral education in mechatronics. The Agder RIS is well connected, and the region has a long history of firm- and system-level collaborations (Normann et al., 2020). One example of a successful collaboration between the firm and system levels in Agder is the process of establishing a local university in 2007. Herstad and Sandven (2017, p. 31) confirmed that the Agder RIS is well connected and functional, noting that 'Agder combines innovation activity levels above the national average with strong local research system linkages.'

In the following section, we examine how the social dimension of regional restructuring influenced the process of establishing the MIL in Agder. Our research question is as follows: To what extent and in what way have structural, relational and cognitive social elements influenced the process of establishing the MIL in Agder?

3.1 Methods and Data Collection

In this chapter, the process of system-level material asset creation is understood as a complex process that includes a wide range of actors and factors. As such, we found a case study design (Yin, 1984) well suited to guide our empirical investigations.

Data were collected between May 2018 and May 2020 using an open interview technique. In total, we conducted 11 in-depth interviews with individuals who held dominant positions in the process of the MIL's initiation and development. The interviewees included rectors and deans at the local university, CEOs of major firms, chairpersons and board members of the MIL, CEOs of the NODE cluster and representatives from local politics, national politics and civil society. Half of the interviews were conducted face-to-face, while the other half were phone interviews.[2] Each interview lasted approximately one hour, and the interviewees were asked to describe and reflect on the process of establishing the MIL from their point of view.

A significant literature review accompanies the interview data. Data were collected from local newspaper archives, the local university's archive, general internet searches and private files. Besides publicly available documents, the literature review also includes key actors' private notes, presentations and speeches held at several milestone events during the process.

In addition to the interview data and public and private documents, the current study is informed by a reanalysis of additional interviews with 34 CEOs of regional firms in 2018. Even though the process of establishing the MIL in Agder was not the core topic in these interviews, parts of the conversation touched on the role of the MIL in firm innovation and the gap that the MIL filled in the RIS when it was established.

4.   EMPIRICAL FINDINGS AND ANALYSIS

4.1   The Establishment of a Mechatronic Innovation Lab in Agder

In Agder, the NODE cluster organisation has played a significant role as a promoter of knowledge sharing and interactive learning among cluster firms. In 2008, the cluster hosted a seminar that aimed to explore alternative joint initiatives that could benefit the future development of NODE firms. The participants made a total of 37 suggestions, 29 of which were discarded. A joint test and piloting lab facility was one of the remaining eight ideas that the industry collectively embraced. The firms argued that testing and piloting innovations were essential because financial institutions favoured proven technology. Thus, a lab for piloting and testing would reduce innovation time to market, thereby benefiting all NODE firms. The firms concluded that the lack of a test and pilot lab in Agder constituted a missing link in the regional innovation structure.

At the local university, a parallel process emerged that sought to reveal how the university could contribute to the region's further advancement. Early in this process, the dean of the Faculty of Engineering and Science proposed the idea of an innovation and mechatronics testing lab. The dean argued that such a lab would effectively serve the local oil and gas industry and drive innovation in additional regional sectors. The dean had first-hand experience in establishing a lab in the information technology sector from his prior position at Ericsson in Singapore. Drawing on knowledge gained from the massive decline of that sector, the dean argued that Agder needed facilities that could promote innovation to make regional industries more robust. This requirement of an innovation lab, he continued, was also shared by the university, which needed to expand its lab facilities to secure future growth. The dean started lobbying the rest of the university about his idea, and after a few years of dedicated work, he and his team managed to elevate the idea of a regional innovation and research lab to become a top priority of the university. The university called the proposed facility Sørlandslab.

NODE applauded the Sørlandslab concept because it seemed to meet the cluster firms' need for piloting and testing facilities. Previous successful collaborations between the industry and academia had fostered a climate that was positive to public–private collaborations and because the project satisfied shared interests, the Sørlandslab idea soon became yet another joint project between academia and industry in Agder. From a business perspective, the idea was that the university, as a neutral partner, would own the Sørlandslab and that local and outside firms would rent its technology and space. During the process of planning and engineering, the Ugland family, who are local industry magnates, agreed to fund the construction of the lab buildings on the university grounds and offered to rent the buildings back to the university. This generous contribution was inspired by positive experiences in past similar arrangements.[3] However, even if the financing of the physical infrastructure was agreed upon, buying state-of-the-art technology within the area of focus was calculated as being very expensive. Therefore, the partners found that this economic burden exceeded what they could manage. The partners, therefore, agreed that the success of establishing the lab relied on their ability to gain state funding.

In August 2011, Sørlandsutvalget – a state-appointed committee – was formed. The committee's task was to propose initiatives that could fuel industrial growth in Agder. Sørlandsutvalget's chairperson was also the university's rector, and the committee consisted of 15 handpicked local representatives. In June 2013, based on a broad dialogue with local representatives, the committee presented its finished report, proposing 19 initiatives that would cost half a billion Norwegian kroner (NOK) to implement. The report positioned Sørlandslab as the committee's top priority and recommended that the state contribute 150 million NOK in funding. Even though Sørlandsutvalget's recommendations were ultimately not implemented, Agder's call for the establishment of a lab to fuel research and innovation was heard by national governments, and a local newspaper reported that the Minister of Trade and Industry was receptive to such a laboratory. 'However', the minister noted, 'projects like this are costly, and we need to prioritise carefully and take things in due time.'[4]

In 2012–13, the Sørlandslab was at the top of the informal regional agenda, and industry, the university and local governments and politicians were united in their message that the region needed Sørlandslab to further develop its strong industry and research. In the spring of 2013, this message was confirmed by regional firms in letters of intent (LOIs), stating that local oil and gas firms were committed to buying 50 million NOK of services from the future lab. This commitment underscored that a gap in Agder's innovation system existed and that there was value in filling it.

In 2013, the NODE cluster appointed a new CEO with significant experience in networking with national governments; subsequently, more efforts went into lobbying the federal government. Furthermore, several parliamentarians were based in Agder and were, thus, motivated to incorporate local initiatives, including Sørlandslab, into the national agenda. Simultaneously, NODE's new CEO argued that the lab's name needed to be changed because it underlined local priorities, which was a drawback when seeking state funding. Accordingly, the name was changed to Mechatronics Innovation Lab.

In 2015, Agder's 30 municipalities signed a letter supporting the MIL project. The message from the municipalities was clear: the Agder region needed state funding to buy cutting-edge technology for the MIL. At this time, a significant drop in oil prices caused severe losses in the oil and gas industry. Therefore, firms in both Agder and the rest of the country were in desperate need of innovation facilities and cutting-edge technology.

Later that year, a revised national budget brought excellent news. The government pledged 20 million NOK to the MIL. Although insufficient, the funding was a great start, and additional funding was awarded to the MIL in the years to come. In her budget speech in 2015, the Minister of Trade and Industry at that time, Monica Mæland, said that the MIL 'will grant businesses across the country access to new knowledge and cutting-edge technology that will contribute to enhancing the competitiveness of the Norwegian oil and gas industry'.[5] The government's funding enabled the MIL initiative to proceed and, soon after, a construction contract was signed. In May 2016, construction began.

The MIL opened on 16 August 2017. By that time, it had spent 46 million NOK on world-class technology and equipment, and another 30 million was earmarked for a second round of investment. Overall, 80 per cent of the lab's machines and technologies were new to Norway, which confirmed that the vision of a cutting-edge lab had been realised. In a speech Mæland delivered at the MIL's opening, she highlighted the massive and unified regional commitment and constant pressure on national authorities as deciding factors in the MIL's development. In the university rector's speech, he offered special thanks to local entrepreneurs, the Ugland family, the GCE NODE cluster's administration, the cluster firms and all supporting partners in the educational and political systems.

Today, the MIL is organised as a commercial firm owned by the university and a national research institute. As such, the MIL needs to finance itself by promoting various services to the industry. In 2018, the MIL lab signed contracts worth 20 million NOK with industrial clients, which pay to gain access to the lab and participate in the various programmes and services offered by the MIL.

4.2   Analysis

The process of establishing the MIL demonstrates that the processes of system-level material asset creation can be time-consuming and costly. Moreover, the MIL case illustrates that system-level material asset creations are social processes influenced by structural, relational and cognitive social elements. In the following, we examine these elements more closely in exploring to what extent and in what way structural, relational and cognitive social elements have influenced the process of establishing the MIL in Agder.

4.2.1   How structural social capital influenced the establishment of the MIL

Over the years, the Agder region had developed a world-leading milieu within oil drilling equipment products and services while simultaneously building a strong knowledge creation subsystem within the field of mechatronics. The Agder RIS had developed into being organisationally thick and specialised in oil- and gas-related industries (Rypestøl, 2018). This organisational structure proved positive to the establishment of the MIL because the need for this particular system-level asset was shared by a critical number of regional actors at both the firm and system levels.

The initial idea of establishing the MIL was formed because regional firms could not afford to build and equip the needed advanced technology and test lab and because such facilities were also not present at the innovation system level. Thus, prior to 2017, the Agder RIS structure was missing what was considered to be an important element: a physically robust building equipped with state-of-the-art technology and knowledge relevant to performing extreme testing within key areas of the oil and gas sector. Such key areas included lifting and handling, pressure, climate, robotics, simulation and more.

Early dialogues between the local node cluster firms and local university revealed alignment with coinciding firm- and system-level interests. Therefore, and because of the scope of the project, key actors such as entrepreneurs, dominating firms, the NODE cluster and the university soon agreed that the need for state-of-the-art lab facilities had to be addressed as a system-level responsibility. This decision to address the establishment of the lab as a collective initiative was facilitated and promoted by a tight regional network structure of successful entrepreneurs, niche firms, world-leading departments of multinational corporations (MNCs), local politicians, representatives from the local university and R&D organisations and representatives from the local governments and local support system. The interviewees highlighted that the initiative to establish the MIL was encouraged by former successes and a dense regional network structure. Tight relations between various actors were seen as favourable to collective initiatives because the actors that needed to connect were easy to recognise and always reachable through informal channels. Thus, the case underlines what we know from social capital theory: that a high level of bonding social capital is supportive of collaboration and cooperation because to a large extent, these types of commitments can be governed from flexible and informal agreements instead of formal and rigid rules and regulations.

In the MIL's case, two successful entrepreneurs and four MNCs were identified as critical key actors (nodes) at the firm level, while the local university, the NODE cluster administration and regional politicians were considered critical regional system-level actors. The leaders in these firms and organisations were influencers in their cliques. Also, the leaders knew each other well, and, thus, effectively bridged the various groups involved. This structure of dense cliques that was connected with well-respected bridging actors was beneficial to the process of establishing and facilitating the asset creation process because the structure secured effective communication, which spread ideas and thoughts effectively among a broad range of regional actors. Although this group of leaders played a vital role in the process, two actors in particular were identified as crucial to its success. This is the first CEO of the NODE cluster administration and the dean of the Faculty of Engineering and Science at the local university. According to our interviewees, without their separate initiatives and ability to collaborate and bridge ideas in an early phase, the MIL would never have been realised.

As the process of establishing the lab developed, a well-connected local network structure was insufficient. Instead, the need for more extra-regional links increased because the region had to put additional pressure on national governments to financially support the lab's establishment. Thus, the need to develop more bridging social capital emerged, and the interviewees described this shift in focus as the second step of the process. The interviewees highlighted that this second stage of development was fuelled when the new NODE cluster leader entered the arena. This new leader had significant contacts at the national level and extended the network by adding more links and increasing pressure on existing channels. The importance of this pressure on national government representatives was highlighted by the Minister of Trade and Industry as significant to receiving national funding.

4.2.2 How relational social capital influenced the establishment of the MIL

Our informants described that a high level of trust existed between the actors in the Agder RIS at the time of the MIL's initiation. Regional actors at both the firm and system levels had positive experiences with previous and simultaneous complex multiscale collaborations, and a basis of trust emerged among the various regional actors because of these experiences. The process of gaining university status is one major example of such multiscale collaboration, while establishing mechatronics as an education programme is another. These were time-consuming processes that required a unified regional message. As such, these successful collaborations were precursors to the process of establishing the MIL and had fostered a high level of relational embeddedness (Granovetter, 1992). Relational embeddedness emerges as accumulative values form from successful collaborations over time, and the MIL case demonstrates that long-term collaborations can foster respect, trustworthy actor bonds, a strong commitment to projects promoting collective value creation and a friendly atmosphere between key actors. Also, embeddedness can facilitate informal obligations and expectations of behaviour in addition to the formal one. In the MIL case, such informal obligations were understood as voicing the demand for the MIL frequently in several channels – both regionally and further afield – to attend meetings and write newspaper articles. Furthermore, the willingness of local firms to form formal obligations was crucial to the success of the MIL case. When the granting authorities required proof that the firms would really benefit from the asset, the local firms signed LOIs worth 50 million NOK. These LOIs played a significant role in documenting that the suggested system-level asset was aligned with the needs of local firms.

Even if the process was a success in the end, several informants referred to an incident at a later stage of the MIL process that put the collaboration to the ultimate test. When structuring the organisation of the MIL, a strategic agreement was disputed by one of the interest groups. This caused confrontations and negatively affected the relational social capital because the regional trust built over the years was threatened. The interviewees were reluctant to comment on this incident and referred to the fact that the incident was solved in closed meetings between the partners involved. Even so, the interviewees stated that the long history of successful regional collaborations and strong community-based commitments built over time were favourable to the successful results of these discussions. Once agreed, the group continued to lobby for the project with one unified voice.

4.2.3 How cognitive social capital influenced the establishment of the MIL

When referring to the underlying cognitive preconditions that support system/asset creation, the MIL case demonstrates that initiatives to form system-level assets can benefit from a history of successful prior collaborations between firm- and system-level actors since such positive experience can lower the barriers for new initiatives.

Further, the MIL case demonstrates that the processes of system-level asset creation can benefit from an institutional setup that favours strong industries. In the Agder region, the RIS is categorised as institutionally supportive of the oil and gas industry (Normann et al., 2020). This skewed prioritisation of the oil and gas sector was beneficial to the establishment of the lab because the local community was relatively easy to convince. This easy-to-convince culture had developed over time and was evidenced as a common understanding stating that initiatives supportive of oil and gas were positive for the region. Thus, the regional actors soon agreed on the importance of the MIL and the questions that were raised during the initiation of the project were more within the category of 'how' rather than 'why'.

The process of establishing the MIL also benefited from parallel related processes. In Agder, two such processes were the process of seeking to establish a centre for research-based innovation in mechatronics and a process that aimed to develop the NODE cluster so that it could be awarded a GCE status by the Norwegian innovation cluster programme. These three related parallel projects in Agder raised massive attention at the national level, and the strong commitment evidenced by a broad range of local actors in these projects spoke with one voice, arguing that the Agder RIS had to be complemented and further developed to support its already strong industry. In retrospect, one could argue that these three mechatronic-related projects contributed to reinforcing Agder as an oil and gas region and forming the strong cognitive regional resonance that was needed to gain acceptance at the national level. The parallel processes were all successful. In June 2014, the NODE cluster received its GCE status. In November 2014, the university was awarded the SFI in mechatronics, and in August 2017, the MIL opened.

5. CONCLUSIONS AND SUGGESTIONS FOR FURTHER RESEARCH

The MIL case is an example of a successful process of system-level material asset creation. The case demonstrates that generating new system-level material assets can be complex, costly and time-consuming. However, it also demonstrates that the creation of this type of asset is a social process that involves multiple actors at multiple scales and geographies.

Overall, in the current study, the proposed analytical framework can be seen as useful for increasing our understanding of how social relations can influence asset modification for regional industrial restructuring. The present study highlights that in various ways, structural, relational and cognitive elements influence the change agency performed by firm- and system-level actors, thus also influencing the process of system-level material asset creation.

When referring to the structural dimension of social interactions, the MIL case highlights that the processes of system-level material asset creation can benefit from a high level of bonding social capital in an early phase because system-level asset creation requires collaboration and cooperation between regional actors. In dense networks high in trust, key actors and gatekeepers are relatively easy to identify, and collaboration and cooperation can be governed by flexible and informal agreements instead of formal and rigid rules and regulations. Furthermore, this case demonstrates that a network structure of cliques can be beneficial if these cliques are connected by actors who hold strategic positions within their cliques. This type of structure will favour a collaborative milieu and facilitate effective communication, which is important in system-level asset creation. The analysis of the MIL case further demonstrates that system-level material asset creation can be costly, thus requiring state funding. As such, the case study highlighted that such projects do not rely on a dense network structure alone. Instead, in a more mature stage, costly projects, such as the establishment of the MIL, also require bonding social capital. Bonding social capital is important because a critical number of strategic external linkages to national governments and administration are needed to ensure that communication and lobbying reach decision makers at the national level.

Referring to the relational dimension of social interactions, the MIL case demonstrates the benefits of hosting a network of strong ties for the initiation and facilitation of system-level asset modification processes. In our case, strong network ties had accumulated over the years from several successful projects in the past and from several major ongoing processes that required strong, trust-based collaborations. Even though the MIL case has turned out to be a successful example of system-level asset creation, the case also demonstrates that system-level asset creation can prove challenging because negotiations, bargaining and compromises can put relationships to the ultimate test.

Referring to the cognitive dimension of social interactions, the case also demonstrates that the processes of system-level asset creation will benefit from community-based rationality and a harmonised worldview among regional actors. Such institutional conditions will be favourable to the processes of system-level asset creation because such processes will require collective action, which can be identified as the will and ability to perform an action that serves the community as a whole. The processes of system-level asset modification will also benefit from a shared understanding of what is more important to the community and what is less important. Such a common understanding is easier to collect if the suggested project responds to the needs expressed by the dominating regional industry rather than if it challenges this dominating industry.

Relevant for both practitioners and policymakers, the MIL case highlights that supporting the preconditions for system-level asset creation includes elements from all the discussed dimensions of social capital. In particular, the case demonstrates that successful system-level material asset creation relies on the complex combination of bonding and bridging social capital. Our case suggests that practitioners and policymakers should aim to strengthen bonding social capital by supporting initiatives that enhance community thinking. The MIL case demonstrates that bonding social capital is particularly important in the initiating and early phases of development, while the need for bridging social capital becomes more evident in the later phases. Bridging social capital can be stimulated by encouraging intraregional linkages at both the firm and system levels. Such links might prove critical because they allow for the flow of information and interactive learning in both directions.

This chapter has analysed the social dimension of regional industrial restructuring in a single case within a coordinated market economy. This case occurred in a regional environment characterised by relatively little regional turbulence and within a region that possesses well-developed social capital. The study further includes a process of system-level material asset creation requiring state funding. These aspects of the case are also its limitations because this case does not offer any knowledge of how structural, relational and cognitive social elements influence the creation of such assets in other contextual settings and in similar projects that are organised and financed differently. We would expect, though, that Norway – as a coordinated market economy – would be more supportive of state funding than countries dominated by an institutional setting that favours more liberal market economies. Therefore, we encourage further research to test whether the proposed analytical framework is useful for understanding such processes in less successful cases and in other contexts. We also encourage a follow-up study on the case of the MIL to analyse whether the MIL has become successful in fulfilling its intended purposes.

NOTES

1. As will be discussed later in this chapter, the MIL is also highly relevant to other industries in Agder.
2. Phone interviews were the only option at this time because of Covid-19-related social restrictions.
3. This is how the university's Grimstad campus was financed, meaning this magnate had already partnered with the university.

4. Cited in *Fædrelandsvennen lørdag*, 31 August 2013.
5. See https://gcenode.no/news/future-engineers-broke-ground-for-mechatronics-in novation-lab/.

REFERENCES

Arthur, W. B. (1988). Self-reinforcing mechanisms in economics. *The Economy as an Evolving Complex System*, *5*, 9–31.

Arthur, W. B. (1989). Competing technologies, increasing returns, and lock-in by historical events. *Economic Journal*, *99*(394), 116–31.

Arthur, W. B. (1994). *Increasing returns and path dependence in the economy*. University of Michigan Press.

Asheim, B. T., & Gertler, M. S. (2005). The geography of innovation: Regional innovation systems. In J. Fagerberg, D. C. Mowery, & R. R. Nelson (Eds.), *The Oxford handbook of innovation* (pp. 291–317). Oxford University Press.

Asheim, B. T., Isaksen, A., & Trippl, M. (2019). *Advanced introduction to regional innovation systems*. Edward Elgar Publishing.

Barney, J. B. (2002). *Gaining and sustaining competitive advantage* (2nd ed). Prentice-Hall.

Bathelt, H., & Glückler, J. (2005). Resources in economic geography: From substantive concepts towards a relational perspective. *Environment and Planning A*, *37*(9), 1545–63.

Boschma, R. A., Coenen, L., Frenken, K., & Truffer, B. (2017). Towards a theory of regional diversification: Combining insights from evolutionary economic geography and transition studies. *Regional Studies*, *51*(1), 31–45. https://doi.org/10.1080/00343404. 2016.1258460.

Bourdieu, P. (1986). The forms of capital. In J. G. Richardson (Ed.), *Handbook of theory and research for the sociology of education* (pp. 241–58). Greenwood.

Burt, R. S. (1992). *Structural holes: The social structure of competition*. Harvard University Press.

Cohen, W. M., & Levinthal, D. A. (1990). Absorptive capacity: A new perspective on learning and innovation. *Administrative Science Quarterly*, *35*, 128–52.

Coleman, J. S. (1988). Social capital in the creation of human capital. *American Journal of Sociology*, *94*(supplement), 95–120.

Coleman, J. S. (1990). *Foundations of social theory*. Harvard University Press.

Cooke, P. (1992). Regional innovation systems: Competitive regulation in the new Europe. *Geoforum*, *23*(3), 365–82.

David, P. A. (1985). Clio and the economics of QWERTY. *American Economic Review*, *75*(2), 332–7.

Foss, N. J. (1996). Higher-order industrial capabilities and competitive advantage. *Journal of Industry Studies*, *3*(1), 1–20.

Gartner, W. B. (1988). 'Who is an entrepreneur?' Is the wrong question. *American Journal of Small Business*, *12*(4), 11–32.

Granovetter, M. S. (1973). The strength of weak ties. *American Journal of Sociology*, *78*(6), 1360–80.

Granovetter, M. S. (1992). Problems of explanation in economic sociology. In N. Nohria, & R. Eccles (Eds.), *Networks and organizations: Structure, form, and action*. Harvard Business School Press.

Grillitsch, M., & Sotarauta, M. (2019). Trinity of change agency, regional development paths and opportunity spaces. *Progress in Human Geography*. https://doi.org/10.1177/0309132519853870.

Grillitsch, M., & Trippl, M. (2016). Innovation policies and new regional growth paths: A place-based system failure framework. *Papers in Innovation Studies*, *26*, 1–23.

Hall, P. A., & Soskice, D. (2001). *Varieties of capitalism: The institutional foundations of comparative advantage*. Oxford University Press.

Herstad, S. J., & Sandven, T. (2017). *Towards regional innovation systems in Norway? An explorative empirical analysis*. Nordic Institute for Studies in Innovation, Research and Education NIFU.

Isaksen, A. (2015). Industrial development in thin regions: Trapped in path extension? *Journal of Economic Geography*, *15*(3), 585–600. https://doi.org/10.1093/jeg/lbu026.

Isaksen, A., Jakobsen, S.-E., Njøs, R., & Normann, R. (2019). Regional industrial restructuring resulting from individual and system agency. *Innovation: The European Journal of Social Science Research*, *32*(1), 48–65. https://doi.org/10.1080/13511610.2018.1496322.

Isaksen, A., Kyllingstad, N., Rypestøl, J. O., & Schulze-Krogh, A. C. (2018). Differentiated regional entrepreneurial discovery processes. A conceptual discussion and empirical illustration from three emergent clusters. *European Planning Studies*, *26*(11), 2200–2215. https://doi.org/10.1080/09654313.2018.1530143.

Isaksen, A., Trippl, M., Kyllingstad, N., & Rypestøl, J. O. (2020). Digital transformation of regional industries through asset modification. *Competitiveness Review*, *31*(1), 130–44.

Jakobsen, S.-E., & Lorentzen, T. (2015). Between bonding and bridging: Regional differences in innovative collaboration in Norway. *Norsk Geografisk Tidsskrift/Norwegian Journal of Geography*, *69*(2), 80–89.

Jolly, S., Grillitsch, M., & Hansen, T. (2020). Agency and actors in regional industrial path development: A framework and longitudinal analysis. *Geoforum*, *111*, 176–88.

Kirchhoff, B. A. (1994). *Entrepreneurship and dynamic capitalism: The economics of business firm formation and growth*. Praeger.

Kirzner, I. M. (1973). *Competition and entrepreneurship*. University of Chicago Press.

Kyllingstad, N., & Rypestøl, J. O. (2018). Towards a more sustainable process industry: A single case study of restructuring within the Eyde process industry cluster. *Norsk Geografisk Tidsskrift/Norwegian Journal of Geography*, *73*(1), 29–38. https://doi.org/10.1080/00291951.2018.1520292.

Kyllingstad, N., Rypestøl, J. O., Schulze-Krogh, A. C., & Tønnessen, M. (2021). Asset modification for regional industrial restructuring: Digitalisation of the culture and experience industry and the healthcare sector. *Regional Studies*, *55*(10–11), 1764–74.

MacKinnon, D., Dawley, S., Pike, A., & Cumbers, A. (2019). Rethinking path creation: A geographical political economy approach. *Economic Geography*, *95*(2), 113–35.

Malecki, E. J. (2012). Regional social capital: Why it matters. *Regional Studies*, *46*(8), 1023–39.

Martin, R. (2010). Roepke lecture in economic geography – rethinking regional path dependence: Beyond lock-in to evolution. *Economic Geography*, *86*(1), 1–27.

Martin, R., & Rypestøl, J. O. (2018). Linking content and technology: On the geography of innovation networks in the Bergen media cluster. *Industry and Innovation*, *25*(10), 966–89. https://doi.org/10.1080/13662716.2017.1343132.

Martin, R., & Sunley, P. (2006). Path dependence and regional economic evolution. *Journal of Economic Geography*, *6*(4), 395–437. https://doi.org/10.1093/jeg/lbl012.

Maskell, P., & Malmberg, A. (1999). The competitiveness of firms and regions: 'Ubiquitification' and the importance of localized learning. *European Urban and Regional Studies*, *6*(1), 9–25. https://doi.org/10.1177/096977649900600102.

Mechatronics Innovation Lab. (2020). https://www.mil-as.no/.

Nahapiet, J., & Ghoshal, S. (1998). Social capital, intellectual capital, and the organizational advantage. *Academy of Management Review*, *23*(2), 242–66.

Njøs, R., & Fosse, J. K. (2019). Linking the bottom-up and top-down evolution of regional innovation systems to policy: Organizations, support structures and learning processes. *Industry and Innovation*, *26*(4), 419–38.

Nooteboom, B., Van Haverbeke, W., Duysters, G., Gilsing, V., & van den Oord, A. (2007). Optimal cognitive distance and absorptive capacity. *Research Policy*, *36*(7), 1016–34. https://doi.org/10.1016/j.respol.2007.04.003.

Normann, R. H., Knudsen, J. P., & Strickert, S. (2020). The Agder region: An innovation policy case study. In M. Gonzàlez-Lòpez, & B. T. Asheim (Eds.), *Regions and innovation policies in Europe*. Edward Elgar Publishing.

North, D. C. (1990). *Institutions, institutional change and economic performance*. Cambridge University Press.

Penrose, E. (1959). *The theory of the growth of the firm*. John Wiley.

Prahalad, C. K., & Hamel, G. (1990). The core competence of the corporation. *Harvard Business Review*, *3*, 79–91.

Putnam, R. D. (2000). Bowling alone: America's declining social capital. In *Culture and politics* (pp. 223–34). Palgrave Macmillan.

Rutten, R., Westlund, H., & Boekema, F. (2010). The spatial dimension of social capital. *European Planning Studies*, *18*(6), 863–71.

Rypestøl, J. O. (2017). Regional industrial path development: The role of new entrepreneurial firms. *Journal of Innovation and Entrepreneurship*, *6*(1), 1–19. https://doi.org/10.1186/s13731-017-0064-1.

Rypestøl, J. O. (2018). Det regionale innovasjonssystemet i Agder. In Agderforskning (Ed.), *Project report* (Vol. 2, p. 70). Agderforskning.

Rypestøl, J. O. (2020). Regional industrial restructuring. In L. Farinha, D. Santos, J. J. Ferreira, & M. Ranga (Eds.), *Regional helix ecosystems and sustainable growth*. Springer International Publishing.

Schumpeter, J. A. (1934). *The theory of economic development: An enquiry into profits, capital, credit, interest and the business cycle*. Harvard University Press.

Schumpeter, J. A. (1939). *Business cycles* (Vol. 1). McGraw-Hill.

Smith, N. R. (1967). *The entrepreneur and his firm: The relationship between type of man and type of company*. Michigan State University, Bureau of Business and Economic Research.

Sotarauta, M., & Suvinen, N. (2018). Institutional agency and path creation. In A. Isaksen, R. Martin, & M. Trippl (Eds.), *New avenues for regional innovation systems: Theoretical advances, empirical cases and policy lessons* (pp. 85–104). Springer.

Stam, E., Bosma, N., Van Witteloostuijn, A., De Jong, J., Bogaert, S., & Edwards, N. (2012). Ambitious entrepreneurship: A review of the academic literature and directions for public policy. *Den Haag: Advisory Council for Science and Technology Policy*, 1–162.

Stam, E., Suddle, K., Hessels, J., & Van Stel, A. J. (2007). High growth entrepreneurs, public policies and economic growth [Hudson Institute Research Paper, NO. 08-02]. *Jena Economic Research Paper* (19), 08–02.

Trippl, M., Baumgartinger-Seiringer, S., Frangenheim, A., Isaksen, A., & Rypestøl, J. O. (2020). Unravelling green regional industrial path development: Regional preconditions, asset modification and agency. *Geoforum*, *111*, 189–97. https://doi.org/10.1016/j.geoforum.2020.02.016.

Yin, R. K. (1984). *Case study research: Design and methods*. Sage.

4. Collective resources in entrepreneurship: a reconceptualisation of resource mobilisation

Karin Wigger and Thomas Lauvås

INTRODUCTION

Entrepreneurial firms – that is, firms that constantly pursue entrepreneurial opportunities (Miller & Friesen, 1982) – can draw on collective resources (i.e. resources that are governed by a collective) to accumulate the variety of resources they need to pursue an entrepreneurial opportunity (Wigger, 2018).[1] Examples of collective resources are natural resources, such as whales (Lawrence & Phillips, 2004) and crabs (Alvarez et al., 2015), and resources developed through social interactions in networks, such as new knowledge co-created in a network initiative (Zhang et al., 2019) or an open innovation project (Garcia et al., 2019). We refer to collective resources as non-exclusive, meaning that the collective resources an entrepreneurial firm draws on to pursue an opportunity are owned and can be used by other actors simultaneously – at least during part of the resource's lifespan.

Because collective resources can be owned by a collective, publicly owned, or are not owned by anyone per se (as is the case for many natural resources), entrepreneurial firms typically need to mobilise collective resources without ownership transfer (Wigger & Shepherd, 2020). This means that the entrepreneurial firm and other actors can simultaneously use collective resources and social contracting is regarded as a promising avenue for commoning practices (Ostrom, 2015/1990). The non-excludability and non-transferability of collective resources can challenge the mobilisation of the resource by the entrepreneurial firm – that is, resource search, access and transfer (Clough et al., 2019) – and thereby jeopardise the planned entrepreneurial activity or degrade the quality of the resources the entrepreneurial firm depends on for opportunity exploitation, for example when the resources are over- or misused (Alvarez et al., 2015; Garcia et al., 2019). The absence of ownership transfer concerning collective resources can result in social dilemmas, caused, for example, by conflicting resource use and interest (Ostrom, 2015/1990) and mobilisation inefficiencies, such as high transaction costs (Coase, 1974; Eggertsson, 1990), in particular because the lack of enforceability leads to the absence of reassuring sustainable resource use and the accessibility of collective resources needs to constantly be reassessed, which implies that entrepreneurial firms need to establish often costly resource-mobilisation arrangements to ensure sustained access and usage of the collective resources needed to pursue opportunities, such as communing practices and other types of social arrangements (Ostrom, 2015/1990).

Prior research highlights the transfer of resources from resource holder(s) to resource seeker(s) as a key activity of resource mobilisation (Clough et al., 2019; Rawhouser et al., 2017) in order to, for example, alleviate dependence between the entrepreneurial firm and the external environment (Pfeffer & Salancik, 2003/1978) and to build a unique heterogeneous resource base (Barney, 1991). Our focus on collective resources provides novel insights into the debate on resource mobilisation without ownership transfer, and it addresses the following question: how do entrepreneurial firms mobilise collective resources for opportunity exploitation?

Prior research discusses the mobilisation of resources without – or at least with indirect – ownership exchange to some extent, for example, bootstrapping (Winborg & Landström, 2001), effectuation (Sarasvathy, 2001) and bricolage (Baker & Nelson, 2005). To illustrate, the concept of effectuation regards resources embedded in the social network of the entrepreneur to be mobilisable, meaning that networks can expand the available resource base of the entrepreneurial firm without gaining ownership of these resources (Berends et al., 2014). While these studies are examples of resources shared amongst a defined or at least known group of actors, this chapter expands the debate by focusing on resources, such as natural resources, which are owned by a larger collective, the public or have no ownership per se.

We utilise insights from well-established resource theories (i.e. resource-based view [RBV], resource dependence theory [RDT], and new institutional economics [NIE]) to conceptually explore how entrepreneurial firms mobilise collective resources to pursue opportunities and to provide a reconceptualisation of the mobilisation of collective resources. We have selected these three theories to gain a broad understanding from three idiosyncratic perspectives on the firm and its relation to resources. For example, RDT uses an outside-in perspective, RBV an inside-out perspective, and NIE a transaction perspective on the relationship between firms and resources (Wigger, 2018). In order to further illustrate and exemplify our arguments, we draw on resource-mobilisation examples from salmon farmers, which utilise various collective resources as their opportunities often build on natural resources.

In doing so, this chapter contributes to the literature on resource mobilisation for entrepreneurship. The excludability and transferability of resources are often assumed in studies on resource mobilisation for entrepreneurship (e.g. Clough et al., 2019; Rawhouser et al., 2017). These assumptions are challenged by the nature of collective resources, and this chapter offers a reconceptualisation of mobilising collective resources with a shared governance by taking into account the non-excludability and non-transferability of collective resources. Moreover, this chapter argues that the shared governance of collective resource requires an idiosyncratic resource-mobilisation approach and presents how four types of resource-mobilisation arrangements (i.e. market arrangement, collaborative arrangement, relational arrangement and institutional arrangement) are designed for collective resources.

RESOURCE MOBILISATION FOR OPPORTUNITY EXPLOITATION

Mobilising resources for opportunity exploitation implies the perception that the novel use of the resources is more worthwhile than the current uses of the resources (Holmén et al., 2007; Penrose, 2009/1959). Established firms consist of a resource endowment (Haynie et al., 2009), and the resources needed to exploit an opportunity can be mobilised internally through, for example, reconfiguring, reallocating and recombining internal resources (Desa & Basu, 2013; Penrose, 2009/1959). Often, however, an entrepreneurial firm does not possess all the resources it needs to exploit an opportunity, or the resources are currently unavailable for reallocation. Consequently, entrepreneurial firms also mobilise resources from organisations in the external environment (Pfeffer & Salancik, 2003/1978). This chapter focuses on the mobilisation of external resources for opportunity exploitation.

Arrangements for Resource Mobilisation

External resources (hereafter referred to as resources) are typically mobilised through arrangements between firms, other types of organisations and institutions, such as those guiding the use of natural resources (Simsek et al., 2003). Arrangements can be contracts as well as socially and institutionally embedded constellations established through interaction between individual and collective actors (Neergaard & Ulhøi, 2006). Hence, arrangements are instruments used to formally and informally govern the mobilisation of resources between different activities throughout the opportunity-development process (Busenitz et al., 2003).

Arrangements come in different forms and can be grouped in different types to transfer and exchange resources. Examples of arrangement types include market arrangements (Eckhardt & Shane, 2003) and collaborative arrangements, such as in the form of inter-organisational arrangements between firms (Drees & Heugens, 2013; Marchington & Vincent, 2004). These arrangements are designed to fit the different motives of the resource holder(s) and resource acquirer(s) as well as the characteristics of the resources, such as ownership and transferability of the resource (Subramani & Venkatraman, 2003).

Resource Ownership: Excludability, Enforceability and Transferability

Resources can have different property rights, as they can be owned by a single actor, a collective or have no ownership as such. The ownership of a resource defines its excludability, transferability and enforceability. Tietenberg and Lewis (2009/1984) argue that these three property right characteristics define efficient resource mobilisation. Excludability means that the resource owner should take on the benefits and costs linked to owning and using the resource; transferability means that ownership of the resource can be transferred from one use to another, and enforceability means that resources are secured from involuntary use and damage (Tietenberg & Lewis, 2009/1984).

Common ownership of collective resources, however, often results in restricted transferability, excludability and enforceability. In order for the entrepreneurial firms to be able to mobilise a collective resource, the resource must be transferable to some degree (Franco & Haase, 2013). Resources with a high degree of transferability include, for instance, financial capital. While some resources are transferable in their usage, ownership exchange through resource mobilisation as a firm-to-firm transaction might not be adequate for collective resources, since this type of resource does not have a single owner or a defined group of owners (Tietenberg & Lewis, 2009/1984).

Given the focus of this chapter on collective resources, we are interested in arrangements established by two or more independent actors, who exchange shared resources for mutual benefit or as a control mechanism of collective resource use.

MOBILISATION OF COLLECTIVE RESOURCES FOR ENTREPRENEURSHIP

To learn more about how the mobilisation of collective resources works, this chapter uses resource mobilisation examples from the Norwegian salmon farming industry and insights from three grand theories on the mobilisation of collective resources. The theories, RBV, RDT and NIE are used to present how the previously defined types of arrangements (i.e. market arrangements,

Collective resources in entrepreneurship 71

collaborative arrangements, relational arrangements and institutional arrangements) are designed for collective resource mobilisation.

Exploring Practices of Collective Resource Mobilisation: Four Examples from the Aquaculture Industry

This section offers empirical insights into the mobilisation of collective resources from the Norwegian salmon farming industry and is based on secondary data and a larger qualitative study by the authors on the aquaculture industry.[2] The use of examples from the real world in conceptual papers (e.g. Lamers et al., 2017; Welter, 2011) has proven to be an effective way to strengthen and illustrate the arguments. Hence, the examples presented below illustrate and exemplify how collective resource can be mobilised for entrepreneurship.

The aquaculture industry is a young but growing industry, which consists of many entrepreneurial firms that innovate to advance production. Moreover, salmon farmers make use of natural resources, such as sea water and production areas and other types of collective resources. Therefore, examples from Norwegian salmon farmers can provide more insight into how collective resources are mobilised.

The aquaculture industry, and especially salmon farming, has received increased international attention due to its potential for value creation based on natural resources (Bjørkan & Eilertsen, 2020). In 2018, the aquaculture industry employed 8,200 persons directly and 12,000 when including the value chain in Norway. The collective output value was 118 billion NOK (11 billion EUR); the industry has one of the highest value creations per capita (Richardsen et al., 2019). Consequently, the Norwegian government intends to increase the growth of the aquaculture industry (NFD & OED, 2017), and Olafsen et al. (2012) estimate a fivefold increase in production by 2050.

However, the main obstacle to achieving these goals is salmon lice, which has negative effects on wild salmon and the quality of farmed salmon. Since salmon lice are naturally found in the ocean, production is affected because the salmon are produced in open cages placed along the Norwegian coastline. If the concentration of salmon lice is too high in the production facilities, the lice may pass on to the wild salmon swimming by the production areas. Until the salmon lice issue is solved, the Norwegian government is limiting new salmon licenses and restraining growth in the sector, and has introduced various measures to limit the effect of the lice on wild salmon.

Traffic light system for salmon production using institutional arrangements to mobilise collective resources

To limit the negative externalities of salmon lice, the Norwegian government introduced the 'traffic light system' in 2017 (Regjeringen, 2017), separating the Norwegian coastline into 13 different production areas for salmon (Ådlandsvik et al., 2015). Based on surveillance and reports regarding salmon lice, an interdisciplinary group of researchers writes a report, which is then evaluated by the Ministry of Trade, Industry and Fisheries. Depending on the perceived risk of salmon lice on the mortality of wild salmon, the Ministry decides which areas are to be identified as green, yellow and red. The rationale is that aquaculture influence on the environment is decisive for its potential growth.

Consequently, the traffic light system determines which sector gets to maintain, increase or decrease its salmon production (Institute of Marine Research, 2020). In practice, this means that a salmon farmer who does not have any issue with salmon lice could face production restrictions if other farmers in the same area struggle to control a lice problem. The traffic light system is an example of regulating institutions defining access to and usage of locations for salmon production. It defines whether the natural resources still can be used if salmon farmers gain access to new natural resources or if they have to stop using the natural resources for a certain timespan.

Auctions and licenses using market arrangements to mobilise collective resources

In 'green light' areas, salmon farmers can buy permits from the government to increase their production. In 2020, for instance, salmon farmers in the nine green areas were allowed 6 per cent growth in biomass. One percentage point was sold at a fixed price of 156,000 NOK (14,300 EUR) per ton, whereas the remaining five percentage points were auctioned by the Directorate of Fisheries (Regjeringen, 2020). The Norwegian government thus decides the value of the natural resources in the form of a defined price per ton of biomass to produce salmon and creates a market-based system to sell and buy natural resources, which no one owns per se. Moreover, buying a permit gives the salmon farmers the right to use the natural resources to produce salmon.

Collective knowledge sharing in networks using collaborative arrangements to mobilise collective resources

From its establishment in the 1970s, the salmon farming industry has been regarded as an open industry, in which knowledge has been shared among the actors regarding how to best produce salmon (Larsen et al., forthcoming). Knowledge related to common challenges is shared openly between the companies, such as salmon lice or concerns over industry reputation. For example, salmon farmers have created a cluster that researches different areas and then

Collective resources in entrepreneurship 73

shares the resulting knowledge among the farmers: 'We have established collective R&D [research and development] projects in the forums on areas that several partners have challenges with, of which participation varies from top management to special expertise ... And knowledge is shared openly on pressing issues in the forums' (interviewee). Salmon farmers collectively create knowledge within the cluster, and this created knowledge is collectively owned by the cluster members, who have established practices about how to use and access this knowledge.

Collaborative smolt production using relational arrangements to mobilise collective resources

The salmon farming industry emphasises biology, and getting the best smolt (young salmon that are ready for entering the sea) is an important part of increasing salmon production. Since economically sound smolt production requires a large volume of smolt, it is not economically viable for single salmon farmers to own their own smolt facility, unless it is a large, listed firm. Regional small and medium enterprises (SMEs) have therefore collectively built smolt production facilities that they also collectively own, which produce top quality smolt available for purchase: 'We initiated a smolt production facility, and we needed others to realise it, so we invited other regional actors to collaborate, which then joined to realise and build the facility' (interviewee). Building such collective arrangements also applies for delousing activities. When the lice 'strike', a whole area is often affected, causing the larger firms who own delousing equipment to use it first. Hence, the SMEs have also collaborated in established delousing firms, which are able to serve their facilities when needed.

Because salmon farmers have licenses determining how much salmon they are allowed to have in their facilities, some of them also lend out their production areas if they have excess capacity (i.e. not using their allowed quota of salmon biomass in the sea). As each ton of salmon is valued at around 150,000–200,000 NOK at the time of writing (Fiskeridirektoratet, 2020), it is beneficial for salmon farmers to utilise the biomass that they have a license for: 'through co-location we can exchange salmon from their [neighbouring firm] localities to ours, or we can have the salmon on their localities ... of which we both benefit from'. Sharing the production area and smolt production is based on trust and social exchange between the salmon farmers.

Theoretical Insights on the Mobilisation of Collective Resources: Three Resource Perspectives

The examples above illustrate that collective resources can be mobilised in various ways and highlight peculiarities of mobilising collective resources.

To gain a more profound theoretical understanding of mobilising collective resources, we apply three theoretical lenses: RDT (Pfeffer & Salancik, 2003/1978), RBV (Barney, 1991; Penrose, 2009/1959), and NIE (Coase, 1991; North, 1990; Williamson, 1985). These three theories are utilised to reconceptualise the debate on mobilising collective resources. We discuss the insights from each of these theories on resource mobilisation regarding the nature of collective resources. The principal aspects of each theory are summarised in Table 4.1.

Moreover, Table 4.1 illustrates that the three theories build on distinct perceptions of the firm and different fundamental issues each theory addresses. This means that the relationship between the firm and resources is conceptualised in three different ways. Hence, applying the logics of the three theories builds a broad foundation to conceptualise the mobilisation of collective resources. We have selected RDT because of the focus on how entrepreneurial firms survive in the long term, despite the dependence on collective resources and issues on how to sustain the accessibility of these resources. Moreover, RBV was selected because it adds a firm-internal aspect to the debate on how to sustain the resource advantages, and thus the entrepreneurial opportunity. Finally, transaction costs and property rights are crucial and define resource mobilisation efficiency. To address the transaction perspective, we have selected NIE.

Mobilisation of collective resources and the RDT

RDT combines theories of the environment of firms in which resources are embedded (e.g. Terreberry, 1968; Yuchtman & Seashore, 1967) and the theory of power to understand the relationship between resource providers in the external environment and resource seekers, such as the entrepreneurial firm (Emerson, 1962). RDT considers resources as exogenous properties before they are eventually acquired by an entrepreneurial firm. Hence, the resources an entrepreneurial firm depends on to exploit an opportunity are often controlled by actors in the external environment. Casciaro and Piskorski (2005) argue that an entrepreneurial firm's ability to manage resource dependences and overcome constraints is determined by the extent of mutual dependence and power imbalance between the resource provider(s) and the entrepreneurial firm. In this line of thinking, the arrangements entrepreneurial firms establish to mobilise resources are designed to create mutual dependence and address power imbalances in order to alleviate resource dependence (Drees & Heugens, 2013).

Research that draws on RDT primarily studies resources that are excludable and transferable, as RDT argues that the most direct method to alleviate dependence is to gain control through ownership, for example through acquisition (Pfeffer & Salancik, 2003/1978). Hence, ownership is a key element under-

Collective resources in entrepreneurship 75

Table 4.1   Theoretical insights on resource mobilisation

	Resource dependence theory (RDT)	Resource-based view (RBV)	New institutional economics (NIE)
Fundamental issue the theory addresses	Firm survival	Competitive advantage (i.e. outperforming other firms)	Existence of the firms
Perception of the firm	Firm as a co-dependent entity	Firm as a bundle of resources	Firm as a nexus of contracts
Nature of collective resources	Increases interdependences between firms benefiting from the resources	Contradicts the logic of internalising critical resources to build a competitive advantage	Increases transaction costs and requires institutions to guide allocation
Issues inherent in collective resources	Power imbalance and interdependences	Heterogeneity issues	Market failures inherent in non-excludability
Level of resource mobilisation	Meso level	Micro level	Micro level (transaction costs) and macro level (property rights)
Motivation for establishing arrangement	Dependences define the arrangements through which resources are mobilised	Creation and internalisation of critical resources to enhance heterogeneity	Institutions provide incentive structures for how resources are mobilised
Type of arrangements	Inter-organisational arrangements	Inter-organisational arrangements	Institutional arrangements

Source: Adapted from Wigger, 2018.

lying the control of resource dependence. Nevertheless, Pfeffer and Salancik (2003/1978, p. 143ff.) acknowledge that an entrepreneurial firm is not always able to gain control through ownership transferability, and they argue that there are alternative arrangements to coordinate mutual dependence and power imbalance to deal with and alleviate resource dependence. For example, RDT considers alternative informal and semiformal inter-organisational arrangements, such as collaborative arrangements and relational arrangements that can be established to coordinate the different interests of both the entrepreneurial firms and actors that control the resources (Gulati & Sytch, 2007; Pfeffer & Salancik, 2003/1978). Consequently, resources can be mobilised through both relational contracting and market contracting (Starr & MacMillan, 1990).

Social coordination through collaborative and relational arrangements is a means to create mutual dependences through relational contracting (Pfeffer & Salancik, 2003/1978). Arrangements based on social agreements are driven by social norms and values. Following this line of thinking, exchange relationships between an entrepreneurial firm and actors controlling the desired resource(s) are defined through rules and norms as well as the emergence and/or development of a relationship (Cropanzano & Mitchell, 2005). Hence, we argue that from an RDT perspective, collaborative and relational arrangements without ownership transferability can be a way to alleviate resource dependence, and they tend to favour the sustainable mobilisation of collective resources. Arrangements that draw on social agreements stabilise resource exchange and the robustness of the relationship as well as reduce uncertainties linked to accessing collective resources (Pfeffer & Salancik, 2003/1978).

Mobilisation of collective resources and the RBV

RBV argues that the basis for value creation is valuable and rare resources (Barney, 1991; Sirmon et al., 2011). Firms internalise resources that are difficult to substitute or to copy in order to build an advantage over other firms for a longer time period (Barney, 1991). Therefore, to internalise critical resources is assumed to be a prerequisite to preserve heterogeneity and thus to limit competition (Peteraf, 1993). Rumelt (1997) coined the term 'isolation mechanism', which refers to strategies and tactics firms apply to protect their resource bundles from imitation. Property rights of resources are one condition included in the isolation mechanism (Rumelt, 1997). Additionally, Peteraf (1993) stresses that private property rights for resources can cause imperfect mobility, which means that these resources are excluded from resource markets and become less valuable to other firms.

The nature of collective resources thus challenges the assumptions of RBV related to how resources and their characteristics lead to sustained competitive advantage (Lavie, 2006). In particular, RBV's emphasis on a heterogeneous resource base and the imperfect mobility of resources is challenged by the non-excludability and non-transferability of collective resources. Lavie (2006) criticises RBV's assumption of firms' independence and extends the theory by arguing that many firms are interconnected and that the interconnectedness includes collective resources, such as network resources. Furthermore, ownership and control of resources are not necessarily a required condition to achieve competitive advantage (Lavie, 2006).

Following Penrose's (2009/1959) suggestion of resources' alternative uses, firms can have access to the services of a resource without obtaining the resource itself. Thus, the imitability of collective resources depends more on the relationship between the actors who aim to use the resource and those who control it. Moreover, the same collective resource acquired or accumulated by a single firm can provide different services for another firm, which, as mentioned earlier, contributes to the heterogeneity of firms.

Mobilisation of collective resources and the NIE

NIE assumes that institutions – formal rules and informal restraints that define social, economic and political interaction – constrain economic behaviours and shape human interactions (North, 1990). Institutions guide interactions and define behaviour during transactions (Garud et al., 2007; North, 1990). Thereby, institutions guide resource mobilisation through, for example, incentives that influence exchange relationships. Hence, institutions affect the mobilisation of resources, as they create order, reduce uncertainties in the exchange process and mitigate opportunistic behaviours (Eggertsson, 1990).

Since institutions shape resource mobilisation, firms establish institutional arrangements to change institutions for more favourable resource allocation (Becker & Ostrom, 1995). NIE scholars focus on the role of property rights when allocating resources (Eggertsson, 1990). This chapter uses Eggertsson's (1990) understanding of property rights, which is defined as a method to assign authority to select how resources are used within institutional constraints by particular individuals organised in firms (as one example). The property rights associated with resources consist of the following three rights: the right to use a resource, the right to earn income from the resource and the right to permanently transfer resource ownership to another party.

Collective resources, such as natural resources, are characterised by the non-exclusive privilege to use the resources, which includes such issues as free-riding, externalities and ineffective resource mobilisation, which can, for example, lead to over-exploitation (Ostrom, 2015/1990). For resources with common ownership or those that are open access, no one holds exclusive rights (Cheung, 1970; Eggertsson, 1990). In this kind of situation, institutions become particularly important because property rights and inherent enforcements are not applicable. Institutional change, such as the establishment of a common fishing ground, can constrain the scope of resource use. However, Ostrom (2015/1990) argues that establishing institutional arrangements to monitor and control resource use can be costly. Thus, the transaction costs connected to the mobilisation of collective resources are likely to be higher for resources with an exclusive ownership structure.

North (1990) argues that when it is costly to mobilise resources, institutions are particularly important. When institutions sub-optimally mobilise collective resources, actors such as firms, other organisations and the state establish institutional arrangements to make more favourable conditions for resource mobilisation. For example, sub-optimal situations can occur when incentive systems fail to prevent over-exploitation (Ostrom, 2015/1990).

Based on the logics from the three different theoretical perspectives, the nature of collective resources influences the mobilisation of these resources for opportunity exploitation. The following issues are revealed when comparing these perspectives: (1) the collective nature of these resources most likely leads to increased interdependences between entrepreneurial firms and other actors; (2) there are challenges linked to how firms draw on collective resources to outperform others; and (3) there will be increased transaction costs for collective resources. Furthermore, mobilisation logics within these perspectives extend arguments based on the assumption of private resource ownership. Starting with this, we now discuss the peculiarities of mobilising collective resources.

FOUR TYPES OF ARRANGEMENTS FOR THE MOBILISATION OF COLLECTIVE RESOURCES FOR ENTREPRENEURSHIP

Drawing on the examples from the salmon farming firms and the theoretical insights from RBV, RDT and NIE, we discuss four arrangements to mobilise collective resources for opportunity exploitation: market arrangements, collaborative arrangements, relational arrangements and institutional arrangements. While these types of arrangements are also used to mobilise exclusive and transferable resources, we argue that for collective resources, these arrangements come with idiosyncratic designs that take into account the common property rights of collective resources. In particular, we draw on these four examples of collective resource mobilisation to gain novel insights into the particularities of collective resource mobilisation. The four arrangements are presented in Table 4.2 and described in terms of access of resources, utilisation of resources, transfer of ownership and theoretical insights.

Mobilisation of Collective Resources Through Market Arrangements

Market arrangements are arrangements that are defined through, for example, sell-and-buy transactions or through renting and borrowing resources, such as a bank loan (Clough et al., 2019). Market arrangements focus on the economic gains of a resource holder and are typically used for resources that have a clearly defined resource holder and instrumental value, such as money. Moreover, resource transfer through market arrangements comes generally with low transaction costs compared to other types of arrangements (Escobal & Cavero, 2012). Typically, when resources are exchanged through market arrangements, the ownership, usership and the resource itself are transferred from the resource holder to the resource seeker. Moreover, market arrangement makes use of market contracts or property right laws, which legally enforce resource users to comply with the defined user and owner right.

A prerequisite for market transaction is that there is a market for the resource that an entrepreneurial venture aims to mobilise to pursue a perceived opportunity. For collective resources, the property rights are not fully allocated, which

Collective resources in entrepreneurship 79

Table 4.2   Arrangements for the mobilisation of collective resources

	Market-based arrangements	Collaborative arrangements	Relational arrangements	Institutional arrangements
Examples from the salmon farming industry	Public auctions and licensing	Knowledge created in networks	Joint smolt production	Traffic light system
Access of resources	To buy access	Access decided by collaborative partners (e.g. network)	Access through social exchange	Access defined by institutions
Utilisation of resources	Sole right to use	Simultaneous usage	Usage comes with social strings	Usage limited by institutions
Transfer of ownership	Public–private transfer	Without ownership transfer	Without ownership transfer	Without ownership transfer
Theoretical insights	RBV and NIE	RDT	RDT and NIE	NIE

Source: Authors' compilation.

leads to market failure (Gardner, 1983), and therefore collective resources typically are not exchanged at markets because of the lack of an assigned value to the resource and because they are not owned by a single resource holder (Hahn & Noll, 1981). Hence, to mobilise collective resources, markets need to be created, as the example of licensing and auction has shown.

In our example, the government designed, created and implemented a 'market-based system' to transfer collective resources, particularly to locations to produce salmon through selling permits defining the location to be used and the maximum salmon biomass to be produced, among other criteria. Using market-like systems to mobilise collective resources demands that there is an institution, such as the government, that has the authority to create such market-based systems that enable the allocation of resources, which prior to the resource mobilisation have been collective resources. Market-like systems have been debated over many years, and are found to be inefficient and unequal, in particular for more exclusive resources (Gardner, 1983; Peterson & Peterson, 1993).

However, drawing on the insights from RBV, mobilising collective resources through market arrangements gives an entrepreneurial venture the sole user-ship of the resources, which means that the resources are excludable and therefore can be internalised in the firm's resource pool. Collective resources mobilised through market arrangements allow the entrepreneurial venture to draw on the isolation mechanism, thereby building a competitive advantage on what before the mobilisation process had been collective resources (Barney,

1991; Rumelt, 1997). The examples from our Norwegian salmon farming firms show that production locations are indeed critical for salmon farmers to build a competitive advantage. Market-like systems for collective resources enable entrepreneurial firms to efficiently mobilise resources once they can buy the resources. As the example of permits and auctions has shown, the resources 'for sale' are highly limited and become exclusive given the high price. Moreover, the government defines the condition for the market and the mobilisation of the resources.

Mobilisation of Collective Resources through Collaborative Arrangements

Collaborative arrangements are arrangements 'in which collaboration replaces arm's length market exchange to a significant extent' (Bailetti & Callahan, 1993, p. 130). This means that the collaboration partners define the access to as well as the usage of the resources. Such arrangements are often used for technologies (Bailetti & Callahan, 1993) and knowledge (Grant & Baden-Fuller, 1995).

While collaborative arrangements to mobilise exclusive resources often draw on formal contracts (Bailetti & Callahan, 1993), relational contracts become essential for collaborative arrangements for collective resources. Collective resources can be jointly owned by a group of actors, such as a network of firms in the same industry – as we have seen in the example of the cluster for salmon farming firms. For example, the knowledge that the firms collectively create through several projects and initiatives in the cluster is collectively owned by the firms in the cluster. Hence, the collective that owns the resources defines the access to and the usage of them, meaning that the collective designs the arrangement to mobilise the joint resources for individual firms to use. Based on insights from RDT, and as our example also illustrates, collaborative arrangements for collective resources draw on mutual benefits and increased dependence on each other (Casciaro & Piskorski, 2005) instead of formal contracts. As our example shows, the joint knowledge applied by several firms simultaneously provides advantages not only for the single firm but also for the industry. However, free-riding is a commonly seen issue when using collective resources in networks (Garcia et al., 2019). Increased co-dependency of the individual actors in a collective can decrease the incentives of free-riding.

Mobilisation of Collective Resources through Relational Arrangements

Relational arrangements through kinship and friendship are regarded as important arrangements to access and acquire necessary resources in entrepreneurship, such as for small business owners and their business founding (Zimmer

& Aldrich, 1987), human capital, for example in form of involving family members (Aldrich & Kim, 2007), or early employees of a start-up that will benefit from venture growth (Clough et al., 2019). A relational contract is not legally formalised, as it is the case for market-based contracts, but is instead based on agreements between the two parties. This means that the enforceability and the scope of usage are often not regulated through legally binding contracts but through social ones.

When resources are owned by one actor, relational arrangements draw on dyadic relationships. Collective resources are typically owned by a collective; the public or ownership is not allotted. Thus, relational contracts underpinning this type of arrangement involve multi-party relationships. Moreover, while kinship and friendship are typically used to mobilise individually owned resources (Aldrich & Kim, 2007; Zimmer & Aldrich, 1987), collective resources are mobilised through social exchange between external actors – in our examples through the collaboration between competing salmon farming firms.

Arrangements become less instrumental when exchange relationships build on joint dependences between entrepreneurial firms and exchange partners (Gulati & Sytch, 2007) – as we have seen in our example of co-producing smolt. Such multi-party relationships can develop a common understanding of mutual beneficial actions, which creates situations that often lead to mutual dependences between the users of the resources (Casciaro & Piskorski, 2005). Thus, we propose that the mobilisation of collective resources likely favours social agreements over market-based contracts and that maximising total dependence results in actors' jointly aiming for mutual benefits. Furthermore, relational arrangements with other users and/or owners of the collective resource can increase trust if it increases the mutual benefit, thus increasing mutual dependences between resource users (Casciaro & Piskorski, 2005). However, if relational arrangements are mismanaged, it could also increase distrust and tensions between the partners.

Mobilisation of Collective Resources through Institutional Arrangements

In situations in which the status quo in institutions hinders effective resource mobilisation, firms may establish *institutional arrangements* aimed at achieving more favourable resource transactions. These arrangements are socially and institutionally embedded constellations shaped by interactions between resource users and resource owners or/and institutional bodies guiding resource allocation (Neergaard & Ulhøi, 2006). Institutional arrangements generally come with high transaction costs (Escobal & Cavero, 2012), as the institutions define how the resources are accessed and used.

While institutional arrangements are often inefficient in mobilising exclusive resources and markets and individual contracts often fail to address the shared governance of collective resources effectively, institutions can be efficient alternatives to govern collective resources (Ostrom, 2015/1990). Using collective resources leads to autonomy challenges, and institutions can define the scope of action within which resource use is accepted. Institutions, such as regulations, can define the use of common property resources (North, 1990), act as legal safeguards and provide sanctions (Eggertsson, 1990). Furthermore, institutions can provide mutually beneficial incentives, which decrease uncertainties related to collective inaction. This is exemplified through our example of the traffic light system, in which both access to increases in salmon production and limits on their production in cases of environmental concern related to salmon lice affecting wild salmon, are defined by institutions. By this, the institution uses a 'carrot and stick' approach, inducing the behaviour necessary to keep infestations of salmon lice down in the 13 production areas.

Institutional arrangements that entrepreneurial firms draw on to mobilise collective resources typically come with higher transaction costs than market exchange (Eggertsson, 1990; North, 1990). Moreover, entrepreneurial firms that mobilise collective resources face uncertainties that they do not encounter (at least not to the same extent) when mobilising more exclusive resources. For instance, extant research has pointed out free-riding issues when resources are created in networks (West & Gallagher, 2006) and instances of inefficient natural resource allocation (Ostrom, 2015/1990). We argue that these issues become even more salient when entrepreneurial firms plan to use collective resources over longer periods, which in turn justifies the use of social and institutional arrangements. To sum up, we propose that arrangements to mobilise collective resources need more creative designs than for resources with individual ownership. Moreover, we suggest that social and institutional dimensions of resource-mobilisation arrangements become particularly important for mobilising collective resources.

CONCLUSION

In this chapter, we argue that particularities of collective resources, such as their low degree of excludability, transferability and enforceability, determine how entrepreneurial firms mobilise resources. While resource mobilisation in the current literature is defined as the activities of searching, creating, accessing and transferring resources (Clough et al., 2019), we argue that collective resources are often mobilised without ownership transfer. To mobilise collective resources, entrepreneurial firms draw more on social aspects, such as trust and co-dependency, than on formal contracts – at least for collaborative and relational arrangements. For collective resources, a market-based system must first be implemented before collective resources can be mobilised through market arrangements – making market-based arrangements less efficient for collective resources than privately owned ones. In turn, we argue that institutional arrangements are more effective for mobilising collective resources than for resources with a clearly defined ownership. Hence, we suggest that resource-mobilisation logics based on the assumption that the resources can be transferred and have a clearly defined ownership structure need to be reconceptualised for collective resources, which we turn to now.

We suggest that when entrepreneurial firms draw on collective resources to pursue opportunities, resource dependence is managed through created co-dependences between the actors with stakes in the collective resources instead of ownership control. These arguments build on those of, for example, Gulati and Sytch (2007), who claim that scholars need to distinguish between inter-dependences and joint dependences to understand resource dependence. Vestrum and Rasmussen (2013) also argue for establishing mutual dependences between community ventures and local resource owners. These studies suggest applying the logic of social embeddedness to understand resource dependence rather than focusing exclusively on dependence advantages and power imbalances. We add to this research by arguing that co-dependency motivates resource users to minimise mobilisation inefficiencies collectively and through social arrangements the entrepreneurial firm can access collective resource by engaging in dependency relations.

Furthermore, entrepreneurial firms establish arrangements that enable them able to mobilise resources that are otherwise not accessible to other firms – at least not accessible at the same cost (Lavie, 2006). In particular, unique relationships facilitate the inimitability of collective resources (Lavie, 2006), which are non-accessible for actors without these relationships. To illustrate, resources that local farming firms collectively build and share, such as smolt production, might not be accessible to firms that do not have the same social relationships with these organisations. Moreover, when collective resources are created and become mutually beneficial for the firms inside the network, spillover rents arise, and the network is likely to become interested in limiting external access to these network resources.

Lastly, given that collective resources often cannot be allocated through ownership exchange, entrepreneurial firms that use collective resources depend on institutions defining how collective resources are accessed and used. Institutions that define the access and usage of resources are key aspects of NIE (e.g. Cleaver, 2000; Ostrom, 2015/1990). We expand on this debate by arguing that institutional arrangements shape the scope of action for entrepreneurial firms mobilising collective resources, which in turn increases their legitimacy and autonomy as long as they follow relevant norms, practices and regulations. In particular, institutional arrangements can be efficient for mobilising collective resources as they provide guidance about how and when resources can be accessed and used.

While our reconceptualisation has important implications for mobilising collective resources, it also opens several avenues for future research on collective resources in entrepreneurship. Further theoretical development is needed to create a common framework of collective resources that incorporates the idiosyncratic elements of this type of resource, including that they are indivisible, non-excludable, non-transferable and non-enforceable. Such development is needed to enhance the knowledge creation of collective resources.

ACKNOWLEDGEMENTS

We thank Siri Jakobsen, Jenny Larsen, Marianne Steinmo and Roger Sørheim for contributing to the data collection. We would also like to thank the anonymous reviewer and editors for their insightful comments. The funding from RFFNORD [269740] is gratefully acknowledged. This funding source was not involved in and did not influence our research.

NOTES

1. This chapter summarises and extends the introductory chapter of Wigger's (2018) doctoral dissertation.
2. For more information regarding the data collection, see Larsen et al. (forthcoming).

REFERENCES

Ådlandsvik, B., Asplin, L., Karlsen, Ø., Sandvik, A., & Svåsand, T. (2015). *Forslag til produksjonsområder: rapport til nærings- og fiskeridepartementet.* Retrieved from https://www.hi.no/resources/publikasjoner/rapport-fra-havforskningen/2015/produksjonsomrader_rapp_20-2015.pdf.
Aldrich, H. E., & Kim, P. H. (2007). Small worlds, infinite possibilities? How social networks affect entrepreneurial team formation and search. *Strategic Entrepreneurship Journal, 1*(1–2), 147–65.
Alvarez, S. A., Young, S. L., & Woolley, J. L. (2015). Opportunities and institutions: A co-creation story of the king crab industry. *Journal of Business Venturing, 30*(1), 95–112.
Bailetti, A. J., & Callahan, J. R. (1993). The coordination structure of international collaborative technology arrangements. *R&D Management, 23*(2), 129–46.
Baker, T., & Nelson, R. E. (2005). Creating something from nothing: Resource construction through entrepreneurial bricolage. *Administrative Science Quarterly, 50*(3), 329–66.
Barney, J. (1991). Firm resources and sustained competitive advantage. *Journal of Management, 17*(1), 99–120.

Becker, C. D., & Ostrom, E. (1995). Human ecology and resource sustainability: The importance of institutional diversity. *Annual Review of Ecology and Systematics*, *26*(1), 113–33.

Berends, H., Jelinek, M., Reymen, I., & Stultiëns, R. (2014). Product innovation processes in small firms: Combining entrepreneurial effectuation and managerial causation. *Journal of Product Innovation Management*, *31*(3), 616–35.

Bjørkan, M., & Eilertsen, S. M. (2020). Local perceptions of aquaculture: A case study on legitimacy from northern Norway. *Ocean & Coastal Management*, *195*, 105276.

Busenitz, L. W., West III, G. P., Shepherd, D., Nelson, T., Chandler, G. N., & Zacharakis, A. (2003). Entrepreneurship research in emergence: Past trends and future directions. *Journal of Management*, *29*(3), 285–308.

Casciaro, T., & Piskorski, M. J. (2005). Power imbalance, mutual dependence, and constraint absorption: A closer look at resource dependence theory. *Administrative Science Quarterly*, *50*(2), 167–99.

Cheung, S. N. (1970). The structure of a contract and the theory of a non-exclusive resource. *Journal of Law and Economics*, *13*(1), 49–70.

Cleaver, F. (2000). Moral ecological rationality, institutions and the management of common property resources. *Development and Change*, *31*(2), 361–83.

Clough, D. R., Fang, T. P., Vissa, B., & Wu, A. (2019). Turning lead into gold: How do entrepreneurs mobilize resources to exploit opportunities? *Academy of Management Annals*, *13*(1), 240–71.

Coase, R. H. (1974). The lighthouse in economics. *Journal of Law and Economics*, *17*(2), 357–76.

Coase, R. H. (1991). The nature of the firm [1937]. *The nature of the firm: Origins, evolution, and development* (pp. 18–33). New York: Oxford University Press.

Cropanzano, R., & Mitchell, M. S. (2005). Social exchange theory: An interdisciplinary review. *Journal of Management*, *31*(6), 874–900.

Desa, G., & Basu, S. (2013). Optimization or bricolage? Overcoming resource constraints in global social entrepreneurship. *Strategic Entrepreneurship Journal*, *7*(1), 26–49.

Drees, J. M., & Heugens, P. P. (2013). Synthesizing and extending resource dependence theory: A meta-analysis. *Journal of Management*, *39*(6), 1666–98.

Eckhardt, J. T., & Shane, S. A. (2003). Opportunities and entrepreneurship. *Journal of Management*, *29*(3), 333–49.

Eggertsson, T. (1990). The role of transaction costs and property rights in economic analysis. *European Economic Review*, *34*(2–3), 450–57.

Emerson, R. M. (1962). Power–dependence relations. *American Sociological Review*, *27*(1), 31–41.

Escobal, J. A., & Cavero, D. (2012). Transaction costs, institutional arrangements and inequality outcomes: Potato marketing by small producers in rural Peru. *World Development*, *40*(2), 329–41.

Fiskeridirektoratet (2020). Auksjon august 2020 [Auction August 2020]. Retrieved from https://fiskeridir.no/Akvakultur/Tildeling-og-tillatelser/Auksjon-av-produksjons kapasitet/Auksjon-august-2020.

Franco, M., & Haase, H. (2013). Firm resources and entrepreneurial orientation as determinants for collaborative entrepreneurship. *Management Decision*, *51*(3), 680–96.

Garcia, R., Wigger, K., & Hermann, R. R. (2019). Challenges of creating and capturing value in open eco-innovation: Evidence from the maritime industry in Denmark. *Journal of Cleaner Production*, *220*, 642–54.

Gardner, B. D. (1983). Market versus political allocations of natural resources in the 1980s. *Western Journal of Agricultural Economics*, *8*(2), 215–29.

Garud, R., Hardy, C., & Maguire, S. (2007). Institutional entrepreneurship as embedded agency: An introduction to the special issue. *Organization Studies*, *28*(7), 957–69.

Grant, R. M., & Baden-Fuller, C. (1995). A knowledge-based theory of inter-firm collaboration. Paper presented at the Academy of Management Proceedings. https://journals.aom.org/doi/abs/10.5465/ambpp.1995.17536229.

Gulati, R., & Sytch, M. (2007). Dependence asymmetry and joint dependence in interorganizational relationships: Effects of embeddedness on a manufacturer's performance in procurement relationships. *Administrative Science Quarterly*, *52*(1), 32–69.

Hahn, R. W., & Noll, R. G. (1981). Designing a market for tradable emissions permits. Social Science Working Paper 398. https://authors.library.caltech.edu/82095/.

Haynie, J. M., Shepherd, D. A., & McMullen, J. S. (2009). An opportunity for me? The role of resources in opportunity evaluation decisions. *Journal of Management Studies*, *46*(3), 337–61.

Holmén, M., Magnusson, M., & McKelvey, M. (2007). What are innovative opportunities? *Industry and Innovation*, *14*(1), 27–45.

Institute of Marine Research (2020). Tema: Trafikklyssystemet – HI sin kunnskap. Retrieved from https://www.hi.no/hi/temasider/akvakultur/trafikklyssystemet-hi-sin-kunnskap.

Lamers, M., Van der Duim, R., & Spaargaren, G. (2017). The relevance of practice theories for tourism research. *Annals of Tourism Research*, *62*, 54–63.

Larsen, J. S. K., Lauvås, T., & Sørheim, R. (forthcoming). In the same boat? The dynamics of embedded salmon farming firms on the periphery. *Entrepreneurship and Regional Development*.

Lavie, D. J. (2006). The competitive advantage of interconnected firms: An extension of the resource-based view. *Academy of Management Review*, *31*(3), 638–58.

Lawrence, T. B., & Phillips, N. (2004). From Moby Dick to Free Willy: Macro-cultural discourse and institutional entrepreneurship in emerging institutional fields. *Organization*, *11*(5), 689–711.

Marchington, M., & Vincent, S. (2004). Analysing the influence of institutional, organizational and interpersonal forces in shaping inter-organizational relations. *Journal of Management Studies*, *41*(6), 1029–56.

Miller, D., & Friesen, P. H. (1982). Innovation in conservative and entrepreneurial firms: Two models of strategic momentum. *Strategic Management Journal*, *3*(1), 1–25.

Neergaard, H., & Ulhøi, J. P. (2006). Government agency and trust in the formation and transformation of interorganizational entrepreneurial networks. *Entrepreneurship Theory and Practice*, *30*(4), 519–39.

NFD, & OED (2017). *Ny vekst, stolt historie: Regjeringens havstrategi*. Retrieved from https://www.regjeringen.no/contentassets/097c5ec1238d4c0ba32ef46965144467/nfd_havstrategi_uu.pdf.

North, D. (1990). *Institutions, institutional change and economic performance*. New York: Cambridge University Press.

Olafsen, T., Winther, U., Olsen, Y., & Skjermo, J. (2012). *Verdiskaping basert på produktive hav i 2050* [*Value creation based on productive oceans in 2050*]. Retrieved from https://www.sintef.no/globalassets/upload/fiskeri_og_havbruk/publikasjoner/verdiskaping-basert-pa-produktive-hav-i-2050.pdf.

Ostrom, E. (2015/1990). *Governing the commons*. New York: Cambridge University Press.

Penrose, E. T. (2009/1959). *The theory of the growth of the firm*. Oxford: Oxford University Press.

Peteraf, M. A. (1993). The cornerstones of competitive advantage: A resource-based view. *Strategic Management Journal, 14*(3), 179–91.

Peterson, M. J., & Peterson, T. R. (1993). A rhetorical critique of 'nonmarket' economic valuations for natural resources. *Environmental Values, 2*(1), 47–65.

Pfeffer, J., & Salancik, G. R. (2003/1978). *The external control of organizations: A resource dependence perspective*. Palo Alto: Stanford University Press.

Rawhouser, H., Villanueva, J., & Newbert, S. L. (2017). Strategies and tools for entrepreneurial resource access: A cross-disciplinary review and typology. *International Journal of Management Reviews, 19*(4), 473–91.

Regjeringen (2017). Nye oppdrettsregler trer i kraft i oktober. Retrieved from https://www.regjeringen.no/no/aktuelt/na-kommer-reglene-for-trafikklyssystemet/id2573185/.

Regjeringen (2020). Regjeringen skrur på trafikklyset i havbruksnæringen. Retrieved from https://www.regjeringen.no/no/aktuelt/regjeringen-skrur-pa-trafikklyset-i-havbruksnaringen/id2688939/.

Richardsen, R., Stoud Myhre, M., Tyholt, I. L., & Johansen, U. (2019). *Nasjonal betydning av sjømatnæringen: En verdiskapings- og ringvirkningsanalyse med data fra 2017 og 2018*. Retrieved from https://www.sintef.no/globalassets/sintef-ocean/pdf/nasjonal-verdiskapning_2018tall_endelig_200619.pdf.

Rumelt, R. P. (1997). A strategic theory of the firm. In N. J. Foss (Ed.), *Resources, firms, and strategies: A reader in the resource-based perspective*. Oxford: Oxford University Press.

Sarasvathy, S. D. (2001). Causation and effectuation: Toward a theoretical shift from economic inevitability to entrepreneurial contingency. *Academy of Management Review, 26*(2), 243–63.

Simsek, Z., Lubatkin, M. H., & Floyd, S. W. (2003). Inter-firm networks and entrepreneurial behavior: A structural embeddedness perspective. *Journal of Management, 29*(3), 427–42.

Sirmon, D. G., Hitt, M. A., Ireland, R. D., & Gilbert, B. A. (2011). Resource orchestration to create competitive advantage: Breadth, depth, and life cycle effects. *Journal of Management, 37*(5), 1390–412.

Starr, J. A., & MacMillan, I. C. (1990). Resource cooptation via social contracting: Resource acquisition strategies for new ventures. *Strategic Management Journal, 11*, 79–92.

Subramani, M. R., & Venkatraman, N. (2003). Safeguarding investments in asymmetric interorganizational relationships: Theory and evidence. *Academy of Management Journal, 46*(1), 46–62.

Terreberry, S. (1968). The evolution of organizational environments. *Administrative Science Quarterly, 12*(4), 590–613.

Tietenberg, T. H., & Lewis, L. (2009/1984). *Environmental and natural resource economics*. New York: Routledge.

Vestrum, I., & Rasmussen, E. (2013). How community ventures mobilise resources. *International Journal of Entrepreneurial Behavior & Research, 19*(3), 283–302.

Welter, F. (2011). Contextualizing entrepreneurship—conceptual challenges and ways forward. *Entrepreneurship Theory and Practice, 35*(1), 165–84.

West, J., & Gallagher, S. (2006). Challenges of open innovation: The paradox of firm investment in open-source software. *R&D Management*, *36*(3), 319–31.

Wigger, K. A. (2018). Mobilization of collective resources for entrepreneurship: Case studies in Nordic peripheries. Doctoral dissertation, Nord University, Bodø.

Wigger, K. A., & Shepherd, D. A. (2020). We're all in the same boat: A collective model of preserving and accessing nature-based opportunities. *Entrepreneurship Theory and Practice*, *44*(3), 587–617.

Williamson, O. E. (1985). *The economic institutions of capitalism: Firms, markets and relational contracting*. New York: Free Press.

Winborg, J., & Landström, H. (2001). Financial bootstrapping in small businesses: Examining small business managers' resource acquisition behaviors. *Journal of Business Venturing*, *16*(3), 235–54.

Yuchtman, E., & Seashore, S. E. (1967). A system resource approach to organizational effectiveness. *American Sociological Review*, *32*(6), 891–903.

Zhang, J., Jiang, H., Wu, R., & Li, J. (2019). Reconciling the dilemma of knowledge sharing: A network pluralism framework of firms' R&D alliance network and innovation performance. *Journal of Management*, *45*(7), 2635–65.

Zimmer, C., & Aldrich, H. (1987). Resource mobilization through ethnic networks: Kinship and friendship ties of shopkeepers in England. *Sociological Perspectives*, *30*(4), 422–45.

5. Innovation and adaptation strategies during the front-end phase of an industry downturn

Jakoba Sraml Gonzalez

1. INTRODUCTION

Innovation in economic crises received increased attention in the years following the financial crisis and recession at the end of the 2000s (Amore, 2015; Archibugi et al., 2013a, 2013b; Filippetti & Archibugi, 2011) and again became an important area of research due to the Covid-19 pandemic. Researchers have been interested in whether or not companies have sustained and invested in innovation during crises and which companies have done so (Alfranseder & Dzhamalova, 2014; Amore, 2015; Archibugi et al., 2013a, 2013b; Filippetti & Archibugi, 2011; Paunov, 2012). The main message of these studies is that cautious spending and retrenchment, defined as the reduction of costs due to economic difficulty, are common strategic responses to economic crises. They also emphasise that there can be exceptions, particularly that start-ups and experienced innovators sustain innovation activities despite economic crises. At the firm level, there is no unanimous conclusion regarding how and why companies innovate in times of economic crisis.

One way to further the understanding of the relationship between economic crises and innovation strategies in companies is to consider the temporal aspect of crises. Economic crises are periods of reduced activity for companies. Crises evolve over time: they have an initial phase, that is, the front end of a downturn, and they deepen and eventually resolve. Arguably, conducting innovation during each phase comes with different challenges and opportunities that companies need to deal with. Consequently, companies may have different abilities and motivations to sustain and engage in innovation activities as the downturn evolves (Martin-Rios & Pasamar, 2018; Mascarenhas & Aaker, 1989).

This chapter contributes to the debate by exploring, specifically, the innovation efforts of companies during the front-end phase of a crisis. It examines how companies adapt and sustain innovation activities during a phase filled with initial uncertainty, scepticism and incredulity about the situation. Yet, companies in this phase need to make important decisions about innovation that will affect innovation outcomes and performance. The chapter goes beyond existing studies that investigate innovation during crises by examining quantitative changes to innovation input and outputs, and nuancing them with insights into social processes surrounding adaptation and innovation choices. The research question is: *How do companies adapt their innovation activities during the front-end phase of an industry crisis, and how do the constrained resources and learned patterns of working affect these activities?*

The empirical case involves a group of suppliers to the oil and gas industry and their innovation activities during the first phase of the industry downturn in 2015–16. Semi-structured interviews with research and development (R&D) and management staff were used as the primary research method. The downturn started in mid-2014 with the oil price collapse and led to a crisis situation marked by reduced investment spending, consequently impacting suppliers (Ramsøy et al., 2016). In retrospect, the situation evolved into a full-scale crisis for the industry, but at the time of conducting the study, the companies were not aware of the phase and the magnitude. The interviews capture the attitudes and the myriad of activities conducted at this specific point in time. With the current knowledge about how the crisis evolved, the interviews generate insight into the front-end phase, that is, how the companies actually adapt and treat innovation when a crisis hits. The study reconstructs the front-end phase of the crisis retrospectively, but it does not retrospectively reconstruct the experience of the companies during the front-end phase. In this sense, this is a prospective study of a specific phase of a crisis. As such, it exposes the complexity and the social nature of a crisis situation for companies wanting to innovate, which may not be captured in retrospective studies.

The structure of the chapter is as follows: relevant literature is reviewed in Section 2, and the case, research design and methods are reviewed in Section 3. The analysis and findings of the study are presented in Section 4. Finally, the chapter ends with a discussion of the findings in Section 5 and concluding remarks in Section 6.

2. LITERATURE REVIEW

2.1 The Temporal Aspect of Industry Economic Crises and Company Adaptation Strategies

Economic crises are periods of fluctuating economic activity. Individual industries can experience similar business cycles with fluctuating activity and periods of crises due to, for example, changes in input and output prices (Mascarenhas & Aaker, 1989). Such crises in business cycles in industries can, to a certain degree, be expected, but their magnitude, periodicity and duration cannot be predicted (Mariscal & Powell, 2014; Mascarenhas & Aaker, 1989). The oil and gas industry, with its fluctuating commodity prices and levels of activity, is a prime example of an industry that regularly goes through phases of industry economic crises. As such, it can serve as a case to discuss how companies that operate within it act and work with innovation in times of crisis.

Economic crises and crises in general evolve as time passes. They have an initial phase, the front end of a downturn, and they can prolong and worsen before eventually resolving. The temporal aspect of crises affects strategy making, as companies need to adapt to the evolving situation and change in conditions (Lawrence & Lorsch, 1967; Webb & Pettigrew, 1999).

The front end of a crisis is characterised by initial uncertainty, scepticism and incredulity about the evolving situation. Companies may experience an initial decline in their activities and need to adopt initial measures. Consequently, companies may need to adopt retrenchment strategies in this initial phase, such as the cutting, downsizing and streamlining of existing activities. These strategies are conducted in parallel with the maintenance of business as usual (Martin-Rios & Parga-Dans, 2016a). Companies in this phase can also dismiss the situation as temporary or as not difficult enough to design a response outside the established patterns of working and operating and initial retrenchment (Martin-Rios & Parga-Dans, 2016a). Nevertheless, general uncertainty about the situation and the outcomes of its evolution generate questions about its consequences and whether the situation may evolve into a 'structural break' and a 'new normal' (Kitching et al., 2009).

The initial phase of a crisis can either resolve or turn into a *phase of deep crisis* if prolonged or if the activity is reduced even more. Companies that do not manage to lower costs and adapt in this phase fail to survive. For example, if a downturn is short, short-term operational and cost-oriented actions may be sufficient to guarantee firm survival (Martin-Rios & Pasamar, 2018). However, if the downturn occurs for a prolonged period and evolves into a deep crisis for an industry, changes that are more radical may be needed. According to previous studies, the surviving and best-performing companies are those that change their existing activities more radically and adopt proactive strategic responses (Martin-Rios & Parga-Dans, 2016a). Mascarenhas and Aaker (1989) showed how drilling companies in the oil and gas industry exposed to volatile market conditions gradually adapted in a more radical fashion as the constraining situation progressed, but their initial strategy was the continuation of business as usual.

Finally, a *crisis resolves* with the return of the levels of pre-crisis economic activity or a normalisation of the conditions, in other words 'a new normal'

(Mascarenhas & Aaker, 1989). This phase offers new opportunities for companies to position themselves in the market.

Arguably, the change in strategies over the phases of an industry economic crisis means that innovation activities and their strategic adaptation also change over time. Conducting innovation during each phase comes with different challenges and opportunities. Consequently, companies may have different capacities and motivations to sustain and engage in innovation activities as the downturn evolves (Martin-Rios & Pasamar, 2018; Mascarenhas & Aaker, 1989). Companies may stop or sustain these activities; there is no clear message about the effects of the crisis on innovation outcomes. This suggests that companies shape *idiosyncratic responses* over the cycle, which depend on the internal workings, strategies and perceptions of the evolution of the environment (Kitching et al., 2009; Martin-Rios & Pasamar, 2018). Nevertheless, qualitative studies hint that there are also common characteristics of crises that affect the responses.

2.2 Innovation Activities during the Front End

The adaptation of the innovation activities in companies has an inherently social aspect, as it is related to the way actors in companies perceive and interpret their environments (Audia et al., 2000; Williams et al., 2017). One important aspect of the front-end phase of a crisis is uncertainty about the existence of a crisis and the future levels of activity and resources available for innovation. The consequence is that, on the one hand, companies can stop innovation activities or put them on hold due to the initial difficulty and choose to cut costs during the front end (Archibugi et al., 2013a; Paunov, 2012). On the other hand, empirical studies find that companies can also aggressively sustain or engage in innovation activities during the front end and subsequent phases. For example, companies can make decisions to build up new capabilities to deal with the crisis more radically (Martin-Rios & Pasamar, 2018; Schmitt et al., 2016; Schmitt & Raisch, 2013) or continue investing despite difficulties (Geroski & Gregg, 1994; Geroski & Walters, 1995; Martin-Rios & Pasamar, 2018).

One reason behind this variety of approaches is the perception of the evolution of the environment and the crisis, sense making and strategizing (Maitlis & Sonenshein, 2010; Weick, 1993). Companies can perceive the sudden challenging environment as inadequate and streamline their innovation efforts. Alternatively, companies can sustain innovation despite uncertainty and financial distress if they expect to benefit from it during and after the crisis. In particular, the perception of existing demand is a driver for sustaining innovation (Kahle & Stulz, 2013).

Another reason why companies decide to sustain innovation during crises is experience with similar events. Exposure to comparable situations improves companies' abilities to invest in R&D when they experience economic and financial constraints (Alfranseder & Dzhamalova, 2014; Amore, 2015; Archibugi et al., 2013a). Companies can approach a seemingly known situation by repeating the activities undertaken previously (Audia et al., 2000). Arguably, companies will have greater confidence in sustaining innovation despite the difficulties during the onset of a crisis if they have relatable experience. This is probably the case for companies in the oil and gas industry. Cyclicity is a characteristic of the industry, and the companies within it are familiar with the intermittent periods of high and low activity (Mascarenhas & Aaker, 1989).

Proposition 1: Experience with similar challenging situations encourages companies to sustain innovation despite retrenchment activities.

The availability of economic resources is important for innovation during the front end and, in general, over the cycle. For example, internal R&D, funding and capabilities are important predictors of sustaining innovation during the different phases of an economic crisis (Amore, 2015; Zouaghi et al., 2018). Similarly, established relationships and sources of external knowledge help companies to weather difficult situations (Ahn et al., 2018; Zouaghi et al., 2018).

However, environmental munificence, the *availability of financial resources* and, in turn, companies' revenues may be severely affected in crises due to the decline in economic activities (Kitching et al., 2009). Firms may enter into a crisis with a backlog of activity and accumulated resources during the front end. This enables them to sustain innovation activities despite the perceptions of a crisis during the front end (Mascarenhas & Aaker, 1989). At the same time, financial resources may become constrained as the downturn progresses, both internally and within the industry or market. Companies may increasingly face threats to their survival and pressures to streamline activities and resources (Martin-Rios & Parga-Dans, 2016a, 2016b; Martin-Rios & Pasamar, 2018). This means that companies may experience several barriers due to constrained resources even though they may want to or have learned how to benefit from sustaining innovation activities during periods of lower activity. One consequence is that they perform retrenchment activities, that is, different ways of cutting costs, to compensate for the loss in revenue (Barbero et al., 2017; Lim et al., 2013). The need to secure their survival may require them to discontinue existing innovation activities or choose not to start new ones (Kitching et al., 2009).

Companies may experience difficulty choosing retrenchment-only strategies. They may decide to stop innovation to save resources or secure their survival. While this may help them to reduce costs and deal with the first shock of reduced activity, it can also shrink internal resources, such as capabilities and sources of knowledge, as well as the ability to survive and adapt to a new environment (Martin-Rios & Parga-Dans, 2016a). Navarro (2005) notes that when the downturn is short, a downsizing approach may be useful, as cost-cutting can enable short-term survival. At the same time, such a stance can also cripple the ability of companies to perform afterwards (Kitching et al., 2009). In fact, the choices of firms during the front end to reduce innovation activities can influence the position and ability of companies to innovate and perform successfully when the crisis resolves and ends.

Proposition 2: Constrained financial resources and uncertainty during the front end force companies to adopt retrenchment strategies and stop innovation activities.

Thus, companies make decisions under uncertainty during the front end without knowing what the outcomes will be and how the environment will evolve. In addition, the front end is pervaded by a specific ambiguity concerning whether the crisis is a major one that they should prepare for. As time goes by or as the crisis worsens, it becomes clearer how to adapt to the situation (Barr, 1998; McKinley et al., 2014).

3. RESEARCH DESIGN AND METHODS

3.1 The Case of Norwegian Oil and Gas Suppliers and the 2014–18 Downturn

This study is based on a case of suppliers to the upstream oil and gas industry in Norway. The upstream segment of the oil and gas industry is structured as a business ecosystem consisting of oil companies, which perform exploration and production activities, and their supply chains. The latter consist of several specialised companies supporting different aspects of exploration and production activities. The array of competences enables the industry to explore and exploit resources (Garcia et al., 2014; Shuen et al., 2014).

The suppliers in the Norwegian context have aggregated into a world-leading cluster distinguished by specific technological competences, which they almost exclusively use to provide technological solutions and solve specific problems of their buyers in the dispersed innovation processes in the upstream oil and gas industry (Ryggvik, 2013; Thune et al., 2018). The innovation processes are distributed across operators and suppliers (Acha & Cusmano,

2005) who assume the roles of technology providers and buyers, although these roles may vary across projects (Burnett & Williams, 2014, p. 134). The operators deploy the capabilities related to the acquisition and deployment of technologies (Garcia et al., 2014; Shuen et al., 2014), while the suppliers have increasingly become a major source of R&D, new technology development, new equipment and materials (Acha & Cusmano, 2005; Maleki et al., 2018; Perrons, 2014). This means that the competences and technological profiles of the suppliers in the cluster vary since they specialise in specific parts of the value chain in the industry. At the same time, the companies are also similar in terms of how they engage in the distributed innovation processes with others in the ecosystem (Hjertvikrem & Fitjar, 2018; Simensen & Thune, 2018).

The oil and gas industry was characterised by high activity in the boom period with high oil prices and investment spending from 2009 until 2014. The boom period was interrupted by a sudden fall in oil prices. The Brent oil price fell from above US$115 per barrel on 19 June 2014 to below US$30 in mid-January 2016. The steep fall put pressure on the profitability of exploration and production activities, forcing the ecosystem to lower the costs of activities (Ramsøy et al., 2016). In addition, the shock came on top of existing initiatives to reduce costs due to low profitability despite high oil prices. The changed situation eventually evolved into an industry crisis for suppliers due to the prolongation of the situation with less and uncertain demand. An upturn of oil prices in 2018 was signalled as the beginning of the end of the downturn in the industry and media (*Financial Times*, 2018).

3.2   The Case Study

The aim of the case study is to understand suppliers' adaptation strategies and their innovation efforts during the front-end phase of the industry crisis. Eleven suppliers operating on the Norwegian continental shelf were selected for the study. The sample consists of two types of suppliers. The first group are the subsea technology companies that provide subsea technology products and services. The second group are subsuppliers, who provide specific products or services to the industry, for example, components or maintenance services. The two types were purposively selected because they represent two important profiles of companies found in the ecosystem that contribute distinctively to the distributed innovation processes. The sample does not represent the entire spectrum of companies in the upstream ecosystem, but it introduces variety. Both groups contribute different technological competences to the dispersed collaborative innovation processes in the industry (Sako, 1995). Despite the different technological profiles and sets of competences in terms of their position in the supply chain, they have internalised some of the same patterns of how economic and innovation activities are conducted in the industry (Hjertvikrem & Fitjar, 2018).

The study is based on semi-structured interviews of five subsea technology suppliers and six subsuppliers (Table 5.1). The companies work both as direct and indirect suppliers, that is, they supply to final customers (operator companies) and to other suppliers. The first round of interviews was conducted in late 2015, approximately one year after the collapse of oil prices. The crisis did not start immediately, as the companies had a backlog of activities and were familiar with drops in prices from previous downturns (e.g. during the financial crisis in 2008). The interviews were conducted during the initial stage when the companies started to consider it as a potentially worse crisis and not a short-term market slump. The second round of follow-up interviews was conducted in mid-2016 to contextualise the information gathered in the first round. Three companies (one subsea and two subsupplier companies) did not follow up. This was compensated for via two additional interviews (one with a subsea and one with a subsupplier company). Access to the companies was hampered due to the stress the companies were experiencing. This resulted in a limited but highly insightful body of data.

3.3   Methods and Data

The semi-structured interviews with R&D and management staff gave insight into the strategies the companies used and the reasons behind them. Interviewees were asked about innovation activities during the downturn (which activities were sustained and how; which new activities were taken up and why), relationships to the buyers, how these had changed and how the company had adapted. Due to the contractual nature of the relations in the oil and gas industry, business and technology dimensions are highly intertwined. The respondents from management and R&D departments were expected to be familiar with the downturn.

The data on economic performance was collected from proff.no and the Rystad Energy database to expose the severity of the situation for the companies. The strong fall in revenues for companies in 2015 compared to 2014 is presented in Table 5.1.

Innovation and adaptation strategies 97

Table 5.1   *Overview of the case companies characteristics and data*

Company	Characteristics of innovation activities	Respondents and number of interviews		Fall in revenues in 2015 compared to 2014
Subsea technology companies				
Company A	Technology and product development for buyers	CEO	2	Established in 2014
Company B	Product development for buyers and for providing services	R&D manager R&D manager	1 1	≤−25%
Company C	Product development for buyers and for providing services	Commercial manager	1	≤−25%
Company D	Product development for buyers and for providing services	R&D manager location 1 R&D manager location 2	2 2	≤−50%
Company E	Product development for buyers and for providing services	Commercial manager	1	≤−50%
Subsupply companies				
Subsupplier A	Product development for buyers and for providing services	CEO	2	≤−50%
Subsupplier B	Selling customised services and products for buyers	CEO	2	≤−50%
Subsupplier C	Product customisation	R&D Manager	1	>0%
Subsupplier D	Product customisation	Commercial manager	2	≤−25%
Subsupplier E	Product development, engineering services	Commercial manager	1	≤−25%
Subsupplier F	Product development	Commercial manager	1	≤−50%
		Total:	19	

3.4   Data Analysis Process

The data analysis process was conducted in four steps. In the first step, the interviews were recorded, transcribed and anonymised. In the second step, the emerging issues and themes related to innovation and crisis were coded. The codes were grouped into two thematic categories: barriers (internal and external) and responses (internally and externally oriented) (Table 5.2).

In the third step, responses to the barriers were linked by closely interpreting the context of the codes. The interpretation of the links resulted in five adaptation strategies and gave insight into how and why innovating companies

98   *Rethinking the social in innovation and entrepreneurship studies*

Table 5.2   *Overview of the codes and thematic categories*

Code	Higher level construct
	Barriers
Internal funding	Internal barriers
Organisation of R&D practices	
Content of R&D	
Focus on business rather than technology	
Inability to do alone	
Costs (efficiency focus in industry)	External barriers
Conservative buyers	
Break of linkage	
Buyers taking more control	
Innovation process changes	
Challenged technology paradigm	
Institutional aspects	
	Response
Reorganisation	Internally oriented
Procurement	
Internal efficiency work processes	
More efficient innovation activities	
Maintaining linkage	Externally oriented
Proposing new	
Collaboration with others	

react to the front end of a downturn (see Section 4.2). In the final step, how the strategies related to each other were analysed and three specific conflicting situations that the companies had faced became apparent. The results of this step unveil the reasons behind choices to adapt and sustain or engage in innovation activities during the front end (see Section 4.3). The findings of the case studies are to be interpreted with care. They offer new insights into an area that has not been sufficiently studied and thus provide directions for further research on innovation in times of crisis. To increase the validity at the data collection stage, I made sure to interview actors in companies that worked with innovation-related activities and were familiar with how the company had been handling the downturn and the effects it had on innovation activities. To ensure the reliability of the findings, I conducted the interviews during the downturn (the aftermath of the sharp fall of the prices and their stabilisation at extremely low levels) to capture the occurrences related to the downturn and avoid post hoc rationalisation of the events. This provides an important insight into how companies deal with innovation when they experience economically uncertain situations. The interviews were based on a protocol and were recorded and transcribed to increase reliability. Software and manual coding were used, and a protocol was kept for all the steps of the analysis to ensure transparency of the analysis process.

4. SUPPLIERS AND THEIR INNOVATION ACTIVITIES DURING THE FRONT END OF THE INDUSTRY DOWNTURN

4.1 The Impact of the First Phase of the Downturn on Suppliers

The period before the oil price collapse was characterised by high activity with an array of different innovation projects for the suppliers in the case study. The suppliers explained in the interviews that they participated in these projects with their innovation competences. Even the smaller suppliers (subsuppliers) usually had at least some form of internal R&D to cater to the different customers since the business logic in the industry favoured customisation. Innovation projects were sometimes based on invitations to collaborate with the buyers or other actors, and, at other times, were based on internal initiatives. In the former type of projects, the companies responded to specific requests, while in the latter, they engaged in upfront R&D for solutions they had imagined the industry would need in the future. The latter were often developed without any formal guarantee of uptake. The booming market provided a guarantee of the sale of the solutions to at least some customers.

The initial phase of the downturn affected the suppliers in two major ways. First, they were affected by a reduced demand for their products and services. Many projects the suppliers hoped to get contracts for were postponed or cancelled as an immediate response to the price collapse. Second, they were pressured to drastically lower the prices of their current solutions as well as the costs of future solutions. The high operation costs of oil and gas production activities and the expense of development projects for future fields meant that profitability in the industry was suddenly very low. This created the necessity to reduce the costs of existing and future operations. Since the suppliers were the source of technological capabilities and competences for innovation in the industry, they were expected to contribute with cost-effective and 'good enough' solutions to restore the feasibility and profitability of the projects.

4.2 Suppliers' Response: Five Adaptation Strategies

The innovation strategies of firms were significantly affected by a lower demand and the need to reduce costs as well as a drop in revenue (see Table 5.1). The interviews show that the companies responded with diverse actions to sustain innovation activities. The analysis exposed five adaptation strategies related to sustaining innovation (Table 5.3). These strategies were not solely

Table 5.3   Five adaptation strategies and the specific sets of actions

Adaptation strategy	Sets of actions
Retrenchment	Cutting costs and downsizing
Content innovation activities	New innovation activities for cost-effective solutions Streamlining existing solutions
Processes/practices	Adapting established practices Introducing new practices
Sustaining relationships with buyers	Getting closer to buyers, trying to understand their new needs
Finding alternative routes	Sustaining business as usual Engaging in innovation despite constrained resources Compensating with external sources/collaborations

related to innovation. The reason is that the crises affected the companies as a whole (operation, marketing, etc.), not only their innovation activities. The strategies were not mutually exclusive and to some degree overlapped. For example, the retrenchment strategy (Strategy 1) was intertwined with the other strategies. The five strategies presented in Table 5.3 were an attempt to disentangle the complex situation the companies found themselves in during the front-end stage of the crisis.

4.2.1   Strategy 1: retrenchment activity

Companies engaged in retrenchment activity; suppliers cut margins and internal costs and downsized their labour force to reduce operating costs. The reduction of operating costs affected R&D activities and particularly their funding, as the business and R&D sides often overlapped.

4.2.2   Strategy 2: adapting existing solutions

The changes in the industry, as well as the deteriorated economic situation of the suppliers, had implications for their internal innovation activities. The companies had to consider adapting the content of their innovation activities. The suppliers engaged in two sets of actions to adapt their own solutions. The first was *streamlining* their existing solutions. Their buyers started evaluating procurement activities and measuring performance to reduce their own project costs. The suppliers – especially the subsuppliers of specialised products and services – felt that they were at risk of being replaced with cheaper competitors and, as a response, the companies tried to reduce the costs of their solutions. This had implications for customisation-related engineering as well as long-term innovation activities. For example, the companies eliminated gold-plated or unnecessary 'nice to have' features of their solutions to retain a good position in a crisis-stricken market:

> We used to be gold plating everything before because the oil and gas industry was booming for many years and we were able to, we had luxury of being able to spend lots of time designing something and overdeciding things and building things more complex and better than what they need to be. But now it's back to what we usually say is 'fit for purpose'. (Company D)

However, the actions geared at streamlining and simplifying were demanding in the face of reduced resources and market uncertainty. Some of the suppliers in the study established new business units for identifying and cutting unnecessary costs. This included optimising their own supply chains to make them as efficient as possible. Nonetheless, making services or products cheaper by stripping them of costly elements was only one part of significantly cutting costs. There were limits to how much they could streamline individual solutions to make them less costly without introducing changes at the systemic level.

The second set of actions was directed at coming up with *new and inherently cost-effective solutions* to provide less costly solutions to buyers. These guaranteed a lower cost base and lifetime costs, therefore handling the challenge in the long run as well. Both suppliers and subsuppliers engaged in designing or in conceptual work for new products and services to cut operating costs in their specific segments of the value chain. For example, the subsuppliers tried to think of alternative products they could offer or changed the design of the services they provided. The subsea technology companies considered alternative technological solutions to be used offshore. This attitude is exemplified by the following quotation:

> That led to [a situation in which] most companies, also X, established teams for price reduction projects. Teams that will look at all bits and details and try to optimise every single bit, making it good enough. Not better than good enough, not too good. That means that one buys a watch that shows time and that's it. Instead of one that checks the pulse and respiration. So, you'll get a watch that only shows time. (Company E)

The novel solutions, mainly at the idea or concept stages, were based on suppliers' specialised competences. The suppliers proposed these new ideas to the buyers as the best possible alternatives to respond to the challenges created by the downturn.

4.2.3 Strategy 3: adapting the practices and processes related to innovation activities

The companies had to consider established practices related to innovation. The strategy of adapting existing solutions required suppliers to sustain innovation-related activities, as they had few standardised solutions. The usual practices for preparing and executing projects neither sufficed nor were adequate in a new situation because the new imagined and demanded solutions were different from the current portfolio of solutions. For instance, changing components with cheaper alternatives (or their complete removal) required additional research, testing and considerations concerning fit with the existing product systems as well as safety.

Engaging in additional innovation activities was necessary, particularly for the suppliers that developed new technologies (i.e. the subsea suppliers). As the engineering manager at subsea technology company D explained, it required significant effort to come up with new solutions when moving from simply cutting down the costs of a solution to an inherently cheaper and simplified solution:

> We need to ask ourselves in all possible ways, how can we do this more efficiently by spending less engineering hours completing a job basically? Not only hours, but how can we design things so that they are cheaper and cost less? (Company D)

To be able to sustain the needed innovation activities (Strategy 2), the companies had to modify existing internal practices. They established stricter criteria for starting new R&D projects that had to be grounded in solid business cases with potential buyers. They prioritised efficient processes, as the above quotation suggests.

4.2.4 Strategy 4: sustaining relationships with buyers

The experienced change in demand and technological uncertainty, together with fewer available internal resources for innovation-related activities, made the established model of doing R&D upfront difficult to sustain despite the effort to do so. It was not clear to the suppliers what kinds of projects they should prioritise to meet the buyers' needs. The supplying companies were dependent on buyers and other actors in the value chain. They could not adapt to the new situation by only introducing changes internally. In fact, decisions to adopt technology depended on the preferences and final decisions of the buyers. The new proposed solutions to tackle the challenges were based on their own interpretations of how to optimise the cost problem in both the short and long term.

Consequently, suppliers started actively seeking new ways to collaborate with buyers. For example, they proposed projects and actively sought collaboration.

> One interesting thing I see is that when we are bidding for these larger umbilical jobs is that projects are getting postponed because the customer is studying it more and waiting for cost reductions. But throughout the process our bidding teams are going through innovation because they are having to find more cost-efficient ways so that we become more competitive. (Company B)

However, buyers were also experiencing downturns and were more risk-averse than usual. The companies explained that they experienced resistance from the buyers in terms of the adoption of new ideas even though they were still encouraged to contribute to the projects in the industry with their competences.

Yet, the suppliers were also flexible in sustaining the innovation effort internally because this was what they had always been expected to contribute in their relationships with the buyers. Not maintaining relationships with the buyers, which provided prospects for work in the long run, was also a risk for the suppliers. The oil and gas industry had experienced similar market uncertainty before. The industry managed to recover relatively fast after the 2008–09 crisis, and there was an overall expectation among the suppliers that this uncertainty was similarly temporary and would eventually end. An upturn would follow with higher levels of activity and margins in the industry. This, as expressed by all the companies, was an industry-wide accepted fact.

4.2.5 Strategy 5: finding alternative routes to sustain/engage in innovation activities

The strategy of being close to the buyers to be able to sustain business as usual constituted a major drive to introduce changes. The difficulty involved in adapting created a strong motivation for the suppliers to engage in *finding alternative ways to sustain innovation activities* despite resource scarcity and uncertainty.

The suppliers also wanted to mitigate the risk of innovating in uncertain times to secure their survival. For example, subsupplier A started testing their solutions in other industries to increase the chances of their solutions being adopted:

> If we can use new technology onshore or maritime industry, maybe we get good references there. It would then, when the oil and gas industry turns around and starts going again, … we have reference projects to show to that this has been used, this worked and the customers are pleased with it. (Subsupplier A)

Another way was to compensate with external resources and competences. For example, some of the companies (both subsuppliers and subsea technology suppliers) applied for public funding for innovation projects that they had funded internally before. Two subsuppliers explained that a new way of engaging in innovation activities was outsourcing part of them to their suppliers:

> We are not waiting for better times, we are working. But like I said, we don't do any R&D ourselves anymore. Because, we don't, we cannot afford to do so. And the way, then maybe the creativity from us is going to the smaller companies and asking them to do it. And they are maybe in an even greater need then we are, so they take that risk. But again, if they, if we cannot sell the invention or that they come with then they will go under. (Subsupplier A)

Finally, engaging in external collaboration also meant compensating for the difficulty of coming up with inherently new solutions. As the above quotation shows, one reason for this was to garner new insights or complementary competences concerning how to respond to a new demand. Furthermore, many of the suppliers engaged in informal talks and collaborations with other actors in the industry, often also competitors. One of the subsea technology companies entered into an alliance with companies that served different parts of the value chain and had complementary knowledge and competences on how to design more cost-effective solutions.

4.3   Conflicting Situations for Innovating Companies during the Front End of an Industry Downturn

The complexity of the situation for firms wanting to sustain and engage in innovation activities resulted in companies engaging in five adaptation strategies. In essence, the strategies were directed at simultaneously balancing innovation and cost-cutting/retrenchment activities during a stage in the downturn in which the companies experienced hardship (constrained resources and drops in revenues) but were still motivated to sustain and/or engage in innovation activities. This balancing act led to companies experiencing three conflicting situations.

Conflicting situation 1: Learned experiences help in sustaining innovation activities, but the willingness to invest is constrained by financial and economic distress.

The learned patterns of collaborating and contributing to the distributed innovation processes were a powerful motivation to sustain innovation activities for all the suppliers. They worked towards, first, finding new and more efficient ways of engaging in and sustaining innovation activities (strategies 2 and 3) and, second, understanding what the new needs of the buyers were and how they could address them (strategy 4). At the same time, the suppliers were

Innovation and adaptation strategies 105

also constrained by economic hardship and experienced uncertainty about future projects (as suggested by strategy 1). The companies had to streamline and retrench to be able to sustain the efforts.

> Hopefully when the oil price comes up again a little bit and the times have become a bit better, we will be a much stronger company than what we used to be because we will have been forced to develop new technologies and forced to simplify how we design conventional structures and equipment. (Company D)

This suggests that companies wanting to innovate during the front-end phase do two distinct and even opposing things. They try to sustain innovation because of the learned experiences that give them confidence, and at the same time, they have to retrench due to the sudden economic hardship.

Conflicting situation 2: Expectations about the resolution of the ongoing situation based on previous experiences drive innovativeness, but the changed context leads to uncertainty and ambiguity.

The companies held specific expectations grounded in the learned experiences from previous downturns and the learned pattern of working in the industry. They expected that the ecosystem would sustain innovation. However, they also experienced ambiguity about the behaviour of the buyers, as discussed under strategy 4. The perceived 'retraction' of buyers was, for some of the suppliers, a source of frustration as it did not fit with their expectations. This suggests that a mismatch between situations that are understood as similar (past and ongoing) may cast doubt on the established understanding of how the company should act in the industry. However, the magnitude of ambiguity and uncertainty is not big enough to put more radical adaptations in motion or to retract fully from engaging in collaborative innovation efforts, as noted by the CEO of subsupplier B:

> [The buyers] don't see that they have a responsibility for supply chain. They don't care if we or other companies are not here anymore in one to two years from now. It's a little bit strange, because … [the buyers] will always be dependent on a supply chain to do the job for them. They are not there anymore. At least that's how we see it. And that's fine, we only want that message in a [clear] way for us to reinvent ourselves marketwise. (Subsupplier B)

This means that the front-end stage is characterised by an introduced uncertainty and ambiguity into the worldviews that guide companies' behaviour. The rupture in the worldview was, however, not strong enough in this phase to trigger more radical adaptation, for example, stopping the innovation activities despite the hardship:

> … innovation and new technology is still important and I guess that the companies that are willing to innovate now will benefit from that in two or three or five years'

time. Whereas those that don't innovate and just try to maintain their business will be worse off in five years. So, I would not say that innovation and that the development has stopped in any way, a lot of companies are still quite innovative but they just stay low and do their work and then when the market turns up it will pay off. (Company A)

In other words, companies made sense of the current situation by drawing on established understandings of how the industry functions despite the perceived divergence.

Conflicting situation 3: Retrenchment and streamlining constrain established innovation practices and activities but also drive companies to engage in novel forms of innovation.

The companies were forced to cut costs and streamline activities, but the motivation to sustain their role as innovators encouraged them to find alternative ways of performing their roles. In particular, slack resources helped them to engage in novel forms of innovation in spite of constraints during the front-end part of the downturn. For example, engineers who did not have projects to work on suddenly had time to work on new solutions:

> Of course we have spare resources at the moment as well and we can do study work. Concept work, how to adapt our technology to their solutions, help them understand in a collaborative way how we can contribute to them reducing their costs. So, that's the story right now. Even though there's not a lot coming out to the market, there's a lot happening in the background. People trying to reduce the cost levels, find solutions. (Company D).

This suggests that innovation during the front end is enabled by a backlog of resources as well as confidence in turnaround, but the threatened survival as well as a changed context in the industry also requires the adaptation of innovation efforts. Suppliers found alternative ways to sustain these efforts in line with a learned understanding of how the industry works (strategy 5).

5. DISCUSSION

The results of the study indicate that the conflicting situations the companies experienced were related to the mismatch between what the companies were used to doing and what they had to do because of the changes in resources and the arising uncertainty and ambiguity during the front-end phase of the crisis. This did not stop innovation efforts, but it sparked a shift in how the companies worked with innovation. For example, they adapted the content and the practices related to innovation and searched for alternative ways of performing their roles in the ecosystem. Interestingly, the pressure was not strong enough to spark a radically novel response outside of the established trajectories of companies, for example, diversification. Rather, companies introduced changes that were still in line with the established pre-crisis understanding of the role of suppliers and their innovation efforts. In fact, the expectations of reversal and the re-establishment of learned patterns of working in the industry were important drivers for innovation activities despite the experienced economic challenges. This result is in line with Proposition 1 that the *experience with similar challenging situations encourages companies to sustain innovation despite retrenchment activities*. The study finds that experiences guide companies' adaptation strategies and innovation activities.

The study further finds that the uncertainty and ambiguity related to the front-end phase are not necessarily strong drivers of more radical adaptation outside of the established trajectory of the companies. One explanation is that the need for a radical response may not be perceived either because there is not enough information about the situation (Kitching et al., 2009) or because confidence in understanding the events based on experiences with similar situations is very strong (Audia et al., 2000). As this case shows, the front-end stage of the crisis was characterised by innovation efforts introduced to sustain business as usual, as opposed to an immediate cessation of innovation. The front-end phase may be in this sense different from subsequent phases that require more radical adaptations because of the threat to survival (Martin-Rios & Parga-Dans, 2016a).

The study extends Proposition 2, which states that *constrained financial resources and uncertainty during the front end force companies to adopt retrenchment strategies and stop innovation activities*. The study shows that the retrenchment and proactive adaptation strategies for innovation were not mutually exclusive and were intertwined throughout the front-end phase. This suggests that even though companies wanted to innovate, they still needed to secure their survival during the front end. This does not necessarily mean that the same strategy holds in the subsequent phases of a crisis. The relationship between innovation and retrenchment may change over time, with companies starting out with retrenchment activities and ending with ambitious innovation efforts over time and vice versa. In fact, innovation may eventually be necessary to survive a deep and prolonged crisis (Martin-Rios & Parga-Dans, 2016a).

Furthermore, the results suggest that factors often considered to hinder innovation can also drive new efforts in times of crises (Kitching et al., 2009). Retrenchment may hinder established practices and projects, but it can also open up avenues for other forms of innovation. In this case, the new efforts were related to both product and process innovation. Product innovation efforts were related to developing new concepts to tackle new needs. Process innovation consisted of new forms of collaboration, new ways of maintaining innovation, and new internal practices and activities. Introducing novel forms of innovation hints at changes to innovation efforts that are qualitative in nature (Archibugi & Filippetti, 2011), for example, increased focus on efficiency and new concepts for increasing the cost-effectiveness of existing solutions. Often, such changes may be invisible on the outside but are part of strategies to sustain innovation in times of crisis. Future studies could look into how the efficiency requirements and cost focus are transformed into novelty (i.e. mapping the qualitative changes to innovation over time).

Another distinct characteristic of the front-end stage is the availability of resources (Proposition 2). The sudden drop in activity did not necessarily mean that the companies could not afford to innovate any more. The drop resulted in slack resources, for example, internal engineers or collaborating firms without projects to work on. The companies could use these slack resources to engage in different innovation efforts. This may mean that the availability of resources may also be a factor behind the adaptation within established trajectories during the front end, as the companies did not have to look for more radical ways to survive and sustain their roles in the industry compared to other phases of crisis (Martin-Rios & Parga-Dans, 2016a; Mascarenhas & Aaker, 1989). This implies that the backlog can mask the severity of the situation in the environment or create doubt about a coming crisis and aversion towards stopping innovation. At the same time, it also implies that there may be a different motivation and ability to sustain and engage in innovation than in a stage of deep crisis when a more radical adaptation of companies is required due to the thinning of available resources and a longer period with reduced economic activity (Martin-Rios & Parga-Dans, 2016a).

6.   CONCLUSION

This chapter has discussed the impact of economic crises on innovation strategies by examining a group of companies during the initial phase of an industry downturn. The empirical setting was a group of suppliers to the oil and gas industry in the first phase of the industry downturn in 2015–16, which lasted until 2018. The chapter addressed *how companies adapt their innovation activities during the front-end phase of an industry crisis and how the constrained resources and learned patterns of working affect them.*

Innovation during the front-end stage is characterised by learned experiences and aligning those with the new situation. Such alignment efforts provide confidence but also bring challenges. The context in which companies functioned well changed, as the three conflicting situations for the companies as innovators in the case study suggest. The findings of the case study also indicate that experiences prevent an in-depth reflection regarding a structural break and potentially constrain more radical responses during the front-end phase. Furthermore, the phase is characterised by a combination of innovation and retrenchment activities – the latter drive new forms of innovation efforts.

Finally, the front-end phase, as opposed to the later phases of a crisis, is characterised by slack resources that companies can deploy and use to sustain innovation activities (Martin-Rios & Pasamar, 2018). This suggests that it is valuable to consider the temporal aspect of a crisis to understand its impact on innovation. Future studies could track how the same companies adapt throughout the different stages of a crisis and compare how their adaptation and innovation strategies differ. This would provide additional knowledge about how a crisis can lead to innovation at the company level.

The findings come with implications for companies facing industry downturns and wanting to sustain innovation activities. A crisis may worsen the conditions in an industry, which means that some of the assumptions and expectations about the industry and/or market may no longer hold. The companies should, in such cases, strive to consider their assumptions relative to the perceived changes in the environment. This would prevent a potential normalisation of a changed situation in line with established expectations and, in turn, prevent a situation in which the company is unable to sustain innovation and, most importantly, survive.

The interpretation and implications of the findings of the case study come with limitations. The front-end period was constructed by the author based on the knowledge of how the crisis had evolved over a period of approximately four years. There is no clear measure of the severity of a crisis, and a different approach could have positioned the timing of the interviews at a different stage (e.g. deep crisis) (cf. Mascarenhas & Aaker, 1989). This issue calls for more conceptual studies on the phases of economic crises. Another limitation is related to the chosen empirical case. In the upstream oil and gas ecosystem, commercial and innovation activities are tightly interlinked due to the nature of work. This means that the suppliers sustain innovation because it is expected of them to do so. Furthermore, the companies in the upstream oil and gas industry are familiar with downturns. This may have additionally increased their eagerness to engage in innovation. Companies in other industries may be less willing to engage in innovation during an economic crisis. Future studies could examine how companies work in terms of innovation in other sectors or industries that face similar dire situations. Another limitation of the study is its small sample, resulting from hampered access during a stressful situation for firms. A bigger sample with more diverse firms may provide a more eclectic picture of the strategies employed. Despite these limitations, the findings of the case study can also be useful starting points for studies investigating innovation during similar situations, such as the Covid-19 pandemic.

REFERENCES

Acha, V., & Cusmano, L. (2005). Governance and co-ordination of distributed innovation processes: Patterns of R&D co-operation in the upstream petroleum industry. *Economics of Innovation and New Technology, 14*(1–2), 1–21.

Ahn, J. M., Mortara, L., & Minshall, T. (2018). Dynamic capabilities and economic crises: Has openness enhanced a firm's performance in an economic downturn? *Industrial and Corporate Change, 27*(1), 49–63. https://doi.org/10.1093/icc/dtx048.

Alfranseder, E., & Dzhamalova, V. (2014). The impact of the financial crisis on innovation and growth: Evidence from technology research and development. Paper presented at the Knut Wicksell Working Paper 2014:8, The Knut Wicksell Centre for Financial Studies, Lund University.

Amore, M. D. (2015). Companies learning to innovate in recessions. *Research Policy, 44*(8), 1574–83.

Archibugi, D., & Filippetti, A. (2011). *Innovation and economic crisis: Lessons and prospects from the economic downturn.* Abingdon: Routledge.

Archibugi, D., Filippetti, A., & Frenz, M. (2013a). Economic crisis and innovation: Is destruction prevailing over accumulation? *Research Policy, 42*(2), 303–14.

Archibugi, D., Filippetti, A., & Frenz, M. (2013b). The impact of the economic crisis on innovation: Evidence from Europe. *Technological Forecasting and Social Change, 80*(7), 1247–60.

Audia, P. G., Locke, E., & Smith, K. (2000). The paradox of success: An archival and a laboratory study of strategic persistence following radical environmental change. *Academy of Management Journal, 43*(5), 637–53.

Barbero, J. L., Ramos, A., & Chiang, C. (2017). Restructuring in dynamic environments: A dynamic capabilities perspective. *Industrial and Corporate Change, 26*(4), 593–615.

Barr, P. S. (1998). Adapting to unfamiliar environmental events: A look at the evolution of interpretation and its role in strategic change. *Organization Science, 9*(6), 644–69.

Burnett, S., & Williams, D. (2014). The role of knowledge transfer in technological innovation: An oil and gas industry perspective. *Knowledge Management Research & Practice, 12*(2), 133–44.

Filippetti, A., & Archibugi, D. (2011). Innovation in times of crisis: National systems of innovation, structure, and demand. *Research Policy, 40*(2), 179–92.

Financial Times (2018). Brent breaks above $70 a barrel to hit highest since 2014 (11 January). https://www.ft.com/content/214ddfa2-f6ed-11e7-8715-e94187b3017e.

Garcia, R., Lessard, D., & Singh, A. (2014). Strategic partnering in oil and gas: A capabilities perspective. *Energy Strategy Reviews, 3*, 21–9.

Geroski, P., & Gregg, P. (1994). Corporate restructuring in the UK during the recession. *Business Strategy Review, 5*(2), 1–19.

Geroski, P., & Walters, C. F. (1995). Innovative activity over the business cycle. *Economic Journal, 105*(431), 916–28.

Hjertvikrem, N., & Fitjar, R. D. (2018). Knowledge networks in the Rogaland subsea industry cluster. In T. M. Thune, O. A. Engen, & O. Wicken (Eds.), *Transformations in the petroleum innovation system: Lessons from Norway and beyond.* London: Routledge.

Kahle, K. M., & Stulz, R. M. (2013). Access to capital, investment, and the financial crisis. *Journal of Financial Economics, 110*(2), 280–99.

Kitching, J., Blackburn, R., Smallbone, D., & Dixon, S. (2009). *Business strategies and performance during difficult economic conditions*. London: Department for Business, Innovation and Skills.

Lawrence, P. R., & Lorsch, J. W. (1967). Differentiation and integration in complex organizations. *Administrative Science Quarterly*, *12*(1), 1–47. https://doi.org/10.2307/2391211.

Lim, D. S. K., Celly, N., Morse, E. A., & Rowe, W. G. (2013). Rethinking the effectiveness of asset and cost retrenchment: The contingency effects of a firm's rent creation mechanism. *Strategic Management Journal*, *34*(1), 42–61.

Maitlis, S., & Sonenshein, S. (2010). Sensemaking in crisis and change: Inspiration and insights from Weick (1988). *Journal of Management Studies*, *47*(3), 551–80.

Maleki, A., Rosiello, A., & Wield, D. (2018). The effect of the dynamics of knowledge base complexity on Schumpeterian patterns of innovation: The upstream petroleum industry. *R&D Management*, *48*, 379–93.

Mariscal, R., & Powell, A. (2014). Commodity price booms and breaks: Detection, magnitude and implications for developing countries. IDB Working Paper Series No. IDB-WP-444. Department of Research and Chief Economist, Inter-American Development Bank.

Martin-Rios, C., & Parga-Dans, E. (2016a). The early bird gets the worm, but the second mouse gets the cheese: Non-technological innovation in creative industries. *Creativity and Innovation Management*, *25*(1), 6–17.

Martin-Rios, C., & Parga-Dans, E. (2016b). Service response to economic decline: Innovation actions for achieving strategic renewal. *Journal of Business Research*, *69*(8), 2890–900.

Martin-Rios, C., & Pasamar, S. (2018). Service innovation in times of economic crisis: The strategic adaptation activities of the top E.U. service firms. *R&D Management*, *4*(2), 195–209.

Mascarenhas, B., & Aaker, D. A. (1989). Strategy over the business cycle. *Strategic Management Journal*, *10*(3), 199–210.

McKinley, W., Latham, S., & Braun, M. (2014). Organizational decline and innovation: Turnarounds and downward spirals. *Academy of Management Review*, *39*(1), 88–110.

Navarro, P. (2005). The well-timed strategy: Managing the business cycle. *California Management Review*, *48*(1), 71–91.

Paunov, C. (2012). The global crisis and firms' investments in innovation. *Research Policy*, *41*(1), 24–35.

Perrons, R. K. (2014). How innovation and R&D happen in the upstream oil & gas industry: Insights from a global survey. *Journal of Petroleum Science and Engineering*, *124*, 301–12.

Ramsøy, O. J., Reve, T., & Nordkvelde, M. (2016). The oil price challenges: Strategic responses of the Norwegian offshore industry. Research Report 1/2016, BI Norwegian Business School.

Ryggvik, H. (2013). *Building a skilled national offshore oil industry: The Norwegian experience*. Oslo: NHO, Avdeling for internasjonalisering og europapolitikk.

Sako, M. (1995). Supplier relationships and innovation. In M. Dodgson & R. Rothwell (Eds.), *The handbook of industrial innovation*. Cheltenham, UK and Northampton, MA, USA: Edward Elgar Publishing.

Schmitt, A., & Raisch, S. (2013). Corporate turnarounds: The duality of retrenchment and recovery. *Journal of Management Studies*, *50*(7), 1216–44.

Schmitt, A., Barker, V. L., Raisch, S., & Whetten, D. (2016). Strategic renewal in times of environmental scarcity. *Long Range Planning*, *49*(3), 361–76.

Shuen, A., Feiler, P. F., & Teece, D. J. (2014). Dynamic capabilities in the upstream oil and gas sector: Managing next generation competition. *Energy Strategy Reviews*, *3*, 5–13.

Simensen, E. O., & Thune, T. M. (2018). Innovation in the petroleum value chain and the role of supply companies in supporting innovation. In T. M. Thune, O. A. Engen, & O. Wicken (Eds.), *Transformations in the petroleum innovation system: Lessons from Norway and beyond*. London: Routledge.

Thune, T. M., Engen, O. A., & Wicken, O. (2018). Transformations in the petroleum supply industry: Innovation, globalisation and diversification. In T. M. Thune, O. A. Engen, & O. Wicken (Eds.), *Transformations in the petroleum innovation system: Lessons from Norway and beyond*. London: Routledge.

Webb, D., & Pettigrew, A. (1999). The temporal development of strategy: Patterns in the U.K. insurance industry. *Organization Science*, *10*(5), 601–21.

Weick, K. E. (1993). The collapse of sensemaking in organizations: The Mann Gulch disaster. *Administrative Science Quarterly*, *38*(4), 628–52.

Williams, T., Gruber, D., Sutcliffe, K., Shepherd, D., & Zhao, E. Y. (2017). Organizational response to adversity: Fusing crisis management and resilience research streams. *Academy of Management Annals*, *11*(2), 733–69.

Zouaghi, F., Sánchez, M., & Martínez, M. G. (2018). Did the global financial crisis impact firms' innovation performance? The role of internal and external knowledge capabilities in high- and low-tech industries. *Technological Forecasting and Social Change*, *132*, 92–104.

6. "Is that my problem?" A study of motivation for knowledge sharing

Stian Bragtvedt

INTRODUCTION

A range of concepts and theories point to the importance of knowledge in contemporary capitalism (Lundvall and Johnson 1994; Høyrup et al. 2012). In order to go from embodied and tacit, to explicit, and thus part of a firm's capability, knowledge has to be shared. The aim of this chapter is to contribute to the discussion of knowledge sharing and, more specifically, what motivates workers to share knowledge. The starting point for the investigation is an empirical puzzle encountered during fieldwork in an aluminum smelter. At Metal Industries, I found that the bonus for participation in knowledge sharing (continuous improvement) had been significantly scaled down. From the perspective of theories underlining incentives as the way to motivate knowledge sharing, this should have led to a decline in the number of incoming suggestions. At Metal Industries, however, the opposite was the case: management were inundated with suggestions for incremental improvements of the production process from shop floor workers.

Herbert Simon points out that "nothing is more fundamental in setting our research agenda and informing our research methods than our view of the nature of the human beings whose behavior we are studying" (1985, 303). Oliver Williamson's (1996) view of transaction cost theory assumes that actors are self-interested and prone to knowledge hoarding, unless incentivized to act differently. What has become known as the knowledge-based view (according to Lam and Lambermont-Ford 2010), emphasizes the social dimension of knowledge sharing, arguing that identification with the firm spurs commitment which in turn enables learning and sharing of knowledge (Nonaka and Takeuchi 1995). As Lam and Lambermont-Ford point out, this perspective implicitly assumes actors are basically benevolent cooperators, sharing knowledge without being rewarded by monetary incentives. I will combine these perspectives to explain how motivation for knowledge sharing changed over time at Metal Industries. In elucidating what caused this change, I will draw on Lindenberg's (2001) and Lindenberg and Foss's (2011) work on intrinsic motivation. The goal is not to argue the superiority of one theoretical approach over another, but rather to show how the different theoretical perspectives help illuminate different aspects of what is going on in the case study.

Metal Industries was a typical J-form organization, adhering to principles of *Lean Manufacturing*, where continuous improvement of production processes is one example of formalized knowledge sharing. Hence, a significant part of Metal Industries' capacity for innovation came from "organization-specific collective competences and problem-solving routines" (Lam 2005, 125, 127). The question thus becomes – why did shop floor workers share their experience-based knowledge for the building of collective competences after the removal of monetary incentives to do so?

Asking why workers were motivated necessitates interpretations of the ideas and beliefs informing practices on the shop floor, such as knowledge sharing. Hence, this project is an interpretative one that sets out to understand social meaning. Its basic assumption about human nature is neither the benevolent cooperators of Nonaka and Takeuchi (1995), nor the opportunist assumed by Williamson, although these assumptions might be correct under the right conditions. Rather, I will start my analysis from the assumption that people are fundamentally intertwined in social meaning, implying that they can be both benevolent cooperators and opportunistic, depending on the meaningful context they find themselves in.

This chapter will show how both "benevolent co-operator" perspective and the "self-interested" perspective can be combined, by arguing that Metal Industries went from knowledge sharing motivated by incentives, to knowledge sharing motivated by the goal of doing the right thing. Hence, the motivation for knowledge sharing went from extrinsic to intrinsic. I will argue that this change in motivation must be understood as intertwined in operators' understandings of everyday work and their responsibilities. Therefore, in order to understand the change from extrinsic to intrinsic motivation for knowledge sharing, it is necessary to understand the changes in how operators understood work. The changing understanding of work was caused by a change in the organization of work, from control and coordination of work by foremen, to control and coordination by team members themselves. After introducing the central theoretical concepts and discussing epistemology and method, I will go on to describe the norms regulating work on the shop floor at Metal Industries. The chapter will conclude with a discussion of how class compromise can play an important role in stabilizing normative frames.

KNOWLEDGE, GOALS AND FRAMING

Nonaka and Takeuchi (1995) argue that the success of Japanese companies stems from their emphasis on the tacit aspect of knowledge, that which cannot be easily explicated. Such knowledge is "deeply rooted in an individual's action and experience, as well as in the ideals, values or emotions" (8). Hence, tacit knowledge is fundamentally intertwined in meaning. This chapter will argue that not only is tacit knowledge rooted in action and experiences, but the motivation for sharing such knowledge is also inherently intertwined in the practices and experiences of everyday work. For Nonaka and Takeuchi, it is workers' commitment to, and identification with, the company that motivates the sharing of knowledge. They offer little guidance, however, for how this state of worker commitment and identification with the company comes about. Furthermore, the sharing of knowledge in continuous improvement practices might lead to rationalization or redundancies. The question of motivation is thus connected to the question of interests; is it in the interest of workers to share knowledge if the knowledge is used to reduce the number of jobs?

Nonaka and Takeuchi do not offer much help in understanding potential conflicts of interest related to knowledge sharing. Instead, they use a living organism as a metaphor for the firm, stressing the importance of a shared understanding of what the company stands for, where it is going and what kind of world it wants to live in (9). This paraphrase points to the implicit assumption of the firm as a unitary actor, or at least an organization where everyone has the same idea where the company is going and what it stands for. To address conflicts of interests related to knowledge sharing, it is therefore necessary to turn to another perspective, which instead of assuming that firms consist of benevolent cooperators, sees people as prone to opportunistic and self-interested behavior.

In the transaction cost view, actors are understood to be "self-interest seeking of a more strategic kind" (Williamson 1996). For a self-interested actor, it might not make sense to share knowledge freely. Instead, knowledge hoarding, or strategic sharing, in order to get something, would be the norm; or even the withholding of knowledge to avoid effectivization that could endanger jobs. Thus, on the one side is the positive view of Nonaka and Takeuchi, which assumes that organizations consist of "benevolent co-operators", who share knowledge willingly (Lam and Lambermont-Ford 2010, 52), and on the other side is the view of the transaction cost tradition, seeing organizations as consisting of people who behave according to strategic considerations, to the best of their ability.

Lam and Lambermont-Ford (2010) seek to bridge these differing views by focusing on different motivational mechanisms, drawing on Siegward

Lindenberg's (2001) work on intrinsic motivation. This chapter will apply Lindenberg's motivational perspective on ethnographic data in order to highlight the motivations and intentions of blue-collar workers participating in continuous improvement. Central to the motivational perspective is the differentiation between intrinsic and extrinsic motivation (Deci 1971). Extrinsic motivation is motivation that comes from outside, such as monetary bonuses for knowledge sharing. An example of intrinsic motivation for knowledge sharing would be the sharing of knowledge because it is enjoyable.

Lindenberg (2001) uses framing theory to further develop the notion of intrinsic motivation, conceptualizing it as either motivated by a normative goal, or a hedonic goal. Central to Lindenberg's understanding of motivation is the goal-driven nature of human behavior. These goals are structured into two hierarchies, substantive goals and operational goals. The former has physical and social well-being at the top while the latter has improvement in one's position. For Lindenberg, social and physical well-being are universal goals. They do, however, take different forms in different contexts. Of relevance for this chapter is *behavioral confirmation* as a means to achieve social well-being. Behavioral confirmation is about doing the right thing in the eyes of relevant others. While such confirmation starts out with overt approval from others, it might continue with approval by the self who has internalized the particular norms. Hence, behavioral confirmation is not limited to explicit actions, but also covers "covert actions such as thinking certain thoughts, agreeing with certain maxims, adopting certain attitudes" (Lindenberg 2001, 327).

In Lindenberg's (2001) theory, there are three basic frames: a hedonic frame (linked to the goal of feeling better), a normative frame (linked to the goal of acting appropriately) and a gain frame (linked to the goal of improving one's condition). These frames are activated when individuals have goals for their behavior, so that a goal of acting appropriately activates a normative frame. The activation of a particular frame means that a particular mode of reasoning is activated: "certain categories and stereo-types are activated; certain heuristics for goal achievement; certain knowledge chunks and attitudes are being mobilized; the individual is becoming sensitive to certain kinds of information; certain options are selected as choice alternatives; and the alternatives will be ordered in terms of their relative contribution to goal realization" (Lindenberg 2001, 322). Hence, a particular goal activates a frame that focuses thinking towards achieving that goal.

Goals compete for "center stage" with other goals, and their related frames. A crucial point for Lindenberg, however, is that the goals that lose out in the competition for taking center stage are not discarded. Rather, they are relegated to the background (322), from where they can either weaken or strengthen the active goal. For example, if my goal in a situation is to act appropriately, and appropriate behavior in the situation is to drink coffee, I will happily drink coffee, both because I act appropriately, but also because it is enjoyable in itself. In this case, the normative frame in the foreground is strengthened by the hedonic frame in the background, making it likely that I will sustain this activity. In the following, I will draw on Lindenberg's concepts to discuss why motivation for knowledge sharing at Metal Industries changed from being extrinsically motivated to intrinsically motivated; that is, from being motivated by monetary incentives and a gain frame, to being intrinsically motivated from a wish to do the right things, a normative frame.

EPISTEMOLOGY AND METHOD

This chapter is based on data from fieldwork in an aluminum smelter, Metal Industries. It is an interpretative study that sets out to understand the meaning behind people's actions. The fundamental assumption informing analysis is from Geertz's writing on thick description, that man is an "animal suspended in webs of significance he himself has spun" (Geertz 1973, 5). The task of the researcher is thus to interpret these webs of significance. The interpretivist approach utilized here is inspired by the work of Isaac A. Reed (2011), who argues for plurality in theory and coherence in meaning. Reed's argument starts from the premise that the use of theory in social sciences is a question of resignification. In what Reed calls the realist epistemic mode, data is resignified into a coherent theoretical framework. In the interpretivist epistemic mode, data is resignified into a deeper interpretation of the case at hand. Hence, the role of theory is to illuminate different aspects of the meanings in the case at hand. The central question put to analytic concepts is not whether it matches the other concepts used in analysis; rather, the criteria on which the relevance of analytic concepts is judged is whether it helps with understanding what goes on in the case. In this way, Nonaka and Takeuchi's (1995) "altruistic" view of motivation can be combined with Williamson's (1996) view of actors as self-interested, because they both serve to illuminate different aspects of motivation for knowledge sharing.

Thus, it is not the theory that sorts and explains the facts, but my interpretation of their symbolic context. Theoretical concepts are brought in to assist with interpretation, rather than the theory structuring the presentation of the facts. What is gained by this approach is an opportunity to grasp the meaning behind people's actions, their intentions and motives. What is lost is the opportunity for generalization that comes from letting the theory order the facts and observations. In the following, my ambitions for generalization are limited to "the orbit of the social actions under scrutiny" (Reed 2011, 92). What is gained by forsaking the aim of generalization is a nuanced understanding of the complexities of motivation for knowledge sharing at Metal Industries.

Data were generated through fieldwork in a Norwegian aluminum smelter over a period of four weeks in 2018. The smelter was chosen for fieldwork because of an interest in Norwegian manufacturing firms successful in global markets that were not located within clusters. This was because I wanted to explore the impact of the institutional framework regulating Norwegian working life, often referred to as the Norwegian model. Norwegian working life is characterized by collective bargaining and cooperation, both on the national level between the main employer and employee associations, and at the micro level between firm and trade union (see e.g. Hvid and Falkum 2018; Levin et al. 2012). The literature on the Norwegian institutional framework typically argues that this is advantageous for firms.

I followed a team of operators during day-, afternoon- and nightshifts. In addition to this I undertook 33 interviews with managers, operators, trade unionists and engineers at the smelter. Fieldwork and interviews complemented each other, so that there was an interplay between unstructured conversations during observation, and the structured interviews. That interviews were structured means that they were done at an agreed time, and while I had prepared specific interview guides for the different interviews, these were often deviated from if the conversation took an unexpected but interesting turn. The data from fieldwork and interviews were analyzed in MaxQda. While thematic coding played a part in indexing the data, the most important part of analysis came by way of writing: from the first jotting down of notes in the field to the later puzzling together of data fragments into narratives, a process which Emerson et al. (2011) liken to a carpenter fitting a door within a doorframe, but where neither the size of the frame nor the door is fixed.

One advantage of observation is the type of data produced, allowing for direct observation of interaction, compared with interviews, where one will get an actor's retrospective interpretation of said interaction. While the combination of interviews and observations yielded a large quantity of data, space here is limited. The data presented here then, are meant as illustrative examples.

KNOWLEDGE SHARING AT METAL INDUSTRIES

Metal Industries is an aluminum smelter located in Lillevik, an industrial town located in the western part of Norway. Its location between mountain and fjord provides both access to hydroelectric power and a harbor from where the metal can be brought to the global marketplace. It is a relatively small smelter on the global level, and thus there is a constant fear that bigger smelters who can rely more on economies of scale can force them out of their market segment. One way to mitigate their relatively smaller size is to adopt the principles of "lean" manufacturing and continuous improvement. As part of the turn to lean, work had since the early 2000s been organized on the principle of autonomous teams. By way of a comprehensive reorganization, foremen and shift leaders were removed, and instead the responsibilities they had were divided up and distributed among the members of the team, typically between 10 and 15 operators, depending on which area of production they have responsibility for. Management and engineers, on the other hand, only work in the daytime so that during weekends and holidays, production is basically run by operators, although with an engineer and a manager available for call out at short notice. The participation of operators in knowledge sharing was deemed vital by management for sustaining competitive advantage. There were several avenues for operators to share their knowledge. In the following, I will examine suggestions for improvements, time studies and informal improvements together. While literature might use different concepts to describe these ways of sharing knowledge, the point in the following is that they were all motivated in the same way.

Just before my fieldwork commenced, Metal Industries had changed the incentive system for coming up with suggestions from one where operators were rewarded with bonuses if they came up with suggestions that improved profitability, to one where the monetary reward for good suggestions was significantly reduced. Instead of a large payout to the operator formulating the suggestion, a symbolic bonus was now given to the team to which the operator belonged. From the view of transaction cost theory and the assumptions of self-interested actors needing incentives to share knowledge, one would expect the number of incoming suggestions to have gone down. At Metal Industries, however, the opposite happened, and management were inundated with suggestions for improvements, so much so that the main bottleneck became not the sharing of knowledge, but management's ability to handle them:

Manager: We started the new way of registering suggestions last year, but we have gotten far more suggestions than we have managed to deal with. We are trying to get better at it. […] We hope that we can achieve our goal of addressing all suggestions in an efficient way. We saw that the response [of operators] was very good to begin with, but we haven't been able to respond to all the suggestions, so that is a challenge.

From this observation, one could draw the conclusion that Nonaka and Takeuchi's (1995) assumption of benevolent cooperators better describes the reality at Metal Industries.

I will demonstrate, however, that knowledge sharing at Metal Industries is best understood as divided into two periods; one period dominated by incentives to motivate knowledge sharing behavior, followed by the current period, where intrinsic motivation was the most important motivation for knowledge sharing. I will argue that it is not the removal of incentives which caused the change from extrinsic to intrinsic motivation. Rather, motivation for knowledge sharing is intertwined in operators' understanding of everyday work and their responsibilities. Therefore, in order to understand the change from extrinsic to intrinsic motivation for knowledge sharing, it is necessary to understand the changes in how operators understood work. The changing understanding of work was caused by a change in the organization of work, from control and coordination of work by foremen, to control and coordination by team members themselves.

The "Old" Way of Knowledge Sharing

Before the introduction of autonomous teams at Metal Industries, each team had a foreman with them at all times, coordinating work and allocating tasks. Odd the operator described the effects of this on work culture:

Odd: Before there were a lot of managers. Shift-foremen, hall-foremen and so on. They told us what to do. You usually just sat down and relaxed until someone told you to do something. We did what was necessary of course [for keeping metal flowing], but everything having to do with maintenance, and such was not done unless the foreman came and told you to do it. Now we do everything ourselves.

Hence, under the system with foremen on the teams, the *locus of authority* (Whitley 1977), the authority to which operators were willing to abide and which coordinated tasks, lay in the managerial hierarchy. If not told what to do by the foreman, workers would sit down and wait; in other words, a way of understanding work which closely resembles the opportunistic actors assume by Williamson (1996). This understanding of work also had consequences for knowledge sharing, and a system of incentives was in place to encourage operators to come up with suggestions for improvements.

Terje the trade unionist had been against the removal of the bonus, and in effect argued that people needed to be incentivized to come up with suggestions for improvements:

Terje: I know of several suggestions that have given operators a nice amount of money. I believe it triggers some people to think about improvements in general. The ordinary operator, who gets 50,000 kroner, that is money. I think that when you remove such incentives, people won't bother coming up with suggestions.

A study of motivation for knowledge sharing 121

Terje argues very much in line with Williamson, in that people who are not incentivized to come up with suggestions will not bother to do so. As mentioned earlier, operators at Metal Industries did indeed bother to come up with new suggestions, even after the removal of the bonus. Truls, the new leader of the trade union, saw the removal of the bonus as a step in the right direction:

Truls: You don't invent the wheel by yourself, you invent it together with other people. It is the same with writing procedures, job observations and all these things. That is why I am against bonuses for improvements. If you give people bonuses for ideas, they start to keep ideas to themselves, because they want the bonus for themselves, and then the idea is perhaps only 30 percent as good as it could have been, and then you might not see the value of it, and you drop it altogether. The idea would be far better if you worked in a larger group, improving it together.

Truls, then, rather than emphasizing extrinsic motivating effect of incentives, argued that suggestions were improved by working together. Incentives, on the other hand, would only encourage knowledge hoarding, with suboptimal improvements as a result. Implicit in Truls's argument is the notion that the common good of the firm is more important than the individual bonus. The quotes from Terje and Truls serve to illustrate the two different views on motivation at Metal Industries: the "old" view of Terje, where incentives are understood as a fair compensation for coming up with suggestions, and the "new" view of Truls, understanding the incentives to encourage knowledge-hoarding and hence the detrimental effect on knowledge sharing. To understand how knowledge sharing at Metal Industries became more aligned with the "new" view of Truls than the "old" view of Terje, it is necessary to grasp the changes in work organization that had taken place at the smelter, changes that altered the experience of everyday work from one of being told what to do to one of operators taking responsibility for production themselves.

Knowledge Sharing: From Incentives to Norms

Among the operators on the autonomous teams, there were no foremen, and thus no formal hierarchy. Still, the work effort was regulated by a set of informal norms. My key to understanding this system of norms was the practice of *making ready*; the idea that a workstation should be left in the state that one would want to encounter it. The system of norms on the shop floor is fundamental to understanding why the removal of the individual bonus did not have a negative effect on motivation for knowledge sharing. This is because the system of norms led to an experience of work where operators saw production as their responsibility, rather than the responsibility of the managerial hierarchy. One consequence of this was that solving the problems of production also was understood as the responsibility of operators. Hence, the introduction of autonomous teams enabled the removal of extrinsic motivation (bonuses) because a system of intrinsic motivation could take over the task of motivating knowledge sharing. Before delving into the complexities of intrinsic motivation, however, it is necessary to go into the system of norms itself.

The system of norms rested on a loose classification of operators into two groups. The lazy workers (literally "lazy dick") and industrious workers. The former category was reserved for those who were seen as shirking their duties, out of which the most important was to *make ready* for the next operator to take over a workstation. Oscar was among the operators on the team whose industriousness was not under question, and he explained to me how a job should be done:

Oscar: When I have made the oven ready for casting, so that I am finished with it, then I immediately go and make ready for the next [oven]. And I do it immediately, so that it is done, and then I can take a break. I rather do it like that, so I don't get behind schedule. Some people, they just go and sit down as soon as an oven is ready, then they wait for the next oven to be ready, and then they go out and make it ready. Then they might use 30–45 minutes to make the oven ready [and fall behind schedule]. There is nothing about this in the procedures, but people get these kinds of things, it is completely normal. It's like you behave at home too, you finish the job before you go and sit down.

During my stay with the autonomous team at Metal Industries, I was able to witness the making of a lazy worker in practice, and some of its consequences.

Ove was a machine driver whose primary job was to load casting ovens with liquid metal. Various other metals would be added to the oven as well, in order to achieve the specific alloy desired by the customer. This was done with a tool mounted on the loader, consisting of a lid with a pipe in it. This tool is used to pick up barrels (containers able to hold liquid metal) and push the lid down on them, and create pressure by adding air, so that metal can be pumped out of the barrel and into the oven. For the barrel to be sealed with the lid on, the gasket on the lid must be relatively new, as they are worn down over time. At the end of Ove's run with the loading truck, he explained to me that we had to change the gasket. Ove left the old gasket on the ground and explained that we had to wait before putting in the new one, as the lid was still too hot from carrying metal in the barrel. This did not stand out to me as anything out of the ordinary in the moment, but the episode would be cast in a different light the following day, when I overheard a conversation between other team members when Ove wasn't present:

Ole-Petter: Other shifts have complained to Frank [the team leader] about him. It has been red on the same place every Monday [implying some problem]. There was trouble with pipes [on the barrel-tool] yesterday and yesterday he had pulled the gasket off the lid, but hadn't bothered to put in a new one.

Oscar: It doesn't look good when one takes over [a workstation] after him. I've let Marko [team-leader] know by writing a deviation report. "Are you writing deviations on your own shift?" he asked me. "I don't know who have done it," I answered.

According to Ove's fellow team members, not only should he put in a new gasket after changing it, but his failure to do so is a recurring problem; so much so that Oscar has tried to sanction him by writing a deviation report to management. A deviation report is written when there is a breach of the procedures regulating work. Operators typically do not write deviations on members of their own team, an informal rule so entrenched that the team leader is surprised that Oscar is doing it. A few days later, Ove again found himself on the receiving end of threats of being reported:

Ottar: Ove, you must go out and work.
Ove: That's not my problem.
Ottar: Yes, it is, because if you don't, the barrels get cold, they can't stay [at the holding shelf] for 6–7 hours. Then the temperature in the casting oven will drop too much.
Ove: Is that my problem?
Ottar: If you don't do it, I will report you. [Ove goes to the truck to start filling ovens.]

Normally, Ottar would not be in a position to threaten anyone on the team with writing a deviation report. This would be a major violation of intra-operator etiquette and would risk Ottar being seen as an operator more loyal to management than to his fellow team members. In this case, however, it was widely understood that Ove was a lazy worker not pulling his weight, thus it was legitimate to use threats of reporting him in order to get him to work. These norms were reproduced in the overlaps between shifts, and were a common topic of conversation – stories about who had not made something ready, and why. Not making something ready for a specific operator can also be a way

124   *Rethinking the social in innovation and entrepreneurship studies*

of sanctioning operators who are seen as not pulling their weight. These notes from overlaps serve as illustrations:

> During talk about who works hard and who hardly works, Mats speaks about how he tries to force another operator to do his part: "I just leave him a lot of barrels [that need cleaning], it is the only way to get him to clean at all."
> Oscar explains why he won't bother making ready for another operator: "I won't make ready for Patrik, he never makes ready for me."
> Oscar lists people he won't make ready for.

The sanctioning of Ottar illustrates how the responsibility for the productive effort of an individual operator is not a question between the operator and management, but between the operator and his or her team. Should conflicts arise over such questions, they are now along a horizontal axis, between team members, rather than along a vertical axis, between management and team. Instead of Ove's unfinished job with the gasket being an issue between him and a foreman, it was an issue between him and his fellow operators. The extraction of work effort is thus the responsibility of the team, rather than the foreman, not because the extraction of work effort has been singled out as a central responsibility of the team, but because the extraction of work effort is necessary for production. Ottar's threat of reporting Ove cannot be reduced to irritation because of Ove not pulling his weight; it is not primarily a moral question. It is a practical question because his lack of work effort risks the metal becoming too cold for casting. Hence, the team not only takes responsibility for work effort, it takes responsibility for the flow of production, and it is against the flow of production that Ottar's actions are judged. That the team saw themselves as responsible for the flow of production meant that solving the problems of production also became a naturalized part of being an operator. In the days of foremen on the team, the experience of work was one of being told what to do. With the removal of the foreman the experience of work changed into one of taking responsibility for production, including responsibility for solving the problems of production, not only in terms of work effort, but also for improving equipment and work routines.

Knowledge Sharing for the Solving of Operators' Problems

I have shown how the problems of production were understood as problems that belonged to the operators' sphere of responsibility, because of the system of norms that had developed after the removal of the foremen from the teams. Magnus the manager's story of operators' response to time studies illustrates the outcome of this logic:

Bragtvedt:	You said you were well received at [place in smelter] when you came to do time studies, why is that do you think?
Magnus:	The preparation. When you enter a place like that, you can't count on being accepted by operators and auxiliary workers, when you tell them that you are there with a stopwatch to record how much time they spend on each operation. But we got really good feedback down there. After the research, we summarized our findings in a meeting with all the workers. And they applauded, they were happy. Before we went down there, we feared we were going to be given a mouthful. Instead, they invited us back: "Can't you guys come to [area] also, we have some trouble over there." So people want to do a good job, they don't come here to shirk their duties.

The function of Magnus's preparation is to negotiate access to the "space" within which the team is responsible. He is not formally obligated to do any such thing, but in respecting the understanding of team autonomy, Magnus negotiates access and acceptance for the time studies project. This ensures that the project is interpreted by operators as a method for solving the problems of production, and hence, solving *their* problems. By respecting team autonomy, Magnus also confirms the status of the operators, related to the goal of social well-being, to the extent that they ask the time-studies team to come back because they have some other problems they need help with as well. One could argue here that time studies are not necessarily an example of knowledge sharing. The point of this example, however, is to show how the logic of solving operators' problems works in practice. Operators enthusiastically participate in projects aimed at increased efficiency, because they see it as their responsibility. Rather than understanding time studies as an attempt to get them to work harder, they see them as offering a solution to problems which are theirs to solve.

The participation in knowledge sharing is thus motivated by the system of norms elaborated on before. In Lindenberg's (2001) terminology, it is behavior with a goal of social well-being, achieved through "doing the right thing" – behavioral confirmation. Behavioral confirmation is doing the right thing in the eyes of significant others, but also regards the adoption of certain attitudes or agreeing with particular maxims (ibid.). In this case, it is about adopting the attitude of responsibility for production and, following on from this, for solving the problems of production. However, there were also examples of knowledge sharing where gain frames, with a goal of improving one's condition, seemed to play the dominant role.

Knowledge Sharing Motivated by Gain Frames

One important part of knowledge sharing at Metal Industries was improvement of equipment used in production. Ole the operator explained how he came up with a way to improve a vehicle used for hauling finished aluminum slabs:

Ole: There is a handle used to turn the seat around, so you can drive both ways; you don't have to back up. That way, you always face the direction you are going. This handle has a safety switch, however, and in the electrolysis halls, there are strong magnetic fields. These would trigger the switch, which then put on the handbrake, because it believed the seat was not fastened in the correct position. So every time the [name of vehicle] was needed inside electrolysis, we had to go to the repair shop to turn off the safety switch. Then you had to wait for the mechanics to fix it. But I suggested we put a key on the switch, so you can turn it off yourself before you enter electrolysis, and now we have such a key.

Ole's improvement thus saved timed in production, as operators did not need to go to the repair shop and wait for mechanics to manually turn off the security switch. A good example of how Ole's experience-based knowledge was used to improve efficiency in production. His motivation for this improvement can be fruitfully understood as a combination of goals; the operational goal of improving one's condition and the goal of increasing physical well-being by increasing stimulation. Ole's goal is to improve his condition by increasing the stimulation offered by his job. To understand how the introduction of the handle key increased stimulation, it is necessary to grasp how operators experienced work.

Of the operators I got to know at Metal Industries, the vast majority preferred afternoon- and nightshifts over day-shifts. This was surprising to me, as I had expected that working during the day would be both more pleasant and convenient. The reason day-shifts were the least favored was because most of the maintenance work was done during that shift, meaning that operators would have to wait for machines or equipment to be ready. Rather than relaxing while waiting for equipment to be fixed, operators preferred to have something to do:

Tim the operator: Time passes quicker during nightshifts, because there is more work to do. Daytime is much worse; you have all the maintenance and the stops.

Oda touched on a similar point during a conversation when I asked if the apprentice she was teaching could do the tasks for her, making her working day more comfortable:

Oda: No, no, you will get crazy from boredom after half a day [...] A good shift is afternoon or the weekend, then we can make up for all the time lost during the weekdays.

In this light, we see that Ole's improvement not only reduces the necessary time for performing a specific task with the vehicle, but it also, and more importantly for Ole, reduces the amount of boring waiting time. The goal motivating the improvement, then, is a combination of the goal of improving his condition, which is improved by the key because it increases his physical well-being at work, by reducing the time spent waiting, and increasing the time spent doing stimulating work. Ole's goal of improving his condition is also compatible with the goal of behavioral confirmation. By improving the production process, he is "doing the right thing" by taking responsibility for solving the problems of production. While the gain frame is activated by Ole's goal of improving his condition, the normative frame is in the background, providing additional support to his behavior, and thus increasing the chance that the behavior is sustained over time.

So far, I have shown how a normative frame (and in particular, behavioral confirmation), plays an important role in motivating knowledge sharing at Metal Industries. For the most part, the normative frame takes center stage while, in the example of Ole's improvement, a gain frame takes center stage, with support from the normative frame in the background. Lindenberg (2001) points out that of the three frames – hedonic, gain and normative – the latter is the most precarious, because it is only indirectly connected to emotions. Hence, behavior motivated by the goal of social well-being (by way of behavioral confirmation), is prone to being pushed aside by behavior motivated by a hedonic (enjoyment) or gain frame (improvement in one's condition). If normative frames are the most precarious, how are they sustained over time in the everyday practice of work at Metal Industries?

DISCUSSION: STABILIZING NORMATIVE FRAMES

Lindenberg and Foss (2011) argue that one way to support normative frames is by cognitive and symbolic management. Common goals must be "embedded in a shared sense of common direction and affect at the level of the firm" (509). They go on to argue that a suitable way to do this is a common mission statement for the firm that is supported by senior management. To understand how a shared sense of common direction is achieved at Metal Industries, however,

Lindenberg and Foss's focus on management is too narrow. Rather than the common vision being a result of the actions of senior management, it was an outcome of the relation between the trade union and senior management – a relation that can be fruitfully understood by Erik Olin Wright's (2015) concept of positive class compromise, where mutual cooperation between trade union and senior management is perceived by both parties as yielding benefits for both sides, greater than what could be achieved without cooperation. The alternative is a negative class compromise, where industrial relations are seen as a zero-sum game where a gain for one side is a loss for the other. At Metal Industries, cooperation between firm and trade union was understood to be integral to the firm's success. This cooperation was based on a formulation of a common interest, namely that of safeguarding the jobs at the smelter for the foreseeable future. Continuous improvement and lean manufacturing were important means to achieve this goal. Hence, the norms motivating participation in continuous improvement that emanated from the practice of everyday work were embedded in a wider narrative of the importance of securing the jobs at Metal Industries. Hence, the shared sense of common direction called for by Lindenberg and Foss (2011) was created in the relation between the trade union and management. This compromise involved concessions from both sides. Executives at Metal Industries had promised that no one was to lose their job from effectivization from continuous improvement. Instead, reductions in jobs were to be achieved by voluntary retirement or reorganization. The trade union, on the other hand, had to commit to supporting continuous improvement.

Thus, rather than understanding the normative frames as supported by the formal values of the company and management's good conduct, they were supported by what Wolfgang Streeck calls an "integrated, internally differentiated system of industrial government" (Streeck 1992, 164, cited in Olin Wright 2015, 199). Such a system is characterized by management and trade union internalizing each other's interests, superseding the system of adversarial industrial relations (ibid.). Truls, the leader of the trade union who earlier spoke warmly of the removal of the bonus, illustrates how the understanding of knowledge sharing was embedded in the larger narrative of securing jobs at Metal Industries, and thus how labor had internalized the values of management:

Bragtvedt: Isn't it reasonable that operators are compensated for their contribution to increased profit [by knowledge sharing in continuous improvement]?

Truls: Or you could say that it is reasonable that you contribute to securing the jobs here in Lillevik. Moreover, maybe the reason you came up with the idea in the first place is that you saw something while on the job; would you have come up with that idea if you were sitting by yourself at home?

For a normative goal frame to be sustainable, it must be embedded in a clear consensual vision (Lindenberg and Foss 2011). While Foss and Lindenberg use formal vision documents from Lego or IKEA as examples, my point here is that in Metal Industries' case, formal visions were of lesser importance when it came to motivating knowledge sharing. While formal visions of an "innovative company" existed at Metal Industries, these were not critical in motivating knowledge sharing. Instead, it was the shared sense of contributing to securing the continued operations at the smelter that kept the normative goal frames in place in everyday work. A clear consensual vision, but different from the formalized language of corporate vision documents.

The norms on the shop floor, designating the problems of production as operators' problems to solve, were sustained by the wider narrative of contributing to securing the jobs in Lillevik. Knowledge sharing at Metal Industries was motivated by norms emanating from the way the everyday practice of work was organized – autonomous teams in which operators took responsibility for production.

CONCLUSIONS

In this chapter, I have demonstrated how knowledge sharing at Metal Industries went from being extrinsically motivated by incentives, to intrinsically motivated by the goal of behavioral confirmation. More specifically, it was motivated by the goal of doing the right thing, which activated a normative frame. This normative frame was sustained because it was supported by a clear and consensual vision (Lindenberg and Foss 2011). This vision and the consensus over it was a result of the positive class compromise at Metal Industries (Olin Wright 2015), where management and trade union cooperated on the basis of what they saw as a shared common interest, namely the safeguarding of jobs in Lillevik. Hence, the participation in knowledge sharing was motivated by a normative frame, "doing the right thing on the shop floor", which in turn was embedded in a larger "clear and consensual vision" to safeguard the jobs in Lillevik. The consensus over the vision at Metal Industries, however, did not trickle down from the level of senior management. Rather, it was a result of the cooperative relations between top management and the trade union. In relation to the theoretical perspectives presented at the beginning of this chapter, the story of motivation for knowledge sharing at Metal Industries provides several key points.

The use of theoretical concepts from different perspectives, not as coherent theoretical frameworks but as aides to interpret data, allows for deeper understanding of motivation for knowledge sharing, in this case because the notion of self-interested actors (Williamson 1996) and benevolent cooperators (Nonaka and Takeuchi 1995) help to describe the dominant forms of motivation for knowledge sharing at Metal Industries before and after the introduction of autonomous teams. Hence, the two perspectives can be fruitfully combined under an interpretative framework, when they are not used as universal assumptions of human nature, but instead as tools to highlight different aspects of motivation. A contribution of ethnography and an interpretative framework focused on social meaning is thus the ability to understand change, from one mode of motivation to another.

The narrative from Metal Industries shows how both opportunism and benevolent cooperation can be brought about by the organization of work. Lindenberg's (2001) framing theory provides a useful way of understanding these behaviors – as motivated by different goals that activate different frames. When organizing work for knowledge sharing, the question to ask is thus: What kind of goal do we want to motivate knowledge sharing? The point made here is not that a normative frame is the best practice. In other contexts, a gain frame would probably work just as well, for example in a work context where employee turnover is high. The point being that motivation is inherently intertwined in local meaning; hence, the ambition of Jurburg et al. (2017) to reach a consensus on exactly what triggers employee participation in knowledge sharing seems too ambitious.

Lindenberg and Foss (2011) argue that a clear and consensual vision helps to maintain the precarious normative frames. They argue that it is the task of senior management to bring about both the vision and the consensus over it. The narrative from Metal Industries illustrates how it is not the formal vision formulated in public documents that is active in creating motivation for knowledge sharing. At Metal Industries, knowledge sharing was understood in light of the larger narrative of securing the jobs in Lillevik. This narrative emanated from the local class compromise between trade union and top management at Metal Industries. Rather than trickling down from senior management, the clear and consensual vision sprang from the integrated industrial governance that had developed at Metal Industries (Streeck 1992, 164, cited in Olin Wright 2015, 199). Hence, the meaning relevant for knowledge sharing in the everyday practice of work might differ considerably from the visions expressed in formal documents. This underlines the relevance of ethnography and thick description for understanding motivation for knowledge sharing. Research that relies only on interviews with management or surveys risks missing the meaning at work in processes of knowledge sharing, and instead reproduces the meaning of management discourse – a discourse which not necessarily reflects the realities of everyday work and the complexities of knowledge sharing.

REFERENCES

Deci, E. L. (1971). Effects of externally mediated rewards on intrinsic motivation. *Journal of Personality and Social Psychology*, *18*(1), 105.

Emerson, R. M., Fretz, R. I., & Shaw, L. L. (2011). *Writing Ethnographic Fieldnotes*. Chicago, IL: University of Chicago Press.

Geertz, C. (1973). *The Interpretation of Cultures: Selected Essays*. New York: Basic Books.

Hvid, H., & Falkum, E. (Eds.) (2018). *Work and Wellbeing in the Nordic Countries: Critical Perspectives on the World's Best Working Lives*. London: Routledge.

Høyrup, S., Bonnafous-Boucher, M., Hasse, C., Møller, K., & Lotz, M. (Eds.) (2012). *Employee-Driven Innovation: A New Approach*. Basingstoke: Palgrave Macmillan.

Jurburg, D., Viles, E., Tanco, M., & Mateo, R. (2017). What motivates employees to participate in continuous improvement activities? *Total Quality Management & Business Excellence*, *28*(13–14), 1469–88.

Lam, A. (2005). Organizational innovation. In Fagerberg, J., Mowery, D. C. & Nelson, R. R. (Eds.), *The Oxford Handbook of Innovation*. Oxford: Oxford University Press, 115–47.

Lam, A., & Lambermont-Ford, J.-P. Knowledge sharing in organisational contexts: a motivation-based perspective. *Journal of Knowledge Management*, *14*(1), 51–66.

Levin, M., Nilssen, T., Ravn, J. E., & Øyum, L. (2012). Demokrati i arbeidslivet. Den norske samarbeidsmodellen som konkurransefortrinn. Bergen: Fagbokforl.

Lindenberg, S. (2001). Intrinsic motivation in a new light. *Kyklos*, *54*(2–3), 317–42.

Lindenberg, S., & Foss, N. J. (2011). Managing joint production motivation: the role of goal framing and governance mechanisms. *Academy of Management Review*, *36*(3), 500–525.

Lundvall, B. Ä., & Johnson, B. (1994). The learning economy. *Journal of Industry Studies*, *1*(2), 23–42.

Nonaka, I., & Takeuchi, H. (1995). *The Knowledge-Creating Company: How Japanese Companies Create the Dynamics of Innovation*. Oxford: Oxford University Press.

Olin Wright, E. (2015). *Understanding Class*. London: Verso Books.

Reed, I. A. (2011). *Interpretation and Social Knowledge*. Chicago. IL: University of Chicago Press.

Simon, H. (1985). Human nature in politics: the dialogue of psychology with political science. *American Political Science Review*, *79*(2), 293–304.

Whitley, R. (1977). Organisational control and the problem of order. *Social Science Information*, *16*(2), 169–89.

Williamson, O. E. (1996). Economic organization: the case for candor. *Academy of Management Review*, *21*(1), 48–57.

PART II

The identification approach

7. Playing around with the 'rules of the game': social entrepreneurs navigating the public sector terrain in pursuit of collaboration

Mikhail Kosmynin

INTRODUCTION

The social plays a significant role in entrepreneurship (Korsgaard & Anderson, 2011). In recent years, social ventures – organizations that combine practices of traditional for-profit firms with non-profit organizations' values – have increasingly been lauded as catalysts for social change (Borzaga et al., 2016; Drencheva et al., 2018; Mair, 2020; Stephan et al., 2016). As social ventures are not restricted by established organizational routines and modes of thinking, they have a significant capacity to foster new innovative solutions to societal challenges addressed by the UN's Sustainable Development Goals (SDGs) (Günzel-Jensen et al., 2020; Muñoz & Dimov, 2015; Saebi et al., 2018).

Indeed, collaboration is a shared feature of social ventures across countries and crucial for attaining SDGs (Günzel-Jensen et al., 2020; Mair, 2020). This chapter is concerned with social venture–public sector collaborations, specifically how social entrepreneurs engage with municipalities when seeking collaboration (Hogenstijn et al., 2018; Seanor, 2018). It is noteworthy that such collaborations go beyond traditional contractual partnerships and move towards co-creation of welfare services, joint projects and the like (Pestoff et al., 2011). However, establishing collaboration in practice is regarded as arduous with many pitfalls (Barinaga, 2020; de Bruin et al., 2016; Salomons, 2020). Prior research has stressed that innovative solutions that deviate from the public sector's current operations and ways of doing things are likely to be met with resistance (Renko, 2013). Further, hybrid organizing and the dual objectives of social ventures as *supplementary* social welfare providers can result in resistance from national constituents and tension-ridden relationships (Hogenstijn et al., 2018; Kibler et al., 2018; Muñoz & Kimmitt, 2019; Seanor, 2018). As a result, social ventures and public authorities often struggle to find common ground, and the road to a reciprocal collaboration appears to be more difficult and time consuming.

While the language of collaboration has permeated policy discourse in many countries (de Bruin et al., 2016; Schaltegger et al., 2018), empirical studies of practices that social entrepreneurs draw on to establish collaboration require greater scrutiny (Barinaga, 2020; Hydle & Billington, 2020; Kibler et al., 2018). Hence, in this chapter, I seek to provide a better understanding of the lived experiences of social entrepreneurs when engaging with municipalities to enact the context for collaboration in a Norwegian welfare state. Accordingly, I focus on the entrepreneurial actions or 'entrepreneuring' in its societal and institutional contexts (Johannisson, 2011; Steyaert, 2007; Watson, 2013a, 2013b) and address the following research question: *How do social entrepreneurs employ different practices to navigate the complex public welfare setting to bring about collaboration with municipalities and facilitate entrepreneurial venturing?*

To elucidate how social entrepreneurs find ways to maneuver in a highly political field as they seek to influence and change the existing practices and the 'rules of the game', this study builds on Michel de Certeau's (1988) practice theory. In this chapter, I extend his notions of 'strategy' and 'tactics' to the context of social venture–public sector collaborations to shed light on the micro-level practices in use by social entrepreneurs to establish collaborations (Barinaga, 2017; Dey & Teasdale, 2016).

To this end, I first outline the theoretical framework that informs my analysis. Before presenting the fieldwork and findings, I flesh out the empirical context and present the methodological approach and two cases. I conclude with some reflections on the broader implications of my findings and the conclusion.

THEORETICAL GROUNDING

Entrepreneurial Practices for Collaboration

Although entrepreneurship scholars have begun to study practices for gaining legitimacy (Anderson et al., 2010; De Clercq & Voronov, 2009; Shepherd et al., 2019; Vestrum et al., 2016) and acceptance from diverse actors (Pret & Carter, 2017), little is known about how social entrepreneurs deal with the 'rules of the game' and settings featured by dominant orders (in this case public authorities) when they seek to bring about collaboration.

In the context of social entrepreneurship, Barinaga's (2017) study using an [actor–network theory] ANT-inspired processual approach, focused on the socio-spatial practices of a social venture used to bring about collaboration. The author suggested the notion of 'tinkering' to underscore the adaptive and fluid nature of the organizational practices and the ongoing everyday work of organizing processes to bring about collaboration. Moreover, her findings indicate that the capacity to continuously adjust the qualities of the eventual social venture to the stakes of potential partners is instrumental to organizing collaborations (Barinaga, 2017).

Prior research also demonstrated that social entrepreneurs employ a set of practices that help overcome the lack of legitimacy and acceptance from external constituents such as the public authorities. For example, Sunduramurthy et al. (2016) theorized that social entrepreneurs utilize a bricoleur-type approach in that they mobilize and leverage collaborations through sustainable mechanisms, such as establishing formal positions to connect varied actors. Their findings suggest that social entrepreneurs create network-linking positions in their ventures to facilitate interaction and intersection of diverse actors. Such staff positions link social ventures with public sector organizations and their surrounding communities. Formalizing such positions in social ventures provides access to distributed agencies including public officials, administrators, community leaders, citizen organizations and other actors (Sunduramurthy et al., 2016; Vestrum et al., 2016).

Furthermore, it has been shown that social entrepreneurs engage in advocacy practices to persuade diverse social actors with heterogeneous motives to provide necessary resources (Di Domenico et al., 2010; Ruebottom, 2013; Seanor, 2018) and skillfully use regulatory influences to support their causes, in an effort to promote their social ventures to a broader audience and increase the credibility of social ventures. A recent study by Günzel-Jensen et al. (2020) suggests that some social entrepreneurs make reference to a meta-narrative of SDGs which acts as a compass and powerful narrative for social ventures to mobilize and enact resources via collaboration with powerful actors such as the public sector.

De Certeau's Notions of Strategy and Tactics

Focusing on the practices in use by social entrepreneurs (i.e. entrepreneurial actions and interactions in their pursuit of collaboration with public authorities), this study draws on de Certeau's (1988) practice theory, which has been creatively applied to diverse entrepreneurial phenomena (e.g. Dey & Teasdale, 2016; Hjorth, 2005; Ramirez-Pasillas et al., 2020). Specifically, inspired by de Certeau's practice theory, I draw on his conceptual idea of the two types of subject's behaviors: the strategic and the tactical. Strategy serves to define and produce regularity thus generating dominant orders. According to de Certeau (1988), strategizing is done by those who have (taken) the power and own the means of control, for example, public authorities and large organizations. In this case, strategy is linked to the 'rules of the game' in a societal and institutional context – governmental policies, regulations and the wider strategies of social policy making which are reinforced by the rhetorical logic in use by politicians who have certain expectations for how, when and why those games are played and by whom.

On the other hand, tactics constitute a calculated action for circumventing or negotiating these 'rules of the game' towards individuals' own objectives and goals. A tactic does not try to dominate or win and makes no attempt to confront the strategy, but tries to fill its needs by hiding behind an appearance of conformity. I embrace the idea that tactics constitute practices that 'constantly manipulate events in order to turn them into "'opportunities'"' (de Certeau, 1988, p. xix; cf. Ramirez-Pasillas et al., 2020). Thus, it must play on and with a terrain imposed on it and organized by the law of a foreign power (de Certeau, 1988). When strategies fail to provide the necessary conditions for social entrepreneurs, leaving little room for maneuvering in the welfare state, tactics provide responses to dealing with the 'everyday' by taking advantage of the occasions and capturing the possibilities offered in a moment. Therefore, tactics represent opportunity generating practices that can be constructive and subtly subversive ways of operating that produce change and outcomes without unsolvable conflicts with preceding orders. In other words, tactics are a form of practices performed by individuals (in this study, social entrepreneurs) when they seek to transform the strategy (in this case 'rules of the game') imposed on them.

THE EMPIRICAL CONTEXT: A STRONG WELFARE STRUCTURE

Given the importance of context in shaping and being shaped by entrepreneurial practices (Shepherd et al., 2019; Thornton, 1999; Welter & Baker, 2020), and its role in determining the 'rules of the game' and expectations, it is important to discuss the context in which social ventures are embedded (Berglund et al., 2012). My empirical setting is the Norwegian welfare state with a strong welfare structure. The Norwegian (and Scandinavian) societal model encompasses a distinct welfare component and a civil society component, which are intertwined (Trætteberg & Fladmoe, 2020). One of the implications is the extensive public supply of social services. Most of the public welfare is produced and provided by public bodies at different levels – municipalities, counties and governmental entities. The Norwegian welfare model is sometimes described as a number of 'welfare municipalities' rather than a welfare state. The Norwegian welfare model is thus characterized by public funding of the health sector and represents an area of comprehensive control management by the government (Bendixsen, 2018). This is a particularly compelling site where social ventures seek to find a suitable position, suggesting interesting dynamics.

Recent decades have witnessed an increasing tendency to open for non-state actors, including social ventures. Social entrepreneurship has recently gained much political attention, as it points to a renewal of the social commitments of the welfare state. Politically, social ventures are pinpointed as a supplement to public welfare services and/or an important resource to renew the public services (Norges forskningsråd, 2018). In addition, the public sector has experienced large structural reforms, implying merging of county administrations and municipalities and centralization of public tasks implemented by the conservative coalition cabinet. There is to some extent also a political divide in Norway on the privatization of welfare: while the conservative parties are pro-privatization, the left has a more ambivalent view.

Norwegian municipalities are partly self-governed and are responsible for delivering services to their citizens, such as child welfare and preschools, education, basic health services, elderly services and others. There is a consensus that welfare ought to be funded by public means. This has far-reaching consequences for the ecosystem in which social ventures operate (European Commission, 2019). For example, one consequence is that social ventures have to find their place in different local contexts. Further, there is no particular official governmental policy directed towards social entrepreneurship in Norway. This makes it challenging for social ventures to find a suitable position inside the traditional Norwegian welfare system (Hauge, 2017).

Although collaboration between social ventures and the local public sector is pinpointed as promising and much needed, there exist numerous challenges that social ventures need to deal with. Actors who hold the strategic power in a welfare state can use their power and influence to shape the social entrepreneurship field of practice and limit the potential of social ventures by co-opting them to serve the actors' own primary interests, instead of recognizing the ventures as equals in collaboration (Hauge, 2017).

METHODOLOGICAL APPROACH

This chapter is a part of a broader doctoral research project and employs a case study approach (Johannisson, 2011; Stake, 2005). I do not intend to compare the cases or find a more generalized pattern. Rather, guided by the principle of 'crystallization' (Berglund et al., 2012), the study seeks to provide a better understanding of how social entrepreneurs deal with the 'rules of the game' in their efforts to bring about collaboration with municipalities.

A purposeful sample was selected to include cases for analysis (Silverman, 2005). The case ventures had to meet the following three criteria. First, social ventures had to operate in the educational, health and social sectors, which are traditionally associated with the public sector in a Norwegian welfare state. The health and social service sector is a particularly important component of the Norwegian welfare state, and it is one in which there has been a lot of emphasis on developing innovative solutions through different forms of collaboration (Vannebo & Grande, 2018). Second, ventures had to have collaborative relationships with municipalities. Although the broader doctoral project focuses on two specific ongoing collaborations between social ventures and municipalities, however, in this chapter, I present the lived experiences of social entrepreneurs not limited to those two collaborations. Third, ventures had to be located in different parts of Norway because local contexts vary and therefore each case might have idiosyncrasies and nuances in terms of collaboration that make them unique from one another. Two cases were eventually selected based on the criteria. Both cases were anonymized to protect the identity of participants.

CASE 1: BETZ

The founder of social venture Betz (anonymized) is a portfolio entrepreneur Helena (pseudonym). The venture was founded in 2009. Its core business idea is to provide a new kind of service to inhabitants with substance abuse problems, thereby addressing the SDG #3 – good health and well-being. At the time of this study Betz had 46 employees: 43 of these are part-time assistants working with users, whereas three employees are permanent staff primarily engaged in administrative tasks. Helena learned the limitations of the Norwegian welfare system after her family's encounter with the municipality as a welfare provider. Betz developed an innovative solution – a personalized treatment program – and provides evidence-based services to inhabitants with substance abuse problems. Betz as a social venture is therefore adding a private layer to the Norwegian welfare system. Betz also recruits people who have previously been outside the labor market, and educates them to provide personalized services, adding another social dimension.

Over several years, Betz has developed a wide-ranging collaboration with different public sector organizations in Norway. During the time of my fieldwork, the venture had ongoing collaboration with Fjord municipality, implying that Betz and municipalities co-create services that fit with the municipality's resources and needs.

CASE 2: NATURE MAGIC

Established more recently in 2016, social venture Nature Magic was set up by three social entrepreneurs. The venture focuses on the well-being of different groups of people who struggle to cope with stress in everyday life. The venture's goal is to strengthen individuals' skills, reduce stress and provide joy in their everyday life. The business has five full-time regular employees, three of which are primarily engaged in management and administrative tasks.

During the time of my fieldwork, Nature Magic entered a collaboration with Rock municipality. The municipality faced a need to strengthen its preventive services for young people and became interested in Nature Magic's solution. However, the municipality's budget was too limited to experiment with innovative solutions. A Norwegian social investor company Anders Capital became interested in supporting the collaboration and provided upfront funding through a social impact bond model. Such collaboration enables Rock municipality to trial an innovative solution delivered by Nature Magic which is eventually expected to be integrated within the municipality.

DATA COLLECTION AND ANALYSIS

Data were collected between 2019 and 2020 using a wide range of sources to understand the lived experiences of social entrepreneurs within a particular context – the Norwegian welfare state. The methods employed are presented in Table 7.1. Interviews with founders and administrative staff that had direct experience of dealing with municipalities were performed face-to-face and lasted from 60 to 150 minutes. The respondents were encouraged to tell their 'stories' in a sequence that made sense to them. After their stories, a semi-structured interviewing technique was employed. The interview guide covered themes such as the characteristics and history of social venture, its services/products, ongoing collaborations with local public sector organizations, the entrepreneurs' experiences related to challenges and tensions arising in such collaborations, and how they navigate those constraints. In addition, follow-up conversations with the founders by Skype or Microsoft teams were performed. All the interviews were (video) recorded with permission from the interviewees and transcribed.

Interviews were supplemented by data collected through ethnography: shadowing the founder of Betz on her trips to Fjord municipality (case 1) and observations during meetings, events and site visits (both cases). Field notes covered anecdotal and chronological data of the entrepreneurs' activities,

Table 7.1 Data collection methods

Method	Case 1	Case 2
Interviews	5 semi-structured interviews (3 with the founder and two with administrative staff) lasting from 60 to 150 minutes	2 semi-structured interviews with two of the founders lasting from 70 to 120 minutes
Shadowing	Ethnography in which a social entrepreneur was shadowed on trips to municipalities, half to full day, fall 2019	
Observations	4 meetings between the founder and representatives of Fjord municipality, half to full day, fall 2019; drawings of the method employed by the social venture	Physical space, size, location, organization; drawings of the method employed by the social venture

information derived during observation and answers to short questions, as well as my ongoing thoughts and reflections. The secondary, archival data included ventures' Facebook homepages and websites.

The transcribed interviews and field notes were analyzed using MAXQDA software. The process was iterative, between cases and relevant literature, as it moved to higher levels of abstraction. The clustering of first-order categories resulted in identification of a number of second-order categories. These second-order categories were then grouped into the overarching practices in use by social entrepreneurs to navigate the public sector setting.

PLAYING AROUND WITH THE 'RULES OF THE GAME'

The Importance of 'System Knowledge'

The analysis of the data suggests that social entrepreneurs are expected to conform to existing rules and meet certain requirements although they may feel resistance to bureaucratic decision-making processes. Respondents from both cases stressed that 'pushing through' social innovations by means of collaboration with municipalities is greatly shaped by bureaucratic rule-following and inflexibility. As one respondent explained:

> I have been in touch with different municipalities to say that we are able to help people with our solution [...] but the answer is 'no' because you cannot choose your help peer.

Respondents also explained that municipalities often are not able to think outside the box in terms of new solutions and collaborative activities, encouraging social entrepreneurs to seek contracts and participate in procurement:

> We have been encouraged to participate in procurement. But we said 'no'. I do not believe in it because this system in the UK does not function and undermines innovation which is so much needed to address social problems [...] I've raised my concerns about it, and it seems like I've been heard.

By drawing on discourses surrounding procurement, the founder of Betz was able to raise awareness among various stakeholders about the dark sides of procurement in terms of enacting social innovations to tackle social problems.

The data suggest that social entrepreneurs' tactical navigation is assisted by their capacity to draw on 'system knowledge', in particular, knowledge of how the public sector is organized and financed, and how it functions. As one respondent highlighted:

> I worked in the public sector and know that municipalities have their regulations to comply with [...] I cannot come to my former colleagues and promote Betz and its activities because they are subject to specific restrictions and conduct of behavior in their positions.

This is further illustrated by a respondent from Nature Magic:

> It is crucial to understand how municipalities are financed and to what extent there is a room and budget for testing innovative solutions.

Indeed, in terms of relationships with municipalities, social entrepreneurs need to fit in with the structural, administrative and cultural patterns in the Norwegian welfare model (Kobro, 2020). For example, social ventures are seen as a *supplement* that can contribute to more social value and innovation in the Norwegian welfare society. One entrepreneur offered an interesting interpretation of this:

> I use the word 'supplement' because it is politically correct and can mean a lot of things. I guess the left-wing and the right-wing put completely different meanings into it. It is a smart word in terms of politics. We do not aim to replace the public health system [...] so in that sense it is definitely a supplement. However, the services we have been delivering are not becoming integrated in the public sector and then we could easily be a replacement.

142 *Rethinking the social in innovation and entrepreneurship studies*

The respondents understood the 'rules of the game' through their prior extensive experience of working or interacting with the public sector and former failures in their collaborative attempts. As the founder recalled:

> We reached out our hosting municipality at a certain point in time ... but right now I understand that we reached it in a wrong way, we were not clever enough to maneuver within municipalities.

Two administrative employees further explained that they met resistance toward their venture from professional personnel responsible for provision of services. The venture was regarded as working in competition to the municipality's own services which can be seen as professional protectionism. Respondents emphasized that this learning process is time-consuming but they consider it essential to gain acceptance and support for their operations in collaboration with public authorities. As one respondent put it:

> It is not like you have a guide book that shows you a right way. It is something completely new and innovation in itself (collaboration).

The data also suggests that social entrepreneurs gained system knowledge by establishing ties developing linkages with key influential organizations, which provide support to social entrepreneurs, and thereby acquired lacking knowledge about existing funding opportunities and potential forms of collaboration. The findings reveal that social entrepreneurs heavily utilize such influential organizations to maneuver within the existing regulatory frameworks. As in the case of Nature Magic, Rock municipality was willing to collaborate with a social venture but the municipality lacked resources to experiment with innovative solutions. However, social entrepreneurs 'made use of the cracks rather than stared at the new walls' (Hjorth, 2004, p. 427) by inviting a social investor company and thereby seizing an opportunity to implement collaboration and integration of new practices in Rock municipality.

As the empirical findings show, social entrepreneurs artfully take advantage of the opportunities stemming from the Norwegian political agenda to initiate collaboration. As the founder of Nature Magic put it:

> It is very important to fit the local political agenda, and our solution, for example, fitted well their political plan to strengthen its preventive services for young people.

Social entrepreneurs proactively use a political agenda to push collaboration forward. For example, Betz, drawing on the need for diversified social services launched by the government, engaged in lobbying for co-creative collaboration of new services based on Betz's successful experience. Hence, the findings underscore the need for social entrepreneurs to demonstrate awareness of

Playing around with the 'rules of the game' 143

system knowledge, local needs and political agendas, and the ways in which they can be addressed and acted on through entrepreneurial practice.

Dynamically Articulating Social Venture's Hybridity

The findings suggest that social entrepreneurs draw on a practice of articulating their venture's hybridity to public stakeholders to enact the context for collaboration. This tactic to 'stand out' from for-profit actors by portraying the entrepreneurs' values and beliefs, often juxtaposed with health profiteers in the Norwegian welfare society, acts as a catalyst for approaching the public sector. As the founder of Betz explained:

> Besides our venture's healthy economy, I have to tell them [municipalities] that this is a solution that has three bottom lines. I point out that this solution brings people employment and we have many years of experience working for this specific group, and that this is very flexible.

For this reason, the founder designed a pictogram to visualize the solution, which is heavily utilized when presenting the organization and solution to external stakeholders. Another respondent from Betz added:

> We tell them [municipalities] that we aim to fill a gap. Because all of them talk about that gap that nobody can fill but we know that we can.

One social change advocated by social ventures often represents deviations from established practices. As a result, it is unlikely that the innovative solutions and processes championed by such ventures will be easily embraced by municipalities embedded in the existing ways of doing things (Renko, 2013). Hence, social entrepreneurs resist skepticism by proactively articulating the 'social' dimension. As one respondent stressed:

> It is the impact and outcome that is a big difference. I have to go through the public sector when it comes to system thinking and explain what quality in services is. Also, I always have to repeat that our employees have been out of the job market due to health reasons.

Furthermore, to articulate the hybridity of their ventures, entrepreneurs sometimes utilize mission statements as an illustration of social mission and proof that profits are reinvested back into the venture. The use of mission statements thus acts as a tactic to convince municipal representatives about the venture's nature. One managerial employee revealed that:

> We've been called health profiteers [...] but I have the answer that we have the mission statement proving that all the income remains in the company for further

development. So it is about selling all the time, not selling services, but selling arguments.

While mission statements play a crucial role in the formulation of ventures' strategy (Berbegal-Mirabent et al., 2019), for social ventures they are an important artifact as they articulate social motives.

The findings echo prior research (Hogenstijn et al., 2018) that the co-existence of the dual mission of financial sustainability and social purpose presents challenges to social ventures as they must advocate a new way of doing things and persuade diverse social actors (Seanor, 2018). The experiences of social entrepreneurs illustrate tactics of acceptance building to differentiate their activities from for-profit companies and to attract municipalities to collaborate. They do this by articulating their venture's hybrid nature, thereby signaling their potential social value attributes, venture viability and member commitment (Jayawarna et al., 2020).

Building Credibility

The findings demonstrate that building credibility is a tactic utilized to gain acceptance and positive perception about the social venture and its mission. This tactic builds on the presentation of a consistent, systematic and moral image to signal their potential social value attributes, venture viability as well as member commitment and competence to deliver a social mission (Jayawarna et al., 2020). As the founder of Betz highlighted:

> I am trying to communicate with pictures and sounds. People who are first negative or skeptical towards the venture or our solution, often change their opinion when they see that picture because our approach is systematic and professional. And I can win their loyalty by doing this.

This 'professional systematic approach' narrative is found to be particularly influential in legitimizing a social venture. The tactic of making their work appealing to municipalities as partners by offering promises to signify the service improvements significantly enhances chances for initiation of collaboration.

It should also be noted that the extent to which social entrepreneurs can build credibility is much shaped by the willingness of municipalities to collaborate, as one respondent explained:

> It does not work if a municipality is forced to engage in collaboration and it is not natural […], the idea should be anchored at all levels of municipality but not pushed top-down.

This reinforces the importance of building credibility on all levels from top political level to the bottom levels of service providers employed in municipalities. In one of the cases, potential collaboration was undermined by a lack of acceptance from the bottom level of a social venture that had succeeded in gaining acceptance and building credibility at top political level.

The above examples show that building credibility with municipalities might potentially lead to diverse forms of collaboration, as in the cases under investigation. As the founder of Betz continued:

> Our story started during the innovation conference. We had a lunch and sat together with two persons from Fjord municipality. They liked what they heard about what we are doing. And this led to certain steps.

In other words, while building credibility can help entrepreneurs to gain acceptance and maintain a positive image, it is of great importance that municipalities embrace a bottom-up approach, have a shared vision and are open to social ventures.

DISCUSSION

This chapter set out to examine how social entrepreneurs navigate the complex public sector terrain to enact the context for collaboration with municipalities and facilitate entrepreneurial venturing. An analysis of the lived experiences of social entrepreneurs advances our understanding of social venture–public sector collaborations by showing that social entrepreneurs remain 'people of agency' (Seanor, 2018) who are able to navigate ambiguous relationships with municipalities. Specifically, this study illustrates that social entrepreneurs draw on various tactics in order to pave the way for potential collaboration although successful navigation in public settings is much influenced by the political forces representing Norwegian municipalities.

The findings resonate with inspiration from de Certeau (1988) and the way he contrasts the logic of 'strategy' with that of 'tactics'. As illustrated by the present study, whether social ventures can gain acceptance and engage in collaboration is shaped by the aspects outside entrepreneurs' reach, such as the dominant position of the Norwegian welfare state, regulatory and financial pressures in the municipal sector, and political forces (European Commission, 2019). As Kobro (2020, p. 8) notes,

> as collaboration between entrepreneurs and bureaucracy/professions takes place across different forms of rationality, the local contexts vary from municipality to municipality, and the Norwegian social policy is spread over many different policy and professional areas, the space for social entrepreneurs to maneuver is therefore fragmented and complicated to understand.

However, the study shows that social entrepreneurs do not take the 'rules of the game' for granted and draw on various tactics to 'constantly manipulate events in order to turn them into opportunities'. In this way, the maneuvering of social entrepreneurs can be seen as a tactical movement towards collaboration in the face of 'rules of the game' and social entrepreneuring appears to be 'an every-day tactic on the public scene' (Steyaert & Katz, 2004, p. 192). This space for playing around with the 'rules of the game' is similar to what Lamine et al. (2021) call 'entrepreneurial space', which is understood as the room for entrepreneuring (Thompson et al., 2020). 'Rules of the game' can determine the scope for social entreprenering and, accordingly, by demarcating a confined space for maneuvering, limit the space for collaboration with public authorities in a Norwegian welfare state.

In relation to the strategically dominant order, the findings illustrate that occasions can be used as opportunities (Hjorth, 2005). For example, the political agenda launched by municipalities can serve as an enabler for social entrepreneurs to engage in different forms of collaboration. As in the case of Betz and Fjord municipality, the political aims of the latter to improve its health and care services by establishing new forms of collaboration were consistent with Betz's vision, and were used by social entrepreneurs as an opportunity for establishing collaboration and playfully experimenting with boundaries between sectors (Hjorth, 2004). In doing so, social entrepreneurs are able to turn such 'cracks' into a resource for social innovation, social change and the venture's growth. The two cases provide good examples of 'openings for change of direction, for playing with the rules differently, for shaping the future in new creative ways' through artful navigation (Berglund & Gaddefors, 2010, p. 142).

This study extends the extant literature by revealing that navigation within the public sector terrain is assisted by the capacity to playfully draw on 'system knowledge' which helps social entrepreneurs shape their offering into one that is likely to be more widely accepted and overcome resistance within the dominated space (Shepherd et al., 2019). Leveraging this 'system knowledge', social entrepreneurs are better positioned to advocate for new solutions and opportunities for collaboration, thus creating bottom-up pressure on the public sector to improve the quality and variety of provided welfare services.

Possessing extensive experience of navigating within the welfare system, social entrepreneurs' own values and beliefs act as an important anchor to guide their attempts to bring about collaboration. Entrepreneurs push forward the viability of alternative, sustainable and systematic approaches to social issues that 'have never been learnt before'. The findings also stress the importance of a mission statement which objectifies and embodies the venture's values. Mission statements as a concrete illustration of a social mission assist social entrepreneurs in recruiting new allies that are aligned and compliant with their solutions. These findings are in line with other studies (e.g. Mersland et al., 2019) which show that advantages of using mission statements go beyond the issue of mission identification and mission statements of social ventures are critical for legitimacy and accountability purposes.

Consistent with prior work, building credibility is an important tactic for changing perceptions and introducing new solutions. In navigating the complex public sector terrain, social entrepreneurs employ different tactics to build a trusted basis for potential collaboration. Building credibility is therefore a tactic that builds on the presentation of a consistent, equal and moral image to signal commitment and competence to deliver a social mission (Jayawarna et al., 2020).

CONCLUSION

This chapter has provided an account of how social entrepreneurs employ different practices to navigate the public sector terrain in order to enact the context for collaboration with municipalities and facilitate entrepreneurial venturing. The focus on one particular context – the Norwegian welfare state – made it possible to contextualize the study to better understand ongoing processes.

The study presented here complements and further develops insights coming from the field of social entrepreneurship. First, this study contributes to social entrepreneurship research by shedding light on practices in use by social entrepreneurs when engaging with municipalities to enact the context for collaboration (Barinaga, 2017; Seanor, 2018) that enhance the capacity to navigate the constraints (Shepherd et al., 2019). Second, building on de Certeau's (1988) practice theory, the study extends the notions of 'strategy' and 'tactics' to the context of social venture–public sector collaboration and provides a better understanding of how social entrepreneurs draw on practices to engage in collaboration and accomplish entrepreneurial work at the micro level. Third, this study also advances scholarly work on 'entrepreneurship in context' by demonstrating how social entrepreneurs navigate the public welfare setting in a context with a well-developed welfare system and seek out new opportunities for collaboration with welfare providers.

There are, of course, limitations to my approach. I acknowledge the limitations of relying on two, albeit in-depth, case studies and purposive sampling for analytical generalizibility. While it is likely that the findings discussed will reflect the experiences of other social entrepreneurs, more research in other contexts is needed. Furthermore, it is noteworthy that initiating collaboration may require different tactics than sustaining it.

REFERENCES

Anderson, A. R., Dodd, S. D., & Jack, S. (2010). Network practices and entrepreneurial growth. *Scandinavian Journal of Management*, *26*(2), 121–33. https://doi.org/https://doi.org/10.1016/j.scaman.2010.01.005.

Barinaga, E. (2017). Tinkering with space: the organizational practices of a nascent social venture. *Organization Studies*, *38*(7), 937–58. https://doi.org/10.1177/0170840616670434.

Barinaga, E. (2020). Coopted! Mission drift in a social venture engaged in a cross-sectoral partnership. *VOLUNTAS: International Journal of Voluntary and Nonprofit Organizations*, *31*(2), 437–49. https://doi.org/10.1007/s11266-018-0019-6.

Bendixsen, S. (2018). The politicised biology of irregular migrants: micropractices of control, tactics of everyday life and access to healthcare. *Nordic Journal of Migration Research*, *8*(3), 167–74. http://doi.org/10.2478/njmr-2018-0020.

Berbegal-Mirabent, J., Mas-Machuca, M., & Guix, P. (2019). Impact of mission statement components on social enterprises' performance. *Review of Managerial Science*. https://www.semanticscholar.org/paper/Impact-of-mission-statement-components-on-social-Berbegal%E2%80%90Mirabent-Mas-Machuca/5371e438b9055f0c77f1 1ca156f28a94931eedce.

Berglund, K., & Gaddefors, J. (2010). Entrepreneurship requires resistance to be mobilized. In *(De)Mobilizing the Entrepreneurship Discourse: Exploring Entrepreneurial Thinking and Action*. Cheltenham, UK and Northampton, MA, USA: Edward Elgar Publishing. https://doi.org/10.4337/9781849806459.00016.

Berglund, K., Johannisson, B. & Schwartz, B. (Eds.) (2012). *Societal Entrepreneurship: Positioning, Penetrating, Promoting*. Cheltenham, UK and Northampton, MA, USA: Edward Elgar Publishing. https://doi.org/10.4337/9781781006337.

Borzaga, C., Fazzi, L., & Galera, G. (2016). Social enterprise as a bottom-up dynamic: part 1. The reaction of civil society to unmet social needs in Italy, Sweden and Japan. *International Review of Sociology*, *26*(1), 1–18. https://doi.org/10.1080/03906701.2016.1148332.

de Bruin, A., Lewis, K. V., & Shaw, E. (2016). The collaborative dynamic in social entrepreneurship: Special Issue Editors. *Entrepreneurship & Regional Development*, *28*(3–4), 310–11. https://doi.org/10.1080/08985626.2016.1140429.

de Certeau, M. (1988). *The Practice of Everyday Life*. Berkeley, CA: University of California Press.

De Clercq, D., & Voronov, M. (2009). Toward a practice perspective of entrepreneurship: entrepreneurial legitimacy as habitus. *International Small Business Journal*, *27*(4), 395–419. https://doi.org/10.1177/0266242609334971.

Dey, P., & Teasdale, S. (2016). The tactical mimicry of social enterprise strategies: acting 'as if' in the everyday life of third sector organizations. *Organization*, *23*(4), 485–504. https://doi.org/10.1177/1350508415570689.

Di Domenico, M., Haugh, H., & Tracey, H. (2010). Social bricolage: theorizing social value creation in social enterprises. *Entrepreneurship: Theory & Practice*, *34*(4), 681–703.

Drencheva, A., McMullen, J. S., Drencheva, A., Folmer, E. C., Renko, M., Tunezerwe, S., Williams, T. A., Burke, G. T., Caldwell, K., Kozlinska, I., Parker Harris, S., Shepherd, D., & Stephan, U. (2018). Social change and social ventures: emerging developments in social entrepreneurship. *Academy of Management Proceedings.* https://doi.org/10.5465/AMBPP.2018.11562symposium.

European Commission (2019). Social enterprises and their ecosystems in Europe. Country fiche: Norway. Author: Lars U. Kobro. Luxembourg: Publications Office of the European Union. http://ec.europa.eu/social/main.jsp?advSearchKey= socenterfiches&mode=advancedSubmit&catId=22.

Günzel-Jensen, F., Siebold, N., Kroeger, A., & Korsgaard, S. (2020). Do the United Nations' Sustainable Development Goals matter for social entrepreneurial ventures? A bottom-up perspective. *Journal of Business Venturing Insights, 13,* e00162. https://doi.org/10.1016/j.jbvi.2020.e00162.

Hauge, H. (2017). Social enterprise in Norway – caught between collaboration and co-optation? Peer Review on "Fostering social entrepreneurship to tackle unmet social challenges", Host Country Discussion Paper, Norway, European Commission. Brussels: European Commission. https://ec.europa.eu/social/BlobServlet?docId= 18812&langId=en.

Hjorth, D. (2004). Creating space for play/invention – concepts of space and organizational entrepreneurship. *Entrepreneurship & Regional Development, 16*(5), 413–32. https://doi.org/10.1080/0898562042000197144.

Hjorth, D. (2005). Organizational entrepreneurship: with de Certeau on creating heterotopias (or spaces for play). *Journal of Management Inquiry, 14*(4), 386–98. https://doi.org/10.1177/1056492605280225.

Hogenstijn, M., Meerman, M., & Zinsmeister, J. (2018). Developing stereotypes to facilitate dialogue between social entrepreneurs and local government. *Journal of Innovation and Entrepreneurship, 7*(1), 3. https://doi.org/10.1186/s13731-018-0084 -5.

Hydle, K. M. & Billington, M. G. (2020). Entrepreneurial practices of collaboration comprising constellations. *International Journal of Entrepreneurial Behavior & Research.* https://doi.org/10.1108/IJEBR-10-2018-0646.

Jayawarna, D., Jones, O., & Macpherson, A. (2020). Resourcing social enterprises: the role of socially oriented bootstrapping. *British Journal of Management, 31*(1), 56–79. https://doi.org/10.1111/1467-8551.12334.

Johannisson, B. (2011). Towards a practice theory of entrepreneuring. *Small Business Economics, 36*(2), 135–50. https://doi.org/10.1007/s11187-009-9212-8.

Kibler, E., Salmivaara, V., Stenholm, P., & Terjesen, S. (2018). The evaluative legitimacy of social entrepreneurship in capitalist welfare systems. *Journal of World Business, 53*(6), 944–57. https://doi.org/10.1016/j.jwb.2018.08.002.

Kobro, L. U. (2020). *Sosialt entreprenørskap – Økt synlighet og større handlingsrom.* https://openarchive.usn.no/usn-xmlui/bitstream/handle/11250/2633885/2019_37 _Kobro.pdf?sequence=3&isAllowed=y.

Korsgaard, S., & Anderson, A. R. (2011). Enacting entrepreneurship as social value creation. *International Small Business Journal, 29*(2), 135–51. https://doi.org/10 .1177/0266242610391936.

Lamine, W., Anderson, A., Jack, S. L, & Fayolle, A. (2021). Entrepreneurial space and the freedom for entrepreneurship: institutional settings, policy, and action in the space industry. *Strategic Entrepreneurship Journal.* https://doi.org/10.1002/sej .1392.

Mair, J. (2020). Social entrepreneurship: research as disciplined exploration. In W. Powell & P. Bromley (Eds.), *The Nonprofit Sector* (pp. 333–57). Redwood City: Stanford University Press. https://doi.org/10.1515/9781503611085-020.

Mersland, R., Nyarko, S. A., & Szafarz, A. (2019). Do social enterprises walk the talk? Assessing microfinance performances with mission statements. *Journal of Business Venturing Insights*, *11*, e00117. https://doi.org/10.1016/j.jbvi.2019.e00117.

Muñoz, P., & Dimov, D. (2015). The call of the whole in understanding the development of sustainable ventures. *Journal of Business Venturing*, *30*(4), 632–54. https://doi.org/10.1016/j.jbusvent.2014.07.012.

Muñoz, P., & Kimmitt, J. (2019). Social mission as competitive advantage: a configurational analysis of the strategic conditions of social entrepreneurship. *Journal of Business Research*, *101*, 854–61. https://doi.org/https://doi.org/10.1016/j.jbusres.2018.11.044.

Norges forskningsråd (2018). Forskningsrådets strategi for innovasjon i offentlig sektor. https://www.forskningsradet.no/no/Arrangement/Lansering_av_ny_strategi_for_innovasjon_i_offentlig_sektor/1254032063210.

Pestoff, V., Brandsen, T., & Verschuere, B. (Eds.) (2011). *New Public Governance, the Third Sector, and Co-Production* (1st edn.). Abingdon: Routledge. https://doi.org/10.4324/9780203152294.

Pret, T., & Carter, S. (2017). The importance of 'fitting in': collaboration and social value creation in response to community norms and expectations. *Entrepreneurship & Regional Development*, *29*(7–8), 639–67. https://doi.org/10.1080/08985626.2017.1328903.

Ramirez-Pasillas, M., Lundberg, H., & Nordqvist, M. (2020). Next generation external venturing practices in family owned businesses. *Journal of Management Studies*. Epub ahead of print. https://doi.org/10.1111/joms.12566.

Renko, M. (2013). Early challenges of nascent social entrepreneurs. *Entrepreneurship Theory & Practice*, *37*(5), 1045–69. https://doi.org/10.1111/j.1540-6520.2012.00522.x.

Ruebottom, T. (2013). The microstructures of rhetorical strategy in social entrepreneurship: building legitimacy through heroes and villains. *Journal of Business Venturing*, *28*(1), 98–116.

Saebi, T., Foss, N. J., & Linder, S. (2018). Social entrepreneurship research: past achievements and future promises. *Journal of Management*, *45*(1), 70–95. https://doi.org/10.1177/0149206318793196.

Salomons, T. (2020). Collaboration between social entrepreneurs and local governments: a causation and effectuation view [Master's thesis, University of Twente]. BMS: Behavioural, Management and Social Sciences. http://purl.utwente.nl/essays/82781.

Schaltegger, S., Beckmann, M., & Hockerts, K. (2018). Collaborative entrepreneurship for sustainability: creating solutions in light of the UN Sustainable Development Goals. *International Journal of Entrepreneurial Venturing*, *10*(2), 131–52. https://doi.org/10.1504/IJEV.2018.092709.

Seanor, P. (2018). Of course, trust is not the whole story: narratives of dancing with a critical friend in social enterprise–public sector collaborations. In P. Dey & C. Steyaert (Eds.), *Social Entrepreneurship* (pp. 159–81). Cheltenham, UK, and Northampton, MA, USA: Edward Elgar Publishing. https://doi.org/10.4337/9781783474127.00019.

Shepherd, D. A., Wennberg, K., Suddaby, R., & Wiklund, J. (2019). What are we explaining? A review and agenda on initiating, engaging, performing, and contextualizing entrepreneurship. *Journal of Management*, *45*(1), 159–96. https://doi.org/10.1177/0149206318799443.

Silverman, D. (2005). *Doing Qualitative Research: A Practical Handbook*. Los Angeles, CA: Sage.

Stake, R. E. (2005). Qualitative case studies. In N. K. Denzin & Y. S. Lincoln (Eds.), *The Sage Handbook of Qualitative Research* (pp. 443–66). New York: Sage.

Stephan, U., Patterson, M., Kelly, C., & Mair, J. (2016). Organizations driving positive social change: a review and an integrative framework of change processes. *Journal of Management*, *42*(5), 1250–81. https://doi.org/10.1177/0149206316633268.

Steyaert, C. (2007). 'Entrepreneuring' as a conceptual attractor? A review of process theories in 20 years of entrepreneurship studies. *Entrepreneurship & Regional Development*, *19*(6), 453–77. https://doi.org/10.1080/08985620701671759.

Steyaert, C., & Katz, J. (2004). Reclaiming the space of entrepreneurship in society: geographical, discursive and social dimensions. *Entrepreneurship & Regional Development*, *16*(3), 179–96. https://doi.org/10.1080/0898562042000197135.

Sunduramurthy, C., Zheng, C., Musteen, M., Francis, J., & Rhyne, L. (2016). Doing more with less, systematically? Bricolage and ingenieuring in successful social ventures. *Journal of World Business*, *51*(5), 855–70. https://doi.org/10.1016/j.jwb.2016.06.005.

Thompson, N. A., Verduijn, K., & Gartner, W. B. (2020). Entrepreneurship-as-practice: grounding contemporary theories of practice into entrepreneurship studies. *Entrepreneurship & Regional Development*, *32*(3–4), 247–56. https://doi.org/10.1080/08985626.2019.1641978.

Thornton, P. H. (1999). The sociology of entrepreneurship. *Annual Review of Sociology*, *25*(1), 19–46. https://doi.org/10.1146/annurev.soc.25.1.19.

Trætteberg, H. S., & Fladmoe, A. (2020). Quality differences of public, for-profit and nonprofit providers in Scandinavian welfare? User satisfaction in kindergartens. *VOLUNTAS: International Journal of Voluntary and Nonprofit Organizations*, *31*(1), 153–67. https://doi.org/10.1007/s11266-019-00169-6.

Vannebo, B., & Grande, J. (2018). Social entrepreneurship and embedded ties – a comparative case study of social entrepreneurship in Norway. *International Journal of Entrepreneurship and Small Business*, *33*(3), 417–48. https://doi.org/10.1504/IJESB.2018.090226.

Vestrum, I., Rasmussen, E., & Carter, S. (2016). How nascent community enterprises build legitimacy in internal and external environments. *Regional Studies*, *51*(11), 1721–34. https://doi.org/10.1080/00343404.2016.1220675.

Watson, T. J. (2013a). Entrepreneurial action and the Euro-American social science tradition: pragmatism, realism and looking beyond 'the entrepreneur'. *Entrepreneurship & Regional Development*, *25*(1–2), 16–33. https://doi.org/10.1080/08985626.2012.754267.

Watson, T. J. (2013b). Entrepreneurship in action: bringing together the individual, organizational and institutional dimensions of entrepreneurial action. *Entrepreneurship & Regional Development*, 25(5–6), 404–22. https://doi.org/10.1080/08985626.2012.754645.

Welter, F., & Baker, T. (2020). Moving contexts onto new roads: clues from other disciplines. *Entrepreneurship Theory & Practice*. https://doi.org/10.1177/1042258720930996.

8. Integrating responsible research and innovation into smart specialization: a question-machine approach

Nhien Nguyen, Jens Ørding Hansen, Are Jensen and Carlos Álvarez Pereira

1. INTRODUCTION

Innovation is a double-edged sword. We may hope that it holds the key to fending off looming and actual calamities, such as climate change, pandemics, loss of biodiversity, accelerating inequality, and the exhaustion of non-renewable resources. We may be equally justified in fearing that it will exacerbate some or all of these. The rapid growth in the disruptive power of technology is matched by an equivalent increase in the urgency with which we must encourage and incentivize innovators to innovate *responsibly*.

Responsible research and innovation (RRI) has attracted increasing interest from academics since the early 2010s (Blok & Lemmens, 2015; Burget et al., 2017; Owen et al., 2012; Schomberg, 2013; Stilgoe et al., 2013). However, since the concept lends itself to a plethora of interpretations and the sparse literature covers enormous ground, virtually every aspect of RRI remains under-researched. For example, the important practical question of how responsible innovation can be stimulated in a systematic fashion through government policy has received little scholarly attention except in specific, narrowly defined contexts (e.g. nanotechnology, robotics, agriculture) and with regard to specific sub-aspects of RRI (e.g. ethical challenges posed by a particular technology).

The point of departure for the present chapter is a lofty vision, promulgated by European policymakers, of establishing self-sustaining regional innovation ecosystems characterized by responsible research and innovation. The vision gave rise to the Horizon 2020 project SeeRRI (see Section 3), which generated the empirical data underpinning this chapter. By combining an examination of existing literature with the analysis of original empirical data from regional innovation planning processes in selected European regions, we seek to answer the research question, *"How can regions apply RRI thinking in the process of developing regional innovation strategies?"*

The remainder of the chapter proceeds as follows. Section 2 introduces the concepts of smart specialization and responsible research and innovation, respectively, and reviews previous attempts in the literature to integrate the two. Section 3 addresses the methodology and assumptions underlying our question-machine approach. The approach itself is presented in Section 4. For illustration, Section 5 describes a case study of how a regional government in Norway attempted to integrate RRI principles into its smart specialization policy by taking steps like those outlined in our suggested approach. Section 6 concludes the chapter.

2.   THEORETICAL BACKGROUND

The approach we will outline is simultaneously practical and abstract. It is practical because we aim to provide useful recommendations for policymakers in charge of regional innovation policy. It is abstract because we adopt a definition of RRI that transcends specific policy agendas and because we deliberately aim to provide "higher-order" recommendations – that is, to advise policymakers on how they can discover for themselves how best to implement RRI, in a manner tailored to their specific context, as opposed to supplying a one-size-fits-all blueprint.

To achieve this, we adopt a holistic perspective on the task of policymakers, practitioners and stakeholders engaged in developing research and innovation (R&I) activities in specific regional contexts. The task of these actors may look daunting since they are faced with multiple demands at the same time. They must identify the best ways to promote R&I processes in their regional context, consistent with smart specialization guidelines; ensure that regional R&I ecosystems are self-sustaining and contribute to regional development; promote RRI in all its dimensions; and ensure that R&I activities effectively address the societal challenges of our times, regionally as well as globally, as expressed through the Sustainable Development Goals (SDGs) defined by the United Nations.

This multiplicity of demands calls for the development of a new approach that goes beyond the existing framing while integrating some of its most valuable aspects. At the conceptual level, advanced knowledge within systems thinking and complexity theory has been a source of inspiration for the development of our question-machine approach (Álvarez Pereira, 2020). We proceed from the assumption that the challenges of governing research and innovation activities in the twenty-first century are so complex and unpredictable that one would be ill-advised to try to translate RRI into a set of hard and fast rules. Indeed, the concept of RRI owes its very emergence to the realization that rule compliance alone is not a sufficient mechanism to keep the potential hazards of technological innovation in check in the modern world (Stilgoe et al., 2013). What one may attempt instead is to rise above policy specifics and consider how to infuse policymaking *processes* with a dose of RRI, which will then hopefully trickle down and leave its benevolent marks throughout the research and innovation ecosystem. The approach we shall present is of this sort. Before describing the approach, we will provide the reader with brief introductions to the concepts of smart specialization and RRI and examine previous attempts at integrating the two.

2.1 Research and Innovation Strategy for Smart Specialization (RIS3)

Smart specialization is a relatively novel approach to regional development policy, conceived around 2009 by an expert group of economists appointed by the European Commission (Foray, 2014). The term "smart specialization" is used more or less interchangeably with what is known in the official parlance of the European Union as "Research and Innovation Strategies for Smart Specialization", or "RIS3". Smart specialization policies are made at the regional level under the auspices of a regional government. Although the concept is barely a decade old, RIS3 is being widely promoted and implemented in the European Union, helped along by financial support from the EU and national governments.[1] While the theoretical foundations of RIS3 are still under development, the approach draws on ideas familiar from economics (Foray, 2014).

The impetus behind the ongoing smart specialization experiment in Europe is a desire to increase the regional diversity of research and development (R&D) investments within the EU (Foray, 2014; Simonen et al., 2015). Proponents of RIS3 argue that a policy of encouraging greater diversity in regional R&D will mitigate the problem of excess R&D duplication in Europe while simultaneously lifting regional development by enabling regions to carve out niches where they can be competitive based on inherent strengths. Smart specialization is a tool for strengthening economic growth at both the regional and the EU level (Foray, 2014, 2018) as well as a building block of a reformed EU cohesion policy (McCann & Ortega-Argiles, 2015, 2016). A growing body of research on smart specialization is leading to refinements in the theoretical and empirical basis of the approach (Ferreira et al., 2021; Lopes et al., 2019) and is helping to shed light on the challenges and opportunities associated with its implementation (Magro & Wilson, 2019; Morgan, 2015; Sorvik et al., 2019).

A "textbook" smart specialization policy in a region has a number of characteristic features (Foray, 2018). First, the policy promotes innovation activities that utilize and enhance the regions' unique strengths and advantages while discouraging blind imitation of other regions' choices. Second, the policy is based on deliberate decisions about which activities to support within the regional economy; it is not, therefore, a "horizontal" (sector-neutral) policy.[2] Third, the aim of the policy is to promote "transformative activities" in the region rather than to support specific sectors as such. For example, the policy might aim to foster linkages among key innovation actors from different sectors. Fourth, the policy is experimental rather than static, and characterized by a strong responsiveness to "entrepreneurial discoveries" by local innovation actors. Some of these actors might be entrepreneurs in the classical sense of the term, but the set of innovation actors comprises all actors involved in the innovation ecosystem and thus could also include established firms, universities, government organizations, and so on.

Because entrepreneurial discovery is a key concept in RIS3 (Foray, 2014; Grillitsch, 2016; Szerb et al., 2020), and since entrepreneurial discoveries may originate from a diverse range of actors unaffiliated with government planners (Estensoro & Larrea, 2016), it would be incorrect to consider RIS3 a purely top-down approach to innovation policy (Nguyen et al., 2020). While RIS3 includes a strong element of government direction, it also acknowledges that innovation is a venture into the unknown and not something for bureaucrats to plan out in isolation (Foray, 2018).

The successful implementation of RIS3 requires considerable effort and sophistication on the part of a regional government. If a region lacks the governance capacity to establish effective processes for identifying and promoting transformative innovation activities, it might be better served by adopting simpler, more horizontal policies (Foray, 2018).

In practical terms, smart specialization in the European Union involves the six activities shown in Figure 8.1. The figure captures the dynamic nature of RIS3 by depicting it as a never-ending cyclical process. *Governance* refers to the establishment and operation of an administrative framework for the entire smart specialization process. Since governance activities take place continuously, in parallel to the other steps of the process, governance is placed outside of the chain of activities in Figure 8.1. *Analysis* refers to collecting information about the regional strengths and weaknesses and other data relevant to developing a smart specialization policy for the region. *Vision* refers to working with regional stakeholders to define a shared vision for the future of the region. *Prioritization* refers to pinpointing specific priority areas (e.g. of a sectoral or technological nature) for the smart specialization strategy to support. *Policy mix* refers to formulating and implementing an action plan for supporting the selected priority areas. Finally, *monitoring and evaluation* refers to watching the progress of the RIS3 implementation with a view to adapting the strategy as the regional context changes.[3]

Figure 8.1   The RIS3 process in action

2.2   Responsible Research and Innovation (RRI)

Responsible research and innovation (RRI) refers to research and innovation activities that are aligned with the values and needs of society. For the last decade, the concept has been evolving along two parallel tracks, one political and one academic (Burget et al., 2017). Politically, the European Union has been the driving force in an ongoing quest to define RRI and promote its practical implementation in Europe and beyond (Schomberg, 2011; Sutcliffe, 2011). Inspired by – and in turn inspiring – this movement, academics have turned various theoretical lenses to the notion of responsibility in innovation, seeking to clarify its meaning and implications (Burget et al., 2017; Lubberink et al., 2018; Ribeiro et al., 2017). Scholars tend to use the terms "responsible innovation" (RI) and "responsible research and innovation" (RRI) interchangeably (Schomberg, 2013; Stilgoe & Guston, 2016). There is considerable overlap between the concept of RRI as championed by the European Commission and the concepts of RI and RRI as used in academia, but there are also salient differences. In particular, whereas the EU has been emphasizing specific policy agendas such as gender equality or science education, academic research has tended to focus on more abstract dimensions of RRI.

The justification for coining a special responsibility concept for innovation, distinct from more general notions of responsibility, lies in the observation that technological innovations are becoming ever more powerful and the scope of their impact ever less predictable. Research and innovation cannot be governed solely by rules because rules are formed in response to the past, not the future (Owen et al., 2012, 2013). Responsibility in innovation requires governance mechanisms that go beyond simple regulation. The literature on RRI explores what these mechanisms might be.

In arguably the most influential conceptualization of RRI in the literature, responsible conduct in research and innovation is broken down into four dimensions: anticipation, reflexivity, inclusiveness and responsiveness (Stilgoe et al., 2013). We will adopt the same view of RRI for the purposes of the present chapter. *Anticipation* refers to systematically considering possible future harmful consequences of research and innovation activities. *Reflexivity* denotes the practice of continuously scrutinizing one's own activities, assumptions, commitments, knowledge and values in order to equip oneself to make responsible decisions in the future. *Inclusiveness* means being open to the views of external stakeholders, including the general public, when making decisions related to the future direction of research and innovation. *Responsiveness* involves taking action to adjust the trajectory of research and innovation activities in response to new knowledge, perspectives and norms (Hansen et al., 2020).

2.3   Integration of RRI and RIS3

The challenge of integrating RRI principles into smart specialization policy is an intriguing one. At least one framework for the integration of RRI and RIS3 has previously been proposed in the literature. Fitjar et al. (2019) analyze the RIS3 policy process with a view to identifying contradictions and complementarities of RIS3 and RRI. The authors define RRI through the four dimensions of anticipation, reflexivity, inclusiveness, and responsiveness. The general conclusion of Fitjar et al. is that RIS3 and RRI are complementary policy frameworks, each addressing weaknesses of the other. For example, RIS3 focuses attention on geography and regional differences – aspects mostly ignored by RRI – while RRI addresses non-economic social interests that are not explicitly considered in RIS3. Moreover, the underlying philosophies of RIS3 and RRI have evident similarities. Both concepts reject top-down approaches to innovation policy in favor of more flexible and inclusive approaches involving interaction with stakeholders. In theory this should facilitate their joint adoption as it allows some of the stakeholder communication efforts required under each of the two policies to be combined into a single process.

On the other hand, the ultimate objectives of RIS3 and RRI are quite different. The former focuses on economic development and growth, the latter on responsible conduct. It is easy to think of scenarios where economic interests clash with other societal concerns, leading to trade-offs in the implementation of the two policies. In a related argument, Fitjar et al. (2019) identify a tension between the two policy frameworks in that the wide stakeholder inclusion prescribed by RRI may thwart the entrepreneurialism at the heart of RIS3. RIS3, like RRI, stresses the need for policymakers to engage with stakeholders, but in RIS3 this is merely a means to an end. In RRI it is a moral imperative; the philosophy of RRI requires not only that innovation policymakers stay in touch with stakeholders but also that they take their opinions seriously and make an effort to strike a balance in catering to their diverse interests. An innovation system that stresses stakeholder consensus is not likely to promote innovation opportunities that will benefit some stakeholders more than others.

Fitjar and his colleagues (2019) provide a useful set of suggestions for how to incorporate each dimension of RRI at each stage of the smart specialization process. The approach we will present in this chapter complements that of Fitjar et al. and highlights how RRI-related processes can be combined with the RIS3 policymaking process and make use of some of its infrastructure, especially with regard to stakeholder engagement. Our approach operates at a high level of generality, compensating for its lack of detail with flexibility: it can be applied in changing environments and requires little in the way of prior commitment to any aspect of innovation policy other than the aspiration to implement RIS3 and RRI. Another difference between our approach and that of Fitjar et al. is that while the latter is purely conceptual, our approach is inspired and supported by empirical data and observations from European regions.

3. FOUNDATIONS FOR THE QUESTION-MACHINE APPROACH

Our objective is to create a consistent and actionable approach to promoting and implementing RRI in a step-by-step manner within the context of the continuously evolving smart specialization policymaking process. In working out the specifics of the approach, we have applied the idea that the process of creating an approach for RRI is in itself an RRI activity and should adhere to RRI principles. If we were to champion an approach for implementing RRI principles while insisting that the process of creating said approach was exempt from the principles of RRI, we would be guilty of hypocrisy and the approach would lack legitimacy. Thus, when designing the approach, we have made it a priority to solicit opinions from relevant stakeholders accessible to us, which in practice means representatives from the pilot territories of the SeeRRI project (see Section 3.1).

3.1 The SeeRRI Project

Our approach is inspired not only by theory but also by empirical observations made while working with stakeholders in European territories on integrating RRI into local smart specialization policies. This work has taken place in the context of the ongoing project *Building Self-Sustaining Research and Innovation Ecosystems in Europe through Responsible Research and Innovation* (SeeRRI), funded by the European Union's Horizon 2020 research program.[4] The project, which runs from January 2019 until October 2021, involves three pilot territories: Nordland (Norway), Lower Austria (Austria), and the B30 industrial area in Catalonia (Spain). Each of the regions had already been carrying out smart specialization activities before joining the SeeRRI project, hence SeeRRI does not focus on formulating smart specialization policy from scratch but on the integration of RRI dimensions into the policy. One of the core activities in the SeeRRI project is a set of stakeholder foresight workshops carried out in each of the three regions. Experiences from the workshops, and from the entire process of working with regional stakeholders to formulate innovation policy, have served as valuable inputs in the development of the approach described in Section 4. Section 5 elaborates in some detail the experiences of SeeRRI in Nordland County, Norway.

3.2 Conceptual Grounding of the Approach

Our approach is underpinned by a set of basic assumptions, summed up in Table 8.1, about the nature of R&I and RRI in modern societies characterized by digitalization and interconnectedness. While the assumptions are drawn substantially from literature on systems thinking and complexity theory (for more details, refer to Álvarez Pereira, 2020), they are also inspired by our experiences in the SeeRRI project, including our conversations with regional policymakers and stakeholders. Assumptions 1–4 listed in the table concern R&I in general without particular emphasis on the responsibility dimension; assumptions 5–7 address RRI directly.

Assumption nos. 1, 2, 3 and 7 follow from our basic tenet, mentioned in Section 2, that R&I ecosystems are highly complex and can profitably be viewed by policymakers through the lens of systems thinking and complexity theory (Álvarez Pereira, 2020). Complex systems do not evolve linearly along a planned roadmap (Anderson, 1999; Byrne & Callaghan, 2013; Manson,

Table 8.1   Summary of assumptions underlying the approach

#	Assumption	Explanation
1	Process philosophy	Focus should be on dynamic processes, not static structures, of R&I
2	Ecosystems	R&I actors should be considered as an integrated system, not in isolation
3	Interdependencies	Focus should be on the interdependencies that bind R&I actors together
4	Communities	Focus should be on local communities (globalization notwithstanding)
5	Wellbeing in biosphere	RRI embodies the aspirations of humankind and defies simple codification
6	Transformations	RRI is transformational; as such, it will inevitably encounter obstacles
7	Mutual learning	RRI is not a planning exercise but an endless process of mutual learning

2001). This entails that we need to abandon any idea of being able to exercise complete central control over the system, like puppet masters, in favor of the more modest notion that actors in the system may hope to seize fleeting opportunities generated in an unpredictable fashion by the complex web of interactivity that composes the system.

Assumption no. 4 may seem obvious since our aim is to build an approach applicable at the sub-national level; clearly we are not studying national, let alone global, innovation structures. Nevertheless, we list this assumption because the importance of local communities and the bonds of culture, language and relationships that hold them together have been brought out by our experience working with stakeholders in the SeeRRI project, and because it is an interesting paradox that despite the steady advance of globalization, the importance of local ties barely seems to have diminished.

Assumption no. 5 relates RRI to the aspiration of the UN Agenda 2030[5] – a vision captured by the phrase, "Equitable human wellbeing within a healthy biosphere". This motto avoids the risks of siloed action in response to only one or a few aspects of the Agenda 2030, which comprises a total of 17 SDGs and more than 200 different indicators.

Assumption no. 6 might also seem obvious – practicing RRI can be costly and may clash with someone's immediate self-interest, hence the imposition of RRI principles is bound to meet resistance – but we include it because our experience of working with even well-intentioned stakeholders in formulating RRI policies has underlined the need for a strong commitment to dialogue with stakeholders, and because it presents an interesting parallel to RIS3, which also focuses on activities of a transformative nature (Schot & Steinmueller, 2018).

4. A QUESTION-MACHINE APPROACH TO INTEGRATING RRI INTO RIS3 POLICY

The practical objective of our approach is to assist policymakers in their search for a viable regional development policy integrating RIS3 and RRI. For reasons discussed above, there can be no simple top-down policy that is universally valid for this purpose. Consequently, our focus is not so much on providing answers as on helping policymakers ask the right questions. Our approach is, essentially, a question machine. The idea is to bring key stakeholders together on a regular basis and engage them in dialogue guided by questions suggested by our approach; the outcomes of the discussions then form the basis for policy. This approach is consistent with the notion that models of complex systems should be open-ended and allow for the expansion of knowledge through processes of mutual learning (Hoffman & McInnis, 2015). Our questions are of a generic nature and need not be used verbatim in stakeholder discussions. On the contrary, they are intended to serve as a starting point for articulating a range of questions specific to the local context. Our generic questions constitute a "question machine" in the sense that they can inspire infinitely many region-specific questions.

Structurally, our approach follows the steps of the RIS3 process described in Section 2.1. The core activity is stakeholder engagement, which is the mechanism for participative governance in RIS3. Stakeholder engagement provides many benefits for research and innovation activities that may lead to a positive impact on society (Hörlesberger et al., 2020, 2021). For example, stakeholder participation leads to stronger and more durable decisions in regional innovation contexts since it increases access to resources and information, improves links and partnerships in regional networks, facilitates learning through sharing of experiences, and creates better communication, awareness, trust and support in the regions.

Practically, we propose that the stakeholder engagement activities should revolve around foresight workshops, conducted either in a physical space or online. Stakeholder engagement activities involving foresight methodology are a means of participative governance that can enable sustainable solutions to grand challenges (Cagnin et al., 2015). Foresight workshops are an important mechanism of our approach because they represent RRI in action. By definition, foresight involves *anticipation*; the involvement of a diverse range of stakeholders in the workshops guarantees *inclusion*; the workshop discussions touching on environmental and social issues embody *reflexivity*; and regular follow-up processes ensure *responsiveness*.

Using stakeholder foresight workshops as a mechanism for participative governance, our approach prescribes three rounds of stakeholder engagement

162   *Rethinking the social in innovation and entrepreneurship studies*

activities, corresponding to step no. 1 (analysis), nos. 2–3 (vision, prioritization), and nos. 4–5 (policy mix, monitoring) of the RIS3 process, respectively. Tables 8.2–8.4 list our proposed generic questions for guiding the dialogue at each round of stakeholder consultation.

4.1   Key Questions for the *Analysis* Stage

Table 8.2 covers the first stage of the RIS3 process, "Analysis". This stage provides a good illustration of how RRI and RIS3 activities are closely related and may conveniently be carried out together, even though they have different goals. The analysis stage of the RIS3 process includes the activity of identifying key regional actors engaged in potentially valuable entrepreneurial discovery processes (EDP). RRI also requires identifying key regional actors to consult on innovation strategy, but for a different purpose: to ensure that a broad range of stakeholders have a say in policymaking.

In the SeeRRI project, after some trial and error, we found that selecting an RRI-related "challenge" or thematic focus for the invited stakeholders to discuss at this stage helped reduce the complexity of the RRI–RIS3 process and create a shared sense of purpose among participants. The thematic focus may be chosen initially by the policymakers who will oversee the process of integrating RRI into RIS3 before other stakeholders are invited to participate in the process. Letting policymakers decide the thematic focus without external stakeholder involvement constitutes a compromise between the ideals of RRI and the realities of organizing complex co-creation processes. The thematic focus should address a grand societal challenge relevant to the region but should also be relevant to the region's smart specialization policy. In the case of Nordland, policymakers chose "responsible coastal management" as the core regional challenge – a challenge closely related to the existing RIS3 priority areas of the region, which were experience-based tourism, seafood, and mineral and chemical processing industries.

Under ideal circumstances, the thematic focus would simultaneously address an important societal challenge *and* contribute to regional development by allowing regional innovation actors to engage in transformative innovation activities as per the theory of RIS3. In this way, the idea is not merely to introduce RRI alongside RIS3 but to search for complementarities between RRI and RIS3 and economize on effort by co-opting some of the methodology and connections already in place for RIS3 and using them to promote RRI-related objectives.

Once the thematic focus is defined, policymakers should identify a group of relevant stakeholders to involve in the consultation process. In SeeRRI, considerable time and effort was invested early on to select relevant stakeholders to invite into the project in each pilot territory. Above all, in the interest

Integrating responsible research and innovation   163

Table 8.2   Smart specialization stages: Analysis

RRI actions in the Analysis stage (Fitjar et al., 2019)
Identify societal needs
Reflect on value system on which analysis is based
Engage stakeholders in analysis
Respond to new knowledge and other perspectives
Key questions based on underlying assumptions (Table 8.1) and suggested RRI actions (Fitjar et al., 2019)
Can you imagine "Wellbeing in Biosphere" being the main design criterion for your regional planning? What could be the initial formulation of challenge in your territory, which would be meaningful and concrete enough to mobilize a wide community of stakeholders? In your territory, who should be concretely mobilized to address the challenge? How can alliances be built to ensure the challenge is properly addressed?

of inclusiveness, priority was given to ensuring that the pool of stakeholders would include representatives from the entire "quadruple helix": government, industry, academia and civil society. The "key questions" listed in Table 8.2 are directed at policymakers rather than external stakeholders, since external stakeholders are not required to enter the RRI–RIS3 process until the next stage of the approach.

4.2   Key Questions for the *Vision and Prioritization* Stage

Once the region's thematic focus is defined and relevant stakeholders identified, the process moves on to the next stage of RIS3 – creating a vision and setting priorities for the region. At this stage, the key stakeholders are again invited to participate in one or more workshops. At these forums, the stakeholders are given the opportunity to collectively reflect on and debate alternative regional future scenarios, and to voice their opinions on how innovation policy can best be employed in the present day to address the challenges and opportunities of the future. In SeeRRI these discussions were guided by several questions, shown in Table 8.3, designed to stimulate critical reflection.

Again, the workshops should address questions relevant to both RIS3 and RRI. Many stakeholders with an interest in RRI will be affected by RIS3 policy, and vice versa. Holding discussions that incorporate both the responsibility and regional development aspects of innovation policy not only saves the participants time but also facilitates policymakers' efforts to integrate the two policies. The workshops should be designed to embrace the four dimensions of RRI: anticipative (through foresight processes), inclusive (by involving a broad range of stakeholders), reflexive (by stimulating critical reflection), and responsive (by encouraging concrete policy suggestions). Our approach capitalizes on the complementarities between RIS3 and RRI pointed out by

Table 8.3 Smart specialization stages: Vision and Prioritization

RRI actions in the Vision and Prioritization stages (Fitjar et al., 2019)
Consider impact of priorities on social and environmental outcomes, including potential negative or unintended ones (anticipation).
Reflect on impact beyond the represented stakeholders and beyond the region, and allow for different perspectives on vision for future (reflexivity).
Include a variety of visions and opinions, and have an open process around prioritization where different voices are heard (inclusion).
Be responsive to critical concerns about the vision, and allow for criticism of prioritization and accept that chosen priorities may be wrong (responsiveness).
Key questions based on underlying assumptions (Table 8.1) and suggested RRI actions (Fitjar et al., 2019)
How can we convince territorial stakeholders that RRI is in their interest? In particular, how can we convince businesses that RRI makes sense as an element of their strategy?
How will the RRI vision affect important characteristics of existing R&I processes? In particular, (1) how does a community-centered vision fit with existing global connections, and (2) how does the open access orientation of RRI fit with existing arrangements regarding intellectual property?
How will RRI impact the "metabolic flows" of existing R&I processes? (These flows refer to: (1) the capture of funding and revenue streams; (2) the attraction of talent; and (3) the creation and capture of new knowledge.)

Fitjar et al. (2019): RRI opens up a space for addressing broader societal concerns within RIS3, while in turn RIS3 helps give life to the abstract ideals of RRI by providing a region-specific context in which those ideals can demonstrate their relevance.

The ultimate outcome of the workshops is a strategic plan outlining how the region will address the core challenge and setting priorities for smart specialization that are complementary to this effort. In practice, the plan is put together by policymakers based on outputs from the workshops. Since the plan is co-created with stakeholders, we will refer to it alternatively as a "shared agenda".

4.3 Key Questions for the *Policy Mix and Monitoring* Stage

Table 8.4 sums up the third and final part of our approach, which covers the RIS3 stages of "policy mix" and "monitoring". In this step, policymakers convert the strategy created at the previous stage into concrete action. This requires careful attention to the issue of how best to achieve complementarities between RRI and RIS3 so that RRI-driven initiatives support rather than undermine RIS3. Our guiding questions reflect these concerns. At this stage policymakers should also reach out to colleagues in other regions for the purpose of knowledge-sharing. In principle, the implementation stage lasts until it is considered appropriate to update the shared agenda through a fresh

Integrating responsible research and innovation 165

Table 8.4   *Smart specialization stages: Policy Mix and Monitoring*

RRI actions in the Policy Mix and Monitoring stages (Fitjar et al., 2019)
Consider unintended outcomes of policy, and evaluate broader effects beyond narrow policy aims (anticipation).
Reflect on diverging interests for different policy mixes, and reflect on the value system of evaluators (reflexivity).
Keep policymaking in democratic forum, and include stakeholders in evaluation (inclusion).
Let dissenting voices be heard, and allow for change in evaluation criteria and results in response to feedback (responsiveness).
Key questions based on underlying assumptions (Table 8.1) and suggested RRI actions (Fitjar et al. 2019)
How can we ensure that processes incorporating RRI are more successful than those which do not take RRI into consideration?
How can we ensure that RRI processes are self-reinforcing?
How do we reflect on future consequences of R&I activities?

round of stakeholder engagement activities, at which point the process starts over. Since in our approach RRI activities are linked to RIS3, and RIS3 policies are subject to periodic review and adjustment, our approach ensures that RRI initiatives are also regularly reviewed.

5.   APPLYING THE QUESTION-MACHINE APPROACH: THE CASE OF NORDLAND, NORWAY

Situated in northern Norway and straddling the Arctic Circle, Nordland County is home to just 4.5 percent of Norway's population but contains 25 percent of its coastline. The economy of the region reflects its geography: marine industries such as fishing and fish farming are of vital importance. By the time the SeeRRI project was launched in 2019, policymakers from Nordland County were working on formulating a regional strategic plan for Nordland, which would also serve as a plan for smart specialization.[6] As a partner in SeeRRI, Nordland County Council (NCC) agreed that SeeRRI would provide Nordland's policymakers with tools to go beyond the formal minimum requirements for stakeholder engagement and co-creation. Norwegian law stipulates that important government planning documents must be presented to the public for feedback before they can be approved, but such stakeholder engagement actions are normally relegated to the latter stages of planning processes. NCC wanted a new approach to stakeholder engagement in which stakeholders were engaged early so that they could contribute inputs to the planning process itself rather than merely comment on already-completed policy proposals.

The SeeRRI process was not formally a part of the RIS3 policymaking process in Nordland since the SeeRRI project does not have a mandate to get directly involved in policymaking. However, Nordland County Council agreed to use the outcomes of the SeeRRI project as part of the knowledge base underlying their smart specialization policy and other regional planning activities.

5.1 Analysis: Laying the Foundation

The key questions listed in Tables 8.2–8.4 served as signposts throughout the SeeRRI process. The questions were contextualized to fit the Nordland region. Consider Table 8.2, which pertains to the first stage of the process. The questions *"Can you imagine 'Wellbeing in Biosphere' being the main design criterion for your regional planning?"* and *"What could be the initial formulation of challenge in your territory, which would be meaningful and concrete enough to mobilize a wide community of stakeholders?"* were never asked verbatim. Rather, they were used as a template to create more context-specific questions such as *"How can we ensure wellbeing and a balance between harvesting from and protecting Nordland's coastline?"* The questions were also localized in the sense that they were asked in Norwegian, not English.

Upon discussion of the questions above, a challenge could be formulated. NCC defined "responsible coastal management" as the core regional challenge for Nordland. At the heart of this challenge lies the problem of how to manage conflicting interests in coastal development – for example, how to strike a socially responsible balance between creating incentives for industry and protecting the environment. As soon as the core regional challenge was settled, NCC started mapping out the regional stakeholder landscape to decide which stakeholders to involve in the next stage of the process, keeping in mind the need for representation of the entire quadruple helix.

The discussions related to the questions, *"In your territory, who should be concretely mobilized around the main challenge and the corresponding vision?"* and *"How can alliances be built to ensure the challenge is properly addressed?"* did not occur in a closed room. At the local level, policymakers consulted with researchers and representatives from civil society organizations (CSOs). At the European level, they discussed these and other questions with SeeRRI partners from across Europe at internal SeeRRI workshops aimed at sharing knowledge and stimulating cross-regional debate among the partners.

5.2 Vision and Prioritization

The vision and prioritization stage of the SeeRRI process centered on a series of workshops where 25–40 invited stakeholders were challenged to think hard about the future of Nordland and participate in a dialogue on future scenarios for the region. The participants included representatives of labor unions, employers' organizations, small firms, large firms, nature preservation NGOs, minority groups (specifically the Sámi), academic institutions, and government bodies from the municipal and county levels. Without such a broad reach, the SeeRRI process would lack the anchoring in the community that lends it legitimacy.

The foresight process was not meant to produce accurate predictions of future trajectories but rather to stimulate discussion and reflection among the participants. The viewpoints expressed during the process were collated and synthesized in an attempt to gain an overview of how Nordland's stakeholders imagined the region's future. The scenarios developed by the stakeholders reflected the importance of trade-offs between economic growth and environmental protection and between local control and global interconnectedness, respectively; these were key dimensions along which the scenarios differed from one another, implying that stakeholders saw them as important variables that are not fixed or predetermined but may be influenced by policy choices.

During the workshops, participants were asked locally adapted forms of the generic questions in Table 8.3. Note that the first question – *"How can we convince territorial stakeholders that RRI is in their interest? In particular, how can we convince a business that RRI makes sense as an element of its strategy?"* – can only be addressed by consulting a broad range of stakeholders, including representatives from industry. Examples of concrete questions used in the workshops, based on the questions in Table 8.3 but tailored to the Nordland context, include: *"How can industry in Nordland share knowledge through an open access orientation while still avoiding intellectual property theft?"* and *"How can science education be used to hinder depopulation and create good jobs in the future?"*

Although workshop participants reached consensus on many issues, we noted that, during the consensus-making process, participants would sometimes resort to abstractions in their search for common ground; these abstractions seemingly served as a bargaining device through which they consolidated their mutual differences. For example, representatives from the oil and gas industry could agree with representatives from environmental NGOs that regional policy should to some extent or other accommodate both the exploitation and the protection of nature. By debating in such general terms, participants could transform their differences from differences in kind to differences in degree.

5.3   Policy Mix and Monitoring

The last stage of the SeeRRI process in Nordland involved a final workshop where project participants gathered to discuss the results of the previous workshops, share lessons learned, and reflect on how the SeeRRI process might be applied going forward. The questions *"How can we ensure that RRI processes are more successful than those who do not consider the importance of RRI?"* and *"How can we ensure that RRI processes are self-reinforcing?"* from Table 8.4 were addressed. Participants were also invited to present their reflections on how their views had changed after partaking in the SeeRRI project. Both learning through *intra-regional* project activities (e.g. the regional foresight processes described in Section 5.2) and learning through *inter-regional* project activities (e.g. some of the activities presented in Section 5.1) were considered. The lessons from the final workshop will be used by the regional government in upcoming planning processes. These planning processes will also incorporate reflections on how future R&I activities can affect the local region and the global community, thus addressing the last of the generic questions in Table 8.4: *"How do we reflect on future consequences of R&I activities?"*

6. DISCUSSION

The smart specialization approach to regional development policy, which has been widely adopted in the European Union, emphasizes the role of regional governments in fostering transformative innovation activities at the regional level (Kroll et al., 2016; Uyarra et al., 2020). In this chapter, we have addressed the question of how regional governments can ensure that smart specialization facilitates responsible research and innovation. Adapting a conceptual framework introduced by Fitjar et al. (2019), we have produced a complementary, more practice-oriented approach that highlights the steps involved in promoting RRI in the context of smart specialization. We aim to contribute to the literature of regional innovation policy in general and RIS3 in particular by connecting the RRI concept to regional planning processes. Although an RRI approach would seem to be compatible with the discourse in regional innovation studies, relatively few RRI studies focus on the regional dimension (Thapa et al., 2019). We propose that the dimension of responsibility in the RIS3 process can be operationalized in the form of a series of questions, formulated based on assumptions from systems thinking and complexity theory, which are answered and debated by local stakeholders in collective sessions that facilitate consensus-building among different interest groups while also helping to clarify the fault lines between them. The knowledge about stakeholder perspectives emerging from this process is the essential input to "responsible regional planning" – that is, planning that takes the values and priorities of the community into account and is sensitive to the need for maintaining a careful balance in catering to competing regional interests.

One important linkage between RRI and RIS3 is a shared concern for sustainability. Whereas RIS3 is concerned mainly with economic sustainability,

RRI takes a broader view, aiming for the alignment of policy with the general interests of society. In the Nordland case, many of the stakeholder discussions came to revolve around sustainability issues with clear relevance for both RRI and RIS3 – for example, the issue of how to halt local population decline. The sustainability connection between RRI and RIS3 may cause synergies in the implementation of the two frameworks. Previous studies have suggested that smart specialization can be used as a vehicle for sustainability transitions (Montresor & Quatraro, 2020; Secundo et al., 2020; Veldhuizen, 2020) and that responsible innovation can contribute to sustainable development (Voegtlin & Scherer, 2017). Although sustainability by itself is not a dimension in the RRI framework we have presented in this chapter, it is considered by some to be an emerging conceptual dimension of RRI (Burget et al., 2017). Others have suggested that RRI may be a useful framework for assessing sustainability (Matthews et al., 2019).

In this chapter, we have described an approach to integrating RRI into RIS3, but we are well aware that our cursory description is not a definitive account of how this integration process may unfold. We hope that future researchers will flesh out the details and, in the spirit of RIS3 and RRI, improve the approach through mutual learning based on real-world experience. As regions in Europe and elsewhere deepen their experiments with policies incorporating RIS3 and RRI, it is vital that research efforts be directed towards gathering more empirical data on the success and failure of efforts to combine these concepts in practice.

Another interesting line of inquiry for future research concerns the question of how to reconcile the mutual tensions and contradictions between RIS3 and RRI that we touched upon in Section 2.3, in particular the tension between the focus of RIS3 on economic growth and the economic costliness of RRI. Is there a credible argument to be made that RRI will bring net economic benefits to its practitioners? If so, this could potentially enhance the popularity of RRI and facilitate its integration into RIS3 policies. If not, we may instead ask ourselves how we, as practitioners, can minimize the costs of practicing RRI without drifting into irresponsibility. For example, RRI mandates broad inclusion of stakeholders, but to engage a diverse range of stakeholders directly on a regular basis is costly and time-consuming and not required by RIS3. To what extent can we rely instead on democratically elected politicians and high-level interest organizations to represent the interests of grassroots stakeholders and still consider our approach responsible?

RIS3 and RRI are evolving concepts, invested with relevance and legitimacy by the policymakers who have allocated resources to their implementation but still perched on fragmentary theoretical foundations. RIS3 has been described by one of its creators as an example of policy running ahead of theory (Foray, 2014), while the efforts to clarify the meaning of RRI have been likened to putting clothes on an emperor who started out naked (Rip, 2016). In years to come, researchers should, above all, continue to refine both frameworks and strengthen their theoretical underpinnings. Doing so will pave the way for new insights into how they can most fruitfully be combined.

ACKNOWLEDGMENTS

The writing of this chapter has benefited from the financial support of the SeeRRI project, funded by the European Union's Horizon 2020 research and innovation program under grant agreement no. 824588, and from the good work done in this project by all its partners. In particular, we wish to thank Dag Bastholm, Liv Rask Sørensen, Eivind Sommerseth, and Anders Paulsen, who formed the core Nordland team, and Marianne Hörlesberger, who played a key role in devising and implementing the foresight methodology. Last but not least, we are grateful to this book's editors and two anonymous reviewers, whose constructive comments inspired significant improvements to the text. We are, of course, entirely responsible for any shortcomings that remain.

NOTES

1. Information about the implementation of RIS3 in the European Union can be found on the EU's Smart Specialization platform: https://s3platform.jrc.ec.europa .eu (retrieved June 14, 2021).
2. However, the adoption of RIS3 does not preclude a region from providing some basic horizontal innovation support as well (Foray, 2018).
3. The figure is adapted from the official EU presentation of smart specialization at http://www.s3platform.eu/how-to-form-ris3 (retrieved June 14, 2021).
4. More details on SeeRRI can be found on the project's website: http://www.seerri .eu.
5. See https://sdgs.un.org/2030agenda.
6. See https://www.nfk.no/tjenester/planer-og-planlegging/pagaende-regionalt-plana rbeid/regional-planstrategi-for-nordland/3-prosess.33071.aspx#31-smart-spesialisering (retrieved June 14, 2021).

REFERENCES

Álvarez Pereira, C. (2020). *Thesaurus and Conceptual Framework of Self-Sustaining R&I Ecosystems* (Deliverable D4.1 of the SeeRRI Project) [Report to the European Commission].

Anderson, P. (1999). Perspective: complexity theory and organization science. *Organization Science*, *10*(3), 216–32. https://doi.org/10.1287/orsc.10.3.216.

Blok, V., & Lemmens, P. (2015). The emerging concept of responsible innovation: three reasons why it is questionable and calls for a radical transformation of the concept of innovation. In B.-J. Koops, I. Oosterlaken, H. Romijn, T. Swierstra, & J. van den Hoven (Eds.), *Responsible Innovation 2: Concepts, Approaches, and*

Applications (pp. 19–35). Springer International Publishing. https://doi.org/10.1007/978-3-319-17308-5_2.

Burget, M., Bardone, E., & Pedaste, M. (2017). Definitions and conceptual dimensions of responsible research and innovation: a literature review. *Science and Engineering Ethics*, *23*(1), 1–19. https://doi.org/10.1007/s11948-016-9782-1.

Byrne, D. S., & Callaghan, G. (2013). *Complexity Theory and the Social Sciences: The State of the Art*. Routledge. https://www.routledge.com/Complexity-Theory-and-the-Social-Sciences-The-state-of-the-art/Byrne-Callaghan/p/book/9780415693684.

Cagnin, C., Johnston, R., & Giesecke, S. (2015). Foresight contribution to grand challenges and participative governance in different cultural settings. *Technological Forecasting and Social Change*, *101*, 182–4. https://doi.org/10.1016/j.techfore.2015.11.020.

Estensoro, M., & Larrea, M. (2016). Overcoming policy making problems in smart specialization strategies: engaging subregional governments. *European Planning Studies*, *24*(7), 1319–35. https://doi.org/10.1080/09654313.2016.1174670.

Ferreira, J. J., Farinha, L., Rutten, R., & Asheim, B. (2021). Smart specialisation and learning regions as a competitive strategy for less developed regions. *Regional Studies*, *55*(3), 373–6. https://doi.org/10.1080/00343404.2021.1891216.

Fitjar, R. D., Benneworth, P., & Asheim, B. T. (2019). Towards regional responsible research and innovation? Integrating RRI and RIS3 in European innovation policy. *Science and Public Policy*, *46*(5), 772–83. https://doi.org/10.1093/scipol/scz029.

Foray, D. (2014). *Smart Specialisation: Opportunities and Challenges for Regional Innovation Policy* (1st edition). Routledge.

Foray, D. (2018). Smart specialization strategies as a case of mission-oriented policy—a case study on the emergence of new policy practices. *Industrial and Corporate Change*, *27*(5), 817–32. https://doi.org/10.1093/icc/dty030.

Grillitsch, M. (2016). Institutions, smart specialisation dynamics and policy. *Environment and Planning C: Government and Policy*, *34*(1), 22–37. https://doi.org/10.1177/0263774X15614694.

Hansen, J. Ø., Jensen, A., & Nguyen, N. (2020). The responsible learning organization: can Senge (1990) teach organizations how to become responsible innovators? *Learning Organization*, *27*(1), 65–74.

Hoffman, R., & McInnis, B. (2015). Concepts for a new generation of global modelling tools: expanding our capacity for perception. *Cadmus*, *2*(5). https://www.cadmusjournal.org/node/507.

Hörlesberger, M., Kasztler, A., Wepner, B., Hansen, J. Ø., Jensen, A., Nguyen, N., & Arino, X. (2021). *Future scenarios for RRI implementation in R&I ecosystems of the three territories* (Deliverable D3.2 of the SeeRRI project) [Report to the European Commission].

Hörlesberger, M., Wepner, B., Kasztler, A., Hartman, A., & Casale, D. (2020). *List of identified stakeholders and list of influencing factors regarding RRI principles in R&I ecosystems* (Deliverable D3.1 of the SeeRRI project) [Report to the European Commission].

Kroll, H., Boeke, I., Schiller, D., & Stahlecker, T. (2016). Bringing owls to Athens? The transformative potential of RIS3 for innovation policy in Germany's federal states. *European Planning Studies*, *24*(8), 1459–77. https://doi.org/10.1080/09654313.2016.1159666.

Lopes, J., Ferreira, J. J., & Farinha, L. (2019). Innovation strategies for smart specialisation (RIS3): past, present and future research. *Growth and Change*, *50*(1), 38–68. https://doi.org/10.1111/grow.12268.

Lubberink, R., Blok, V., van Ophem, J., van der Velde, G., & Omta, O. (2018). Innovation for society: towards a typology of developing innovations by social entrepreneurs. *Journal of Social Entrepreneurship*, *9*(1), 52–78. https://doi.org/10.1080/19420676.2017.1410212.

Magro, E., & Wilson, J. R. (2019). Policy-mix evaluation: governance challenges from new place-based innovation policies. *Research Policy*, *48*(10), 103612. https://doi.org/10.1016/j.respol.2018.06.010.

Manson, S. M. (2001). Simplifying complexity: a review of complexity theory. *Geoforum*, *32*(3), 405–14. https://doi.org/10.1016/S0016-7185(00)00035-X.

Matthews, N. E., Stamford, L., & Shapira, P. (2019). Aligning sustainability assessment with responsible research and innovation: towards a framework for Constructive Sustainability Assessment. *Sustainable Production and Consumption*, *20*, 58–73. https://doi.org/10.1016/j.spc.2019.05.002.

McCann, P., & Ortega-Argiles, R. (2015). Smart specialization, regional growth and applications to European Union cohesion policy. *Regional Studies*, *49*(8), 1291–302. https://doi.org/10.1080/00343404.2013.799769.

McCann, P., & Ortega-Argiles, R. (2016). The early experience of smart specialization implementation in EU cohesion policy. *European Planning Studies*, *24*(8), 1407–27. https://doi.org/10.1080/09654313.2016.1166177.

Montresor, S., & Quatraro, F. (2020). Green technologies and smart specialisation strategies: a European patent-based analysis of the intertwining of technological relatedness and key enabling technologies. *Regional Studies*, *54*(10), 1354–65. https://doi.org/10.1080/00343404.2019.1648784.

Morgan, K. (2015). Smart specialisation: opportunities and challenges for regional innovation policy. *Regional Studies*, *49*(3), 480–82. https://doi.org/10.1080/00343404.2015.1007572.

Nguyen, N., Mariussen, Å., & Hansen, J. Ø. (2020). The role of smart specialization in providing regional strategic support for establishing sustainable start-up incubation ecosystems. In A. Novotny, E. Rasmussen, T. Clausen, & J. Wiklund (Eds.), *Research Handbook on Start-Up Incubation Ecosystems* (pp. 19–39). Cheltenham, UK, and Northampton, MA, USA: Edward Elgar Publishing. https://www.elgaronline.com/view/edcoll/9781788973526/9781788973526.00008.xml.

Owen, R., Macnaghten, P., & Stilgoe, J. (2012). Responsible research and innovation: from science in society to science for society, with society. *Science and Public Policy*, *39*(6), 751–60. https://doi.org/10.1093/scipol/scs093.

Owen, R., Stilgoe, J., Macnaghten, P., Gorman, M., Fisher, E., & Guston, D. (2013). A framework for responsible innovation. In *Responsible Innovation* (pp. 27–50). John Wiley & Sons. https://doi.org/10.1002/9781118551424.ch2.

Ribeiro, B. E., Smith, R. D. J., & Millar, K. (2017). A mobilising concept? Unpacking academic representations of responsible research and innovation. *Science and Engineering Ethics*, *23*(1), 81–103. https://doi.org/10.1007/s11948-016-9761-6.

Rip, A. (2016). The clothes of the emperor. An essay on RRI in and around Brussels. *Journal of Responsible Innovation*, *3*(3), 290–304. https://doi.org/10.1080/23299460.2016.1255701.

Schomberg, R. von. (2011). *Towards responsible research and innovation in the information and communication technologies and security technologies fields*. Publications Office of the European Union. https://data.europa.eu/doi/10.2777/58723.

Schomberg, R. von. (2013). A vision of responsible research and innovation. In R. Owen, J. Stilgoe, P. Macnaghten, M. Gorman, E. Fisher, & D. Guston (Eds.),

Responsible Innovation (pp. 51–74). John Wiley & Sons. https://doi.org/10.1002/9781118551424.ch3.

Schot, J., & Steinmueller, W. E. (2018). Three frames for innovation policy: R&D, systems of innovation and transformative change. *Research Policy*, *47*(9), 1554–67. https://doi.org/10.1016/j.respol.2018.08.011.

Secundo, G., Ndou, V., Del Vecchio, P., & De Pascale, G. (2020). Sustainable development, intellectual capital and technology policies: a structured literature review and future research agenda. *Technological Forecasting and Social Change*, *153*, 119917. https://doi.org/10.1016/j.techfore.2020.119917.

Simonen, J., Svento, R., & Juutinen, A. (2015). Specialization and diversity as drivers of economic growth: evidence from high-tech industries. *Papers in Regional Science*, *94*(2), 229–47. https://doi.org/10.1111/pirs.12062.

Sorvik, J., Teras, J., Dubois, A., & Pertoldi, M. (2019). Smart specialisation in sparsely populated areas: challenges, opportunities and new openings. *Regional Studies*, *53*(7), 1070–80. https://doi.org/10.1080/00343404.2018.1530752.

Stilgoe, J., & Guston, D. H. (2016). Responsible research and innovation. In U. Felt, R. Fouche, C. A. Miller, & L. Smith-Doerr (Eds.), *The Handbook of Science and Technology Studies* (chapter 29), 4th edition. MIT Press.

Stilgoe, J., Owen, R., & Macnaghten, P. (2013). Developing a framework for responsible innovation. *Research Policy*, *42*(9), 1568–80. https://doi.org/10.1016/j.respol.2013.05.008.

Sutcliffe, H. (2011). *A report on responsible research and innovation*. https://citeseerx.ist.psu.edu/viewdoc/download?doi=10.1.1.226.8407&rep=rep1&type=pdf.

Szerb, L., Ortega-Argiles, R., Acs, Z. J., & Komlosi, E. (2020). Optimizing entrepreneurial development processes for smart specialization in the European Union. *Papers in Regional Science*, *99*(5), 1413–57. https://doi.org/10.1111/pirs.12536.

Thapa, R. K., Iakovleva, T., & Foss, L. (2019). Responsible research and innovation: a systematic review of the literature and its applications to regional studies. *European Planning Studies*, *27*(12), 2470–90. https://doi.org/10.1080/09654313.2019.1625871.

Uyarra, E., Mikel Zabala-Iturriagagoitia, J., Flanagan, K., & Magro, E. (2020). Public procurement, innovation and industrial policy: Rationales, roles, capabilities and implementation. *Research Policy*, *49*(1), 103844. https://doi.org/10.1016/j.respol.2019.103844.

Veldhuizen, C. (2020). Smart specialisation as a transition management framework: driving sustainability-focused regional innovation policy? *Research Policy*, *49*(6), 103982. https://doi.org/10.1016/j.respol.2020.103982.

Voegtlin, C., & Scherer, A. G. (2017). Responsible innovation and the innovation of responsibility: governing sustainable development in a globalized world. *Journal of Business Ethics*, *143*(2), 227–43. https://doi.org/10.1007/s10551-015-2769-z.

9. Making a thousand diverse flowers bloom: driving innovation through inclusion of diversity in organisations

Marte C.W. Solheim

> It is hardly possible to overrate the value (…) of placing human beings in contact with persons dissimilar to themselves, and with modes of thought and action unlike those with which they are familiar (…) Such communication has always been, and is particularly in the present age, one of the primary sources of progress.
>
> (Mill, 1848)

The quotation by Mill is easily applicable in contemporary society,[1] as one of the pivotal strategic challenges in modern work-life is changing the demographics of the workforce (Abramovic & Traavik, 2017). Augmented diversity is a reality across organisations, industries and countries (Mor Barak, 2005); employees in today's workplaces are more likely than before to engage with people with different backgrounds (Guillaume et al., 2014). This increased diversity stems from increased and more complex migratory patterns (Özden et al., 2011), ageing populations, anti-discrimination measures, more women entering the workforce, educational and skill upgrading of the workforce (Parrotta et al., 2014) and augmented job-hopping (Czaja, 2020). Together, these factors (and more) lead to increased diversity in the contemporary workforce in terms of work-life experiences, gender, educational background and skill mix, birthplace diversity and age, to mention a few.

Concomitantly, a vast amount of research has pointed to the benefits of a diverse workforce (e.g. Cox, 1994; Richard, 2000; Solheim and Fitjar, 2018) and has been highlighted by practitioners (e.g. Hunt et al., 2015). The commonly painted picture herein is that a diverse workforce boosts creativity and innovation. Past research discusses, on the one hand, diversity bringing new perspectives and ideas (Ottaviano & Peri, 2006), and on the other hand, reducing trust and increasing conflict among actors (Basset-Jones, 2005). Thus, there are mixed and often contradictory results in the context of culturally diverse teams (Stahl et al., 2010). Diversity has, therefore, often been depicted as a 'double-edged sword' (Milliken & Martins, 1996) or a 'mixed blessing' (Williams & O'Reilly, 1998).

Making a thousand diverse flowers bloom 175

Innovation comprises a set of processes carried out by individuals and assemblies of individuals that are 'stimulated, facilitated and enhanced – or the opposite, by a set of macro-structural conditions' (Kanter, 2000, p. 205). Kanter herein addresses the importance of management of the innovation process in empowering the individuals who facilitate 'connecting the dots'.[2] However, in considerable research on skill inflows, these processes are taken for granted, as if the integration of diverse knowledge take place (or not) independently of firm efforts (Timmermans & Boschma, 2014). In line with this, van Knippenberg and Schippers (2007) have signalled that it has been difficult to predict under which conditions diversity might have negative or positive effects on organisational outcomes. Stegmann et al. (2012, p. 20) argue that 'the underlying mechanisms which translate diversity into individual and organizational outcomes, as well as the factors that moderate these relationships, are not sufficiently understood.'

Moreover, van Knippenberg and Schippers (2007, p. 534) argue that diversity research should pay more attention to the social categorisation and information/decision-making processes and intergroup biases that underlie the potential effects of diversity. In line with this, this chapter argues that firms can gain a competitive advantage only if they can integrate the knowledge and expertise of their workforce in meaningful ways (Hu et al., 2009). Traavik (2019, p. 215) argues that 'Today's workplaces, filled with a variety of people, need to create environments where people can develop a sense of belonging and self, contribute successfully to organizational goals and outcomes, collaborate and cooperate with one another and flourish.' Even though employees might come up with creative ideas and innovate (put those creative ideas into practice), they must also feel confident that their attempts to innovate will be well received. We therefore arrive at a crucial point of marrying diversity, innovation and inclusion. This is increasingly important in the knowledge economy, where business success depends on bringing in and joining diverse perspectives 'on purpose' (Edmondson & Besieux, 2021).

Consequently, the purpose of this chapter is to marry lessons learned from social psychology and management with those learned from innovation studies. The field must move beyond the automatic assumption of association between diversity and innovation or studying either the good or bad effects of diversity on innovation (separated from mechansisms at play to increase utilisation of such), and rather, shed light on inclusion or stimuli that leverage the potential in a diverse workforce fostering innovation.

DIVERSITY

The concept of diversity is context-dependent and is interpreted in 'a variety of ways ranging from gender to age to culture to people with disabilities'

(Traavik, 2019, p. 216). For the purpose herein, the chapter builds on the rather broad understanding of diversity being typically understood 'as referring to differences between individuals on any attribute that may lead to the perception that another person is different from self' (van Knippenberg & Schippers, 2007, p. 517). This interpretation could be understood as the underpinnings of how Mor Barak (2005) defines diversity, which could potentially affect how one is being treated in the workplace.

Diversity covers many differences within a given social unit, such as a work team, a department, or an organisation (Harrison & Sin, 2006). These differences might become apparent in various forms but are often divided into primary (ascribed) and secondary (acquired) diversity characteristics (Horwitz & Horwitz, 2007; Milliken & Martins, 1996; Ruef et al., 2003).[3] Usually, the primary characteristics are traits that one cannot change, such as birthplace, and the secondary characteristics refer to the things that one can change (or not), such as education. The research underpinning this chapter draws upon various diversity characteristics, and hence, is not restrained to a particular type; however, particular emphasis is placed on primary diversity characteristics, such as those highlighted through the evolution of diversity management discussed below.

The term 'diversity' has its origins in the USA, 'beginning in the 1960s and 1970s with the equal rights and affirmative action legislation aimed at addressing gender and race imbalances in the workplace' (Traavik, 2019, p. 216). With that, diversity management came in the organisation and management discourse in the late 1980s in the USA and in Europe around ten years later, and in Scandinavia around the year 2000 (Holvino & Kamp, 2009). Holvino and Kamp (2009) report that the increased interest amongst academics and practitioners for diversity management in Scandinavia was centred around a debate about including ethnic minorities in the workforce. This discussion was, moreover, concerned with an increase in birthplace diversity in the workforce. Later, we see that this train of thought has shifted from seeing diversity as something one must include to be considered a competitive advantage (Traavik, 2019) or a liability (Stahl et al., 2010). Stahl et al. (2010, p. 440) argue that we know less 'about the positive dynamics and outcomes associated with cultural diversity than we know about the problems and obstacles caused by cultural differences'. In the last ten years, however, more research has addressed the benefits of diversity, such as Solheim and Fitjar (2018) demonstrating positive linkages between high-skilled, foreign-born workers and the breadth of international collaboration which they find to be positively associated with firm-level innovation. However, a recent contribution by Moss and Solheim (2021) addresses the shifting diversity discourses, discussing diversity not only as a concept but also as an associated value and moving from multiculturalism towards narrower monoculturalism, nationalism and prejudice. Moss and Solheim (2021) draw on feeling rules, social identity theory and critical discourse analysis, and highlight how discourses emphasising 'us' and 'them' are shifting. Using Brexit as a case, they argue that a 'sea change' or an 'unveiling of racism' is being observed, and subsequently, could be considered a backlash to the past development of diversity as a practice that offered distinct perspectives and world views.

DIVERSITY AND INNOVATION

As put forward in a metaphor by Kanter (2000, p. 167), innovations, 'like flowers, start from tiny seeds and have to be nurtured carefully until they blossom: then their essence has to be carried elsewhere for the blossom to spread. And some conditions – soil, climate, fertilizer, the layout of the garden – produce larger and more abundant flowers.' This metaphor adds a perspective of fostering innovation through nurturing and creating a healthy environment. In her seminal work, Kanter also states that contact with people that see the world differently is a logical prerequisite as to seeing it differently ourselves (p. 173). She refers to pivotal work by Pelz and Andrews (1966) that found that the most creative and productive research scientists were those who had more contacts outside of their fields and spent more time with people who did not share their beliefs or values. Another example is the story of how the Polaroid company gained success going from black and white film to sepia. At the time, Polaroid was under the management of Meroë Morse, who had an art background, rather than chemistry or physics. She influenced this transformation due to her strong interest and expertise in colours and her strong commitment (Grant, 2016).

This chapter focuses on the inclusive processes *within* an organisation, but innovation is also often studied through networks and collaboration beyond the organisation. This approach speaks to Burt (1992) and 'structural holes' where bridging could lead to information benefits gained by interacting with people holding knowledge and networks that complement what is already known to the firm (Granovetter, 1973). Albeit the focus of this chapter is on internal processes, this is not to say that innovation does not benefit from inter-organisational ties as well as internal integration (Kanter, 2000), and they are obviously connected.

Innovation is a social phenomenon and a product of an interactive process (Lundvall, 1992; Van der Ven et al., 1989). Innovation often occurs when a variety of knowledge intersects (Carlile, 2004), and the creation of boundary-crossing interactions becomes pivotal. Diversity could influence innovation and the innovation process by bringing in new perspectives (Østergaard et al., 2011) that could shed light on not only what the process should be, but also on what the challenge in question is understood to be.

More heterogeneous teams outperform homogenous teams because they have broader knowledge bases, skills and competence. These advantages provide that group with a broader pool from which to draw knowledge that, combined, can generate new knowledge (Van Engen & Van Woerkom, 2010), as innovation is *re-combination of already-existing knowledge and resources* (Schumpeter, 1934).

Diversity could affect innovation beyond bringing in new perspectives, however, through challenging the 'of-course' assumptions held within organisations (Solheim, 2017). In line with this, Phillips et al. (2009) argue that heterogeneous teams performed better than homogenous teams, despite the former reporting feeling less confident. From this, we understand that the road to the finish line might have been curvier and full of more perceived setbacks for the heterogeneous team, whilst in the homogenous team, 'the ride' was a more comfortable, straightforward one. This analogy speaks to what Clearfield and Tilcsik (2018) refer to as 'the speed bump effect' of diversity. Diversity is less comfortable and makes us more sceptical and vigilant, which in turn, enables us to catch errors and to 'call out the naked emperor' (Clearfield & Tilcsik, 2018). Clearfield and Tilcsik (2018, p. 182) furthermore argue that diversity 'feels strange. It's inconvenient. But it makes us work harder and ask tougher questions.' In more heterogeneous teams, people are challenged in different ways, they must take a stand and put forward arguments for one's meanings and values, and they were able to convert 'effective pains into cognitive gains' (Phillips et al., 2009). We can see two main perspectives arising within human resources management studies,[4] namely the 'similarity attraction paradigm' and the 'cognitive resource diversity theory' (Horwitz, 2005). The former upholds the 'birds of a feather flock together' (McPherson et al., 2001) theory, and that there is a tendency of people to prefer to work with others whom they perceive to be similar to them (i.e. based on some common attribute; see van Knippenberg and Schippers, 2007). This theory posits that when we work with 'like' people, communication flows easier, we feel more comfortable, and operations run more smoothly and with less friction (see Solheim and Herstad, 2018).

In line with this, and 'microfoundations' of the categorisations mentioned above, is the social identity theory approach (Tajfel & Turner, 1979; Turner et al., 1987) and the creation of in- and out-groups.[5] The in-group is a group in which one psychologically identifies as a member, whilst the contrary is the case for the out-group (Turner et al., 1979). Stets and Burke (2000, p. 225) note that:

> In social identity theory, a social identity is a person's knowledge that he or she belongs to a social category or group (…). A social group is a set of individuals who hold a common social identification or view themselves as members of the

same social category. Through a social comparison process, persons who are similar to the self are categorized with the self and are labelled the in-group; persons who differ from the self are categorized as the out-group.

This effective understanding of in- and out-groups has implications for social perception, interaction and behaviour (see Gaertner and Dovidio, 2000 for a review) as people tend to more pro-socially orient towards in-group members than towards out-group members (Vos & van der Zee, 2011), which could potentially affect how one is being treated in the workplace (Mor Barak, 2005) and inclusion in work processes (such as innovation). It can also be related to well-being in the workplace. A recent contribution investigating Swedish firefighters highlights that well-being in the workplace pertains to homosocial group (Jacobsson et al., 2020), much in line with social identity theory upholding that differences within groups are minimised, whilst differences between groups are maximised (Tajfel, 1982). People like in-group members more than they do out-group members, prefer to cooperate with them, trust them more and are more prone to help them out, and retain more positive information about them (Gaertner & Dovidio, 2000). A critical challenge for the future of the rescue service (in the Swedish case), therefore, is transforming firefighting to be more inclusive whilst upholding the well-being that is in place (Jacobsson et al., 2020).

Another study serves as an illustrative example herein. In a large study of American banks, Almandoz and Tilcsik (2015) investigated why some banks failed, and some did not. When they investigated the details, they discovered that the banks with the highest percentage of bankers on the board of directors were more likely to fail. In *Meltdown: why our systems fail and what we can do about it*, Clearfield and Tilcsik (2018, pp. 192–3) lay out the details from Almandoz and Tilcsik's research and highlight three main points. The first point was related to 'baggage' (relied too much on their experience), the second was overconfidence (too focused on what had worked in the past), and the third was a lack of constructive discussion and productive conflict. Clearfield and Tilcsik (2018, p. 193) note: 'Boards that weren't dominated by experts behaved like racially diverse teams. The directors argued and questioned each other's judgment. They took nothing for granted. Bankers didn't speak the same language as doctors and lawyers, so even "obvious" things had to be spelled out and debated.' If one sees this from a diversity, inclusion and innovation point of view, it refers to the need to have diverse backgrounds, and also the need to have practices that actually create constructive dynamics between groups.

The 'cognitive resource diversity perspective', however, is based on the premise of rewards that stem from working with diverse others. An increase in the knowledge base and absorptive capacity, a larger pool from which

180　　*Rethinking the social in innovation and entrepreneurship studies*

extract knowledge, and broader networks are among some of the traits often mentioned as important when discussing the benefits of a diverse workforce. Another advantage is 'socio-cognitive horsepower' (Carpenter, 2002), which, in turn, could deliver more creative solutions than similar teams due to boundary-crossing interactions (Jackson et al., 1995). Increased diversity could increase conflicts and miscommunication, however (Basset-Jones, 2005). This tension is exemplified by Smith et al. (2017, p. 305), who state that:

> Heterogeneity often implies innovation and change but diversity also confirms stability (…). Diverse teams open a larger pool of knowledge than homogenous teams, which may enhance creative solutions, but diversity can also hinder innovation because of categorization of the ingroup by the outgroup and lack of shared understanding.[6]

One could argue that relatedness or proximity (Boschma, 2005) employed in innovation studies represents an in between position in the debate of the similarity attraction and the cognitive resource diversity perspective (Solheim, 2017). Some proximity facilitates interaction, but too much could lead to lock-in situations due to a lack of openness and novelty brought in (Boschma, 2005). This situation is what Boschma and Frenken (2010) refer to as the proximity paradox, which has clear connections to the opposing views put forward above in the gains and pains of diversity (Solheim, 2017).[7] Evolutionary economic geography and innovation studies often conceptualise this position as related variety (RV) (mirroring cognitive complementarity) and unrelated variety (URV) (mirroring cognitive distance). Herein, we could envision these through placing RV within the framework of similarity attraction perspective and URV to the cognitive resource diversity perspective. URV and RV are often employed to understand and encapsulate cross-fertilisation and mobility flows between firms (Aarstad et al., 2016; Solheim et al., 2020; Timmermans & Boschma, 2014). However, these are categorisations, and in the following we will dig deeper into how to leverage the potential of benefitting from the variety within.

DIVERSITY, INCLUSION AND INNOVATION

Diversity is much easier to attain than inclusion (Shore et al., 2018). Inclusion

> involves equal opportunity for members of socially marginalized groups to participate and contribute while concurrently providing opportunities for members of non-marginalized groups, and to support employees in their efforts to be fully engaged at all levels of the organization and to be authentically themselves. (Shore et al., 2018, p. 177)

In line with this definition comes the understanding that a company does not automatically get rewards by employing people with diverse characteristics. A business must 'trigger' inclusion; it is dependent on the creation of a creative and constructive dynamic between the different groups (Kvålshaugen, 2003). This requirement, moreover, speaks to innovation understood as micro-processes (such as individual creativity and talent) and the activation and support of innovation through macro-processes (Kanter, 2000).

Managers of innovative teams must balance the effects of 'thought worlds' and organisational routines (Dougherty, 1992) because 'innovation is an interpretive process, so the management of innovation must involve the management of the interpretive schemes that shape and frame how people make sense of their work' (Dougherty, 1992, p. 195). This requirement points to management responsibilities about directing diversity and inclusion. Inclusive management styles have been referenced as important to foster diverse, inclusive workplaces. However, Brimhall (2019, p. 719) argues that there is limited empirical evidence pointing towards any form of leadership directly creating inclusive workplaces. Instead, evidence suggests that 'a leader's ability to encourage the participation of all organisational members and express value for the unique perspectives given aligns with the theoretical foundation for creating a climate for inclusion.' Li et al. (2017) find that, for teams holding high cultural diversity, a high-inclusion climate boosted team information sharing and employee information elaboration, and the opposite was found when the inclusion climate was low.

This refers to the need to 'integrate – in order to innovate' and the need to move beyond studying the good or bad effects of diversity on innovation (Axtell et al., 2000). Businesses also need to move beyond 'counting diversity' and assuming automatic links to innovation to leverage the potential of diversity to drive innovation. Van Knippenberg and Schippers (2007) call for increased understanding of the complex conceptualisations of diversity, and state that exploring potential curvilinear effects could provide new insights and contribute to explaining some inconsistencies in diversity research, such as demonstrated by Solheim et al.(2020).

CREATING A SENSE OF BELONGING

Various measures of how well companies leverage the potential of a diverse workforce have been investigated (see Shore et al., 2018). These studies often take place apart from the literature on diversity and innovation. There is much to learn from past studies in social psychology. As an example of an important contribution, consider the cross-cutting themes highlighted by Shore et al. (2018): psychological safety, involvement in the work-group, feeling respected and valued, influence on decision making, authenticity, and recognising, honouring and advancing diversity. Underpinnings herein, is the role of empathy, and perspective-taking, motivation to know and learn more about and from 'different others' through active listening, and creating a sense of belonging.

To create an inclusive work climate, workers need to start with the motivation to get to know and engage with different others. In other words, workers need 'diversity mindsets' (van Knippenberg & Schippers, 2007). These mindsets are facilitated through constructive and creative dynamics through perspective-taking, empathy (Stegmann et al., 2012) and the creation of psychological safety (Edmondson, 1999). The latter emphasises the importance of creating a culture that tolerates mistakes, asks questions, and seeks help (Edmondson, 1999). Companies must create a culture where it is not only acceptable to voice an opinion, but also to allow room for workers' views and opinions to be heard. In these cultures, it is permitted to fail and, as such, the company creates a safe place for people to partake and learn from one another. More than voicing your opinion, it is also a matter of doing so productively (Edmondson & Besieux, 2021). As companies suffer when people are afraid to speak up, ensuring that diverse voices are *in* the conversation is pivotal. Fostering good conversations is, in today's diverse workplaces, increasingly important (see Edmondson & Besieux, 2021, p. 5 for productive conversation in which the 'aspiration is to ensure everyone's knowledge and experience are engaged – so that their diverse experiences and expertise can be integrated efficiently').

Edmondson (1999) reports on a team climate that is characterised by interpersonal trust and mutual respect that allows people to feel comfortable being themselves. Establishing a climate where people can bring 'their whole selves' to work and reveal their true selves (Shore et al., 2018) is pivotal. This refers to belonging, which is a fundamental human need as well as a huge driver for motivation in organisational participation (Traavik, 2019). Traavik (2019, p. 226) exemplifies this through a 'Zulu greeting: "Sawubona" which means "I see you". "Ngikhona" "I am here", the meaning is, "until you saw me, I did not exist".' Creating a sense of belonging entails that the workers feel seen and have the experience of being an important member of the workgroup 'through experiencing treatment that satisfies his or her needs for belongingness and uniqueness' (Shore et al., 2011, p. 1265).

Practical examples of creating a climate like this include emphasising, among other things, time allocations in meetings, ensuring that people's voices are being heard, such as the 'Google Aristotle study', and investigating what makes some teams more successful than others. The study identified, amongst others, the importance of time allocation and listening to your team members (Duhigg, 2016), suggesting effective ways to ensure that people feel they can voice their opinions. This practice could ensure that various views are counted and being included in the innovation process. Companies that practice such behaviours face timely questions: who is involved in innovative processes? Whose voices are being heard? Reflecting upon innovation practices, and taking an active stand on them, becomes important (see also Edmondson & Besieux, 2021 on good conversations, and effective and inclusive meetings).

CREATING ROOM FOR DIVERSITY

This chapter has addressed the nexus between diversity and innovation by focusing on inclusion. Diversity has been pointed out as a 'mixed blessing' with the benefits of having varied perspectives with associated costs. A vast amount of research addresses the benefits of workplace diversity, such as increased creativity and variety of perspectives that could result in better decision-making, innovation and increased profits. Diversity works because it makes us question the consensus and how we do things (Clearfield & Tilcsik, 2018). The insecurity employees feel when working in diverse groups could be what makes the project better (Phillips et al., 2009). Disagreeing or having to take a stand could lead to more well-thought-through decisions (Loyd et al., 2013). This premise also holds that friction, emphasised through the cognitive resource diversity perspective, might lead to increased distrust and morale that could hamper productivity and innovation (Basset-Jones, 2005).

The core issue raised in this chapter is that the benefits of diversity, such as innovative capacity, do not occur automatically and in every situation. When I have been involved in diversity, equity and inclusion (DEI) projects, it often becomes apparent that leaders lack the language to address issues related to DEI. Leaders often find it uncomfortable to address issues related to diversity and do not know where to start, and might find the task daunting. As a starting point, managers must emphasise the importance of top-level commitment to DEI and the creation of an inclusive work environment, through training and time allocation. Herein, I uphold that diversity can be fostered through creating room in which people feel safe, valued, and (feel they) can contribute. This entails motivation to engage with others different from self and knowledge of others (see Stegmann et al., 2012 on the empathy-stimulating effect of diversity). Herein, active listening and putting mentor-programmes into action might facilitate and foster knowledge-sharing and bridging. It is important to create a sense of belonging, a place where people can go to work and experience that they can be fully themselves (if they want to). Such inclusion practices entail that employees perceive being seen, respected and valued as essential, which entails staff having access to important information and being invited to partake both formally and informally in the organisation's work (Traavik, 2019). Moreover, companies must create a safe and sound environment, and focus on building psychological safety and trusting workgroups to allow diverse voices to be heard.

An automatic relationship between various workforce characteristics and innovation potential is often assumed, in both theory and practice, where diversity is counted and measured towards innovation as output. It is important to move beyond the mere counting of diversity through 'diversity washing', towards the adoption of actual practices of inclusion. Companies must move from (solely focusing on) diversity as 'tokenism' towards incorporating diversity and inclusion practices into formal and informal organisational routines and structures. It is about moving from thinking about diversity as a goal in itself, towards incorporating diversity and inclusion practices into organisational routines and structures (as exemplified through the case of gender mainstreaming in the Swedish Ministry of Foreign Affairs (Solheim & Moss, 2021)). Future research should furthermore aim at disentangling and viewing the relationship between formal and informal diversity and inclusion practices within organisations.

This chapter has addressed the importance of looking into the relationship between diversity and innovation from a relational point of view/inclusion, referring to past research, particularly in social psychology and diversity research and measures undertaken to spur inclusiveness in the workplace. Including a variety of voices is particularly important for innovation, as innovation does not take place in isolation but in collaboration with others and when a variety of knowledge intersect. Kanter (2000, p. 205) says that

> making a thousand flowers bloom is not a fully random or accidental process unless we are satisfied with spindly, fragile wildflowers. Instead, the flowers of innovation can be cultivated and encouraged to multiply in the gardens (…) where the growth rhythm of innovation is well understood.

There is, unfortunately, no 'one size fits all' recipe. Herein, leaders must acknowledge that they need to get to know their employees and increase understanding as to what works for *their* specific employees in *their* specific setting. Future research should, therefore, aim at studying links between diversity, inclusion and innovation in various countries and contexts.

NOTES

1. See also Van Der Vegt and Bunderson (2005) and Solheim (2017, p. 27).
2. The title of this chapter is referring to Kanter's seminal chapter "When a thousand flowers bloom: structural, collective, and social cognitions for innovation in organziations", see Kanter (2000).
3. Or divided between surface-level and deep-level diversity characteristics.

4. Within psychology, these are referred to as the 'social categorisation perspective' and the 'information/decision perspective'. For reviews, see van Knippenberg and Schippers (2007, p. 507) who moreover argue that these perspectives are not clear-cut, and they instead frequently 'represent a more loosely defined emphasis on either the preference to work with similar others or the value of diverse information, knowledge, and perspectives'. Herein, it is also important to note that these are 'ideal types', and 'change and innovation not only that results from clashes between poles, but also that emerges within each pole' (Smith et al., 2017).
5. A sidenote, but an important one, is that both diversity and social identity are dynamic, social constructs. Diversity is complex and compiled of multiple identities and complexity, such as intersectionality (Traavik, 2019, p. 217). This could become apparent inter alia through *salience* of identity. Salience refers to activation of an identity in a situation (Stets & Burke, 2000). People have several social group memberships, such as sister, mother, Latin, doctor, and so forth, but we are most often reduced to pertain in one category (Traavik, 2019) when people sort themselves and others into in- or out-groups.
6. Moreover, Solheim (2017, p. 34) argues that the concepts of the similarity attraction paradigm and the cognitive resource diversity perspective 'relate to the seminal work by Granovetter (1973) regarding the strong and weak ties. The similarity attraction could be tied to the strong ties, and weak ties could represent the cognitive resource diversity perspective.' See Solheim (2017, p. 34) for more on the dynamic nature of ties in reference to these perspectives.
7. Solheim (2017, pp. 32–3) argues that antecedent to this paradox from developmental psychology, we can find work by, for example, Vygotsky (1962) and the 'Zone of Proximal Development', and Nooteboom (2000) on 'cognitive complementarity and 'cognitive distance' that were based on a constructivist, interactionist view of knowledge.

REFERENCES

Aarstad, J., Kvitastein, O. A., & Jakobsen, S.-E. (2016). Related and unrelated variety as regional drivers of enterprise productivity and innovation: A multilevel study. *Research Policy, 45*(4), 844–56.

Abramovic, G., & Traavik, L. E. M. (2017). Support for diversity practices in Norway: Depends on who you are and whom you have met. *European Management Journal, 35*(4), 454–63.

Almandoz, J., & Tilcsik, A. (2015). When experts become liabilities: Domain experts on boards and organizational failure. *Academy of Management Journal, 59*(4), 1124–49.

Axtell, C. M., Holman, D. J., Unsworth, K. L., Wall, T. D., & Waterson, P. E. (2000). Shopfloor innovation: Facilitating the suggestion and implementation of ideas. *Journal of Occupational and Organizational Psychology, 73*, 265–85.

Basset-Jones, N. (2005). The paradox of diversity management, creativity and innovation. *Creativity and Innovation Management, 14*, 169–75.

Boschma, R. (2005). Proximity and innovation: A critical assessment. *Regional Studies, 39*, 61–74.

Boschma, R., & Frenken, K. (2010). The spatial evolution of innovation networks: A proximity perspective. In R. A. M. Boschma (Ed.), *Handbook of Evolutionary*

Economic Geography (pp. 120–35). Cheltenham, UK, and Northampton, MA, USA: Edward Elgar Publishing.

Brimhall, K. C. (2019). Inclusion is important … But how do I include? Examining the effects of leader engagement on inclusion, innovation, job satisfaction, and perceived quality of care in a diverse nonprofit health care organization. *Nonprofit and Voluntary Sector Quarterly*, *48*(4), 716–37.

Burt, R. (1992). *Structural Holes: The Social Structure of Competition*. Cambridge, MA: Harvard University Press.

Carlile, P. R. (2004). Transferring, translating, and transforming: An integrative framework for managing knowledge across boundaries. *Organization Science*, *15*(5), 555–68.

Carpenter, M. A. (2002). The implications of strategy and social context for the relationship between top team management heterogeneity and firm performance. *Strategic Management Journal*, *23*(3), 275–84.

Clearfield, C., & Tilcsik, A. (2018). *Meltdown: Why Our Systems Fail and What We Can Do About It*. London: Penguin Press.

Cox, T. (1994). *Cultural Diversity in Organizations: Theory, Research and Practice*. Oakland, CA: Berrett-Koehler.

Czaja, S. J. (2020). Setting the stage: Workplace and demographic trends. In S. J. Czaja & J. James (Eds.), *Current and Emerging Trends in Aging and Work*. Dordrecht: Springer.

Dougherty, D. (1992). Interpretive barriers to successful product innovation in large firms. *Organization Science*, *3*(2), 179–202.

Duhigg, C. (2016). What Google learned from its quest to build the perfect team. https://www.nytimes.com/2016/02/28/magazine/what-google-learned-from-its -quest-to-build-the-perfect-team.html.

Edmondson, A. (1999). Psychological safety and learning behavior in work teams. *Administrative Science Quarterly*, *44*(2), 350–83.

Edmondson, A. and Besieux, T. (2021). Reflections: Voice and silence in workplace conversations. *Journal of Change Management*, *21*(3), 269–86.

Gaertner, S. L., & Dovidio, J. F. (2000). *Reducing Intergroup Bias: The Common Ingroup Identity Model*. Philadelphia, PA: The Pshycology Press.

Granovetter, M. S. (1973). The strength of the weak ties. *American Journal of Sociology*, *78*, 1360–89.

Grant, A. (2016). *Originals: How Non-Conformists Move the World*. London: Penguin Books.

Guillaume, Y. R. F., Dawson, J. F., Priola, V., Sacramento, C. A., Woods, S. A., Higson, H. E., Budwar, P.S., & West, M. A. (2014). Managing diversity in organizations: An integrative model and agenda for future research. *European Journal of Work and Organizational Psychology*, *23*(5), 783–802.

Harrison, D. A., & Sin, H.-P. (2006). What is diversity and how should it be measured? In A. M. Konrad, P. Prasad, & J. K. Pringle (Eds.), *Handbook of Workplace Diversity* (pp. 191–216). London: Sage.

Holvino, E., & Kamp, A. (2009). Diversity management: Are we moving in the right direction? Reflections from both sides of the North Atlantic. *Scandinavian Journal of Management*, *25*(4), 395–403.

Horwitz, S. K. (2005). The compositional impact of team diversity on performance: Theoretical considerations. *Human Resource Development Review*, *4*(2), 219–45.

Horwitz, S. K., & Horwitz, I. B. (2007). The effects of team diversity on team outcomes: A meta-analytic review of team demography. *Journal of Management, 33*, 987–1015.

Hu, M.-L. M., Horng, J.-S., & Sun, Y.-H. C. (2009). Hospitality teams: Knowledge sharing and service innovation performance. *Tourism Management, 30*(1), 41–50.

Hunt, V., Layton, D., & Prince, S. (2015). Why diversity matters. https://www.mckinsey .com/~/media/McKinsey/Business%20Functions/Organization/Our%20Insights/ Why%20diversity%20matters/Why%20diversity%20matters.pdf.

Jackson, S., May, K. E., & Whitney, K. (1995). Understanding the dynamics of diversity in decision making teams. In R. A. Guzzo & E. Salas (Eds.), *Team Effectiveness and Decision Making in Organizations* (pp. 204–61). San Francisco, CA: Jossey-Bass.

Jacobsson, A., Backteman-Erlanson, S., & Sjolander, A. E. (2020). Diversity, preventive work and education – matters of health and well-being in firefighter discourse. *International Journal of Qualitative Studies on Health and Well-being, 15*(1), 1–12.

Kanter, R. M. (2000). When a thousand flowers bloom: structural, collective, and social cognitions for innovation in organizations. In B. Staw & R. Sutton (Eds.), *Research in Organizational Behavior*, Vol. 22 (pp. 167–210). Amsterdam: Elsevier Science.

Kvålshaugen, R. (2003). *Likevekt, motvekt og mangfold. Om kvinner og innflytelse. [Equilibirium, counterbalance and diverity. About women and influence].* ISCO Group Communication, 15(2), 1–5.

Li, C.-R., Lin, C.-J., Tien, Y.-H., & Chen, C.-M. (2017). A multilevel model of team cultural diversity and creativity: The role of climate for inclusion. *Journal of Creative Behavior, 51*(2), 163–79.

Loyd, D. L., Wang, C. S., Phillips, K. W., & Lount, R. B. J. (2013). Social category diversity promotes premeeting elaboration: The role of relationship focus. *Organization Science, 24*(3), 757–72.

Lundvall, B.-Å. (1992). *National Systems of Innovation: Towards a Theory of Innovation and Interactive Learning.* London: Pinter Publishers.

McPherson, M., Smith-Lovin, L., & Cook, J. M. (2001). Birds of a feather: Homophily in social networks. *Annual Review of Sociology, 27*, 415–44.

Mill, J. S. (1848). *Principles of Political Economy.* London: Longmans, Green and Co.

Milliken, F. J., & Martins, L. L. (1996). Searching for common threads: Understanding the multiple effects of diversity in organizational groups. *Academy of Management Review, 21*(2), 402–33.

Mor Barak, M. E. (2005). *Managing Diversity: Toward a Globally Inclusive Workplace.* Thousand Oaks, CA: Sage.

Moss, S. M. & Solheim, M. C. W. (2021). Shifting diversity discourses and new feeling rules? The case of Brexit. *Human Arenas.* https://doi.org/10.1007/s42087-020 -00177-9.

Nooteboom, B. (2000). *Learning and Innovation in Organizations and Economies.* Oxford: Oxford University Press.

Østergaard, C. R., Timmermans, B., & Kristinsson, K. (2011). Does a different view create something new? The effect of employee diversity on innovation. *Research Policy, 40*, 500–509.

Ottaviano, G. I. P., & Peri, G. (2006). The economic value of cultural diversity: Evidence from US cities. *Journal of Economic Geography, 6*(1), 9–44.

Özden, Ç., Parsons, C. R., Schiff, M., & Walmsley, T. L. (2011). Where on Earth is everybody? The evolution of global bilateral migration 1960–2000. *The World Bank Economic Review, 25*(1), 12–56.

Parrotta, P., Pozzoli, D., & Pytlikova, M. (2014). Labor diversity and firm productivity. *European Economic Review*, *66*, 144–79.

Pelz, D. & Andrews, F. (1966). *Scientists in Organizations*. London: John Wiley & Sons.

Phillips, K. W., Liljenquist, K. A., & Neale, M. A. (2009). Is the pain worth the gain? The advantages and liabilities of agreeing with socially distinct newcomers. *Personality and Social Psychology Bulletin*, *35*(3), 336–50.

Richard, O. C. (2000). Racial diversity, business strategy, and firm performance: A resource-based view. *Academy of Management Journal*, *43*(2), 164–77.

Ruef, M., Aldrich, H. E., & Carter, N. M. (2003). The structure of founding teams: Homophily, strong ties, and isolation among U.S. entrepreneurs. *American Sociological Review*, *68*(2), 195–222.

Schumpeter, J. A. (1934). *The Theory of Economic Development: An Inquiry into Profits, Capital, Credit, Interest and the Business Cycle*. Cambridge, MA: Harvard University Press.

Shore, L. M., Cleveland, J. N., & Sanchez, D. (2018). Inclusive workplaces: A review and model. *Human Resource Management Review*, *28*(2), 176–89.

Shore, L. M., Randel, A. E., Chung, B. G., Dean, M. A., Holcombe Ehrhart, K., & Singh, G. (2011). Inclusion and diversity in work groups: A review and model for future research. *Journal of Management*, *37*(4), 1262–89.

Smith, K. W., Erez, M., Jarvenpaa, S., Lewis, M. W., & Tracey, P. (2017). Adding complexity to theories of paradox, tensions, and dualities of innovation and change: Introduction to organization studies [special issue]. *Organization Studies*, *38*(3–4), 303–17.

Solheim, M. C. W. (2017). Innovation, space, and diversity (doctoral dissertation no. 327), University of Stavanger.

Solheim, M. C. W., Boschma, R., & Herstad, S. J. (2020). Collected worker experiences and the novelty content of innovation. *Research Policy*, *49*(1), 103856.

Solheim, M. C. W., & Fitjar, R. D. (2018). Foreign workers are associated with innovation, but why? International networks as a mechanism. *International Regional Science Review*, *41*(3), 311–34.

Solheim, M. C. W., & Herstad, S. J. (2018). The differentiated effects of human resource diversity on corporate innovation. *International Journal of Innovation and Technology Management*, 15(5). https://doi.org/10.1142/S0219877018500463.

Solheim, M. C. W. & Moss, S. M. (2021). Inter-organizational learning within an organization? Mainstreaming gender policies in the Swedish ministry of foreign affairs. *The Learning Organization*, 28(2), 181–94.

Stahl, G. K., Mäkelä, K., Zander, L., & Maznevski, M. L. (2010). A look at the bright side of multicultural team diversity. *Scandinavian Journal of Management*, *26*(4), 439–47.

Stegmann, S., Roberge, M.-É., & van Dick, R. (2012). Getting tuned in to those who are different: The role of empathy as mediator between diversity and performance. In B. Beham, C. Straub, & J. Schwalbach (Eds.), *Managing Diversity in Organizations* (pp. 19–44). Wiesbaden: Gabler Verlag.

Stets, J. E., & Burke, P. J. (2000). Identity theory and social identity theory. *Social Psychology Quarterly*, *63*(3), 224–37.

Tajfel, H. (1982). Social psychology of intergroup relations. *Annual Review of Psychology*, *33*(1), 1–39.

Tajfel, H., & Turner, J. (1979). An integrative theory of intergroup conflict. In W. G. Austin, & S. Worchel (Eds.), *Psychology of Intergroup Relations* (pp. 33–47). Brooks/Cole.

Timmermans, B., & Boschma, R. (2014). The effect of intra- and inter-regional labour mobility on plant performance in Denmark: The significance of related labour inflows. *Journal of Economic Geography*, *14*, 289–311.

Traavik, L. E. M. (2019). Where differences dwell: Inclusion and the healthy workplace. In R. J. Burke, & A. M. Richardson (Eds.), *Creating Psychologically Healthy Workplaces* (pp. 215–34). Cheltenham, UK, and Northanpton, MA, USA: Edward Elgar Publishing.

Turner, J. C., Brown, R. J., & Tajfel, H. (1979). Social comparison and group interest ingroup favouritism. *European Journal of Social Psychology*, *9*(2), 187–204.

Turner, J. C., Hogg, M. A., Oakes, P. J., Reicher, S. D., & Wetherell, M. S. (1987). *Rediscovering the Social Group: A Self-Categorization Theory*. Oxford: Basil Blackwell.

Van Der Vegt, G. S., & Bunderson, J. S. (2005). Learning and performance in multi-disiplinary teams: The importance of collective team identification. *Academy of Management Journal*, *48*(3), 532–47.

Van der Ven, A. H., Angle, H. L., & Poole, M. S. E. (1989). *Research on the Management of Innovation: The Minnesota Studies*. London: Harper & Row.

Van Engen, M., & Van Woerkom, M. (2010). Learning from differences: The relationships between team expertise diversity, team learning, team performance, and team innovation. In M. Van Woerkom & R. Poell (Eds.), *Workplace Learning: Concepts, Measurement and Application* (pp. 131–47). London: Routledge.

van Knippenberg, D., & Schippers, M. C. (2007). Work group diversity. *Annual Review of Psychology*, *58*(1), 515–41.

Vos, M., & van der Zee, K. (2011). Prosocial behavior in diverse workgroups: How relational identity orientation shapes cooperation and helping. *Group Processes & Intergroup Relations*, *14*(3), 363–79.

Vygotsky, L. S. (1962). *Thought and Language*. Cambridge, MA: MIT Press.

Williams, K. Y., & O'Reilly, C. A. (1998). Demography and diversity in organizations: A review of 40 years of research. *Research in Organizational Behavior*, *20*, 77–140.

PART III

The essentialist approach

10. Schumpeter's social ontology: before and beyond pure economics

Beniamino Callegari

1. INTRODUCTION

As innovation and entrepreneurship scholars labor to discover, explore and operationalize the connections between the social and their own understanding of the economic consequences of novelty generation and exploitation (Abu-Saifan, 2012; Mulgan, 2012), Schumpeter is rarely considered a source of inspiration, despite his vast influence over these fields (Fagerberg & Verspagen, 2009). The abstract tones of his theory, coupled with his explicit efforts to separate scientific work and philosophical discussion (Schumpeter, 2010) justify present attitude. This chapter argues, however, that beyond a severe disciplinary façade lies a complex and consistent social ontology, informing and supporting all key methodological and theoretical choices characterizing the Schumpeterian edifice. The reconstruction of Schumpeter's social ontology is aimed towards two objectives. The first is to illuminate some areas of the Schumpeterian theoretical framework, providing an explanation for some of Schumpeter's more controversial choices, still debated today. The second is to illustrate the relevance of social ontology for economic theory and methodology, even in the context of a strict disciplinary approach aimed towards the generation of pure, abstract economic theory. Social ontology is a necessary component, explicit or implicit, of all work in the field of social science; current efforts aimed towards integration of the social within innovation and entrepreneurship studies should engage with the ontological foundations of their discourse, in order to strengthen the platform on which they hope to stand. In this regard, Schumpeterian ontology offers both an example and a potential first stepping stone: we can take it or refuse it with good reasons, but it should not be ignored.

Following this brief introduction, Section 2 reconstructs the monistic foundations of Schumpeter's social ontology, and the crucial issue of the relationship between natural phenomena, the social process and economic theory, a theme that provides the basis for most of the following discourse. Section 3 describes how Schumpeter's social ontology frames his most notorious contribution, the theory of economic development, and the methodological choices that led to its construction. Section 4 delves into the first defining feature of the theory of economic development, individual agency, and the resulting conflict between agent and system, which provides the mechanism for the entrepreneurial process. Section 5 describes the economic consequences of agency, namely the endogenous generation of novelty, and the ontological foundation of the specific Schumpeterian conceptualization. Section 6 completes the review by describing the enabler of individual agency and novelty in the context of the Schumpeterian framework, namely the monetary system, and how through the latter a social element enters the theory of economic development, separating it irreversibly from pure economics. Section 7 concludes by drawing some implications both for our interpretation of Schumpeterian theory, and for the development of present debates on the role of the social in innovation and entrepreneurship studies.

2. ONTOLOGICAL FOUNDATIONS: SOCIAL REALITY AND ECONOMICS

The ontological foundations of Schumpeterian thought are introduced as assumptions underpinning the scientific discourse, "underlying large truths (…) [which] we sense more than that we can actually prove" (Schumpeter, 2002, p. 140). The defining characteristic of Schumpeter's ontology is that phenomena are assumed to be neither separated nor separable, but rather connected in an indivisible whole, developing in historic time (Schumpeter, 1954, p. 12). This monistic assumption, however, does not imply that all phenomena are qualitatively the same. Social phenomena can be distinguished from material phenomena from the nature of their primary causal mechanisms. Phenomena can be described as social if their primary cause is found in human will and purposeful behavior, while material phenomena have primarily material causes (Waters, 1952).

Social phenomena are still affected by material factors: "In spite of the relative independence of all areas, (…) every element in every area, at any time, is connected with every element in every other area" (Schumpeter, 1912, p. 545). The qualitative causal distinction is not absolute, identifying at best an area of relative autonomy, characterized by higher density of similar causal relations (Schumpeter, 2002). Since the dominant underlying causal mechanisms are qualitatively different, scientific analysis, understood by Schumpeter as a primarily causal inquiry (Schumpeter, 1954), benefits from operating a distinction between social and natural phenomena, giving rise to separated social and natural sciences, which, for Schumpeter, is a functional distinction with an ontological basis.

If the social process is an indivisible whole, then disciplinary separation of social sciences requires a justification. Schumpeter argues that the irreducible complexity of the social process prohibits the identification of phenomenological areas of relative autonomy. However, significant qualitative differences nevertheless exist in terms of the causal mechanisms active in the social process (Schumpeter, 2010). From this ontological position it follows that the scientific study of the social process must be theoretical, because it must go beyond the phenomenological complexity, and requires disciplinary separation, not in order to reach separate truths, but rather to bring different contributions to the development of a single underlying truth.

The complexity of the social process, however, has important epistemological and methodological consequences for the social sciences. Schumpeter tackled the issue from the perspective of economics. In order to establish itself as a separate discipline, economics needed to identify a specific object of analysis. However, for Schumpeter this object cannot be a phenomenon, but rather an analytical artifact: "Out of [the social process'] great stream, the classifying hand of the investigator artificially extracts economic facts" (Schumpeter, 1934, p. 3). The argument is the following. Social phenomena are identified as being caused by human conduct. Correspondingly, economic phenomena should be identified by a specific dimension of purposeful human behavior, namely economic conduct, defined as "conduct directed towards the acquisition of goods" (ibid.). But "A fact is never exclusively or purely economic; other – and often more important – aspects always exist" (ibid.): while a specifically economic dimension of human behavior exists, it is insufficient to act as a primary cause of specific phenomena, and therefore cannot identify an area of phenomenological relative (causal) autonomy.

Actual processes of production, acquisition and consumption of goods are social phenomena, or, in Schumpeterian parlance, social facts. Production takes place through work, a social process affected by and affecting all aspects of human life. Through work we contribute to the development of our community and our society, realize our ambitions, socialize with our peers, establish boundaries, enter into conflict, and so on. We also produce goods and services. By abstracting from all other aspects, reducing work to the sole production of goods, pursued for the sole purpose of acquiring goods for consumption or exchange, we obtain the economic "fact" of production. Exchange, consumption and innovation can be treated similarly, leading to the creation of the foundational "facts" of economic theory. Such "facts", however, are too distant from reality to qualify as anything other than instrumental abstractions produced for analytical purposes. The designation of a fact as "economic" conveys the proposition that, in the process of analysis, we are abstracting from all non-economic aspects, despite their factual causal relevance. Schumpeter did not mince words in describing the results: "Is that, which we

194   *Rethinking the social in innovation and entrepreneurship studies*

are left with not just as worthless as it is lifeless? It could almost appear this way" (Schumpeter, 2010, p. 410).

Non-economic mechanisms are involved in all economic "facts". Their elimination from pure economic theory does not imply denial or disinterest; it is an unfortunate necessity dictated by the complexity of the social. "The specifically technical factor and the specifically sociological factor are moreover alike alien to the economic factor, and it is the erroneous confusion of the former with the economic essence of production and of the latter with the economic essence of distribution that impedes insight" (Schumpeter & Takata, 1998, p. 10). The abstraction involved in economic theorization is meant to identify the economic essence of the actual processes of production, distribution and consumption. It is claimed that such an essence, qualitatively different from sociological, technical and all other relevant elements, exists. It is *not* claimed that these elements could be reduced to such economic essence, nor that the latter holds a dominant claim over the others in the determination of actual human conduct. Rather than minimizing or ignoring the social and natural factors, abstraction enables the identification of the narrow limits within which the economic essence operates, thus enabling, in the empirical moment of analysis, the study of its factual interaction with other, "alien" mechanisms.

While economic "facts" are abstract, they are not unreal. "Everyone must, at least in part, act economically; everyone must either be an 'economic subject' or be dependent upon one" (Schumpeter, 1934, p. 3). Life cannot be reduced to subsistence, but subsistence is nevertheless a necessary fact of life. Work is much more than production of goods; yet without the purpose of production work would lose its meaning. The economic agent is unsatisfactory as a description of human behavior, just as a pure economic system is an unsatisfactory description of society. However, any description of society which ignores economic "facts" is equally unsatisfactory. Therefore, "we speak of economic facts in science just as in ordinary life and with the same right" (ibid.). The undeniable truth of the economic dimension of life is the source of this right. Economics is a necessary component of our efforts to understand the social process, but we cannot substitute economics for the social process; social complexity will always stand between economic theory and its application to real life.

While abstractions are not necessarily unreal, they can certainly be so, when they are not conceived to reflect actual mechanisms, but are purely convenient fabrications. The example used by Schumpeter in this regard is both telling and relevant for current debates:

> Any theory involves abstractions and therefore will never fit reality exactly, hence economic theory is inevitably unrealistic in this sense; but its premises are induced

from realistic observation of the profit-seeking and calculating businessman; the premises of political theory (style James Mill) are (…) *postulated* from a completely imaginary agent, the rational voter; therefore these premises, hence results that are derived from them, are not merely abstract but also unrealistic *in a different sense*. (Schumpeter, 1954, p. 430, n6)

The passage highlights a key Schumpeterian methodological principle, the principle of correspondence, which disciplines the process of abstraction. Abstract theoretical concepts must reflect actual tendencies of social phenomena. When this correspondence between concept and phenomena is missing, the abstraction is pure ideation and therefore entirely unreal, and should not be included within the analysis.

What are the "facts" admitted by Schumpeter as the main objects of study of economics, to which all other phenomena of disciplinary interest can be ultimately reduced? Only two. On one side, the tendency of commodities' quantities and price towards systemic consistency, the *magna carta* ensuring that the subject of economics "is a cosmos and not a chaos" (Schumpeter, 1939, p. 41). On the other, the ability of individual agency to destroy and recreate such a system: the "fact" of economic development, for the defense of which Schumpeter spent his entire academic career.

3. TWO "FACTS", TWO THEORIES: SYSTEM AND DEVELOPMENT

The first economic "fact" acknowledged by Schumpeter is that any given socioeconomic context at any given time includes a specific set of commodities, distributed among economic agents, and that the relations between the quantities of the commodities form a coherent system: the system of relative prices. These relations are not causal, but functional (Schumpeter, 2010): they connect quantities with quantities, identifying an immanent "logic of things" (Schumpeter, 1915, p. 102). Price relations determine exact quantities under given conditions at a given time; they neither describe nor determine human behavior. The discovery of the systemic nature of prices provided the necessary object of study for the historical development of a scientific discipline of economics (Schumpeter, 1954): the theory of the economic system. This is a theory of quantitative relations, devoid of agency – approaching the study of the social process with instruments that proved effective in the natural sciences (Schumpeter, 2010). This is, however, not simple imitation, but the most appropriate approach to this specific object of study.

For Schumpeter, the economic system is an abstraction of an actual social tendency towards systemic consistency, a tendency supported and reinforced by market mechanisms. In the social process, such tendency is constantly contrasted, overshadowed and confused by many other forces that make its phenomenological study almost impossible. Therefore, abstraction is necessary to bring it to the fore, to realize its full potential in order to study its internal mechanisms. To bring this logic of things in full display, agency must be subordinated to the economic variables and their relations. "We want to describe the changes, or better, a certain type of changes, as if they would happen automatically, without looking at the people who are responsible for those changes" (Schumpeter, 2010, p. 71). It is only from this perspective that Schumpeter defended the individualist approach to economics (Shionoya, 2007): as a purely methodological assumption aimed at neutralizing agency and limited to the context of the theory of the economic system.

Methodological individualism removes agency by dropping from the analysis all forms of collective action and setting preferences as exogenous, thus eliminating all social mechanisms affecting their formation. The isolated individual, however, may still disrupt the economic system by refusing to conform their activities to systemic data: this possibility is eliminating by assuming a rational economic individual, implying, among other things, that individual action is predicated on the existing price structure (Schumpeter, 1984). Methodological individualism creates the conditions for the systemic tendency to reach its maximum extent, namely general equilibrium, but at a cost: the resulting economic analysis cannot support either descriptive statements or normative statements regarding actual human conduct, as essential causal factors affecting it are excluded from the analysis. Only the ontological claim that actual human behavior is essentially individualistic could make economic theory realistic; but such a claim is starkly rejected by Schumpeter as ridiculous (Schumpeter, 1954).

Although unrealistic, the mechanisms highlighted by the theory of the economic system are present in the social process. Furthermore, their influence is mediated by the ruling institutional arrangements: they are stronger under capitalism and weakest under communist, or, more generally, planned economic configurations (Schumpeter, 1909). These considerations, however, are only relevant for the process of derivation of practical implications from theoretical analysis; the pure theory of the economic system remains free from institutional considerations. This makes the resulting theory general in scope, rather than bounded to a specific socioeconomic context, although at the cost of further complications in regard to its practical applicability (Schumpeter, 1942). Furthermore, Schumpeter generally supported a parsimonious approach to theoretical development, aiming at limiting as much as possible the amount of "facts" included within the process of analysis, again for ontological reasons.

If the tendency towards equilibrium is a specifically economic mechanism, the introduction of non-economic elements in the analysis cannot be integrated in a consistent system. Extending purely economic analysis to larger and larger areas of the social process implies either ontological or methodological frictions, or both, as it requires the abandonment of either the assumption of the unreality of pure economics, or the pluralist goal of a single, interdisciplinary truth, or both (Schumpeter, 2010). What is consistent with Schumpeterian ontology, however, is to identify and introduce to economic theory new economic "facts". This is the task that would occupy most of Schumpeter's academic career, the introduction of the second great economic "fact": development.

The parsimonious methodology of theoretical development favored by Schumpeter, however, implied that the introduction of a new economic "fact" is not a pure gain to be celebrated, but rather an analytical cost that must be justified. The argument employed by Schumpeter to justify the introduction of development to economics had both a negative and a positive component. Firstly, Schumpeter observed that the theory of the economic system of his time could not offer a satisfactory theorization of several phenomena which should have fallen under the purview of economic conduct: namely the business cycle, innovation, entrepreneurship, profits, credit, interest and capital (Schumpeter, 2010). Secondly, Schumpeter argued that the introduction of a single "fact", economic development, would be sufficient to provide a satisfactory theorization of all other elements, thus greatly enlarging the field of application of economics without unduly complicating its analytical apparatus (Schumpeter, 1934).

In order to abstract an economic concept from the actual phenomena of development, Schumpeter first excluded those phenomena that, although often associated with development, are in fact qualitatively different and may be satisfactorily handled by the theory of the economic system. These are the phenomena associated, on the one hand, with the process of gradual adaptation to modest social and natural variations, and, on the other, with growth, defined as continuous quantitative expansion of economic activities along pre-existing lines of production, distribution and consumption. Also excluded from the analysis are large-scale exogenous shocks: while their effects cannot be effectively analyzed through application of the theory of the economic system, their causal mechanisms are by definition non-economic, and therefore cannot provide a foundation for the concept of economic development (Schumpeter, 1934). The Schumpeterian concept of development therefore corresponds only to those phenomena of endogenous, qualitative, intentional change.

To underline the abstract nature of the new economic "fact", Schumpeter clarified that his analysis did not include "the fact of historical change, whereby social conditions become historical 'individuals' in historical time" (Schumpeter, 1934, p. 58). Schumpeterian economic development does not coincide with the actual process of development taking place through histori-cal time:

> [Real] economic development is so far simply the object of economic history (…) Because of this fundamental dependence of the economic aspect of things on everything else, it is not possible to explain *economic* change by previous *economic* conditions alone. For the economic state of a people does not emerge simply from the preceding economic conditions, but only from the preceding total situation. (ibid.)

Since economics cannot analyze the entire social process, the social phenom-ena of development cannot be explained by economics alone.

What can be done is to abstract from actual development phenomena a pure economic "fact", reflecting the essential economic mechanism operating within the social process. This economic "fact" is the main object of study of the Schumpeterian theory of economic development. None of the previ-ously mentioned limitations affecting the theory of the economic system are overcome: the theory of economic development does not represent a general advancement over the theory of the economic system. Superiority is claimed exclusively regarding those phenomena which can be analyzed by the theory of the economic system only through unrealistic distortions of their essential economic mechanisms, namely endogenous qualitative change, business cycles and monetary phenomena, including profits, interest, capital and credit. It is not a modest claim, but nevertheless a limited one, recognizing the neces-sity and usefulness of the theory of the economic system. Furthermore, the foundational "fact" of the economic system, the systemic tendency towards order, is affirmed, and in fact made into a necessary component of the theory of economic development, although under a different guise.

The "fact" of economic development is thus reduced to the intentional implementation of a new production function (Schumpeter, 1939, p. 87). The focus on implementation does not imply disregard for the role of creativity and ideation (cf. Solo, 1951), but only that these mechanisms, while critical for the actual development process, are not essentially economic, and therefore cannot be meaningfully integrated within pure economic theory. The term "produc-tion function" summarily conveys the idea that economic development is part of the production process, and that it can involve any combination of changes affecting inputs, outputs and their relations (Schumpeter, 1934). Despite this apparently limited conceptualization, the "fact" of development introduces to economic analysis the missing concepts of individual agency and novelty, which combine to introduce a distinction between systemic and individual level of analysis, thus creating the necessity for explicitly social elements to enter pure economic analysis, thus creating a divide between the theory of the economic system and the theory of economic development. Therefore,

Schumpeterian ontology can be said to provide the foundational justification for a separate economic theory of innovation and entrepreneurship.

4. INDIVIDUAL AGENCY AND THE LOGIC OF THINGS

The theory of the economic system describes a "logic of things", a set of functional relations determining the quantities of commodities and their relative prices. While individual preferences inform and, through their interactions, shape these relations, the individual agent's behavior is dictated by the distribution of endowments and technology, to which the individual adapts. The question of individual and social agency becomes moot, as agency is assumed away from the economic system. Being closed, the economic system cannot generate change endogenously (da Graça Moura, 2002); it can only reproduce continuous trends and drifts taking place in logical time (Vickers, 1994). The analysis of endogenous economic change requires the introduction of agency to make individual behavior at least partially free from systemic conditions. Only through the introduction of individual, exceptional and indeterminate behavior can economic agency be conceptualized (Schumpeter, 1947).

Agency is not compatible with the pure, abstract economic system (da Graça Moura, 2002), but it is compatible with the real tendency towards systemic order on which such system is based. Output prices are necessarily related to the relevant inputs' prices, and both are necessarily connected to all other economic variables: development and agency affect but do not overwrite the first economic "fact". "Novelty always exists together with a wide area of circumstances and processes that, in principle, are deterministic" (Schumpeter, 2005, p. 113). A theory of economic development requires a reconceptualization of the systemic tendency towards consistency in a form compatible with the novelty introduced by indeterminate individual agency. Similarly, creative agency must be conceptualized in a way compatible with a continuous tendency towards systemic order, although one that cannot see its full realization.

Schumpeter's solution is to split economic conduct into two behavioral archetypes: the adaptive response and the creative response (Schumpeter, 1947). The former identifies the normal behavior of all economic agents, characterized by passive adaptation to systemic data; the latter is an exceptional, temporary and indeterminate response taken in deliberate opposition to a subset of systemic prices, motivated by the objective aim of modifying them. For this distinction to emerge, it is necessary for systemic prices to be at least partially independent and additional to the interaction of economic agents. In other words, the "fact" of economic development requires the emergence of a temporary systemic configuration in which individual behavior and systemic data are partially inconsistent. Therefore, the economic system acquires now a specifically social, and not simply aggregated, essence. When systemic prices suffice to determine individual behavior, the latter can be described as adaptive. The creative response emerges when systemic prices are insufficient to determine individual behavior: the creative response coincides with individual agency.

The result is a potential contrast between systemic prices and individual economic actions and interactions. This implies the emergence of systemic expectations, defined as the set of prices that would result in the absence of creative response. In this scenario, systemic expectations and outcomes coincide, and the Schumpeterian circular flow emerges. While the circular flow is the counterpart of the general equilibrium, the two should not be confused, as they belong to two different theoretical frameworks: they are supported by different assumptions, contain different propositions, and are instruments developed to reach different aims. When, by instrumental assumption, economic agency is muted, the circular flow is superficially identical with general equilibrium. However, while general equilibrium obtains from the result of present adaptive interactions of economic agents, the circular flow is dependent on the past:

> Past economic periods govern the activity of the individual (...) All the preceding periods have (...) entangled him in a net of social and economic connections which he cannot easily shake off. They have bequeathed him definite means and methods of production. All these hold him in iron fetters fast in his tracks. (Schumpeter, 1934, p. 6)

While general equilibrium is a timeless present, the circular flow requires a definite past in order to enable a different future.

The conflict between systemic prices and individual activities, however, must be exceptional, if the logic of things is not to break down completely.[1] Thus, adaptive behavior describes most economic conduct, while the creative response is extraordinary, temporary and partial. While all agents are potentially creative, only a few engage in creative behavior, and even fewer succeed. Furthermore, while the adaptive response is a-temporal, the creative response has a definite beginning and end: the entrepreneur is a temporary, not a permanent, role (Schumpeter, 1934). Although the creative agent can challenge systemic prices, such a challenge is localized: only a limited, often marginal, number of economic variables are directly affected by entrepreneurial agency, although the systemic nature of the economy may produce significant consequences in the fullness of time. Furthermore, outside the narrow scope of entrepreneurial activities, even the creative agent's behavior is determined by systemic prices. These qualifications ensure the potential cohabitation of individual freedom and systemic order, although this odd couple is not without its tensions (da Graça Moura, 2015).

The implications of this ontological separation between systemic data and economic conduct are numerous. First, it enables a degree of individual agency, as described above. Second, it creates conditions for a new type of economic process to emerge, namely entrepreneurship, providing an economic explanation and conceptualization for the missing key phenomena: innovation, business cycles, profits, credit, interest and capital. Third, it provides minimum conditions for economic novelty to be meaningfully defined. Finally, to admit the possibility of partially autonomous individual economic behavior raises the question of how such activities can be funded, thus revealing a specific role for credit. While the concept of economic innovation, and therefore novelty, is the most well-recognized of Schumpeter's contributions, individual agency provides the foundations on which the theory of economic development can be built in autonomy from the received theory of the economic system.

5. ECONOMIC NOVELTY AND PRICES

The key concept behind economic innovation is novelty (Schumpeter, 1934). The introduction of novelty disrupts the economic system: "Novelty is the true core of everything that must be accepted as indeterminate in the most profound sense" (Schumpeter, 2005, p. 113). An effective definition of novelty requires three elements: a specific characteristic of the object and/or process being evaluated; a general term of reference, comparable with the selected characteristic; and a precise relation between the two, at least sufficient to establish the presence or absence of novelty. Novelty is a complex concept, potentially applicable to a wide variety of heterogeneous phenomena, each characterized by specific terms of comparisons. These difficulties are well known to the scholars who have tackled the issue of innovation measurement in recent decades (Nelson et al., 2014). However, the empirical task of measuring actual novelty is different from the theoretical task of operationalizing the concept of economic novelty. While modern definitions have been developed for the purpose of supporting surveys able to generate meaningful innovation data, Schumpeter strove to introduce a definition that could operate a clear distinction between the two abstract concepts of adaptive and creative behavior, described above. The difference in aims provides an explanation for the significant, although rarely noticed, difference between some of the most influential present definitions of innovation (e.g. OECD & Eurostat, 2019) and the Schumpeterian conceptualization (Schumpeter, 1939).

Consistently with his methodology, Schumpeter approached the issue by abstracting from the actual phenomenon of novelty to the more limited concept of economic novelty. The three constitutive elements of economic novelty must be economic in nature: the characteristic and the term of reference must therefore indicate a price or a quantity, and the relation between them must be a quantitative relation. Schumpeterian methodology imposes two additional constraints, previously introduced. First, the principle of correspondence states that the concept should be abstract but not unreal: it should reflect a real mechanism, although not necessarily the most relevant. Second, the conceptualization should be consistent with the existing theoretical framework, and should not, if possible, rely on the introduction of any additional economic "facts", in order to minimize complexity (Shionoya, 2007).

The quantitative relation requirement implies that both the object's characteristic to be evaluated and the term of reference must be expressed in a common unit of measurement. It cannot be a specific physical unit of measure, since economic novelty should be a general concept, applicable across all potential economic products and processes. Since novelty is a quality referring to a singular instance of the object of study, it cannot be a pure number, which would always be unitary. The only economic characteristic satisfying the requirements is price: all economically relevant resources can theoretically be priced, directly or indirectly, and quantitative comparison is the raison d'être of prices. Furthermore, prices have a clear term of reference: the price structure which composes systemic data. Thus, the Schumpeterian conceptualization of economic novelty is the following. A specific production function implies novelty, that is, is innovative, if the prices implied by the function are inconsistent with the current price structure. Such inconsistency might arise because the output and/or inputs of the production function under analysis do not have a market price, or because the production function is economically unviable when evaluated according to current market prices.

The rationalist condition associated with methodological individualism implies that the individual expectations of the creative agent performing the innovative production function, expressed in terms of prices, are such as to make the latter economically viable. This implies the temporary coexistence of two sets of prices: systemic prices, including an implicit set of systemic price expectations, and entrepreneurial prices, identifying the set of prices that the entrepreneurial agent expects to obtain as a consequence of their activities (Schumpeter, 1939). The entrepreneurial process begins when the economic activities required to implement the innovative production function begins, and completes when the discrepancy between entrepreneurial prices and systemic prices disappears. Successful (failed) innovation takes place when systemic (entrepreneurial) prices adapt to entrepreneurial (systemic) prices.

The Schumpeterian operationalization of novelty has several advantages. First, it can be used as foundations of a purely economic conceptualization of development, the primary Schumpeterian theoretical aim. Second, it is a general conceptualization, applicable to all economic objects, despite phenomenological heterogeneity. Third, it satisfies the Schumpeterian correspondence principle, as sudden, endogenous price changes are an empirically verifiable phenomenon intimately linked with innovation and entrepreneurship, not merely convenient ideation. Fourth, it is equally applicable to so-called "marginal" and "radical" innovation, avoiding a qualitative distinction between the two, while maintaining the possibility of measuring a quantitative difference in terms of prices changes, consistent with Schumpeter thinking on the subject:

> Marshall, therefore, distinguishes these, which he calls "substantive" inventions (...) from inventions which, being of the nature of more obvious applications of known principles, may be expected to arise in consequence of expansion itself. (...) This view, however, cuts up a homogeneous phenomenon, the elements of which do not differ from one another except by degree. (Schumpeter, 1928, p. 378, n1)

Fifth, it neither imposes nor requires an arbitrary calendar time period, being applicable to processes of any duration. Sixth, it does not imply a normative stance, as success and failure conditions only describe which price set changes, with no social welfare implication.

An important consequence of the Schumpeterian conceptualization of novelty is that, before completion of the entrepreneurial process, there is no way to distinguish between successful innovation, failed innovation and irrational, meaning suboptimal, economic activity. This inability to assess innovation *ex ante*, but only *ex post*, is a crucial characteristic of the phenomenon (Schumpeter, 1947), with significant consequences for the study of its economic mechanisms. Schumpeterian entrepreneurship implicitly relies on the presence of mechanisms allowing a distinction between systemic entrepreneurial prices to both emerge and be reconciled. If development is to occur, creative agents must be allowed to achieve control over the required resources on the basis of economically unviable production plans. This, for Schumpeter, is the systemic function played by credit, and, more generally, monetary transaction within market economies. Thus, while economic novelty is the final cause of credit, credit is the efficient cause of economic novelty, its monetary counterpart (Schumpeter, 1934).

6.   MONEY AND THE SOCIAL CONTEXT

Schumpeter described the theory of the economic system of his own times as predicated on a single type of functional relation: the barter relation (Schumpeter, 2010). The term does not indicate a specific historical type of human interaction, but rather the abstract economic conceptualization of a transaction as potential frictionless exchange of commodities against commodities. The resulting concept can be used to describe a system of relations connecting all economic quantities and relative prices: the first economic "fact". Thus, Real Analysis is sufficient for the theory of the economic system (Schumpeter, 1954). However, the barter relation cannot meaningfully describe the "fact" of development. A theory of economic development requires the barter relation to be complemented by the monetary relation, identifying the potential frictionless exchange of commodities against general purchasing power. The latter is the factor enabling individual economic agency within a functional economic system and the consequent temporary divergence between the systemic norm, operationalized as a price structure, and actual economic activities. Therefore, the Schumpeterian theory of development can only be expressed in a Monetary Analysis framework (Schumpeter, 1954).

The monetary aspects of Schumpeterian theory are described in detail in the rarely read *Treatise on Money* (Schumpeter, 2014). In the theory of the economic system, a complete set of relative prices implies that all commodities are fungible. Once novelty is introduced, however, relative prices become uncertain, and economic coordination requires the introduction of a mechanism *"foreign to the meaning of the calculation process"* (ibid., p. 233), at least partially resistant to "the apparatus of supply and demand" (ibid., p. 241). Since it escapes the confines of pure economic relations, such mechanism is described by Schumpeter as a *social* accounting system. The choice of the term implies that while the economic function of the mechanism can be identified, its workings cannot be inferred exclusively based on economic conduct and must therefore be introduced to the analysis as an assumption. While the assumption must still be expressed in economic form, in order to be integrated within the theoretical framework, it corresponds to a specific phenomenon, linked to a specific context.

The specifically capitalist vehicle of social accounting is the modern banking-centered monetary system. Systemic funding of the creative response is solved under capitalism by the provision of general purchasing power through the balance sheet of an economic entity at least temporarily and/or partially excepted from market evaluation. While transactions defying systemic prices normally imply a temporary wealth loss, bank funding does not: the balance sheet of the banking system is not subject to conventional systemic pricing rules. This implies that, on one side, the price of their liabilities used as means of payment is not determined by the price of their assets. On the other, acquisition of assets lacking a systemic price does not entail any immediate wealth loss for the banking system. Therefore, the capital process avoids the temporary loss of wealth implied in the operation of the entrepreneurial function within a market system. The theoretical alien monetary element corresponds to the capability of banks to issue systemic IOUs on the basis of individual IOUs (Callegari, 2021). This exorbitant privilege enables the banker to take the role of the ephor of capitalist development (Schumpeter, 1934, p. 74).

Lakomski-Laguerre recently observed how "money appears to be a norm that helps organize economic life, reducing uncertainty in a changing world"

(Lakomski-Laguerre, 2016, p. 497). Money is an "alien element" to the logic of the economic system. Yet, social accounting systems, human creations, partially ruled by human logic, also introduce a principle of meaning and order, although necessarily transient and potentially fragile. The credit-based monetary system enables the entrepreneurial process within a capitalist setting, but also provides a reliable store of value function, offering options to adaptive agents to mitigate the economic effects of uncertainty (Keynes, 1936) and constrain discontinuous price changes mostly to financial markets, thus maintaining systemic order outside of the context of pathological crises (Schumpeter, 1939).

The theory of the economic system claims to be a general theory, due to its lack of reliance on institutional, context-specific assumptions. However, Schumpeter argues that, while potentially general (Schumpeter, 1942), its meaningful field of application is limited to individualist economies, as collective socioeconomic systems are likely to be dominated by different mechanisms (Schumpeter, 1909). The monetary assumptions introduced by Schumpeter to enable novelty to be implemented and economic development to take place makes the theory of economic development a theory of the capitalist economy, defined as an individualist economy characterized by private control of the processes of monetary creation and destruction, or, in other words, a private banking system (Schumpeter, 1928, 1943). Within the disciplinary approach favored by Schumpeter, social elements cannot be integrated into the analysis, acting instead as boundary conditions for the related theoretical propositions. Compared to the theory of the economic system, the theory of economic development is simultaneously phenomenologically broader, for it can account for development and monetary phenomena, and less general, for its propositions are dependent on the validity of context-specific assumptions.

7.   CONCLUSIONS

For Schumpeter, the social identifies the domain of the real. This domain lies beyond the reach of the scientific approach; even multidisciplinary analysis can lay very limited claims on it. The scientific process of social research, the collective and disciplined creation and accumulation of knowledge, is limited to the analysis of abstractions. Such abstractions are not necessarily unreal, as they are derived from observation of a single facet of reality, yet they can neither substitute social reality, nor even be considered a simplified version of it. Complexity is a necessary characteristic of the social process; a simplified social process is an oxymoron. Between the abstract "fact" and social reality lies an impassable divide.

From this perspective, no contradiction exists between the idea that all actual innovation is inherently social and complex, and the practice of studying innovation as a pure economic object, defined in its emergence, development and diffusion exclusively through prices. The inescapable corollary is, however, that any economic theory of development won't be directly applicable to the analysis of actual development. Schumpeterian theory requires mediating interdisciplinary efforts to enter in contact with the domain of the real. The crowning achievement of the Schumpeterian system is neither policy recommendations, nor normative evaluations, but *histoire raisonnée*, comprehensive long-term historical analysis resting on multidisciplinary scientific work (Shionoya, 2007). Economics is a required, but ancillary, component of a much more ambitious analytical effort: a sobering thought in the age of economics imperialism (Mäki, 2009). However, this clear ontological blueprint is not entirely consistent with the actual contents of Schumpeter's theory of economic development.

Despite his best attempts, Schumpeter had to conclude that development resisted reduction to pure economic "fact", and that its introduction within economic theory would necessarily entail the introduction of supporting "facts" extraneous to the pure theory of the economic system, which he adopted as a starting point. More precisely, intentional entrepreneurial activity can only be meaningfully conducted through monetary transactions, and the essence of the latter cannot be provided by pure economics, as the introduction of money necessarily entails a supporting discourse of power and social relations. Thus, through monetary analysis, an "alien" element enters the picture, separating the theory of the economic development from "pure" economic theory. The result is a dualistic, and, therefore, potentially pluralistic, approach to economics, based on two related yet necessarily distinct theoretical frameworks, differentiated according to the foundational "facts", supporting assumptions, analytical goals and field of application.

Is Schumpeterian theory of development "social" then? No, it is not. The divide between theory and social process cannot be bridged by the introduction of a few assumptions to pure economic theory. What Schumpeter did claim for his theory was that it provides a better supporting framework for the analysis of such phenomena as money, debt, interest, profit and, crucially, capital. The costs are high, though. Besides being analytically distinct from what is now the mainstream economic core, Schumpeterian theory is also reliant on a specific institutional localization. The contents of the theory depend on the shifting landscape of the monetary system, leaving its propositions limited not only to capitalism, which would make its field of application rather wide indeed today, but to specific capitalist regimes (Schumpeter, 1939). Given the mutability of capitalism (Hall & Soskice, 2001), the actual applicability of Schumpeterian theory in space and time should never be taken for granted.

Despite the narrow disciplinary approach favored by Schumpeter, his social ontology underlies, supports and explains both his methodology and his theory. His theory of economic development is predicated on a sophisticated exploration of the nature of the social process, the possibilities and limits of its scientific analysis, the meaning and value of scientific results for practical life. The Schumpeterian approach is disciplinary in order to be ultimately multidisciplinary and holistic. Scientific rigor is both an analytical necessity and a sign of distance from actual phenomena. The crowning achievement of social science is not precise mathematical modeling, but grand historical narrative (Georgescu-Roegen, 1971). His approach has clearly failed to achieve dominance within the field of economics, at least for now.

Its influence, however, is alive and well in innovation and entrepreneurship studies. After all, many authors active in these fields are profoundly influenced by Schumpeterian thought, which still provides the foundations of our economic understanding of innovation (Fagerberg & Verspagen, 2009). The firm commitment to multidisciplinary understanding (Baregheh et al., 2009), methodological and theoretical pluralism (Martin, 2013), and the willingness to go beyond the boundaries of mainstream economic theories (Castellacci et al., 2005) identify an undeniably large area of common ground between Schumpeter's own approach and the dominant practices of innovation and entrepreneurship studies. What is presently missing is a consistent, ample metatheoretical discourse (Shionoya, 2007), solidly grounded in an explicit ontological discourse acknowledging the relevance of the social process, the analytical challenges it poses, and its key role for the development of theoretical insight into practical, normative implications for policymakers and practitioners alike. This chapter has endeavored to show that these ontological foundations can be provided by the Schumpeterian heritage. Besides offering a better understanding of its theoretical and methodological foundations, which many of us still share, Schumpeterian ontology can provide solid ground for a better understanding of the social in innovation and entrepreneurship studies. Schumpeter's approach may not satisfy many, perhaps most. By standing on his shoulders we may, and perhaps should, gain a better view than he ever glimpsed. What we cannot do is turn away from the task.

NOTE

1. In that case, the tendency towards systemic order would not result from economic interaction, but could be maintained only by assumption, and therefore implicitly classified as non-economic in nature, a position entirely inconsistent with Schumpeterian ontology.

REFERENCES

Abu-Saifan, S. (2012). Social entrepreneurship: definition and boundaries. *Technology Innovation Management Review*, *2*(2), 22–7.

Baregheh, A., Rowley, J., & Sambrook, S. (2009). Towards a multidisciplinary definition of innovation. *Management Decision*, *47*(8), 1323–39.

Callegari, B. (2021). *Foundations of Post-Schumpeterian Economics: Innovation, Institutions and Finance*. New York: Routledge.

Castellacci, F., Grodal, S., Mendonca, S., & Wibe, M. (2005). Advances and challenges in innovation studies. *Journal of Economic Issues*, *39*(1), 91–121.

da Graça Moura, M. (2002). Metatheory as the key to understanding: Schumpeter after Shionoya. *Cambridge Journal of Economics*, *26*(6), 805–21.

da Graça Moura, M. (2015). Schumpeter's conceptions of process and order. *Cambridge Journal of Economics*, *39*(4), 1129–48.

Fagerberg, J., & Verspagen, B. (2009). Innovation studies: the emerging structure of a new scientific field. *Research Policy*, *38*(2), 218–33.

Georgescu-Roegen, N. (1971). *The Entropy Law and the Economic Process*. Cambridge, MA: Harvard University Press.

Hall, P. A., & Soskice, D. (2001). *Varieties of Capitalism: The Institutional Foundations of Comparative Advantage*. Oxford: Oxford University Press.

Keynes, J. M. (1936). *The General Theory of Employment, Interest, and Money*. London: Macmillan.

Lakomski-Laguerre, O. (2016). Joseph Schumpeter's credit view of money: a contribution to a "monetary analysis" of capitalism. *History of Political Economy*, *48*(3), 489–514.

Mäki, U. (2009). Economics imperialism: concept and constraints. *Philosophy of the Social Sciences*, *39*(3), 351–80.

Martin, B. R. (2013). Innovation studies: an emerging agenda. In J. Fagerberg, B. R. Martin, & E. S. Andersen (Eds.), *Innovation Studies: Evolution and Future Challenges*, 168–86. Oxford: Oxford University Press.

Mulgan, G. (2012). The theoretical foundations of social innovation. In A. Nicholls & A. Murdock (Eds.) *Social Innovation: Blurring Boundaries to Reconfigure Markets*, 33–65. London: Palgrave Macmillan.

Nelson, A., Earle, A., Howard-Grenville, J., Haack, J., & Young, D. (2014). Do innovation measures actually measure innovation? Obliteration, symbolic adoption, and other finicky challenges in tracking innovation diffusion. *Research Policy*, *43*(6), 927–40.

OECD, & Eurostat (2019). *Oslo Manual 2018: Guidelines for Collecting, Reporting and Using Data on Innovation*. Paris: OECD Publishing; Luxembourg: Eurostat.

Schumpeter, J. A. (1909). On the concept of social value. *Quarterly Journal of Economics*, *23*(2), 213–32.

Schumpeter, J. A. (1912). *Theorie der Wirtschaftlichen Entwicklung*. Leipzig: Dunker & Humblot.

Schumpeter, J. A. (1915). *Vergangenheit und Zukunft der Sozialwissenschaften*. Munich and Leipzig: Duncker & Humblot.

Schumpeter, J. A. (1928). The instability of capitalism. *Economic Journal*, *38*(151), 361–86.

Schumpeter, J. A. (1934). *The Theory of Economic Development: An Inquiry into Profits, Capital, Credit, Interest, and the Business Cycle*. Cambridge, MA: Harvard University Press.

Schumpeter, J. A. (1939). *Business Cycles: A Theoretical, Historical and Statistical Analysis of the Capitalist Process*. New York: McGraw-Hill Book Co.

Schumpeter, J. A. (1942). *Socialism, Capitalism and Democracy*. New York: Harper and Brothers.

Schumpeter, J. A. (1943). Capitalism in the postwar world. In S. E. Harris (Ed.), *Postwar Economic Problems*. New York: McGraw-Hill Book Co.

Schumpeter, J. A. (1947). The creative response in economic history. *Journal of Economic History*, 7(2), 149–59.

Schumpeter, J. A. (1954). *History of Economic Analysis*. New York: Oxford University Press.

Schumpeter, J. A. (1984). The meaning of rationality in the social sciences. *Zeitschrift für die gesamte Staatswissenschaft/Journal of Institutional and Theoretical Economics* (H.4), 577–93.

Schumpeter, J. A. (2002). The economy as a whole: seventh chapter of *The Theory of Economic Development*. *Industry and Innovation*, 9(1/2), 93–145.

Schumpeter, J. A. (2005). Development. *Journal of Economic Literature*, *43*, 108–20.

Schumpeter, J. A. (2010). *The Nature and Essence of Economic Theory*. New Brunswick, NJ: Transaction Publishers.

Schumpeter, J. A. (2014). *Treatise on Money*. Aalten: Wordbridge Publishing.

Schumpeter, J. A., & Takata, Y. (1998). *Power or Pure Economics?* Basingstoke and London: Macmillan.

Shionoya, Y. (2007). *Schumpeter and the Idea of Social Science: A Metatheoretical Study*. Cambridge: Cambridge University Press.

Solo, C. S. (1951). Innovation in the capitalist process: a critique of the Schumpeterian theory. *Quarterly Journal of Economics*, *65*(3), 417–28.

Vickers, D. (1994). *Economics and the Antagonism of Time: Time, Uncertainty, and Choice in Economic Theory*. Ann Arbor, MI: University of Michigan Press.

Waters, W. (1952). Entrepreneurship, dualism, and causality: an appreciation of the work of Joseph A. Schumpeter. Unpublished PhD dissertation, Georgetown University, Washington, DC.

11. The naturalized disharmony of a socio-technical system: understanding safety in the oil and gas drilling industry

Stefania Sardo

1. INTRODUCTION: SYSTEM STABILITY AND DIFFUSED VALUE COHERENCE

Innovation scholars interested in socio-technical systems construction and change – such as Transition theorists (e.g. Bergek et al., 2008; Geels & Schot, 2016; Sovacool et al., 2018) – distinguish between periods of socio-technical *quasi-stability*, where a system changes incrementally, and periods of *transition*, where the existing system is either substituted with a new one or otherwise radically changed. Crucial in this differentiation is the role of social values and their respective translations into *socio-technical codes*, that is, the variables and metrics employed to assess the worth of a given technological development. These codes "define an object in strictly technical terms, in accordance with the social meaning it has acquired" (Feenberg, 1999, p. 88; see also Feenberg, 2010). Indeed, innovation scholars argue that technological systems are not only aimed at fulfilling technical requirements; that is, they are not value-neutral. Moral and societal agendas are embedded in technological designs, in rules and regulations: ideologies and techniques are inevitably blended together. However, during periods of *stability*, socio-technical codes are assumed to be fixed, pervasive and capillary. They are shared among organizations and individuals belonging to the same industry, and especially to the same relevant actor group (Geels, 2002). Discourses, contracts, relationships, technologies, procedures, standards, routines and imaginaries about the future are all imbued with the same values. All together, these elements constitute a socio-technical *framework* or *paradigm*, that is, the semi-coherent set of formal and informal rules, regimes and institutions providing constraining and enabling contexts for actors (Geels, 2004, p. 903; see also Bijker, 1987, 1995; Geels & Schot, 2007). Giovanni Dosi (1982, p. 148; 1984) describes a technological paradigm as "an 'outlook', a set of procedures, a definition of the 'relevant' problems and of the specific knowledge related to their solution. (…) A paradigm defines its own concept of 'progress' based on its specific technological and economic trade-offs"; progress is meant to achieve greater technological efficiency. Because everyone is looking in the same direction when it comes to socio-technical advancements, the *quasi-stability* of a socio-technical system is theoretically self-explaining (Geels & Schot, 2016; Hughes, 1983): nothing is really surprising in this period, as changes are somehow predictable. Socio-technical codes are invisible standpoints contributing to the system stability, or better, to its "incremental optimization" (Geels, 2004). This literature resorts to the concept of *framework* also to make sense of how entities can work together in the making and maintaining of a socio-technical system, despite having clearly different goals and roles. Coordination is possible because rules are reproduced through concrete actions in local practices, such as organizational and cognitive routines that channel research and development (R&D) activities (Dosi, 1982, p. 156; see also Nelson & Winter, 1974, 1982). Few conflicts or mismatches characterize this *not-in-transition* period and, when emerging, they will be solved by applying the framework's logics, thus maintaining a substantial internal coherence (Scott, 1995; Turnheim & Geels, 2013).

On the opposite side, *revolutions* are extraordinary periods where the radical change or the complete disruption of the existing socio-technical system is somehow possible again. They might be triggered, for example, by scarcities or the abundance of critical inputs, by shocks in prices, deviations in demand patterns, or industrial conflicts (Dosi et al., 1990), but also by cultural and political transformations (Geels, 2002). The disruption can also be enforced by the emergence of alternative systems having the same socio-technical functionality but based on incommensurable logics, values, languages and meanings.[1] To simplify this point, think about the environmental movement and its involvement in questions of technology since the 1970s – together with more recent calls from the European Union, for example, towards more sustainable and *just* ways of living: to what extent is this care for *environment* compatible with existing chemical industries, energy-intensive industrial processes, and systems of consumption? Differently for the *not-in-transition* period, revolutions are theoretically described as highly uncertain and full of confusion, also because agents employ different metrics and technical values to evaluate the worth of technologies and to imagine a possible future for society. *Transition periods* and new system creations have been at the centre of scholarly work since the 1980s, but recently the attention has been directed towards how to practically bring about revolutions (Unruh, 2002; Urry, 2004). *Not-in-transition* periods, instead, have not received the same kind of attention as their counterparts. One reason for this is because the literature does not problematize its own assumptions on what *not-in-transition* periods are, or how they change, which relates to the assumed consistency of socio-technical values. Instead, concepts such as stickiness, path dependence and lock-in (Arthur, 1989; David, 1985; Unruh, 2002) have been widely adopted and are used to justify (and perpetuate) this lack of interest – as if we already knew everything about these periods. Inasmuch as the essence of technical codes is taken for granted by the industry operators, so it is by innovation scholars.

Instead, what I argue in this chapter is that it is fundamental to investigate the socio-technical values characterizing not-in-transition industries, if we want to understand the extent to which they change and how. First of all, industrial and innovation activities cannot be separated from social values, as they affect each other. Therefore, it is critical to understand which (and whose) criteria are employed in the design of technologies and operations. Second, if we assume social values in the industry to be homogenous, we might not be able to understand why certain problems – like accidents – irrupt. The aim of this chapter is therefore to open the black box of socio-technical code making, and its relation to industrial stability. In particular, I will show: (1) How a social value is translated into a socio-technical code, how it is constructed and enforced in a *not-in-transition* industry through regulations and standards, and by whom; (2) The relationship between system stability and code homogeneity; (3) The implications of this relationship for understanding innovation processes.

The chapter employs concepts from Science and Technology Studies (STS) as analytical lenses. STS is a discipline that understands the making of science and technology as social and material activities. In this sense, STS does not treat technologies as apolitical, but as connected to power and politics. Also, it explores questions of justice and democracy in relation to the consequences of such activities.

The empirical focus of this work is the making of safety in the Norwegian offshore oil and gas (O&G) drilling industry. Within a Global North perspective, safety is considered crucial for the industry. It has become the bargaining chip of a tacit contract between industry and society, in exchange for the permission to extract and produce precious resources for sustaining our modern ways of living. Because safety is de facto one of the criteria used to keep the industry accountable for its actions, it is implemented in organizational routines and technologies by means of regulations, standards and risk assessments. Moreover, it is proudly displayed by operators, manufacturers and related governmental departments as a trophy, after being accurately translated into reports and digestible statistics. Safety is also employed as a rationale to push for technical and organizational transformations, conveying a sort of *precautionary approach* towards uncertain O&G operations. At first glance, safety appears as a *naturalized element*, a standard criterion routinely applied. However, a close analysis reveals that it is instead the loose outcome of a distributed – but hierarchical – surveillance system. Tensions and debates on safety constantly tear the industry apart; rather than being stable, safety is continuously in the making.

The remainder of this chapter are structured as follows. In Section 2, we engage with concepts from STS – such as boundary objects, workarounds and articulation work – that offer a different perspective on system cohesion and homogeneity. Section 3 focuses on the methodology, research design and empirical case selection. Sections 4 and 5 contain the empirical findings and their analyses, while Section 6 draws the conclusions and broader implications of this work.

2.   CHANGING ASSUMPTIONS: LIVING WITH DISHARMONY

Within STS, scholars have been interested in understanding how stability is produced in practice, starting from the empirical evidence that actors (individuals and collective) have their own way of interpreting facts and are guided by different goals. Nevertheless, while we would expect to experience continuous controversies, in reality groups (or *social worlds*, see Clarke, 1990; Fujimura, 1988) coexist and collaborate despite diversity. How can this possibly happen, and how is diversity maintained?

By analysing different ways of producing knowledge, Gieryn (1982, 1995) introduced the concept of *boundary work*. Gieryn was interested in how "people contend for legitimacy or challenge the cognitive authority of science" (Gieryn, 1995, p. 405); but also about how boundaries are drawn between disciplines and between what is considered as science, and what is not. For example, standards of practices help in defining how knowledge should be produced within a certain discipline in order for it to be perceived as "credible". Building on this line of work, Star and Griesemer (1989; see also Star, 1995, 2010) explored the mechanisms allowing collaborations among various groups of amateurs, professionals and administrators working at and with the Museum of Vertebrate Zoology in California, and developed the concept of *boundary objects*. A boundary object is "a set of work arrangements that are at once material and processual (…) allow[ing] groups to work together without consensus [and despite] differences in expertise, goals, and interests" (Star, 2010, pp. 602–4). This happens because boundary objects are "weakly structured in common use and (…) strongly structured in individual-site use" (Star & Griesemer, 1989, p. 393); tailored for one's own purposes, but still recognizable by different social worlds (Guston, 2001; Star, 2010).[2] In this sense, these objects "ensure reliability and simultaneously retain disciplinary, institutional, and social integrity" (Fujimura, 1992, p. 172). On the one hand, a boundary object provides coherence for participants, by establishing a shared syntax or language (Carlile 2002, p. 451). On the other hand, it allows for diversity, because of its *polysemic* character: in fact, it embeds multiple functions and accommodates different understandings. Boundary objects are characterized by what STS scholars have defined as *interpretative flexibility* (Pinch & Bijker, 1984), by referring to the fact that, for example, technologies are open to more than one interpretation regarding form and function. However, while normally we would expect consensus to emerge at a certain point from interactions around it, a boundary object maintains its polysemy intact.

The term *object* includes everything from technologies, infrastructures, software and measures to ideas, concepts and processes: boundary objects can be abstract or concrete (Star & Griesemer, 1989). What is important is that these arrangements emerge from a need to collaborate. They can be thought of as a sort of space of interaction between otherwise incommensurable social worlds. Therefore, they are never stable, but subject to constant renegotiations (Harvey & Chrisman, 1998).

Boundary objects are not the only conceptual tool to understand the management of tensions between divergent opinions or ways of doing things. Both *work-arounds* (David & Bunn, 1988; Gasser, 1986; Pollock, 2005) and *articulation work* (Star, 1999) were coined to explore the different ways people accommodate and organize "the local circumstances of their activities [when they] do not match prescribed categories or standards" (Bowker & Star, 2000, p. 293). These concepts emerge from scholarship highlighting the power of design decisions encoded in infrastructures such as standards and regulations, or in technologies, which impose visions and values on what is "right" and "wrong", what should be included and excluded, what is the average user, and so on. The problem of both standards and technology designs is that they tend to flatten varieties and exclude the anomalies and unconformities of our ordinary lives and cultural practices. A workaround, then, emphasizes the mechanisms and the efforts to overcome the imposed constraints of a technology and fits them to localized circumstances. For example, Akrich (1992) talks about users adjusting photoelectric kits, while Pollock (2005) explores how programmers rewrite software codes. "All-encompassing and codified rules for executing work are an illusion, since they can never cover the richness and variability of situated practice, which require informal improvisation and workarounds" (Nooteboom, 2012, p. 353; see also Jackson & Barbrow, 2015). Differently from the literature reviewed in the previous section, rules, framings and standards are not solely structuring action, but action is vital to locally reframe rules, so that they can fit with reality. What is interesting to note is that these forms of work to mitigate incompatibilities and bring "things back on track" (Jackson & Barbrow, 2015; see also Ribes & Lee, 2010; Star & Ruhleder, 1996) are often "invisible to rationalized models of work" (Star,

1991b, p. 275), and thus taken for granted. Problems of misfit might be perceived by single individuals and not communicated because these individuals do not have a voice until their problems are taken on by powerful groups, or until they organize themselves into a group.

In this chapter, the notions of boundary object and articulation work are mobilized to examine this seeming homogeneity of safety, and to make sense of how the dynamic stability of an industry can be preserved even though there is a lack of coherence in the construction and use of socio-technical values.

As previously stated, safety is a pervasive value in the O&G drilling socio-technical system: it is understood by respondents as a *conditio sine qua non* to operate and one of the fundamental criteria for technological developments. This is especially true after major accidents, as they bring societal concerns and avoidance of human and environmental damage to the forefront. Certainly, the concept of safety influences new and old technologies, entities and relationships, and it is used as a criterion to evaluate who/what can be included/excluded from the industry. However, as we will see in the following sections, behind an apparent agreement on the crucial importance of safety, there is a messy reality where several definitions co-exist, are enforced through rules and mechanisms, and emerge. The system is not only less internally homogeneous than how it is theoretically defined, but also unpredictable in how it will develop.

3. METHODOLOGY

The theoretical premises are illustrated through a qualitative case study on the Norwegian O&G offshore drilling socio-technical system. The drilling segment can be defined as being not in transition according to the Innovation Studies (IS) categorization. In fact, it is a dynamically stable socio-technical system progressing in an incremental fashion along a socially constructed trajectory (Dosi, 1982; Rip & Kemp, 1998). The first mechanism used to drill was the cable tool, but since the 1900s, the rotary method is considered to be the standard (Baker, 2001; Long, 2006). While there have been several innovations (e.g. horizontal drilling and automated systems), there is no other way to reach oil and gas offshore than through the drilling of holes into the ground (Mitchell & Miska, 2011). Therefore, I consider the way this function is fulfilled as stable, and the industry as mature.

Starting from this case selection, I studied the socio-technical code of safety, which is one of the social values characterizing the Norwegian O&G offshore drilling industry and its development. To understand whether one could consider this value as being homogeneous and unproblematic, I have explored where and how safety definitions are formally produced, how they are integrated into rules and standards, how they are surveilled, to what extent they are counteracted and negotiated, and what consequences these activities have on the industrial evolution. This exploration moved in two directions. The first involved the investigation of the making of formal safety rules and regulations, because these represent a window into the structural aspects of the industry. Also, they clearly define what is allowed under a certain regulatory regime, who can participate in safety activities and in the making of rules, and how regulations should be monitored and enforced. As highlighted in Section 2, laws and regulations are here conceived as socially defined (i.e. they are not politically neutral), and as not necessarily shared or agreed upon. Among rules, I have included standards, as they are a means of coordinating people and things, thus employed to favour efficiency and predictability. Standards themselves produce social order, while emerging from it: they "elevate some values, things, or people at the expense of others" (Timmermans & Epstein, 2010, p. 83). They embed ethical judgements of how the world should be seen and classified, thus setting boundaries and producing exclusions (Bowker & Star, 2000).

The second direction uncovers the interpretative flexibility of safety. I have conducted 37 semi-structured interviews (between 2016 and 2017) and carried out an extensive document analysis to collect different viewpoints and perspectives (Star, 1991a; Star & Griesemer, 1989). The interviews were conducted during the oil price crisis that started in 2014 and marked a moment of disruption in the industry. The crisis unveiled existing controversies on safety, as well as those workaround activities that usually reside in the background (Bowker, 1994; Sims, 2007; Wynne, 1988). First, *landscape interviews* were conducted with organizations selected by virtue of their expert status in the sector and their position in specific organizations (Creswell, 2009). Then, a *snowballing sampling method* was adopted to increase the heterogeneity of perspectives. In most cases, respondents were CEOs, CFOs, CTOs, project managers, technology directors, HSE directors, supply chain and operation managers (especially related to drilling operations), R&D managers, and directors of specific divisions/departments within the public sector that deal with O&G. The interviewed entities were public institutions, industrial associations, research centres, mechanical firms, oil companies, international certification bodies, and organizations operating in robotics and automation. Information was gathered on the definitional production, spread and monitoring of safety. In parallel, documents were collected on themes connected with the interview topics, among which were public laws and regulations (e.g. those related to work and environmental safety); technological development programmes and strategies for the industry; firms' communications reports; and O&G-related newspapers. Finally, I have attended seminars and conferences on the O&G industry. The data analysis started by developing *open coding categories* based on the background theories, further refined during

The interview rounds as the research and the understanding of the case moved on (Charmaz, 2000, 2006; Creswell, 2009; Dubois & Gadde, 2002, 2013). Summarizing, instead of forcing predefined categories of what safety is to my empirical field, I have explored the processes through which it is contextually defined. This means analysing collective actions built through "processes of negotiation, articulation, translation, triangulation, debating, and sometimes even coercion" (Fujimura, 1992). As will be explained in Section 5, the concepts of boundary objects and workaround can be employed to make sense of how safety can appear as a homogeneous and uncontested socio-technical value, while pointing to some intrinsic theoretical and practical problematics.

4. THE MAKING OF "FORMAL" SAFETY: A TALE OF CO-EXISTING REGIMES

Safety in the O&G drilling industry is constructed at the intersection of formal rules and standards – the main instances of stabilization and points of coordination in the system. Indeed, rules are continuously embedded in material components and operational routines. Yet, even these instances of stability appear to be less stable than the innovation literature assumes. In the following sections, I will present different settings where safety as a socio-technical code is collectively constructed. First, I will explore that of national regulations (Section 4.1), then that of standards and risk assessments (Section 4.2) and finally the rules produced by oil companies (Section 4.3). Separating these settings was analytically crucial to further dig into who defines safety, to what extent definitions spread throughout the whole system, where different definitions are encountered (and where not), and whether oppositional voices (in terms of different safety definitions) emerge.

4.1 The National Regulatory Framework

The regulatory framework for petroleum activities in Norway is under the responsibility of the Norwegian Parliament. In its role of designing and applying policies, the Parliament is supported by specific ministries, directorates and agencies (e.g. the Petroleum Safety Authority (PSA), the Norwegian Environment Agency, the Norwegian Directorate of Health, the Ministry of Petroleum and Energy, and the Ministry of Labour). When it comes to safety, the basic requirements for organizing and carrying out petroleum activities are set out in the Health, Safety and Environment (HSE) Framework Regulation (Royal Decree 12 February 2010; hereafter FR). This has to be combined with the Management, Facility, Activity, Technical and Operational Regulations.[3] The supervision of the Norwegian legislation is a task carried out by both the Norwegian Petroleum Directorate (NPD) and the PSA – subject to the Oil and

Energy Ministry. While the NPD is responsible for resource management, the PSA is responsible for the working environment and safety levels.

The governmental risk-based regime is guided by the following principles:

1. Activities should be prudent, based on the assessment of factors related to health, safety and the environment (Section 10 and 11).
2. "Risks (…) shall be reduced beyond the regulations minimum level if this can take place *without* unreasonable cost or drawback. [Otherwise], it has to be reduced to the extent possible" (Section 10 and 11).
3. "In reducing the risk, the responsible party[4] shall choose the (…) solutions that offer the best results, provided the costs are not significantly dispro-portionate to the risk reduction achieved" (Section 11).
4. "If there is insufficient knowledge concerning the effects that the use of [these] (…) solutions can have on health, safety or the environment, solu-tions that will reduce this uncertainty shall be chosen" (Section 11).

Summarizing, the HSE framework recognizes that safety is a dynamic social value that will necessarily change in response to technological, economic and demographic developments.[5] It is based on performance-based (*functional*) requirements: it does not concretely advise on how issues have to be solved, but what the operating entities have to achieve (i.e. the safety goal). What it means is that regulations recognize that there are risks and uncertainties, but it is up to the operators to quantify and reduce them (e.g. by developing their own control systems) (Kringen, 2009), and to demonstrate compliance with regulations. Such an approach was designed to encourage the industry to come up with better and more cost-effective solutions to meet requirements, while trusting the industry in its ability and willingness to introduce risk-reducing measures when needed. However, on the one hand, this system does not prac-tically impose the introduction of safer technologies – as long as minimum requirements of safety protection are met. On the other, it is difficult in practice to understand what the required safety level is, as it is by principle dynamic.

The HSE framework is revised yearly by the Parliament, but major legisla-tive steps are usually taken in response to accidents. For example, a profound change happened after the Ekofisk Bravo (1977) blow-out and the capsizing of the Alexander Kielland (1980), as Parliament pushed for a redesign of the regulatory principles to operate in the Norwegian Continental Shelf (NCS).[6] The Framework revision is based on the *tripartite collaboration* model (Braut & Lindøe, 2010; Karlsen & Lindøe, 2006). The PSA organizes regulatory forums (*regelverksfora*) where the authority, industrial associations and unions discuss draft revisions, as well as safety and working environment issues. On these occasions, parties would support or oppose regulations changes, thus opening up controversies that might last for a long time.[7] As some respondents explained, "the three-party cooperation is very much dependent on balance in power" (cit. drilling company), and final decisions "depend on who is going to have the power to say no and yes [to regulatory changes]" (cit. industrial association). This is especially true when changes in regulations might nudge companies towards changes to existing technologies and infrastructure in order to meet higher safety levels. Needless to say, there is not a common and overarching rationale for implementing new regulations because, as already stated, the same concept of safety changes over time, and the parties involved in these changes will in any case fight for having their own ideas on safety embedded in new regulations.

In order to monitor safety and the development of risk level in the NCS, the *Risikonivå i norsk petroleumsvirksomhet* (RNNP, i.e. Risk Level in Norwegian Petroleum activities) was introduced at the end of the 1990s. The RNNP illustrates risk levels of the NCS stemming from, for example, major hazards related to emergency preparedness, risk perception and cultural factors (Bang & Thuestad, 2014), by using as a basis relevant information about accidents and near misses provided by the industry (Vinnem, 2010). These data are partially used as a basis for discussing emerging issues in the industry, and whether revised regulations, technical developments or assessments are needed. The intrinsic value of the RNNP report relies on the collaborative and transparent attitude of the involved entities (i.e. research institutions, the O&G industry, and trade unions).

4.2 Standards and Risk Assessments: Cumulated Knowledge and New Calculations

The second setting where safety is formally produced is that of *standards and risk assessments* (i.e. the set of tools that the industry designs and employs to define the extent to which technologies, procedures and operations are safe). As we have previously seen, while the FR is quite vague, at the same time the government provides non-binding guidelines and recommendations to help understand how to possibly meet it. In there, one can find reference to many worldwide legal, industrial and professional standards. By stating that the responsible operator can comply with the requirements by making use of a standard recommended in the guidelines, the FR (Section 12) is somehow delegating the standards, and their classification societies, to a regulatory role. However, due to the non-legally binding character of the guidelines, an operator can also decide to meet regulations in an alternative way, including developing its own processes and systems – as long as it can be documented as compliant (FR, Section 24). Standards and risk assessments translate safety into risks, which are "measures of physical observable things, while safety is not a 'physical observable thing'. So [one has] to deduce, infer, what is the actual safety level from the indicators. That in itself is difficult, but the indicators are very useful, nevertheless" (cit. safety issuing organization). Yet, there is a fundamental difference between the two tools. Risk assessments, instead, have to be performed for one-off situations, where few data are available on the specific case under review (cit. safety consultant organization). Standards define general technical requirements for operators and suppliers, and they are "the cumulative experience repository of the industry" (cit. standard organization). Each standard

> summarize[s], through stochastic modelling or frequentist approaches, a deep phenomenological understanding of processes, technologies, operations. Therefore, they can be applied only to something that is "certain enough" and whose risks can be managed. [For example], if you have a lot of similar kind of equipment that you have gained experience with, you may consider building this into a standard. (cit. safety consultant organization)

Indeed, standards should be thought of as a sort of shortcut for those designing a process or a technology, indicating what one has to check. By following them, the industry saves time and money deriving from the duplication of unnecessary detailed and special requirements. The shortcut role of standards works only if they are continuously updated, by adding data, technologies, scenarios and so on. Updates normally happen after some years, often resulting from joint industry projects that "try to follow the industrial development and to keep up [with it] – otherwise, they will be disregarded at a certain point" (cit. private research centre). They emerge from experts' discussion forums, selected by the issuing organization because of their up-to-date knowledge and experience in a specialized field or technology. These individuals belong to the industry (most likely oil companies, rig owners and large technology providers), governmental agencies, and consulting groups.

The O&G industry is filled with standards issued by different organizations (e.g. DNV-GL, the European Committee for Standardization, the International Organization for Standardization, the Norwegian Oil and Gas Association, the Federation of Norwegian Industries, and the Norwegian Shipowners' Association). One of the reasons why so many different standards are available is because they are proprietary and in competition with each other; this also means that the data each of them is built upon (i.e. datasets and models to calculate risk) are not necessarily shared among issuing organizations. Therefore, the knowledge embedded in every standard is somehow partial. In the description of standards, safety is broken down into risk matrices and models, which are meant to help the technology users in taking decisions when employing the technology, by highlighting the loci of possible uncertainties. "By making the risk concept operational, we [experts] make a lot of assumptions, which are included in the model error (…)" (cit. standard issuing organization). Indeed, the process of construction of the tools and instruments to determine risk is often not shared with the final users (e.g. drilling operators); it is hidden behind the final schemes and formulae. For example, it is typically difficult to get information on residual model errors resulting from its simplification of reality (and what these errors imply):

> This has practical implications when you go into operations, because it might happen that the model assumptions are broken. The indicators can look very nice, but all of a sudden the foundations upon which they were based completely erode, and having a green indicator does not make you safe. (cit. standard issuing organization)

As explained before, the cases in which standards cannot be employed are those where there is a lack of specific data on future scenarios stemming from the adoption of a new technology or process. The operationalization of safety into the probability of some risky events to occur is carried on by the "technicians designing the technology, together with some involved field experts, and other available knowledge" (cit. safety consultant organization and technology suppliers). The case-by-case risk identification and quantification relies on probabilities identified and imagined by the enrolled experts. Indeed, a high level of ambiguity is involved in this judging process:

> The risk on safety is a social construction. It is a subjective belief and you can achieve it inter-subjectively, you can have different experts that will agree, but still it is subjective. It cannot be measured per se, only through derived indicators. And those indicators have some shortcomings. (cit. standard issuing organization)

There is no doubt that risk assessment experts have increasingly acquired a powerful role in the Norwegian O&G industry. While the important functions of producing data and provide standards are delegated, at the same time they have created knowledge boundaries between them and the rest of the industry, including the government. Because of this, experts are often hired as "surveillants" in between the government and the operating companies, for example to invigilate on how the latter deal with an accident. As a rig owner company stated, "[they are] specialists towards the government, so when they say: 'We strongly recommend [to do something or to replace a component]', then we do it".

4.3 Oil Companies' Regulations: Controlling and Anticipating

The third setting where safety definitions are produced connects to oil companies. These organizations are ultimately responsible for what is happening during a drilling campaign, and they have to create a "health, safety and environment culture" (FR, Section 15). A drilling campaign is full of risks that have to be calculated ahead of time: operators go through possible hazards and discuss with the PSA and safety consultants whether they need to adopt new equipment or modify operations previously codified.

> Operators and regulators establish what is the de facto acceptable fatal accident ratio, KPIs [key performance indicators] (…). When you apply the risk thinking in all the areas of a project (e.g. acceptable delay, acceptable overrun, etc.), you are setting the criteria of what is meaningful and useful, depending on the project and your risk appetite. (cit. standard issuing organization)

The "risk appetite" is a way of expressing what is behind decisions at all levels: considerations about environmental risks, personnel risks and commercial risks, and their related aspects. Of course, it relates to both future (e.g. accident consequences) and present costs (e.g. new technologies and training). Every campaign is then unique, because of the specificities of the drilling site (type of well and reservoir, environmental conditions, distance from the shore, etc.), and because of the risk perception and willingness to risk of each operator.

To supplement the functional – and purposefully vague – regulatory requirements, oil companies have to design: (1) administrative and organizational safety management systems. In this case, they partially recur to HSE guidelines and industry standards, and partially add requirements and procedures by referring to their own experience and organizational safety culture. (2) Drilling plans and ad hoc risk assessments to evaluate environmental damage, personnel, and commercial risks. Of course, these internal systems and plans have to be approved by authorities, who can intervene in case they believe companies are not carrying out safe practices. Indeed, besides the role of prescribing norms, the state has the *duty* to see to it that norms are properly followed. In non-compliance cases, authorities can impose individual and legally binding requirements, which are normally very specific compared to the FRs (Kaasen, 2014). This process somehow assumes a transparent relation between authorities – who should gain insights into the petroleum activities – and the companies – who should submit reports and all the necessary documents for supervision (FR, Section 23).[8] Indeed, the internal control system constitutes a crucial element to ensure and prove safety, from both the industry and the government side.

4.4   Emerging Definitions: Safety as Bureaucracy and Costs

Oil companies control a wide range of technologies and suppliers, while keeping at bay the uncertainties of the drilling environment. To ease these tasks, they predefine basic conditions to be part of the drilling endeavour (e.g. suppliers have to be certified and economically sustainable), and impose or strongly advise suppliers to comply even with detailed safety features. "Even for small things like gloves, we are prone to find out what is the opinion of the oil company. They might have preferences for a certain type of glove, tool, or for a certain type of new technology" (cit. drilling owner). Constructing safety comes also with the production of documents to receive certified approvals. However, oil companies' detailed and peculiar requirements are reported to increase the costs and time spent by suppliers in filling out paperwork, to the detriment of actual safety supervision. "Sometimes safety is not seen as an integrated part of the business, but as something someone 'takes care of' in their offices" (cit. safety consultant). Suppliers have always found this quite a problematic issue, but before the oil crisis they would execute this work without objecting – as it was paid enough:

> The companies delivering are paid to produce papers, so they would produce whatever they are asked to (…). The good economic times have been the driver here: as long as you get paid for something, then you produce it. As an example, a rig company was called up from a store (…), saying that they had a 20 foot container with documentation that no one had ever asked for. (cit. industrial association)

This proliferation of ad hoc oil company specificities also follows from the intrinsic competition with each other on HSE results (e.g. lack of accidents/ quasi accidents). This means that suppliers delivering to several oil companies have to produce different documentation and at times change their technologies according to each requirement. This is evident from the following:

> [All this] paper work is a huge challenge for small companies. (…) The operator A wanted to exceed B with respect to having a HSE focus; B wanted to exceed C, etc. [As a supplier, you had to follow different regulations] when dealing with A, B, or C. Sometimes it seemed like they were inventing things that they needed to have, [just to be] different from the others, because "we don't copy and paste anything". (cit. drilling rig owner)

> Some of the requirements have become too big, and everyone makes their own versions of the general standards. As an example, for subsea equipment there are thirty or forty shades of yellow for paint. (…) You could have one yellow paint, and that would be much cheaper for everyone. (cit. safety consultant)

Following from this, many respondents reported that safety procedures might be perceived as the act of mechanically going through checklists and analyses, while others might be disregarded as unnecessary and redundant. As highlighted in previous sections, the lack of direct involvement of suppliers and workers in the design of "formal" safety definitions and routines might cause misunderstandings in terms of how and when risk models and relative tools should be used, and ignorance regarding their built-in limitations and errors. All these specifics, instead, end up "threatening the credibility of the safety system and lowering people's attention" (cit. safety consultant). As a follow-up result, this perception of safety bureaucracy and rules uselessness sometimes enters into a joke dimension:

> The strong focus [on minor risks like] cutting fingers has defocused some of the attention towards major accidents. (…) When people start making jokes and saying: "safety is ridiculous", then you start to expose. I have seen expert A attacking [safety] by taking up examples like people who needed new protective shoes and had to make a 50-page report on that (…). [But all this] can drown the key message: i.e. what are the few things that can kill you?" (cit. safety consultant)

Besides this bureaucratic side of safety, in the aftermath of the 2016 oil crisis another translation of this social value surfaced, as safety was juxtaposed to costs. Of course, this parallel is not new (cf. Hovden, 2002, about the 1990s cost-cutting phase), but it appears that "Today you are allowed to ask questions [like]: 'Is this cost for the safety issue really worth it?' Because you can't drive the costs to the roof for safety" (cit. technology supplier). The definitional limits and the materialization of safety are then questioned, together with the idea of what progress-in-safety looks like. "In the old offshore days, they had men in a sleeping room. Then they moved into single cabins, which have two beds (…). It is a balance of costs for the company operating, of the context of the society, and of the expectations of the people working there" (cit. public safety authority). In good economic times, "the costs of a living quarter with a little bit more comfort is minute"; but in a cost-cutting regime, the industry allows itself to reframe this definitional line. Also, in this moment of turbulence the role of safety experts is questioned as well:

> The specialists are making standards. In these meetings, they can add a particular requirement, (…) but maybe, in the bigger picture, it was only another element driving the costs or adding documentation requirements. [These meetings] are a food for specialists to live out their dreams, and [this] can be very dangerous. (cit. drilling company)

Important questions have been raised about the extent to which "lowering" the safety level should be considered as a crime, or if this level is in any case "too high" due to "unnecessary" elements that can instead be removed. After having reached in the past a political compromise on the importance of specific safety features (e.g. in the *tripartite* meetings), removing them or lowering some safety thresholds might require a very similar process. Once again, this shows that safety is not just "technical" – it is (and always will be) a "social" judgement.

5. DISCUSSION: THE NORMAL INCOHERENCE OF STABILITY

This chapter investigates the making of the socio-technical value of safety throughout the O&G offshore drilling industry, and in particular the assumption of its coherence in an industry not in transition, as put forward by innovation scholarship. I looked into how safety is institutionally designed and how it is locally problematized in the O&G drilling industry. The empirical results run counter to some of IS assumptions, in that it is clear that heterogeneity characterizes this not-in-transition industry. Because safety as a "social value" is an immaterial concept, this raises some issues regarding its unambiguous translation into practices and technologies. Instead, this translation process relies highly on cumulated experience and existing rules, and also on a personal attitude towards risks, on power relationships, and on ways through which controversies unfold. The empirics highlight three main interconnected formal settings producing their own translations of what safety is, and embedding them into ad hoc routines, contracts and operations, as well as technologies. The Framework Regulations somehow dominate the industry, but they provide only a general understanding of safety, and suggest non-compulsory ways of interpreting regulations. The industrial standards setting is an experts' domain, governed by certificatory organizations that produce their own data, models, cumulated knowledge and practices. Standards are employed to certify "known" technologies, while ad hoc risk assessments are constructed when technologies are new and when the potential interactions with already installed bases are unknown. Finally, oil companies govern safety to protect themselves from inevitable scandals related to unsafe operations. They design rules and practices that are a patchwork of existing regulations, standards and procedures, adapted to their own safety appetite, commercial interests and experience. Borrowing from Wynne (1988, p. 151), oil companies have developed "*ad hoc* judgments and assumptions, (…) creating more private informal 'rules' beneath the discourse of formal rules and check procedures". "Safety" has become, at least in principle, a distributed responsibility, delegated to oil companies' safety–cultural silos.

Yet, while only partially sharing an understanding of safety as a social value, all of these settings participate in the emerging landscape where "safety" is negotiated: "safety" comprises a complex web of entities and practices. Even though this is an interesting finding in itself that can contribute to the IS literature, it is still quite puzzling how an industry like the offshore O&G drilling can keep on operating notwithstanding the dissonance in one of its core values. By referring to previous STS scholarship (Star, 2010; Star & Griesemer, 1989), I suggest two different theoretical moves. The first is to conceptualize safety as an *immaterial boundary object*. The second is to foreground the invisible *workaround* carried on by several entities to solve the discrepancies and conflicts emerging when discordant safety definitions are encountered.

As a social value maxim, safety is largely employed by every organization, group and individual involved – whether to avoid the risk of societal shame or intrinsically embracing it. Safety, as a boundary object, represents heterogeneous solutions to the same problem of producing a safe drilling environment. Safety is a plastic boundary object. Its definitional vagueness is formally allowed by the NF regulations, which follow a functionally based approach and do not impose a unique way of defining and practising safety. The definitional plasticity and vagueness facilitate the communication among organizations around safety, as they are not forced to agree on a precise meaning, nor on how to translate it into risk calculations, practices and so on. Indeed, the industry is characterized by different risk regimes and risk cultures – at times incommensurable; for example, whether one would consider too expensive the introduction of a certain technology that might save drillers from injury, or whether the routines implemented by an organization to produce safe behaviours are deemed insufficient or useless by those enforced to use it. Safety, then, is both *ideal* and *material* (Cole, 1996), in the sense that its importance is somehow agreed upon, but the way it is transformed, inscribed into texts and embedded into technologies is determined by the interactions among a variety of entities through time. In this sense, safety is a politically successful boundary object, even though it relies on a somehow elitist set of institutional and industrial agreements. To summarize, safety as a boundary object works only because we have relaxed Framework Regulations, and because there is commitment and acceptance on all sides with them being this way.

Of course, it is not that safety as a boundary object is a magic bullet that makes conflicts disappear when different understandings of safety are encountered. Contrary to the assumption employed by the IS scholarship of regulations, standards and technical requirements as coordinating mechanisms (Geels, 2002; Rip & Kemp, 1998), we experience them as reproducing additional definitions and controversial behaviours, instead of clarity and solidification. The concept of *workaround* (Akrich, 1992; David & Bunn, 1988; Gasser, 1986; Wynne, 1988) helps, then, in understanding how multiplicity is partially kept together, and why the industry does not fall apart. In this study, workaround is about constantly mending inconsistencies between safety definitions at a local level. The industry is full of "adaptors" and "converters" of mismatched safety regimes (i.e. single entities that absorb incoherence and in return produce an apparent unity, or of spaces where definitions are discussed and closure is found around them). In general, this workaround and local tailoring remains invisible to both innovation researchers but also, as Bowker and Star (2000) remind us, to those benefitting from it (in this case, e.g. oil companies, standard organizations, experts, policymakers, and industrial associations).

One example is the work done at the supply chain level to deal with different safety procedures and regulations imposed by multiple clients (e.g. oil companies). This produces additional paperwork, technical specificities, risk evaluations and training. The supply chain acts as a sort of boundary organization, in the sense of internalizing conflicts and the boundaries between different safety regimes, and thus avoiding the complications that can result from their clashes. These companies have more than one principal, they pursue the interests of all of them, and their actions are constrained by contracts. During the "good times" of the industry, this extra bureaucratic or technical work for safety is paid for: monetary compensations somehow justify the safety variety persistence and keep at bay disappointments at the suppliers' level for the extra work. But in times of trouble, such as during an oil price crisis, the limits of managing safety as a *boundary object* and of workarounds as glue for incoherence emerge. Under cost-cutting pressures, the work of transforming incoherence into coherence becomes harder, as these companies cannot deal with multiple requests under financial constraints. Safety as a boundary object then risks reaching its practical limits, and we can see it as it is translated into the realms of *costs*, *bureaucracy* and *irony*.

A second example of workaround relates to the tripartite discussions centred on changes to HSE regulations and guidelines, which normally highlight divergent opinions held by the government, industrial associations, unions and their experts. While being highly political spaces, these controversies relate to circumscribed issues, and therefore solutions do not overcome higher-level discrepancies in understanding and calculating safety between the involved actors and also depend on which group or individual is able to impose a certain vision over others.

A third final example relates to geography and time. Some of the regulatory changes are not retroactive, which means that the industry is filled with coexisting technologies designed according to different safety regimes. Rigs navigate the same sea, but they are partially independent safety islands. Physical distance allows variety to coexist, until workers are moved from one rig to another. Then, they have to deal with inconsistent safety regimes and go through additional training. This burden is normally taken on by workers themselves, and by the organizations they work for. Safety, then, is not only multiple; it is also asynchronous and in motion. Its boundaries are continuously reframed and adjusted; they are malleable.

What emerges from this analysis is that if we want to understand innovation processes in a complex environment like the O&G drilling industry, we have to study also the socio-technical codes upon which it develops. The IS literature instead has for long time flattened out these values, not engaging with how socio-technical they are constructed and enforced, and whether they are actually shared in practice. What is then missed is the importance of "the social" for technological developments, as well as the political and controversial aspects behind them. The fact that *safety* is widely accepted in its general definition, and ethically legitimatized, hides the politics of safety in terms of who is allowed to take part in those spaces where safety is formally framed. The O&G is an oligarchical industry, not only when it comes to organizing petroleum operations, but also when it is about the enforcement of specific safety regimes on less powerful entities (Sardo et al., 2021). Safety is mostly left in the hands of a few organizations, and especially back to the industry, which is considered to be the most knowledgeable when it comes to drilling operations. The industry, the government and a few other organizations inevitably shape the way in which innovations and regulations are developed and adopted. What is important here is to ask what kind of innovation emerges out of this complexity, when the definitions of what a socio-technical value is are pretty much left in the hands of a few well-known organizations that necessarily compromise their organizational efficiency and interests with safety.

While safety as a boundary object helps in avoiding continuous conflicts in the industry, at the same time it justifies some organizations in carrying on in their own interests without being questioned (Harrison et al., 2018). Therefore, it is actually debatable whether safety as a boundary object ends up being productive, destructive, or both, and whether it really produces a more democratic (and safe) environment. By separating "the social" from "the technical", we end up simplifying not only the conditions for innovation to emerge, but also the work done by several entities to keep the industry going.

6.   CONCLUSIONS

Summarizing, this chapter revolves around not-in-transition periods, theoretically characterized by shared and almost fixed socio-technical codes, which are traded off when deciding on the worthiness of socio-technical advancements. I have investigated the status of *safety* as a value, and its relation to industrial stability; in particular, how it is constructed, by whom, and how it is embedded in the social and technical aspects of the O&G industry. At first glance, safety appears as a naturalized element. However, its definitions and practical transpositions into risks are rather variegated and inconsistent. Even if individuals and organizations constantly enact and "talk safety", generally agreeing on it being the "absence of unacceptable risks", this neat definition overlooks inconsistency. It assumes (1) a shared process of transforming safety into quantitative risks; (2) the same concerns over work culture, economic pressures, and environment; and (3) safety as neutral, that is, that entities involved in controversies over safety have the same power to enforce one definition over others. The industry is characterized by a patchwork of definitions that are at times hierarchical, overlapping and isolated. Decisions, planning, technological developments and even single actions are based on a mixture of standardized and ad hoc safety definitions.

This raises questions about whether value homogeneity and coherence are theoretically necessary conditions for explaining the dynamic stability of industries *not in transition*. Studying how safety is embedded in the industry – and not only how formal regulations are produced and reproduced – forces us to employ different theoretical concepts and to twist our understanding of stability as being *intrinsically* incoherent. By looking at safety as a boundary object and by revealing the workarounds necessary to overcome clashes between safety regimes, we can provide a better explanation of how the dynamic stability of an industry can be preserved even though there is a lack of coherence in the construction and use of socio-technical values.

Besides these theoretical considerations, assuming that socio-technical values are shared (and therefore theoretically unimportant) and that decisions on innovations and policies are value- and power-neutral hinders a more democratic construction of safety. The question is whether leaving the responsibility of safety – which should be considered a *public concern* – in the hands of the industry (even within a tripartite collaboration arena) is actually prioritizing innovations for safety and the embedding of safety in technological innovations. This is especially problematic when a few powerful actors trade "safety" for other concerns such as costs and efficiency. Rule- and regulation-making emerge from an intricate bundle of politics and economics, while single workers and suppliers are left with the ultimate responsibility of following procedures, stopping machines or pushing for new innovations for safety. While I am not claiming that the O&G industry is in absolute terms unsafe, a more transparent and democratic evaluation of the worth of innovation will certainly produce better results in overall terms for workers and environmental safety. Issues of power, legitimacy and public interest should be discussed openly, as well as who is allowed to mediate between moral and societal considerations and innovation processes. This work contributes to existing Innovation Studies and opens up a theoretical and practical discussion on how to design technologies in accordance with the moral values of society.

NOTES

1. This distinction was first theorized by Kuhn (1970, 1982), when describing the emergence of scientific paradigms. Incommensurability means that one cannot "define all the terms of one theory in [terms] of the other" (Kuhn, 1982, p. 669).
2. "A social world (…) is a unit of analysis that cuts across formal organizations, institutions like family and church, and other forms of association such as social movements" (Bowker & Star, 2000, p. 294).

230   *Rethinking the social in innovation and entrepreneurship studies*

3. It should be noted that other norms might apply for the personnel working on float-
    ing devices (e.g. the 2007 Ship Safety and Security Act and the 1977 Seamen's
    Act). Another important regulation is the Working Environment Act (2005). For
    a more detailed description of the complexity of the regulatory framework, see
    Kaasen (2014).
4. That is, "the licensee, the onshore facility owner, the operator and others partici-
    pating in the activities are responsible pursuant to the regulations" (FR, Section 7).
5. Section 1 of the Decree states: "The purpose of these regulations is to (…) further
    develop and improve the health, safety and environmental level".
6. The new principles were those of *internal control* (1981) of licences and the *Act
    of Petroleum Activities on the Continental Shelf* (1985). The former indicates that
    the industry has the responsibility of establishing a system "for identifying rele-
    vant requirements, checking that these were adhered to, implementing corrective
    measures if needed and reporting all these activities to state authorities" (Kaasen,
    2014, p. 105).
7. Roughly speaking, unions are more concerned about workers' well-being and
    push for better working environments; industrial associations usually fight against
    measures that would increase costs without anyone "sufficiently" proving that
    they lead to safer operations; the PSA represents the government, which in turn
    gives voice to societal concerns.
8. The government does not carry out physical control of the platforms, which is
    instead done by either classification societies, or industry employees themselves
    (and then reported in the internal control system).

REFERENCES

Akrich, M. (1992). The De-Scription of Technical Objects. In W. E. Bijker & J. Law
    (Eds.), *Shaping Technology, Building Society: Studies in Sociotechnical Change*
    (pp. 205–24). Cambridge, MA: MIT Press.
Arthur, W. B. (1989). Competing technologies, increasing returns, and lock-in by
    historical events. *Economic Journal*, 99, 116–31.
Baker, R. (2001). *A Primer of Oilwell Drilling* (6th edn.). Austin, TX: Petroleum
    Extension Service.
Bang, P., & Thuestad, O. (2014). Government-enforced self-regulation: the Norwegian
    case. In P. H. Lindøe, M. Baram, & O. Renn (Eds.), *Risk Governance of Offshore Oil
    and Gas Operations* (pp. 243–73). New York: Cambridge University Press.
Bergek, A., Jacobsson, S., Carlsson, B., Lindmark, S., & Rickne A. (2008). Analyzing
    the functional dynamics of technological innovation systems: a scheme of analysis.
    Research Policy, 37(3), 407–29.
Bijker, W. E. (1987). The social construction of Bakelite: toward a theory of inven-
    tion. In W. E. Bijker, T. P. Hughes, & T. Pinch (Eds.), *The Social Construction of
    Technological Systems* (pp. 159–87). Cambridge, MA: MIT Press.
Bijker, W. E. (1995). Socio historical technology studies. In S. Jasanoff, G. E. Markle,
    J. C. Peterson, & T. Pinch (Eds.), *Handbook of Science and Technology Studies*
    (pp. 229–56). London: Sage Publications.
Bowker, G. C. (1994). *Science in the Run: Information Management and Industrial
    Geophysics at Schlumberger, 1920–1940*. Cambridge, MA: MIT Press.
Bowker, G. C., & Star, S. L. (2000). *Sorting Things Out: Classification and Its
    Consequences*. Cambridge, MA: MIT Press.

Braut, G. S., & Lindøe, P. H. (2010). Risk regulation in the North Sea: a common law perspective on Norwegian legislation. *Safety Science Monitor*, 14(1). https://www .semanticscholar.org/paper/Risk-regulation-in-the-North-Sea-%3A-a-common-law -on-Braut-Lind%C3%B8e/6b6a269bc1ad2baae233375785043fbec3ba1e40.

Carlile, P. R. (2002). A pragmatic view of knowledge and boundaries: boundary objects in new product development. *Organization Science*, 13(4), 442–55.

Charmaz, K. (2000). Constructivist and objectivist grounded theory. In N. K. Denzin & Y. S. Lincoln (Eds.), *Handbook of Qualitative Research* (2nd edn., pp. 509–35). Thousand Oaks, CA: Sage.

Charmaz, K. (2006). *Constructing Grounded Theory: A Practical Guide Through Qualitative Analysis*. London: Sage.

Clarke, A. (1990). A social worlds adventure: the case of reproductive science. In S. E. Cozzens & T. F. Gieryn (Eds.), *Theories of Science in Society* (pp. 15–42). Bloomington: Indiana University Press.

Cole, M. (1996). *Cultural Psychology: A Once and Future Discipline*. Cambridge, MA: Belknap Press of Harvard University Press.

Creswell, J. W. (2009). *Research Design: Qualitative, Quantitative and Mixed Methods Approaches* (3rd edn.). Thousand Oaks, CA: Sage Publications.

David, P. A. (1985). Clio and the economics of QWERTY. *The American Economic Review*, 75(2), 332–7.

David, P. A., & Bunn, J. A. (1988). The economics of gateway technologies and network evolution: lessons from electricity supply history. *Information Economics and Policy*, 3, 165–202.

Dosi, G. (1982). Technological paradigms and technological trajectories: a suggested interpretation of the determinants and directions of technical change. *Research Policy*, 11(3), 147–62.

Dosi, G. (1984). *Technical Change and Industrial Transformation*. London: Macmillan.

Dosi, G., Pavitt, K., & Soete, L. (1990). *The Economics of Technical Change and International Trade*. Brighton: Wheatsheaf.

Dubois, A., & Gadde, L. E. (2002). Systematic combining: an abductive approach to case research. *Journal of Business Research*, 55, 553−60.

Dubois, A., & Gadde, L. E. (2013). Systematic combining—a decade later. *Journal of Business Research*, 67(6), 1277–84.

Feenberg, A. (1999). *Questioning Technology*. New York: Routledge.

Feenberg, A. (2010). *Between Reason and Experience: Essays in Technology and Modernity*. Cambridge, MA: MIT Press.

Fujimura, J. H. (1988). The molecular biological bandwagon in cancer research: where social worlds meet. *Social Problems*, 35(3), 261–83.

Fujimura, J. H. (1992). Crafting science: standardized packages, boundary objects, and "translation". *Science as Practice and Culture*, 168, 168–9.

Gasser, L. (1986). The integration of computing and routine work. *ACM Transactions on Office Information Systems*, 4(3), 205–25.

Geels, F. W. (2002). Technological transitions as evolutionary reconfiguration processes: a multi-level perspective and a case-study. *Research Policy*, 31(8–9), 1257–74.

Geels, F. W. (2004). Understanding system innovations: a critical literature review and a conceptual synthesis. In B. Elzen & F. W. Geels (Eds.), *System Innovation and the Transition to Sustainability: Theory, Evidence and Policy* (pp. 19–47). Cheltenham, UK, and Northampton, MA, USA: Edward Elgar Publishing.

Geels, F. W., & Schot, J. (2007). Typology of sociotechnical transition pathways. *Research Policy*, *36*(3), 399–417.

Geels, F. W., & Schot, J. (2016). Towards a new innovation theory for grand societal challenges. *Working Paper for SPRU Anniversary conference*.

Gieryn, T. (1982). Boundary work and the demarcation of science from non-science: interests in professional ideologies of science. *American Sociological Review*, *48*(6), 781–95.

Gieryn, T. (1995). *Cultural Boundaries of Science: Credibility on the Line*. Chicago, IL: University of Chicago Press.

Guston, D. (2001). Boundary organizations in environmental policy and science: an introduction. *Science, Technology & Human Values*, *26*(4), 399–408.

Harrisson, D., Hoholm, T., Prenkert, F., & Olsen, P. I. (2018). Boundary objects in network interactions. *Industrial Marketing Management*, *74*, 187–94.

Harvey, F., & Chrisman, N. (1998). Boundary objects and the social construction of GIS technology. *Environment and Planning A*, *30*(9), 1683–94.

Hovden, J. (2002). The development of new safety regulations in the Norwegian oil and gas industry. In B. Kirwan, A. Hale, & A. Hopkins (Eds.), *Changing Regulation* (pp. 57–78). Amsterdam: Elsevier Science.

Hughes, T. P. (1983). *Networks of Power*. Baltimore, MD: Johns Hopkins University Press.

Jackson, S. J., & Barbrow, S. (2015). Standards and/as innovation: protocols, creativity, and interactive systems development in ecology. *Proceedings of the 33rd Annual ACM Conference on Human Factors in Computing Systems*, 1769–78.

Kaasen K. (2014). Safety regulation on the Norwegian continental shelf. In P. H. Lindøe, M. Baram, & O. Renn (Eds.), *Risk Governance of Offshore Oil and Gas Operations* (pp. 103–31). New York: Cambridge University Press.

Karlsen, J. E., & Lindøe, P. H. (2006). The Nordic OSH model at a turning point? *Policy and Practice in Health and Safety*, *4*(1), 17–30.

Kringen, J. (2009). Culture and control: regulation of risk in the Norwegian petroleum industry (doctoral dissertation). Oslo: University of Oslo.

Kuhn, T. (1970). *The Structure of Scientific Revolutions* (2nd edn., with postscript). Chicago, IL: University of Chicago Press.

Kuhn, T. (1982). Commensurability, comparability, communicability. *PSA: Proceedings of the Biennial Meeting of the Philosophy of Science Association*, 669–88.

Long, R. C. (2006). Emerging drilling technologies. In R. F. Mitchell (Ed.), *Petroleum Engineering Handbook: Volume II, Drilling Engineering* (pp. 571–88). Richardson, TX: Society of Petroleum Engineers.

Mitchell, R. F., & Miska S. Z. (2011). *Fundamentals of Drilling Engineering*. Richardson, TX: Society of Petroleum Engineers.

Nelson, R. R., & Winter, S. G. (1974). Neoclassical versus evolutionary theories of economic growth. *Economic Journal*, *84*, 886–905.

Nelson, R. R., & Winter, S. G. (1982). *An Evolutionary Theory of Economic Change*. Cambridge, MA: Belknap Press.

Nooteboom, B. (2012). Embodied cognition, organization and innovation. In R. Arena, A. Festré & N. Lazaric (Eds.), *Handbook of Knowledge and Economics* (pp. 339–68). Cheltenham, UK, and Northampton, MA, USA: Edward Elgar Publishing.

Pinch, T. J., & Bijker, W. E. (1984). The social construction of facts and artefacts: or how the sociology of science and the sociology of technology might benefit each other. *Social Studies of Science*, *14*(3), 399–441.

Pollock, N. (2005). When is a workaround? Conflict & negotiation in computer systems development. *Science, Technology, & Human Values, 30*(4), 496–514.

Ribes, D., & Lee, C. (2010). Sociotechnical studies of cyberinfrastructure and e-research: current themes and future trajectories. *CSCW, 19*(3–4), 231–44.

Rip, A., & Kemp, R. (1998). Technological change. In S. Rayner & E. L. Malone (Eds.), *Human Choice and Climate Change* (vol. 2, pp. 327–99). Columbus, OH: Battelle Press.

Sardo, S., Parmiggiani E., & Hoholm, T. (2021). Not in transition: inter-infrastructural governance and the politics of repair in the Norwegian Oil and Gas offshore industry. *Energy Research and Social Science, 75*, 102047.

Scott, W. R. (1995). *Institutions and Organizations: Foundations for Organizational Science*. Thousand Oaks, CA: Sage.

Sims, B. (2007). Things fall apart: disaster, infrastructure, and risk. *Social Studies of Science, 37*(1), 93–5.

Sovacool, B. K., Lovell, K., & Ting, M. B. (2018). Reconfiguration, contestation, and decline: conceptualizing mature large technical systems. *Science Technology and Human Values, 43*(6), 1066–97.

Star, S. L. (1991a). Power, technology and the phenomenology of conventions: on being allergic to onions. *Sociological Review, 38*(S1), 26–56.

Star, S. L. (1991b). The sociology of the invisible: the primacy of work in the writings of Anselm Strauss. In D. Maines (Ed.), *Social Organization and Social Process: Essays in Honor of Anselm Strauss* (pp. 265–83). Hawthorne, NY: Aldine de Gruyter.

Star, S. L. (1995). *Ecologies of Knowledge: Work and Politics in Science and Technology*. Albany, NY: SUNY Press.

Star, S. L. (1999). The ethnography of infrastructure. *American Behavioural Scientist, 43*(3), 377–91.

Star, S. L. (2010). This is not a boundary object: reflections on the origin of a concept. *Science, Technology & Human Values, 35*(5), 601–17.

Star, S. L., & Griesemer, J. R. (1989). Institutional ecology "translations" and boundary objects: amateurs and professionals in Berkeley's Museum of Vertebrate Zoology, 1907–39. *Social Studies of Science, 19*(3), 387–420.

Star, S. L., & Ruhleder, K. (1996). Steps toward an ecology of infrastructure: design and access for large information spaces. *Information Systems Research, 7*(1), 111–34.

Timmermans, S., & Epstein, S. (2010). A world of standards but not a standard world: toward a sociology of standards and standardization. *Annual Review of Sociology, 36*, 69–89.

Turnheim, B., & Geels F. W. (2013). The destabilisation of existing regimes: confronting a multi-dimensional framework with a case study of the British coal industry (1913–1967). *Research Policy, 42*(10), 1749–67.

Unruh, G. C. (2002). Escaping carbon lock-in. *Energy Policy, 30*, 317–25.

Urry, J. (2004). The 'system' of automobility. *Theory, Culture, Society, 21*(4–5), 25–39.

Vinnem, J. E. (2010). Risk indicators for major hazards on offshore installations. *Safety Science, 48*, 770–87.

Wynne, B. (1988). Unruly technology: practical rules, impractical discourses and public understanding. *Social Studies of Science, 18*(1), 147–67.

12. Interactions in innovation processes of medical devices: systemic and network perspectives

Olga Mikhailova

1. INTRODUCTION

Innovation is a key driver for the expansion of the medical device sector, which has been consistently growing over recent decades (Ciani et al., 2016; Consoli et al., 2015). Developing and implementing medical devices is a complex process characterized by strict regulations, diverse actors, cross-disciplinary knowledge and high resource demand. Recent studies underline that healthcare innovation is relatively overlooked within the field of innovation studies (Proksch et al., 2019; Thune & Mina, 2016). Furthermore, according to Ciani et al. (2016), medical technologies should be studied as a separate category within healthcare innovation due to the special interdisciplinarity that characterizes this specific innovation context (Galbrun & Kijima, 2010; Littell, 1994).

It is well known that healthcare is distinguished by a wide context of participants, their relationships and their contextual knowledge; therefore, innovation processes, including their development and implementation, to a large extent depend on connecting different actors (Proksch et al., 2019). Cross-complementarity of agents thus becomes necessary to perform tasks and activities under the innovation umbrella. As a result, multiple and mutual dependencies of actors continuously attract scholars' attention.

In this chapter, I study the interactions/interdependencies between elements in the innovation process of medical devices from two different perspectives. I focus on systems and network approaches to discuss the features of these processes. Even though the concepts of networks and systems are often used interchangeably (Consoli & Ramlogan, 2009), these two approaches focus on different types of interactions. While both approaches emphasize the relevance of relationships between agents and their heterogeneity, the systemic perspective provides an overview of all agents involved in medical innovation processes and enables the analysis of the healthcare function in its totality (Consoli & Mina, 2009). The network approach is instead centered on the agent, focusing on the actual relationships and interdependences influencing their choices and decisions (Chiambaretto & Dumez, 2016).

I use a case study approach building on innovation process of Transcatheter Aortic Valve Implantation (TAVI) in Danish hospitals to illustrate the differences and complementarities in studying interactions in the medical innovation process through healthcare innovation systems and interactive network lenses, respectively. By analyzing interactions within producer–practitioner networks at the early stages of technology implementation, I provide evidence for the position that a systemic view provides a working model for explaining medical device innovation across various contexts. However, I also emphasize how the actual complexity of social relationships within networks cannot be properly analyzed within the systemic framework. The networking approach provides the required instrument to understand the challenges faced by each individual agent within specific innovation processes. While these two frameworks provide different views and results from analysis of the same process, for analytical purposes these perspectives are complementary and need to be applied interchangeably to understand the medical innovation process in its entirety.

The reminder of this chapter is structured as follows. Section 2 reviews the systemic and network perspectives on interactions in the medical innovation process; Section 3 describes the study methods; Section 4 presents the TAVI case; Section 5 compares the systemic and network perspectives based on the case analysis; finally, Section 6 draws conclusions and identifies some general implications.

2. REVIEW OF SELECTED LITERATURE

While there are different bodies of literature that can be used to look into the connection between the agents or components within the medical device innovation process, I turn my attention to systems and network perspectives. I further describe the main assumptions and characteristics of each approach to identify situations in which they can be applied.

2.1 Systemic View of the Healthcare Innovation Process

One of the approaches to understand the relationship between different elements within the innovation process is to look at these interdependencies as a feature of the systemic quality of innovation in the healthcare sector (Consoli & Mina, 2009; Windrum & Garcia-Goni, 2008). The growing interest of scholars in systemic perspective is driven by its overall goal of nurturing present and future innovativeness through identifying and adequately rewarding current innovations (Ciani et al., 2016). The system perspective reflects on innovativeness at the aggregate level; with regard to medical technologies, this perspective addresses the need to find a pattern behind development of technological solutions for existing problems in the healthcare sector. Scholars have already highlighted the link between healthcare medical technology and the concept of Health Innovation Systems (HIS) (Consoli & Mina, 2009). This link has been supported by many successful attempts to explore specific medical technologies through the lens of (sectoral) innovation systems (Consoli et al., 2015; Larisch et al., 2016; Metcalfe et al., 2005; Petersen et al., 2016).

The concept of HIS was first introduced by Ramlogan et al., (2007), who connected the healthcare context with the literature on innovation systems. Building on this work, Ramlogan and Consoli (2008) presented HIS as a synthesis of institutions, agents and their interactions that contribute to the creation, diffusion and implementation of new technologies in modern healthcare. Hence, HIS represents "the logical structure that connects the purpose for which a system exists to the set of activities that are set out to achieve it" (Consoli, 2007, p. 76). By mapping the institutionally bound interactions among agents, or gateways of innovation, HIS scholars try to capture the network-shaped structure behind the knowledge creation that leads to new trajectories of change, or pathways of innovation (Consoli & Mina, 2009). Based on this conceptualization of the HIS, interactions are viewed from a functional perspective, consolidating patterns behind chaotic relationships contributing to knowledge development. Along these lines, each connection between agents has an underlying function to generate knowledge, whereas the overall function of the system is to coordinate the emerging knowledge (Consoli & Ramlogan, 2009). As a result, a system is "an emerging property that reflects the employment of either an implicit or agreed strategy to achieve a collective scope" (Consoli & Ramlogan, 2009, p. 4). However, while the systemic perspective builds upon the assumption that all agents are driven by a common goal to stimulate innovations in healthcare, on the agent level the functions portfolio may be more diverse (Thune & Mina, 2016). To further explore this diversity and contribute to the systems-oriented literature, a micro-level investigation of particular cases of medical device innovations must be conducted.

HIS draws particular attention to knowledge, as medical devices entail knowledge reconfiguration across interconnected institutional, organizational and technical domains (Metcalfe, 2002). Studying the diversity of knowledge bases involved in the medical device innovation, Metcalfe et al. (2005) emphasize the reciprocal dependence between science and technology as distinctive characteristic of HIS. In line with this thinking, Davey et al. (2010) conceptualize health innovation as "complex bundles of new medical technologies and clinical services emerging from a highly distributed competence base" (p. 22). Taking a closer view on the knowledge component of the system,

Barberá-Tomás and Consoli (2012) claim that the development and application of knowledge are bound to the "grip of history" (p. 932).

The value of knowledge and the idea of better informing practice with research findings has been dominant in healthcare (Dearing & Kee, 2012). The expectation is that those who allocate funding and those who run health services and deliver care to patients, use the most up-to-date findings from medical research to inform their decisions. Consequently, healthcare practitioners rely on research results in their search for new treatment and procedures. Based in this logic, the published results from clinical trials of new practices serve as a starting point for innovation implementation and spread. Yet, knowledge application is more complex in reality. Colditz and Emmons (2012) assert that innovation studies in healthcare commonly indicate that discovery on its own does not lead to use of knowledge, and evidence from clinical studies does not lead to uptake of new practices. The predominant view of knowledge development and application being a technical exercise that places products into events has been critiqued by social scientists. Lomas (2007) claims that these tasks are as much social as technical. Dearing and Kee (2012) affirm that it is useful to consider the interplay between the technical rationalities of knowledge producers and users' narrative rationalities. Indeed, HIS scholars admit that even though "a system thrives on the diversity of the forms of specialization within", it "requires coherence through coordination across the activities in which knowledge is embodied" (Consoli, 2007, p. 76). This brings forward the role of interaction between various agents pointing at the need to study different aspects of interaction or interactive processes within a system.

According to Consoli and Ramlogan (2009), the structure of a network cannot be divorced from the dynamics of the knowledge supporting it; therefore, epistemic networks are the operational tool in the HIS studies. Indeed, network analysis is the underlying method used to trace the trajectories of change. Both Mina et al. (2007) and Ramlogan et al. (2007) use a network analysis of scientific publications and collaborations for glaucoma and cardiovascular disease, connecting a multitude of "medical micro innovation systems" (Mina et al., 2007, p. 791) and specific medical research spread across geopolitical boundaries. Barberá-Tomás and Consoli (2012) implement connectivity analysis on patent citations data studying multiple trajectories in artificial disc technology. Consoli and Ramlogan (2009) use a unique longitudinal dataset of scientific articles studying the long-term evolution of medical scientific research in ophthalmology. By capturing the growing variety of scientific knowledge, they concentrate explicitly on network evolution of medical research. Thus, a system approach to healthcare innovation seeks to "synthesize the patterns traversed by those who, over time, engineered solutions in the attempt to overcome the limitations of existing techniques" (Consoli

& Ramlogan, 2008, p. 32). Analyzing the trajectories provides a long-term overview of the process, yet some of the intricacies can be overlooked if only knowledge production is in focus. For example, patents and scientific articles may not always lead to new products and services. Small variations in innovation implementation may also be excluded from the analysis, thus creating a partial picture of a single innovation process.

There are some examples of a systemic view being used for studying healthcare innovation within a certain geographical scope. Larisch et al. (2016) use a functional dynamics approach to analyze a regional health innovation system in Stockholm suggesting it as a basis for designing and evaluating innovation policy. Weigel (2011) studies a regional health innovation system in Switzerland, scrutinizing the role of specific actors in the Bern region. Analyzing the pattern of hospital–industry interactions in the medical device industry, he affirms the complementarity between agents in industry and healthcare in terms of their resources (practical medical knowledge of healthcare agents versus engineering know-how and commercialization) to achieve a certain goal (scientific recognition by their peers for the healthcare agents versus commercial success for the industry actors). Indeed, an HIS perspective stresses the relevance of relationship between users or clinicians and the industry and serves as an important tool for policymakers alike to understand how the systems function. However, this perspective results in a fixed conceptualization of the relationships among agents disregarding the diversity of social structures embedded in the context that provides insights on how medical innovation processes are shaped in different settings. Functional interaction within systems is static in nature and connects elements that are necessary to replicate innovation processes. An HIS perspective provides the model showing how the connected agents achieve the best possible result (highlighting the role of lead users). Yet, a single innovation process is insignificant in this system as HIS's concern is to trace technological trajectory across various domains and to combine all the necessary elements driving the innovation process in its totality. This reductionist approach focuses on successful cases that do not represent the diversity of the actual fluid interaction between actors which poses difficulties for understanding short-term dynamic changes. Thus, using an HIS perspective to study innovation processes of medical devices, we have an incomplete understanding of actors' intentions and intricacies of the innovation process itself.

2.2 Network View of the Healthcare Innovation Process

Another way to look at the connection between elements is by taking a networked approach (Chiambaretto & Dumez, 2016; Dahl et al., 2016). According to this approach, networks are socially embedded structures (Baum

& Dutton, 1996; Oliver, 1997) characterized by the reciprocal relationship between structure and interaction (Håkansson et al., 2009). In other words, the network is both the structure within which interactions take place and the interactions' results. From this perspective, the healthcare sector can be viewed as a network of inter-organizational networks (Albert-Cromarias & Dos Santos, 2020; Lega & De Pietro, 2005; Westra et al., 2017). Building on the work of innovation scholars (Oliver, 1990; Van de Ven, 1976), Westra et al. (2017) define inter-organizational networks in healthcare as networks "of various types of temporary or long-lasting inter-organizational relations through which resources are transferred between organizations, underpinned by various organizational motives" (p. 43). Therefore, networks constitute various structural interdependences between and amongst actors, implying that strategic actions of actors and organizations are influenced by the social context in which they are embedded.

Scholars reveal that the initiation and implementation of relationships among healthcare organizations are influenced by several ambiguities that impact both the governance and the structuring of collaborative relationships. Palumbo et al. (2020) inform us that an inability to bring awareness and deal with these ambiguities will shape an impaired understanding of collaborative relationships among actors and the emergence of conflicting relationships. Albert-Cromarias and Dos Santos (2020) advocate for envisioning healthcare as a bundle of interactive networks when studying medical technologies, due to specific structures associated with healthcare organizations, primarily due to the presence of various powerful professional groups and regulatory systems influencing decision-making and implementation of healthcare innovations (Radnor et al., 2012). In terms of medical devices, innovation processes are advised to be studied across organizations to avoid incomplete understanding of the process.

Inter-organizational relationships as the basis of collaboration has been claimed to play a key role in situations characterized by faster industrial dynamics and therefore higher uncertainties (Bouncken et al., 2015). In terms of healthcare innovation, mutual ties between hospitals stimulate knowledge sharing and inter-organizational learning (Peng & Bourne, 2009; Westra et al., 2017). Lega and De Pietro (2005) demonstrate that healthcare institutions are embedded in network alliances or informal agreements of cooperation, whereas Chiambaretto and Dumez (2016) point at the multiplicity of these alliances, as hospitals engage in several simultaneous collaborative agreements. Studying relationships in alliances in healthcare, Zuckerman and D'aunno (1990) argue that they may vary depending on a range of dimensions, including announced purpose, structural forms (e.g. profit or non-profit; degree of control or autonomy), governance and management structure. Among various reasons for inter-organizational collaborations, scholars identify economic benefits, cost

240   *Rethinking the social in innovation and entrepreneurship studies*

reduction, better access to healthcare and incorporation of specialized services (Lega & De Pietro, 2005).

Indeed, relationships in networks are generally considered to have positive connotations indicating opportunities for collaboration, benefits of membership, and information and knowledge flow in a group. At the same time, negative effects materialize in controversy, disagreement or even conflicts. This dual nature of relationships can be explained by diametrically different logics behind relationships. On the one hand, individuals act to maximize their own interest driving the competition against each other to best fulfill their own self-interests (Bengtsson & Kock, 2000). On the other hand, the social structure that surrounds individuals creates the conditions for cooperation that motivate people to act collectively to create a win–win relationship (Axelrod & Hamilton, 1981).

Peng and Bourne (2009) explore the duality of relationships by studying how Taiwanese healthcare networks with different structures compete and cooperate with each other. The term "competition" has been historically restricted to private firms and it is rarely associated with healthcare organizations (Albert-Cromarias & Dos Santos, 2020). Some studies have drawn attention to the limitations of competition – additional expenditure, duplicated services, spread of insufficient resources in healthcare and citizen dissatisfaction (Gee, 2000; LeTourneau, 2004). Gee (2000) concludes that competition in healthcare simply does not have the desired result. Despite that, Peng and Bourne (2009) highlight some positive outcomes of competition across hospitals and networks; among those are adoption of medical devices and technologies, support of public relations and decreased cost of procurement. This is consistent with the claim, advanced by scholars in strategic management, that cooperation and competition can be parts of one and the same relationship (Bengtsson & Kock, 2000; Nalebuff et al., 1996) – they call it coopetition. Building on the resource-based view, strategic management scholars assert that, to a certain extent, concurrence of competition and cooperation can be explained by homogeneity and heterogeneity in resources. Similarity of resources (e.g. provided services or treatments) create common ground for competing organizations to engage in joint development, innovation project and quality assurance. Peng and Bourne (2009) illustrate that cooperative strategies emerge in situations with high uncertainty and fragility, for example when new medical teams are created, or economic sustainability is at stake. It can be attributed to the fact that alliances create opportunities to access scares resources, such as knowledge, expertise or tangible assets. Lomi et al. (2014) highlight that if cooperative inter-organizational healthcare networks are well structured, they can serve as an efficient resource distribution mechanism that consequently contributes to improved quality of care.

Table 12.1   Comparison of system and network perspectives

	Systems perspective	Network perspective
Relationships	Functional	Actual
Time dimension	Static	Dynamic
Main object of study	The capabilities of the collective to generate, diffuse and utilize technologies that have economic value	The building, managing and exploitation of interdependencies by actors
Foundational elements	Agents, relationships and their attributes	Interactions, actors, activities and resources
Boundaries	Minimum number of qualitatively diverse activities necessary to perform the theoretically determined function	Empirically determined

Earlier research highlights the relevance of applying the concept of coopetition in healthcare (Barretta, 2008; Gee, 2000; Mascia et al., 2012; van den Broek et al., 2018; Westra et al., 2017). Albert-Cromarias and Dos Santos (2020) provide empirical evidence that coopetition takes place in healthcare, LeTourneau (2004) has discussed strategies for building a foundation for coopetition, while Gnyawali and Park (2011) identify inter-network coopetition as a prospect for future research. Studying interactions between two networks, Peng and Bourne (2009) assert that it depends on the network management activities, which according to Harland et al. (2004) include many elements – "partner selection, resource integration, information processing, knowledge capture, social coordination, decision-making, risk and benefit sharing, conflict resolution, and motivating" (pp. 8–9). Essentially, coopetition calls for selecting "what to share, with whom, when, and under what conditions" (Levy et al., 2003, p. 4) resulting in more complex structural interdependence (Ireland et al., 2002).

According to Westra et al. (2017), enhanced competitiveness and innovativeness as beneficial outcomes of coopetition can be achieved when tensions distinctive to the dual nature of relationships are guided and supervised. However, further research must be conducted to enhance our knowledge and understanding of the ambiguous and perplexing concept of coopetition in the complex and equally ambiguous healthcare context (Albert-Cromarias & Dos Santos, 2020).

To summarize the main aspects of systems and networks perspectives Table 12.1 provides the general characteristics of each of the approaches (establishing grounds for the discussion).

3.   METHODS

This chapter empirically draws on the process of TAVI transformation from an academic invention to an established medical procedure. TAVI is a minimally invasive procedure for treating patients with severe aortic valve calcification that became an alternative to standard open-heart surgery for inoperable, as well as high- and intermediate-risk patients. Implementation of the TAVI technology requires the engagement of a multidisciplinary team, including interventional cardiologists, thoracic surgeons and anesthesiologists, among others, and involves significant changes in organization and cross-disciplinary practice.

Together with a team of researchers, I was a part of the project "From breakthroughs in knowledge to integration in medical practice" funded by the Research Council of Norway (grant no. 210511). We conducted a qualitative study to investigate TAVI adoption and implementation at a total of ten hospitals in Norway, Denmark and Sweden. In this chapter, I selected the Danish user–producer network as my research setting for three reasons. First, among Scandinavian countries, Denmark has been leading in TAVI procedures from the early phase of the TAVI innovation process, which allows studying the emergence of TAVI networks. Second, the underlying concept of TAVI has been developed by Henning Rud Andersen, cardiologist at Århus University Hospital (ÅUH-S), Denmark (Nielsen, 2012). The license of the patent has been later acquired by Edwards Lifesciences, a major TAVI producer. The connection between Edwards and ÅUH-S was particularly suitable for investigating the interplay between users and producers in the TAVI industry networks. Third, there were practical reasons. Limiting this study to Danish hospitals allows circumvention of differences among healthcare systems and focuses on the dynamics within the network. All the hospitals in this study are Danish research-oriented university hospitals that combine specialized and top clinical healthcare delivery, scientific healthcare research and professional training.

In my data collection, I rely on a combination of interviews, non-participant observations and extensive document analysis. The overview of the interviews is presented in Table 12.2. To supplement the interview data, I also participated in meetings and conferences wherein TAVI-related topics were discussed among participants. In addition to the hospital visits and interviews, I collected extensive empirical material from publicly available reports on both the technology producers and the hospitals, including articles in medical journals, press releases, reports produced by regulatory health authorities, practice guidelines provided by professional associations, national TAVI registries, reports from TAVI conferences and news from internet sources.

Interactions in innovation processes of medical devices 243

Table 12.2   Interviews overview

Informant group	Affiliation	Number of interviews
Practitioners at Danish university hospitals	Århus University Hospital (ÅUH-S)	4
	Ålborg University Hospital (ÅUH)	6
	Rigshospitalet, Copenhagen (RH)	2
Producers	Medtronic	1
	Edwards	1

In the analysis, I focused on the interactions between different groups of practitioners and producers. I started by analyzing the interview data which I supplemented with various documentary sources. Then I reconstructed the interdependent chain of events that I wrote into a case narrative, the primary task of qualitative inquiries (Patton, 1990). Finally, I combined this material with corresponding theoretical perspectives by systematically combining and recombining collected material, in line with Dubois and Gadde (2002).

4.   THE TAVI CASE

4.1   Emergence of the Global TAVI Network

Back in 1989, a cardiologist from Århus University Hospital in Denmark created the first prototype, filed patents and, after some struggles, published results of successful insertion of a balloon expandable aortic valve through the blood vessels on pigs (Andersen et al., 1992). This idea was not accepted by either surgeons who dominated the domain of structural heart diseases or relevant business actors; therefore, it remained unattended until the exclusive license of this patent was acquired by a startup Percutaneous Valve Technologies (PVT) located in New Jersey, USA. The PVT team, with world leading interventional cardiologists and bioengineers, finally put in use the Andersen license and developed the first useable prototype applied in the first in-man successful operation performed at Rouen University Hospital, France in 2002 (Cribier et al., 2002). In 2004, PVT was acquired by Edwards Lifesciences, an industry incumbent who sought to maintain and grow its traditional surgical markets. Therefore, it became critical that the valve could be used by both surgeons and cardiologists. Edwards invested in creation of the delivery system for the valve that would allow surgeons to get on board. At the end of 2007, Edwards' valves eventually received a quality certificate from the European Conformity Marking Competent Authorities (Conformité Européenne [CE]), and the first commercially viable version of TAVI appeared on the European market the same year. However, by that time, Edwards had gained a competitor – a startup, CoreValve. The company was founded in France in 2001 and moved its HQ to Irvine, California in 2005. The company developed a similar technology based on a self-expanding valve. CoreValve was first implanted in man in 2004 and the company received CE approval of their valves for the same group of patients in 2007. That was the beginning of a competitive race in Europe between Edwards and CoreValve.

Even though TAVI was evaluated by medical professional associations confirming that the device was feasible, the European professional associations advised restricting access to high-volume centers with both cardiology and cardiac surgery departments to guarantee patient safety (Vahanian et al., 2008). Producer companies were also interested in initiating TAVI programs at the main European university hospitals, but in addition to safety and efficiency, they had strategic reasons. At the early stage of TAVI dissemination, Edwards would consult new TAVI medical teams on patient selection, the choice of access point and valve size, yet the assistance of practitioners during the first operations was crucial for the smooth introduction of TAVI into the market. To address this issue, producer companies invested in recruiting already engaged practitioners to train new hospital teams who start with TAVI programs. These assistants were called proctors. To become a proctor, a practitioner had to perform at least 40 TAVI operations. Not having enough proctors was a critical bottleneck for TAVI expansion; thus, producers had to concentrate their marketing on the hospitals that performed sufficient number of procedures to hire new proctors.

CoreValve promoted their product to cardiologists, while Edwards ran into a puzzling situation. As Edwards' primary customer, surgeons openly showed distrust and skepticism towards TAVI (Walther et al., 2012). This forced Edwards to develop a new strategy that would engage both surgeons and cardiologists in the TAVI innovation process. As a result, TAVI was introduced as complementary option, rather than competing with open-heart surgery treatment. For this reason, only inoperable and high-risk patients were included in the clinical trials at the beginning.

In late 2009, CoreValve was acquired by Medtronic Inc., another industry incumbent. Shortly after, Medtronic and Edwards were involved in extensive patent litigation. After a series of disputes, Medtronic agreed to pay Edwards $750 million with ongoing royalties based on a percentage of sales of at least $40 million annually through April 2022. Additionally, the Anderson patent was set to expire in 2011. These events gave Edwards an advantage and the company obtained a market monopoly in the U.S. market that lasted until January 2014, when Medtronic also received approval from the U.S. Food and Drug Administration (FDA). Despite these conflicts, the diffusion of TAVI grew exponentially during this period. In 2007, the aggregated number of TAVI procedures conducted across the world was approximately 1,000.

Interactions in innovation processes of medical devices 245

Two years later, the number grew to 10,000, and by early 2014, it had risen to 100,000.

4.2   The National TAVI Network of Producers and Practitioners

In 2008, Danish health authorities officially approved TAVI as a treatment for selected patients (Özcan et al., 2016). This allowed university hospitals to engage with experimental implementation of TAVI technology and major Danish university hospitals started TAVI programs in 2007–08. In collaboration with TAVI producers, teams at university hospitals were developing their signature techniques. Copenhagen University Hospital (RH) adopted a self-expanding TAVI technology by CoreValve, and established a dedicated team led by a cardiologist focused on performing one technique (transfemoral approach). The team was initially trained by Jan Claude Labarde who performed the first in-man CoreValve TAVI procedure. The Odense University Hospital (OUH) later joined the CoreValve network, but they also started a second TAVI program with Edwards.

ÅUH-S participated in pre-approval experimental procedures in 2006. A close relationship between the inventor cardiologist and Edwards gave Århus an opportunity to engage with TAVI before CE approval. However, due to poor results, this initiative was suspended until February 2008 when Edwards was looking for new centers after CE approval. This time the TAVI program was led by the surgeons and ÅUH-S was among the leading investigator hospitals partnering with Edwards and became a core center for TAVI with the transapical approach (Wendler et al., 2011).

Two leading Danish national centers, RH and ÅUH-S were perfect targets for the TAVI producers. Both centers performed enough TAVI procedures to be involved in proctoring and to produce evidence supporting the spread of the new medical technology. Both ÅUH-S (Edwards) and RH (CoreValve) initiated independent studies comparing the TAVI technologies from the corresponding provider with the open-heart procedure.

The Notion study initiated by RH in 2008 compared transfemoral TAVI with an open-heart valve replacement, leading to several publications (Thyregod et al., 2013; 2015). Based on the results of this study, CoreValve managed to receive CE approval for an additional group of patients, the intermediate risk group. The Stacatto study initiated at the same time by ÅUH-S together with Odense University Hospital aimed at comparing transapical TAVI with open-heart surgery (Nilsen, 2015). This project was funded by the Danish Heart Foundation (Van Brabandt et al., 2012), but unfortunately it was terminated by the Data Safety Monitoring Board due to poor results with the transapical treatment. Staccato investigators concluded that TAVI should remain restricted to surgically inoperable patients. Edwards, in its turn, concentrated on the larger and more extended U.S.-based PARTNER multi-center trial that later was included in the FDA application. The results of the studies split the Danish TAVI market into two regions. Even before the studies, Danish university hospitals did not have a unified TAVI registry system. There were two separate registries – Eastern (RH) and Western (ÅUH-S and OUH), and hospitals in each region were looking for more patients to treat with TAVI. As a result, the split between the regions became more explicit, leading to unequal access to patients.

In 2010, the Danish National Committee restricted the TAVI program to only hospitals that could perform at least 40 TAVI procedures per year. This change was enforced at the time when Ålborg University Hospital (ÅUH) decided to launch the TAVI program. ÅUH was formally a part of ÅUH-S until 2013 and did not have enough patients to begin with. Yet after the unsuccessful Staccatto study, Edwards was looking for new centers and after long negotiations, ÅUH started a TAVI program in collaboration with ÅUH-S and Edwards in 2011 (Figure 12.1).

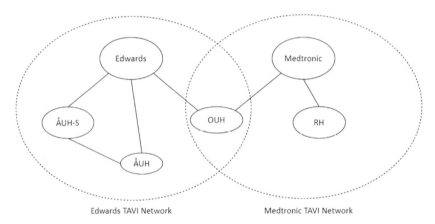

Figure 12.1   Illustration of the TAVI networks in Denmark

Data show that the number of TAVI procedures in Denmark hospitals significantly increased after 2011 (De Backer et al., 2016). Until then, there were only two TAVI technologies commercially available on the market, and hospitals tended to order valves from either provider (Edwards or CoreValve/Medtronic). However, in 2011, the Andersen patent expired, and new companies entered the TAVI industry. By 2014, several startups were offering various CE-approved TAVI technologies. At that point the Danish health authorities introduced the tender system for TAVI valves and hospitals organized meetings with providers to discuss different options. At the time,

Danish centers had accumulatively performed more than one thousand TAVI procedures, among these approximately 400 operations at ÅUH-S and 550 operations at RH. ÅUH had performed 96 TAVI operations; despite the lower quantity, the ÅUH team achieved good results and were chosen by Edwards to be the first to engage with the next version of Edwards TAVI.

5. DISCUSSION

The purpose of this study was to understand the features of the innovation process of medical devices. I offered two conceptually different perspectives to shed light on the interactions between the elements within the medical innovation process.

5.1 Complementarity of System and Network Perspectives

Since innovation by definition involves the creation and implementation of novelty (Van de Ven, 2017), actors operate in highly uncertain conditions. The systemic view allows abstraction from these uncertainties, instead searching for the constant in the chaotic reality. Thus, the systemic approach isolates the necessary elements that ensure a system's functioning. For this reason, the HIS perspective can be used as an analytical tool for tracing the long-term evolution and development of the technology and practice that draws on the nexus of functional interactions among agents. The outcome of this analytical exercise is a blueprint – a model composed of equally important connected elements in a network-shaped structure that describes how to reproduce or improve technology-based medical practices in healthcare. The TAVI case confirms that the connection between the elements of HIS (Consoli & Mina, 2009) should be well functioning for a successful outcome of the innovation process. The link between the science and technology system (including scientific communities and professional associations, as well as the technology market) and health delivery system (both in terms of practitioners and the service that they provide) is crucial for safe and efficient implementation of the TAVI medical device. In particular, the essential role of the relationship between technology producers and practitioners is highlighted by the case analysis. This is aligned with the results of the study on hospital–industry interactions which emphasize the complementarity of these agents both in means and in ends (Weigel, 2011). Indeed, the TAVI innovation process from the patent filing until the approval of commercial implementation of this technology in the U.S. market has shown that, on an aggregated level, practitioners and producers concur in their activities to solve an existing problem in the domain of structural heart diseases; hence the TAVI technology has been continuously improved through multiple contributions of practitioners applying TAVI in practice. Yet, by studying interactions in the provider–practitioner TAVI networks one might describe the TAVI innovation process as a chain of strategic choices simultaneously shaping the innovation trajectory; some of these choices did not contribute to the technology development but were necessary for integration of the new solution into existing social structures. For example, TAVI operations could have been mainly performed by cardiologists (what inevitably happened after some time); however, without involving surgeons in the process and building on their expertise it was impossible to introduce this medical procedure safely.

The case also illustrates that the decisions were not purely based on scientific knowledge; rather, it was a range of contextually embedded trade-offs that depended on social structures and available resources at particular moments in particular contexts. The case demonstrates that the multiple frictions among professional groups (cardiologists and surgeons), producers (Edwards and CoreValve), and hospitals (both among leading hospitals across regions and among hospitals within a region) create both divergence and convergence that pave the innovation pathway. Thus, studying the TAVI innovation process in the extended network of actors allows identification of the controversy, disagreements and conflicts that remain unattended in the systemic model of the medical device innovation process, as the systemic perspective does not regard elements or relations that do not "function". Nevertheless, they indicate areas for improvement, dealing with which may also increase the innovativeness of the healthcare system.

Inattentiveness to multiple ambiguities in the systemic view is not surprising, considering that the HIS focuses on the necessary connected elements enabling innovation reproduction. Overloading the system with less important elements is irrational, as the system may lose its balance. Therefore, the system should consist of robust elements proven to contribute to its functioning. This static structure, however, becomes less predictable under conditions of high complexity and heterogeneity (Riley et al., 2017). In these situations, an enhanced understanding of the medical innovation process can be achieved by adopting a network perspective. This perspective allows observation of the actual interactions and relationships within networks of agents. The analysis of these open and divergent interactions focuses on the meaning or intent assigned by the agents to their actions. Indistinguishably, studying processes in an extended network of actors demonstrates how parallel interactions co-evolve around multiple problem areas, eventually contributing to the establishment of a new medical treatment.

5.2 The Complexity of Social Relationships

Epistemic networks collectively acting to accumulate knowledge across domains and geographies do not entirely illustrate the interactive dynamics within the innovation process. According to Dearing and Kee (2012), there is a discrepancy between the state of the science, what researchers collectively know, and the state of the art, what researchers collectively do. Evaluating the current state of scientific knowledge is an important step, but acting upon it is equally important. The capacity of a practitioner to find and use knowledge effectively is dependent on the context in which knowledge is applied. Therefore, the mechanisms behind the transformation of scientific results into medical practice require the analysis of the contextual network within which the practitioner can act. While interactions in a system are balanced and neutrally laden, network relationships are imbalanced, reflecting uneven power distribution. The analysis of interactions in the TAVI producer–user network illustrates the complexity of actual social relationships. This complexity cannot be compressed into a single systemic model and calls for detailed analysis of multiple interests and intentions of actors in the innovation network. Suitable for this purpose, the network perspective is used to illuminate how interdependencies influence the strategic choices of actors in the TAVI network consequently shaping the innovation process.

The existence of multiple heterogeneous actors entails the emergence of dynamics of competition within networks. Producers may compete for hospitals; hospitals may compete for patients and resources; whereas practitioners may compete for status and prestige. The competitive dynamics occur not only between individuals but can also be traced at the global network of producers, between practitioners on the national level, or between networks of practitioners and producers of different medical technologies. For instance, strong relationships between Edwards and ÅUH-S on one side and between CoreValve and RH on the other side created a competitive environment on the national level. Both university hospitals partnered with TAVI providers and engaged in studies that collected evidence to support the corresponding technology. Exploring competition allows us to perceive the outline of hierarchies as currently shaped by the development of ongoing innovation processes. The choices made in the emerging constellations of actors, in the network of both leading users and producers, determine the direction of the next step of technology and practice development, which then requires new connections between actors with knowledge and resources crucial for successful outcomes. Strategic networking and aligning interests through interactions enable actors to meet challenges and navigate global medical innovation processes. In these situations, taking a broader and more open-ended perspective of network boundaries and composition enables better evaluation of strategic choices within and between relationships while managing medical innovation processes locally.

In terms of engaging with new radical technologies, local actors strongly benefit from cooperation with those who hold stronger network positions than they do themselves. In these instances, cooperation serves as a source of power and influence as well as of knowledge and resources. Local leaders are likely to establish relationships with global manufacturers as they scale the implementation of innovation at a fast pace and become involved in experimental trials contributing to incremental improvements of the new medical practice and assisting other hospitals. For example, ÅUH-S became one of the leading investigators in the Edwards network by aligning its implementation strategy with the strategy of the technology producer to extend the market of surgical artificial valves with TAVIs. Engaging with the newly introduced TAVI with transapical approach, the ÅUH-S team chose to specialize and develop skills in this technique. Consequently, they were trained by the lead practitioners in Edwards' network. Eventually ÅUH-S established themselves in a stronger position in the TAVI network and began proctoring other centers starting TAVI programs. However, high-involvement relationships, like the one between ÅUH-S and Edwards, create interdependences between actors that last beyond the point of usefulness and might later become a burden. In fact, while other hospitals diversified their portfolio of TAVI technologies by adding a second supplier, ÅUH-S partnered solely with Edwards, concentrating its efforts on promoting Edwards TAVI. This partnership was efficient during the early implementation of TAVI at the hospital; however, the rapid scaling of the TAVI procedure revealed issues related to budgeting and organizing, forcing ÅUH-S to reconsider TAVI procurement at the hospital.

Smaller hospitals that cannot link directly with global manufacturing and research networks often rely on local leaders to integrate with global innovation processes. This situation creates a local hierarchy formed by a community of small actors in relation to a single central leader. While leading university hospitals often focus on research opportunities aimed at strengthening their position, smaller hospitals are more concerned with securing access to the diverse medical procedures to match with major regional centers. In the ÅUH case, close partnerships with ÅUH-S and the alignment of local activities with Edwards' marketing strategies created an opportunity for ÅUH to engage with the TAVI program despite the restrictions of the Danish National Committee. Competition dynamics can be consciously manipulated by central actors, like Edwards. By connecting and managing local hierarchies, global actors can leverage network resources into a dynamic position of strength. For example, the opportunity to start the TAVI program at ÅUH emerged due to power redistribution in the national network of TAVI hospitals resulting from different outcomes of the Notion and Stacatto studies. At that point, both Edwards and ÅUH-S were looking for new opportunities to increase the number of operations performed with Edwards' technology. As a result, ÅUH was taken on board. These examples of complex social relationships in the innovation process of TAVI technology are evidence in favor of the hypothesis that, while collaboration among competitive actors is not without costs, it also creates the necessary conditions to adapt to the emergent needs generated by innovation processes.

5.3 Heterogeneity and Dynamic Dimensions in Medical Innovation Processes

The strong heterogeneity among actors, activities and resources in the innovation process of a medical device is managed by actors through strategic choices related to the inclusion and exclusion of relationships. However, for analytical purposes, this heterogeneity needs to be organized from both a systemic and a network perspective. The HIS framework traces technological trajectories across multiple domains over time, enabling researchers to break down complex processes and to identify the main elements contributing to change (Consoli & Mina, 2009; Metcalfe et al., 2005; Ramlogan & Consoli, 2008). This perspective is particularly appropriate for understanding the nexus of interactions between actors operating under different institutional conditions. The TAVI case shows how the underlying concept of the TAVI technology stems from accumulated knowledge of different agents, including among others professional communities of surgeons and cardiologists, bioengineers, and market incumbents. Furthermore, the full impact of TAVI followed from the development and adoption of long sequences of innovation in materials (bovine or pig tissue), techniques (delivery systems, balloon valve placement in the aortic valve), and complementary equipment (3D CT scanner and other imaging modalities). By focusing on the technological trajectory of the innovation process, the HIS perspective moves toward a macro view of actors and the inter-related processes and inter-connected relationships through which innovation occurs. Yet, identifying these elements on the aggregated level results in a robust structure characterized by static heterogeneity of elements and their connections. Consequently, the HIS approach provides a functional view of the medical innovation process in the form of an impersonal holistic system that integrates important elements necessary for medical device reproduction obscuring the specific agent perspective. On the contrary, the network perspective is centered on the agent and lacks the common objective behind the activities of the interdependent agents. According to the network perspective, connections between different elements are based on contextually embedded interactions influencing the strategic choices and decisions of the agent that consequently restructure the relationships in the network. This structure embraces the actual dynamic heterogeneity of actors and their relationships, yet it loses sight of the "vector" of the innovation process. As a result, these two perspectives highlight different aspects of reality: from the system perspective a practitioner contributes to TAVI development as an agent in the system who generates knowledge on the aggregated level and facilitates further development of the technology, but from the network perspective each practitioner in the TAVI network is driven by personal strategic goals and objectives. Depending on the analyzed structure – system or network, the same agents can be a necessary element contributing to knowledge development or a decision maker who needs to evaluate opportunities and set the priorities concerning a new medical technology. Despite the differences between the two approaches, in the practice of analysis one needs to shift between these analytical tools to have a better understanding of the innovation process of medical devices.

6.   CONCLUDING REMARKS

While broad actor types and structured relationships are exclusively subject to very long-term processes of change, the relevance of actors, resources, activities, and their interactions is constantly changing, following the unfolding of simultaneous innovation processes. These dynamic processes are shaped by the concomitant strategic choices of the actors involved aimed at exploiting current circumstances and securing advantageous positions for future development. The systemic approach highlights how heterogeneity is organically organized to enable the reproduction and development of healthcare activities at all levels – from patient treatment to experimental research. The network approach highlights how the resulting system is not an equilibrium of perfectly counteracting forces but rather an ever-changing network of dynamic interactions. Functional stability is predicated on relational creative destruction as new actors, resources, activities and interactions appear and disappear over time. At the systemic level, the heterogeneity of actors, resources, activities and interactions can be understood as a stable, necessary feature. From the perspective of the actors themselves, however, the same elements are subject to constant processes of reconfiguration and re-evaluation due to ongoing innovation activities. Thus, the contextual situations in which actors, resources, activities and interactions take shape are organized in temporary hierarchical structures revealing opportunities, weaknesses and conflicts of interest. These structures, relatively invisible from a systemic perspective, are created, sustained and modified by network interactions and provide fundamental motivations for actors' activities.

To target the increase of innovativeness in the medical device sector, policies should account for complex social relationship of innovation processes. Policymakers tend to adhere to systemic views, consistent with a functional perspective. Indeed, from a systemic and functional perspective, policies on medical innovations should be fixed. However, dealing with specific innovation processes, policies should account for the interactive dynamics in relevant networks. This reconsideration has two important implications. First, to stimulate innovation, it might be more effective to support leaders by providing resources that are relatively valuable in the particular context at the given point in time. These leaders can be identified by their connectedness to other actors in the global and local networks. Second, the leading actors should be continuously re-evaluated. For this matter, reconfiguration within networks can serve as an indicator for policy re-adjustments.

REFERENCES

Albert-Cromarias, A., & Dos Santos, C. (2020). Coopetition in healthcare: Heresy or reality? An exploration of felt outcomes at an intra-organizational level. *Social Science & Medicine, 252*, 112938.

Andersen, H., Knudsen, L., & Hasenkam, J. (1992). Transluminal implantation of artificial heart valves. Description of a new expandable aortic valve and initial results with implantation by catheter technique in closed chest pigs. *European Heart Journal*, 13, 704–8.

Axelrod, R., & Hamilton, W. D. (1981). The evolution of cooperation. *Science, 211*(4489), 1390–96.

Barberá-Tomás, D., & Consoli, D. (2012). Whatever works: Uncertainty and technological hybrids in medical innovation. *Technological Forecasting and Social Change, 79*(5), 932–48.

Barretta, A. (2008). The functioning of co-opetition in the health-care sector: An explorative analysis. *Scandinavian Journal of Management, 24*(3), 209–20.

Baum, J., & Dutton, J. (1996). The embeddedness of strategy. In P. Shrivastava, A. S. Huff, & J. Dutton (Eds.), *Advances in Strategic Management* (pp. 3–40). Greenwich, CT: JAI Press.

Bengtsson, M., & Kock, S. (2000). "Coopetition" in business networks—to cooperate and compete simultaneously. *Industrial Marketing Management, 29*(5), 411–26.

Bouncken, R. B., Gast, J., Kraus, S., & Bogers, M. (2015). Coopetition: a systematic review, synthesis, and future research directions. *Review of Managerial Science, 9*(3), 577–601.

Chiambaretto, P., & Dumez, H. (2016). Toward a typology of coopetition: a multilevel approach. *International Studies of Management & Organization, 46*(2–3), 110–29.

Ciani, O., Armeni, P., Boscolo, P. R., Cavazza, M., Jommi, C., & Tarricone, R. (2016). De innovatione: The concept of innovation for medical technologies and its implications for healthcare policy-making. *Health Policy and Technology, 5*(1), 47–64.

Colditz, G. A., & Emmons, K. M. (2012). The promise and challenges of dissemination and implementation research. In R. C. Brownson, G. A Colditz, & E. K. Proctor (Eds.), *Dissemination and Implementation Research in Health: Translating Science to Practice*, 3–22. Oxford: Oxford University Press.

Consoli, D. (2007). Services and systemic innovation: A cross-sectoral analysis. *Journal of Institutional Economics, 3*(1), 71–89.

Consoli, D., & Mina, A. (2009). An evolutionary perspective on health innovation systems. *Journal of Evolutionary Economics, 19*(2), 297–319.

Consoli, D., & Ramlogan, R. (2008). Out of sight: Problem sequences and epistemic boundaries of medical know-how on glaucoma. *Journal of Evolutionary Economics, 18*(1), 31–56.

Consoli, D., & Ramlogan, R. (2009). *Scope, Strategy and Structure: The Dynamic of Knowledge Networks in Medicine*. https://www.researchgate.net/publication/23795436_Scope_Strategy_and_Structure_The_Dynamics_of_Knowledge_Networks_in_Medicine.

Consoli, D., Mina, A., Nelson, R. R., & Ramlogan, R. (2015). *Medical Innovation: Science, Technology and Practice.* New York: Routledge.

Cribier, A., Eltchaninoff, H., Bash, A., Borenstein, N., Tron, C., Bauer, F., … Leon, M. B. (2002). Percutaneous transcatheter implantation of an aortic valve prosthesis for calcific aortic stenosis: first human case description. *Circulation*, *106*(24), 3006–8.

Dahl, J., Kock, S., & Lundgren-Henriksson, E.-L. (2016). Conceptualizing coopetition strategy as practice: A multilevel interpretative framework. *International Studies of Management & Organization*, *46*(2–3), 94–109.

Davey, S. M., Brennan, M., Meenan, B. J., & McAdam, R. (2010). The health of innovation: Why open business models can benefit the healthcare sector. *Irish Journal of Management*, *30*(1), 21–40.

De Backer, O., Luk, N. H., Olsen, N. T., Olsen, P. S., & Søndergaard, L. (2016). Choice of treatment for aortic valve stenosis in the era of transcatheter aortic valve replacement in Eastern Denmark (2005 to 2015). *JACC: Cardiovascular Interventions*, *9*(11), 1152–8.

Dearing, J. W., & Kee, K. F. (2012). Historical roots of dissemination and implementation science. In R. C. Brownson, G. A Colditz, & E. K. Proctor (Eds.), *Dissemination and Implementation Research in Health: Translating Science to Practice*, chapter 3. Oxford: Oxford University Press.

Dubois, A., & Gadde, L.-E. (2002). Systematic combining: An abductive approach to case research. *Journal of Business Research*, *55*(7), 553–60.

Galbrun, J., & Kijima, K. J. (2010). Fostering innovation in medical technology with hierarchy theory: Narratives on emergent clinical solutions. *Systems Research and Behavioral Science*, *27*(5), 523–36.

Gee, E. P. (2000). Co-opetition: The new market milieu. *Journal of Healthcare Management*, *45*(6), 359–63.

Gnyawali, D. R., & Park, B.-J. R. (2011). Co-opetition between giants: Collaboration with competitors for technological innovation. *Research Policy*, *40*(5), 650–63.

Håkansson, H., Ford, D., Gadde, L.-E., Snehota, I., & Waluszewski, A. (2009). *Business in Networks*. Chichester: Wiley-Blackwell.

Harland, C., Zheng, J., Johnsen, T., & Lamming, R. (2004). A conceptual model for researching the creation and operation of supply networks. *British Journal of Management*, *15*(1), 1–21.

Ireland, R. D., Hitt, M. A., & Vaidyanath, D. (2002). Alliance management as a source of competitive advantage. *Journal of Management*, *28*(3), 413–46.

Larisch, L.-M., Amer-Wåhlin, I., & Hidefjäll, P. (2016). Understanding healthcare innovation systems: The Stockholm region case. *Journal of Health Organization and Management*, *30*(8), 1221–41.

Lega, F., & De Pietro, C. (2005). Converging patterns in hospital organization: Beyond the professional bureaucracy. *Health Policy*, *74*(3), 261–81.

LeTourneau, B. (2004). Co-opetition: An alternative to competition. *Journal of Healthcare Management*, *49*(2), 81–3.

Levy, M., Loebbecke, C., & Powell, P. (2003). SMEs, co-opetition and knowledge sharing: The role of information systems. *European Journal of Information Systems*, *12*(1), 3–17.

Littell, C. L. (1994). Innovation in medical technology: Reading the indicators. *Health Affairs, 13*(3), 226–35.

Lomas, J. (2007). The in-between world of knowledge brokering. *BMJ, 334*(7585), 129–32.

Lomi, A., Mascia, D., Vu, D. Q., Pallotti, F., Conaldi, G., & Iwashyna, T. J. (2014). Quality of care and interhospital collaboration: A study of patient transfers in Italy. *Medical Care, 52*(5), 407–14.

Mascia, D., Di Vincenzo, F., & Cicchetti, A. (2012). Dynamic analysis of interhospital collaboration and competition: Empirical evidence from an Italian regional health system. *Health Policy, 105*(2–3), 273–81.

Metcalfe, J. S. (2002). Knowledge of growth and the growth of knowledge. *Journal of Evolutionary Economics, 12*(1), 3–15.

Metcalfe, J. S., James, A., & Mina, A. (2005). Emergent innovation systems and the delivery of clinical services: The case of intra-ocular lenses. *Research Policy, 34*(9), 1283–304.

Mina, A., Ramlogan, R., Tampubolon, G., & Metcalfe, J. S. (2007). Mapping evolutionary trajectories: Applications to the growth and transformation of medical knowledge. *Research Policy, 36*(5), 789–806.

Nalebuff, B. J., Brandenburger, A., & Maulana, A. (1996). *Co-opetition*. London: HarperCollins.

Nielsen, H. H. M. (2012). Transcatheter aortic valve implantation. https://pubmed.ncbi .nlm.nih.gov/23290293/.

Nilsen, P. (2015). Making sense of implementation theories, models and frameworks. *Implementation Science, 10*(1), 53. https://doi.org/10.1186/s13012-015-0242-0.

Oliver, C. (1990). Determinants of interorganizational relationships: Integration and future directions. *Academy of Management Review, 15*(2), 241–65.

Oliver, C. (1997). Sustainable competitive advantage: Combining institutional and resource-based views. *Strategic Management Journal, 18*(9), 697–713.

Özcan, C., Juel, K., Lassen, J. F., von Kappelgaard, L. M., Mortensen, P. E., & Gislason, G. (2016). The Danish Heart Registry. *Clinical Epidemiology, 8*, 503–8.

Palumbo, R., Manesh, M. F., Pellegrini, M. M., & Flamini, G. (2020). Exploiting inter-organizational relationships in health care: a bibliometric analysis and literature review. *Administrative Sciences, 10*(3), 57. https://doi.org/10.3390/admsci10030057.

Patton, M. Q. (1990). *Qualitative Evaluation and Research Methods*. Los Angeles, CA: Sage Publications.

Peng, T. J. A., & Bourne, M. (2009). The coexistence of competition and cooperation between networks: Implications from two Taiwanese healthcare networks. *British Journal of Management, 20*(3), 377–400.

Petersen, A. M., Rotolo, D., & Leydesdorff, L. (2016). A triple helix model of medical innovation: Supply, demand, and technological capabilities in terms of Medical Subject Headings. *Research Policy, 45*(3), 666–81.

Proksch, D., Busch-Casler, J., Haberstroh, M. M., & Pinkwart, A. (2019). National health innovation systems: Clustering the OECD countries by innovative output in healthcare using a multi indicator approach. *Research Policy, 48*(1), 169–79.

Radnor, Z. J., Holweg, M., & Waring, J. (2012). Lean in healthcare: The unfilled promise? *Social Science & Medicine, 74*(3), 364–71.

Ramlogan, R., & Consoli, D. (2008). Knowledge, understanding and the dynamics of medical innovation. Manchester Business School Working Paper, No. 539, The University of Manchester, Manchester Business School, Manchester.

Ramlogan, R., Mina, A., Tampubolon, G., & Metcalfe, J. (2007). Networks of knowledge: The distributed nature of medical innovation. *Scientometrics*, *70*(2), 459–89.

Riley, B., Willis, C., Holmes, B., Finegood, D., Best, A., & McIsaac, J. (2017). Systems thinking in dissemination and implementation research. In R. C. Brownson, G. A Colditz, & E. K. Proctor (Eds.), *Dissemination and Implementation Research in Health: Translating Science to Practice*, chapter 9. Oxford: Oxford University Press.

Thune, T., & Mina, A. (2016). Hospitals as innovators in the health-care system: A literature review and research agenda. *Research Policy*, *45*(8), 1545–57.

Thyregod, H. G., Søndergaard, L., Ihlemann, N., Franzen, O., Andersen, L. W., Hansen, P. B., … Gluud, C. (2013). The Nordic Aortic Valve Intervention (NOTION) trial comparing transcatheter versus surgical valve implantation: Study protocol for a randomised controlled trial. *Trials*, *14*(1), 1–10.

Thyregod, H. G., Steinbrüchel, D. A., Ihlemann, N., Nissen, H., Kjeldsen, B. J., Petursson, P., … Clemmensen, P. (2015). Transcatheter versus surgical aortic valve replacement in patients with severe aortic valve stenosis: 1-year results from the all-comers NOTION randomized clinical trial. *Journal of the American College of Cardiology*, *65*(20), 2184–94.

Vahanian, A., Alfieri, O. R., Al-Attar, N., Antunes, M. J., Bax, J., Cormier, B., … Kappetein, A. P. (2008). Transcatheter valve implantation for patients with aortic stenosis: A position statement from the European Association of Cardio-Thoracic Surgery (EACTS) and the European Society of Cardiology (ESC), in collaboration with the European Association of Percutaneous Cardiovascular Interventions (EAPCI). *European Journal of Cardio-Thoracic Surgery*, *34*(1), 1–8.

Van Brabandt, H., Neyt, M., & Hulstaert, F. (2012). Transcatheter aortic valve implantation (TAVI): Risky and costly. *BMJ*, *345*, e4710.

Van de Ven, A. H. (1976). On the nature, formation, and maintenance of relations among organizations. *Academy of Management Review*, *1*(4), 24–36.

Van de Ven, A. H. (2017). The innovation journey: You can't control it, but you can learn to maneuver it. *Innovation*, *19*(1), 39–42.

van den Broek, J., Boselie, P., & Paauwe, J. (2018). Cooperative innovation through a talent management pool: A qualitative study on coopetition in healthcare. *European Management Journal*, *36*(1), 135–44.

Walther, T., Kempfert, J., & Mohr, F. W. (2012). Transcatheter aortic valve implantation: Surgical perspectives. *Archives of Cardiovascular Diseases*, *105*(3), 174–80.

Weigel, S. (2011). Medical technology's source of innovation. *European Planning Studies*, *19*(1), 43–61.

Wendler, O., Walther, T., Schroefel, H., Lange, R., Treede, H., Fusari, M., … Thomas, M. (2011). The SOURCE Registry: What is the learning curve in trans-apical aortic valve implantation? *European Journal of Cardio-Thoracic Surgery*, *39*(6), 853–60.

Westra, D., Angeli, F., Carree, M., & Ruwaard, D. (2017). Coopetition in health care: A multi-level analysis of its individual and organizational determinants. *Social Science & Medicine*, *186*, 43–51.

Windrum, P., & Garcia-Goni, M. (2008). A neo-Schumpeterian model of health services innovation. *Research Policy*, *37*(4), 649–72.

Zuckerman, H. S., & D'aunno, T. A. (1990). Hospital alliances: Cooperative strategy in a competitive environment. *Health Care Management Review*, *15*(2), 21–30.

Index

Aaker, D. A. 91
"absence of unacceptable risks" 228
adaptation strategies 89
  adapting practices and processes
    related to innovation
    activities 102
  existing solutions 100–101
  industry economic crises and
    company 90–92
  retrenchment activity 100
  suppliers' response 99
  sustain/engage in innovation
    activities 103–4
  sustaining relationships with buyers
    102–3
adaptive behavior 200
adversarial industrial relations 128
Agder RIS 53, 57, 59, 60
agency
  firm-level 43, 46
  in regional industrial restructuring,
    change 45–6
  strategic change 12, 43
  system-level 43, 46, 52
agent-driven process 27
Akrich, M. 214
Albert-Cromarias, A. 239, 241
Almandoz, J. 179
analysis stage of the RIS3 162–3
Andersen, H. 242–4, 246
Anderson, A. R. 10
Andrews, F. 177
animal behaviour studies 28
anticipation 157, 161
ANT-inspired processual approach 134
aquaculture industry, examples from
  71–3
Århus University Hospital (ÅUH-S) 242,
  245–7, 249, 250
Arthur, Bryan 45
articulation work 214, 215

Asheim, B. T. 45–6
asset creation process 58
asset destruction 47
asset modification 12, 48, 50
  in firms and systems 52
  processes 51
  for regional industrial restructuring
    (RIS) 44, 46–9, 51, 52, 61
asset reuse 44, 47
asset types and scales 48
auctions and licenses 72–3
augmented diversity 174
ÅUH-S see Århus University Hospital
  (ÅUH-S)

Baba, Y. 7
Barak, Mor 176
Barberá-Tomás, D. 237
Barinaga, E. 134
Bathelt, H. 47
Beal, D. 10
Beckman, C. M. 28–9, 34
behavioral confirmation 116, 125, 127,
  129
belonging, sense of 175, 181–3
beneficial incentives 82
"benevolent co-operator" perspective
  114, 115
Betz 138, 142–4, 146
Boeker, W. 29
Boschma, R. 180
boundary objects 213–15, 217, 226–9
boundary organization 227
boundary work 213
Bourdieu, P. 49
Bourne, M. 240, 241
Bowker, G. C. 226
Bragtvedt, Stian 14
bricoleur-type approach 135
Brimhall, K. C. 181
building credibility 144–7

Building Self-Sustaining Research and Innovation Ecosystems in Europe through Responsible Research and Innovation 159
bureaucratic decision-making processes 140
Burget, M. 8
Burke, P. J. 178
Burt, R. 49, 177
Burton, M. D. 28–9, 31, 34
buyers, sustaining relationships with 102–3

Callegari, Beniamino 16
'carrot and stick' approach 82
Casciaro, T. 74
case-by-case risk identification and quantification 221
case of Nordland 165
    analysis 166
    policy mix and monitoring 167–8
    vision and prioritization 166–7
Cavalieri, M. 10
change agents and change agency in regional industrial restructuring 45–6
Chiambaretto, P. 239
Ciani, O. 234
Clearfield, C. 178, 179
cognitive regional resonance 60
cognitive resonance 50
cognitive resource diversity
    perspective 179, 180, 183, 185
    theory 178
cognitive social capital 50, 51, 60
Colditz, G. A. 237
Coleman, J. S. 49
collaboration 58, 60, 61, 80, 81, 137, 138, 140, 142, 146
    entrepreneurial practices for 134–5
    firm- and system-level 53
    inter-organizational 239
    public–private 55
    regional 59
    social venture–public sector 15, 133, 145, 147
    with TAVI producers 245
collaborative arrangements to mobilise collective resources 72–3, 80
collaborative smolt production 73

collective knowledge sharing in networks 72–3
collective resources 67, 68, 71, 73, 74, 76–9, 81, 83, 84
    common ownership of 70
    mobilisation of (*see* mobilisation of collective resources in entrepreneurship)
    particularities of 82
    shared governance of 69, 82
collective socioeconomic systems 205
common ownership of collective resources 70
common property resources 82
community-based commitments 59
company adaptation strategies 90–92
complexity of social relationships 235, 248–51
complexity theory 153, 159, 168
conceptual grounding of approach 159–60
concomitantly 174
consensus-making process 167
Consoli, D. 236, 237
cooperative inter-organizational healthcare networks 240
CoreValve 244–6, 248–9
creative behavior 200, 201
credit-based monetary system 205
critical realism 9
cross-complementarity of agents 234
'crystallization' 137
CSOs *see* civil society organizations (CSOs)
cumulated knowledge and new calculations 219–21

Danish National Committee 246, 250
data analysis process 97–9
D'aunno, T. A. 239
Davey, S. M. 236
David, Paul 45
Dearing, J. W. 237, 249
de Certeau, M. 15, 134, 135–6, 145, 147
decision-making process 26, 140
DEI projects *see* diversity, equity and inclusion (DEI) projects
De Pietro, C. 239
distributed innovation processes 95, 104
diversity 16, 174–6, 185

creating room for 183–4
and inclusion 180–181
and innovation 177–81
management 176
sense of belonging 181–3
diversity, equity and inclusion (DEI)
projects 183
Dosi, Giovanni 210
Dos Santos, C. 239, 241
Dubois, A. 243
Dumez, H. 239
dynamic evolutionary progression 45
dynamic socio-technical framework 17

easy-to-convince culture 60
economic activities 10, 90, 93, 108, 197,
202
economic crises 89–91, 108, 109
economic novelty and prices 201–3
economics imperialism 206
economic theory 4, 10, 17, 191, 193–4,
196–9, 206
Edmondson, A. 182
EDP *see* entrepreneurial discovery
processes (EDP)
EEG approach *see* evolutionary
economic geography (EEG)
approach
Eggertsson, T. 77
Emerson, R. M. 118
Emmons, K. M. 237
enforceability 68, 70, 81
entrepreneurial activities 67, 200
entrepreneurial change agent 46
"entrepreneurial discoveries" 155
entrepreneurial discovery processes
(EDP) 162
entrepreneurial firm 13, 67–71, 74, 75,
78, 80–83
entrepreneurial opportunity 6, 8, 67, 74
'entrepreneurial space' 146
entrepreneurial team (ET) formation
as antecedent of position imprinting
33–8
firm founding and position
imprinting 29–30
imprinting theory 26, 27–9
perspectives on position creation
30–32
position imprinting 28–9

entrepreneurship
collective resources in 67–70
humanistic conceptualization of 3
literature 6
mobilisation of collective resources
in (*see* mobilisation of
collective resources in
entrepreneurship)
Schumpeterian 43, 45, 203
social (*see* social entrepreneurship)
social ontology of 10
environmental movement 211
environmental munificence 93
essentialist approach 2, 9, 16–18
essentialist conceptualizations 11
ET formation *see* entrepreneurial team
(ET) formation
ethnographic case study approach 15
ethnography 130, 139
EU cohesion policy 154
European Conformity Marking
Competent Authorities 243
evolutionary economic geography (EEG)
approach 47, 180
excludability 69, 70
experience-based knowledge 114, 126
external resources 36, 69, 104
extrinsic motivation 116, 122
Eyde cluster firms 51

financial resources 93, 94, 107
firm founding and position imprinting
29–30
firm-level actors 43, 60, 61
firm-level agency 43, 46
firm-level assets 12, 44
firm-level entrepreneurs 46, 51
firm-level idiosyncrasies 29
firm–system alignment 51
firm-to-firm transaction 70
Fitjar, R. D. 157–8, 164, 168, 176
Fjord municipality 138, 139, 146
foresight workshops 159, 161
formal contracts 13, 80, 82
"formal" safety 217–24
Foss, N. J. 114, 127–30
framing theory 116, 130
free-riding 77, 80, 82
Frenken, K. 180

front-end phase of industry downturn 89, 107–9
    industry economic crises and company adaptation strategies 90–92
    innovation activities during 92–4
    research design and methods 94–9
    suppliers and their innovation activities during 99–106
functional dynamics approach 238
functional stability 252

Gadde, L.-E. 243
gain frames, knowledge sharing motivated by 126–7
GCE *see* Global Centre of Expertise (GCE)
Gedajlovic, E. 6
Gee, E. P. 240
Geels, F. W. 9
Geertz, C. 117
Ghoshal, S. 49, 50
Gieryn, T. 213
Global Centre of Expertise (GCE) 53
Global TAVI network 243–5
Glückler, J. 47
Gnyawali, D. R. 241
Gonzalez, Jakoba Sraml 13, 14
governmental risk-based regime 218
government rules and regulations 33
Granovetter, M. S. 48, 185
Griesemer, J. R. 213
Grillitsch, M. 43, 45
Gulati, R. 83
Günzel-Jensen, F. 135

Hall, P. A. 50
Harland, C. 241
Health, Safety and Environment (HSE) Framework Regulation 217, 218, 227
health and social service sector 138
healthcare ecosystem 18
healthcare function 235
healthcare innovation process 235–41
healthcare innovation system 235
healthcare organizations 239, 240
health delivery system 247

Health Innovation System (HIS) 18, 236, 247, 251
Herstad, S. J. 53
Holvino, E. 176
"horizontal" (sector-neutral) policy 155
hospital–industry interactions 238, 247
human capital 32, 81
human resource 178

idiosyncratic arrangements 13
idiosyncratic positions and jobs 30
idiosyncratic resource-mobilisation approach 69
I&E studies *see* Innovation and Entrepreneurship (I&E) studies
immaterial boundary object 226
imperfect mobility of resources 76
imprinting literature 26, 27, 38, 39
imprinting process 12, 26, 27, 38
imprinting research 27, 36
imprinting theory 26–9, 33
    organizational 12, 26
    and position imprinting 28–9
inclusion and diversity 175, 180–181, 183, 184
inclusive management styles 181
inclusiveness 157
incremental innovation processes 14
incremental operational improvements 14
"incremental optimization" 211
industry economic crisis 90–92
informal inter-organisational arrangements 75
'information/decision perspective' 185
innovation activities 90
    adapting practices and processes related to 102
    during front end of industry downturn 92–4, 99–106
    sustain/engage in 103–4
innovation and diversity 177–81, 183, 184
Innovation and Entrepreneurship (I&E) studies 2–6, 8, 9, 11
innovation policy 158, 159, 163, 238
    regional 153, 168
    top-down approach to 155, 157
innovation process of medical devices 234

complementarity of system and network perspectives 247–8
complexity of social relationships 248–51
healthcare innovation process 235–41
heterogeneity and dynamic dimensions in medical innovation processes 251–2
methods 242–3
TAVI case 243–7
innovation projects 99, 104
innovation-related activities 98, 102
innovation strategies 109, 162
economic crises on 89, 108
of firms 99
innovation studies (IS) 7, 9, 13, 17, 175, 234
categorization 215
economic geography and 180
in healthcare 237
regional 168
Innovation System approach 7
"innovative company" 129
innovative production function 202
institutional arrangements to mobilise collective resources 72, 77, 81–4
institutional change 77
institutional endowments 47, 51
institutional imprinters 28
integrated industrial governance 130
intentional entrepreneurial activity 206
interactions
constructive 11
functional 18, 238, 247
hospital–industry 238, 247
in innovation process of medical devices (*see* innovation process of medical devices)
social (*see* social interactions)
internal control system 222
internal idiosyncratic jobs 30
international markets 33
inter-organisational arrangements 70
inter-organizational networks in healthcare 239
inter-organizational relationships 239
interpretative flexibility 214, 216
interpretivist epistemic mode 117
IS *see* innovation studies (IS)

Isaksen, A. 43
'isolation mechanism' 76, 79

Jevnaker, B. 33
J-form organization 114
Johnson, V. 26, 38
Jung, H. 30
Jurburg, D. 130

Kamp, A. 176
Kanter, R. M. 177, 184
Kee, K. F. 237, 249
Kirchhoff, Bruce 46
knowledge-based view 113
knowledge sharing, motivation for 113, 130
epistemology and method 117–18
knowledge, goals and framing 115–17
at Metal Industries 118–27
stabilizing normative frames 127–9
Kobro, L. U. 145
Korsgaard, S. 10
Kosmynin, Mikhail 15
Kriauciunas, A. 27
Kuhn, T. 229
Kyllingstad, N. 45, 47, 51

Labarde, Jan Claude 245
Lakomski-Laguerre, O. 204
Lam, A. 113, 115
Lambermont-Ford, J.-P. 113, 115
Lamine, W. 146
Larisch, L.-M. 238
Lavie, D. J. 76
Lazar, M. 33
lean manufacturing 114, 118, 128
Lega, F. 239
LeTourneau, B. 241
Lewis, L. 70
Li, C.-R. 181
"liability of newness" 27, 31
Lindenberg, S. 114–17, 125, 127–30
LOIs *see* letters of intent (LOIs)
Lomas, J. 237
Lomi, A. 240

MacKinnon, D. 47
Mæland, Monica 56

Malecki, E. J. 49
Malmberg, A. 47
market arrangements to mobilise
    collective resources 70, 72,
    78–80, 83
market-based contracts 81
market-based system 72, 79, 82–3
market contracts 75, 78
market transaction 78
Marquis, C. 27–9
Mascarenhas, B. 91
Maskell, P. 47
Mathias, B. D. 26, 37
Mechatronic Innovation Lab (MIL) 44,
    52–61
medical devices, innovation processes
    of 234
    complementarity of system and
        network perspectives 247–8
    complexity of social relationships
        248–51
    healthcare innovation process
        235–41
    heterogeneity and dynamic
        dimensions in medical
        innovation processes 251–2
    methods 242–3
    TAVI case 243–7
medical innovation processes 235, 238,
    248, 249, 251–2
"medical micro innovation systems" 237
Metal Industries, knowledge sharing at
    113, 114, 117–19, 128–30
    from incentives to norms 121–4
    motivated by gain frames 126–7
    "old" way of knowledge sharing
        120–121
    solving operators' problems 124–5
Metcalfe, J. S. 236
methodological individualism 196, 202
Mill, J. S. 174
Miller, C. J. 10
Mina, A. 237
Miner, A. 31
Misganaw, B. A. 12, 33
mobilisation logics 78
mobilisation of collective resources in
    entrepreneurship 70
    examples from aquaculture industry
        71–3

theoretical insights on 73–8
through collaborative arrangements
    80
through institutional arrangements
    81–2
through market arrangements 78–80
through relational arrangements
    80–81
Monetary Analysis framework 204, 206
monetary compensations 227
Moss, S. M. 176, 177
Mulgan, G. 1
municipalities 133, 134, 139, 140, 142–4,
    146, 147
    credibility with 145
    Norwegian 137
    social ventures and 138
    welfare 136

Nahapiet, J. 49, 50
National Innovation System perspective
    4
national regulatory framework 217–19
National TAVI network of producers and
    practitioners 245–7
natural resources 67–9, 71, 72, 77, 82
Nature Magic 139, 141, 142
Navarro, P. 94
NCC see Nordland County Council
    (NCC)
NCS see Norwegian Continental Shelf
    (NCS)
neoclassical economics 17
network-based approaches 18
new institutional economics (NIE) 68,
    70, 77–8
NODE cluster 53–8, 60
NOK see Norwegian kroner (NOK)
Nonaka, I. 114, 115, 117, 119
non-compliance cases 222
non-economic mechanisms 194
non-excludability of collective resources
    67, 69, 76
non-transferability of collective resources
    67, 69, 76
Nooteboom, B. 185
Nordland County Council (NCC) 165–6
normal incoherence of stability 225–8
North, D. C. 77
Norway 62, 138

Index 263

case of Nordland (*see* case of
    Nordland)
oil and gas industry in 94
petroleum activities in 217
on privatization of welfare 137
regional government in 153
social enterprises in 15
social entrepreneurship in 137
system-level material asset in 13
Norwegian aluminum smelter 14, 118
Norwegian Continental Shelf (NCS) 95,
    218, 219
Norwegian innovation cluster program
    53, 60
Norwegian model 118
Norwegian municipalities 137, 145
Norwegian offshore oil and gas drilling
    industry 212, 215
Norwegian oil and gas industry 221
Norwegian Oil and Gas Suppliers 94–5
Norwegian salmon farmers 71
Norwegian salmon farming firms 80
Norwegian welfare model 136, 141
Norwegian welfare society 141, 143
Norwegian welfare state 134, 136, 138,
    139, 145–7
Norwegian welfare system 15, 137, 138
not-in-transition industries 17, 212, 225
not-in-transition period 211–12, 228

oil and gas industry 14, 53, 54, 56, 60,
    90, 91, 93–6, 103, 108, 109, 167,
    220, 229
    system stability and diffused value
        coherence 210–213
oil companies' regulations 221–2
Olafsen, T. 71
opportunity-development process 69
opportunity exploitation 67–70, 77, 78
organizational imprinting 39
    process 27
    research 27
    theory 12, 26, 38
organization theory 31
orthodox economic theory 10
Ostrom, E. 77
ownership transferability 75, 76

Palumbo, R. 239

Park, B.-J. R. 241
path restructuring, preformation phase
    of 47
Pelz, D. 177
Peng, T. J. A. 240, 241
Penrose, E. T. 76
Percutaneous Valve Technologies (PVT)
    243
performance-based (functional)
    requirements 218
Peteraf, M. A. 76
Pfeffer, J. 75
Phillips, K. W. 178
Piskorski, M. J. 74
place-based leadership 45
policy mix and monitoring stage 164–5
Pollock, N. 214
position creation 35, 36
    and assignment process 34
    perspectives on 30–33
position imprinting
    ET formation as antecedent of 33–8
    firm founding and 29–30
    imprinting theory and 28–9
    literatures 38
private banking system 205
private property rights for resources 76
producer–practitioner networks 235
'professional systematic approach'
        narrative 144
property right 77
    laws 78
    of resources 76
public sector organizations 135, 138, 139
public welfare 136, 137, 147
Putnam, R. D. 49

"quadruple helix" 163, 166
quasi-stability of socio-technical system
    211
question-machine approach 152–3
    case of Nordland, Norway 165–8
    foundations for 158–60
    to integrating RRI into RIS3 policy
        161–5
    Research and Innovation Strategy
        for Smart Specialization
        (RIS3) 154–8

Ramlogan, R. 236, 237
Rasmussen, E. 83
rational model 32, 33, 35
RBV *see* resource-based view (RBV)
R&D *see* research and development (R&D)
RDT *see* resource dependence theory (RDT)
Reed, Isaac A. 117
reflexivity 157, 161
regional actors 50, 57–61, 73
regional development policy 154, 161, 168
regional health innovation system 238
regional industrial restructuring 43, 45
    analytical framework 51–2
    asset modification for 44, 46–9, 51, 52, 61
    change agents and change agency in 45–6
    empirical findings and analysis 54–60
    presentation of case, research questions and methods 52–4
    social dimension of 48–51
regional innovation actors 162
regional innovation ecosystem 15, 152
regional innovation planning processes 152
regional innovation policy 153, 168
regional innovation strategy 153
regional innovation system (RIS) 46, 48, 51, 53, 54, 60
regional institutional framework 51
regional planning processes 166, 168
regional small and medium enterprises (SMEs) 73
related variety (RV) 180
relational arrangements to mobilise collective resources 73, 75, 80–81
relational contracts 80, 81
relational embeddedness 59
relational social capital 50, 59
research and development (R&D) 90
    activities 211
    funding programmes 1
    investments 154
research and innovation (R&I) activities 9, 16, 153, 156, 157, 161

Research and Innovation Strategy for Smart Specialization (RIS3) 154–8, 169
    policy, integrating RRI into 161–5
resource-based view (RBV) 13, 46, 47, 68, 70, 74, 76, 79, 240
resource dependence analysis 32
resource dependence theory (RDT) 68, 70, 74–6, 80
resource endowment 69
resource mobilisation 36, 74, 79
    arrangements for 13, 68–70, 82
    collective 71–3
    institutions guide 77
    logics 83
    for opportunity exploitation 69–70
    theoretical insights on 75
resource ownership 70
resource-seeking strategy 35
resource theories 68
"responsible coastal management" 162, 166
"responsible regional planning" 168
responsible research and innovation (RRI) 7–9, 15, 16, 152–4, 156–65, 167–9
responsiveness 157, 161
retrenchment 14, 106
    activities 14, 93, 100, 107, 109
    strategy 91, 100
R&I activities *see* research and innovation (R&I) activities
RIS *see* regional innovation system (RIS)
RIS3 *see* Research and Innovation Strategy for Smart Specialization (RIS3)
Risikonivå i norsk petroleumsvirksomhet (RNNP) 219
"risk appetite" 222
Ruef, M. 32
'rules of the game' 133, 146–7
    articulating social venture's hybridity 143–4
    building credibility 144–5
    data collection and analysis 139–40
    De Certeau's notions of strategy and tactics 135–6
    entrepreneurial practices for collaboration 134–5

Index

importance of 'system knowledge'
140–143
methodological approach 137–9
welfare structure 136–7
Rumelt, R. P. 76
RV *see* related variety (RV)
Rypestøl, J. O. 12, 13, 44–6, 51
Rystad Energy database 96

Salancik, G. R. 75
salience 185
salmon farming industry 70, 71, 72, 73,
78, 80, 81
Sandven, T. 53
Sardo, Stefania 17, 18
Schippers, M. C. 175, 181
Schumpeter, J. A. 17, 46
social ontology (*see* social ontology
of Schumpeter)
theory of economic development
16, 206
Treatise on *Money* 204
Schumpeterian conceptualization 192
of economic novelty 202
of innovation and entrepreneurship
17
of novelty 203
Schumpeterian economic development
197–8
Schumpeterian entrepreneurship 43, 45,
203
Schumpeterian heritage 207
Schumpeterian methodological principle
195
Schumpeterian ontology 191, 197, 199,
207
Schumpeterian operationalization of
novelty 202
Schumpeterian theory 17, 192, 198, 204,
206
Schumpterian meta-theoretical blueprint
17
Science and Technology Studies (STS)
17, 212, 213
SDGs *see* Sustainable Development
Goals (SDGs)
SeeRRI project 152, 159, 160, 162, 163,
165–8, 170
self-interested actors 115, 119, 130

"self-interested" perspective 114
semiformal inter-organisational
arrangements 75
semi-structured interviewing technique
139
semi-structured interviews 90, 96, 139,
216
sense of belonging 49, 175, 181–3
Shepherd, D. A. 7
Shinkle, G. 27
Shore, L. M. 181
'similarity attraction paradigm' 178, 185
Simon, Herbert 113
Simsek, Z. 28
smart specialization 158, 165, 169
approach 15, 168
in the European Union 155
policies 15, 16, 153, 154, 157, 159,
162, 166
policymaking process 158
and RRI 154
smart specialization stages
analysis 163–4
policy mix and monitoring 164–5
vision and prioritization 163–4
Smith, K. W. 180
Smith, Norman 46
smolt production facilities 73
social accounting system 204, 205
social arrangements 68, 83
social capital
bonding 13, 50, 61–2
cognitive 60
definition of 49
elements of 52
mobilizing 8
relational 59
relational and cognitive 51
structural 57–8
theory 6, 7, 44, 48, 51, 58
social categorisation perspective 32, 185
"social change" 8, 15, 133, 143
social conditions 10, 12, 27, 34, 38, 39,
197
social coordination 75
social dimension 143
in innovation and entrepreneurship
studies 3–11
of knowledge sharing 113

of regional industrial restructuring
(*see* regional industrial
restructuring)
residual 2
social embeddedness 83
social entrepreneurs 1, 15, 133, 136, 137,
140–144, 146, 147
activities of 8
in advocacy practices 135
lived experiences of 134, 138, 139,
145
social entrepreneurship 1, 7, 134
activities of 8
in Norway 137
research 147
social identity theory 32, 178–9
social innovation 1, 7, 8, 140, 141, 146
social interactions 6, 18, 44, 49
in networks 67
relational dimension of 61
social networks 7, 49, 68
social ontology of Schumpeter 191
economic novelty and prices 201–3
individual agency and logic of
things 199–201
money and social context 203–5
social reality and economics 192–5
system and development 195–9
social phenomena 5, 11, 192, 193, 195,
198
social-psychological model 32–4
social reality and economics 192–5
social relations 5, 8, 12, 13, 44, 48, 51,
52, 61, 83, 206, 235, 248–52
"Social Structure and Organizations" 26
social structures 12, 26, 28, 238, 240,
248
social value 8, 18, 141, 210, 212, 215,
218, 224–6
social venture–public sector
collaboration 145, 147
social ventures 133–7, 141, 142, 145,
147
hybridity 143–4
and municipalities 138
'socio-cognitive horsepower' 180
socio-psychological model 33, 34
socio-technical code 17, 210–212, 215,
217, 227, 228

socio-technical framework or paradigm
210
socio-technical quasi-stability 210
socio-technical system
boundary work 213
interpretative flexibility 214
methodology 215–17
system stability and diffused value
coherence 210–213
socio-technical value 18, 212, 215, 217,
225, 228, 229
Solheim, M. C. W. 176, 177, 181, 185
Sørlandsutvalget 55
Soskice, D. 50
Sotarauta, M. 43, 45
'speed bump effect' 178
Stahl, G. K. 176
stakeholder communication 158
stakeholder engagement 158, 161, 165
stakeholder foresight workshops 159,
161
stakeholder participation 161
Stam, Erik 46
standards and risk assessments 219–21
Star, S. L. 213, 226
state funding 55, 56, 61, 62
state of middle-range theory 8
state-of-the-art technologies 53, 55, 57
Stegmann, S. 175
Stets, J. E. 178
Stinchcombe, A. L. 12, 26–8, 31, 36
strategic change agency 12, 43
Streeck, Wolfgang 128
'structural holes' 177
structural social capital 57–8
STS *see* Science and Technology Studies
(STS)
sub-optimal situations 77
subsea technology companies 95, 101,
102, 104
Sunduramurthy, C. 135
Sustainable Development Goals (SDGs)
133, 135, 153
'system knowledge' 140–143, 146
system-level actors 60, 61
system-level agency 43, 46, 52
system-level asset 12, 43, 44, 51, 57, 60
modification processes 61
preconditions for 62
system-level entrepreneurs 46, 51

Index 267

system-level material asset 13, 52, 53, 57, 60–62
systems thinking 153, 159, 168
Sytch, M. 83

Taiwanese healthcare networks 240
Takeuchi, H. 114, 115, 117, 119
TAVI *see* Transcatheter Aortic Valve Implantation (TAVI)
theory of economic development 16, 17, 192, 198, 199, 201, 204–7
theory of the economic system 195–9, 201, 203–6
Tietenberg, T. H. 70
Tilcsik, A. 27–9, 178–9
'tokenism' 184
Traavik, L. E. M. 175, 182
trade union 121, 130
    firm and 118
    management and 129
    and senior management 128
traditional Norwegian welfare system 137
    for salmon production 72
transaction costs 68, 77, 78, 81, 82
    and property rights 74
    theory 113, 119
    tradition 115
transactive memory system 29
Transcatheter Aortic Valve Implantation (TAVI) 235, 242, 248–52
    Global TAVI network 243–5
    national TAVI network of producers and practitioners 245–7
    technology 18
transferability 69, 70, 75, 76
transformative innovation activities 155, 162, 168

transition periods 211
transition processes 9
Treatise on Money (Schumpeter) 204
tripartite collaboration model 218
Triple Helix perspective 4
Trippl, M. 44, 47

UN Agenda 2030 160
UN's Sustainable Development Goals (SDGs) 133
U.S. Food and Drug Administration (FDA) 244

"vacancy assumption" 31
van Knippenberg, D. 175, 181
venture-founding process 26, 27, 36, 38–9
Vestrum, I. 83
vision and prioritization stage 163–4
volatile market conditions 91
von Schomberg, R. 9
Vygotsky, L. S. 185

Walsh, J. P. 7
Weigel, S. 238
'welfare municipalities' 136
Westra, D. 239, 241
Williamson, O. E. 113, 114, 117, 120, 121
work-arounds 214
Working Environment Act (2005) 230
workplace diversity 183
Wright, Erik Olin 128
Wynne, B. 225

Zafirovski, M. 10
Zuckerman, H. S. 239